The Architect's
Portable Handbook

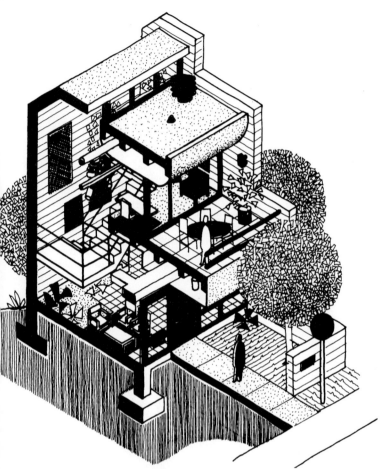

THE ARCHITECT'S
PORTABLE HANDBOOK
FIRST STEP RULES OF THUMB FOR BUILDING DESIGN

BY PAT GUTHRIE
ARCHITECT

SECOND EDITION

McGraw-Hill, Inc.

New York   San Francisco   Washington, D.C.   Auckland   Bogotá
Caracas   Lisbon   London   Madrid   Mexico City   Milan
Montreal   New Delhi   San Juan   Singapore
Sydney   Tokyo   Toronto

Library of Congress Cataloging-in-Publication Data

Guthrie, Pat.
    The architect's portable handbook : first step rules of thumb for
building design / by Pat Guthrie. — 2nd ed.
        p.   cm.
    Includes bibliographical references and index.
    ISBN 0-07-025303-X
    1. Architectural design—Handbooks, manuals, etc.   I. Title.
NA2750.G87   1998
721—dc21   98-11896
                                                                CIP

    4 5 6 7 8 9 0   DOC/DOC   0 2 1 0

ISBN 0-07-025303-X

*The sponsoring editor for this book was Wendy Lochner, and the
production supervisor was Pamela A. Pelton. It was set in Times Ten
by North Market Street Graphics.*

Printed and bound by Donnelley/Crawfordsville.

This book is printed on acid-free paper.

Dedicated to:

- *Bill Mahoney of BNI (Building News Inc.) who encouraged me in the first edition*
- *Joel Stein, editor of the first edition*
- *My family (Jan, Eric, and Erin)*

Contents

How to Use This Book   xiii

Use this table as a checklist for the design of buildings.

How to Use This Book

The concept of this book is that of a *personal tool* that compacts the 20% of the data that is needed 80% of the time by *design professionals* in the preliminary design of *buildings* of all types and sizes.

This tool is meant to always be at one's *fingertips* (open on a drawing board or desk, carried in a briefcase, or kept in one's pocket). It is never meant to sit on a bookshelf. It is meant to be *used every day!*

Because design professionals are individualistic and their practices are so varied, the user is encouraged to *individualize this book* over time, by adding notes or changing data as experience dictates.

The addition of rough construction **costs** throughout the book (making this type of handbook truly unique) will "date" the data. But building laws, new technologies, and materials are changing just as fast. Therefore, this book should be looked on as a *starter of simple data collection* that must be updated over time. New editions *may* be published in the future. See p. 35 for more information on **costs.**

Because this book is so broad in scope, yet so compact, information can be presented only at one place and not repeated. There is little room for examples of how to use the information provided. Information is presented by simple ratios or coefficients that leave the need for *commonsense judgment.*

The whole book is laid out in checklist format, to be quickly read and checked against the design problem at hand.

Where ( ) is shown, refer to p. 543 for further explanation of references.

This book is *not a substitute* for professional expertise or other books of a more detailed and specialized nature, but will be a continuing everyday aid that takes the more useful "cream" off the top of other sources.

The Architect's Portable Handbook

<u>NOTES</u>

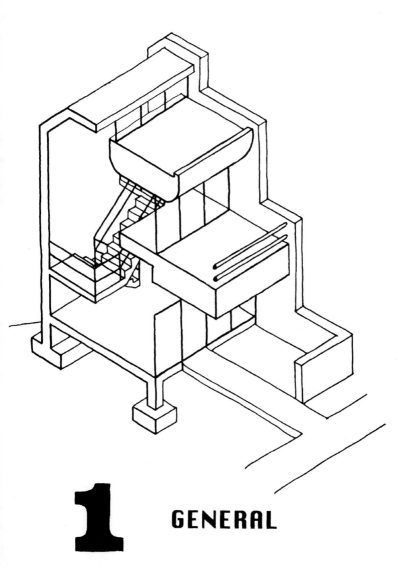

1 GENERAL

NOTES

__ A. PRACTICE ⑤ ㉑ ㊷

__ 1. <u>Services</u>: Use "Schedule of A/E (Architectural/Engineering) Services" on pp. 6–15 to plan the services for building design.

__ 2. <u>Compensation</u> (A/E Fees)

    __ *a.* See App. A, item E for A/E fees as a percentage of construction cost by building type.

    __ *b.* Total fees can be broken down as follows:

__ Schematic design phase	15%	or
__ Design development	20%	25% Preliminary design
__ Construction documents	40%	50% Const. doc.
__ Bid/negotiation	5%	25% Const. adm.
__ Construction administration	20%	
	100%	100%

    __ *c.* Of the total A/E fees, standard *consultants' fees* can be broken out as follows:

        __ (1) Civil engineering and landscape architect ..... 2.5 to 6%
        __ (2) Structural engineering ..... 1 to 2.5%
        __ (3) Mechanical engineering ..... 4 to 10%
        __ (4) Electrical engineering ..... 4 to 10%
        __ (5) Other

__ 3. <u>Rules of Thumb for Business Practice</u>

    __ *a.* Watch *cash flow:* For a small firm, balance checkbook. For a medium or large firm, use cash statements and balance and income statements. Estimate future cash flow based on past, with 15% "fudge factor," plus desired profit.

    __ *b.* Have *financial reserves:* Six months' worth.

    __ *c.* Monitor *time* by these *ratios:*

        __ (1) Chargeable ratio $= \dfrac{\text{direct job labor cost}}{\text{total labor cost}}$

    This tells what percent of total labor cost is being spent on paying work. The higher the percent the better. Typical range is 55 to 85%, but lower than 65% is poor. However, principals often have a 50% ratio.

        __ (2) Multiplier ratio $= \dfrac{\text{dollars of revenue}}{\text{dollars of direct labor}}$

This ratio is multiplied times wages for billing rates. Usually *2.5 to 3.0.* Will vary with firm and time.

___ (3) Overhead rate: looks at total indirect expenses as they relate to total direct labor. An overhead rate of 180 means $1.80 spent for ea. $1.00 working on revenue-producing projects.

___ (4) Profit: measured as total revenue minus expenses. Expressed as percent of total revenue.

___ *d.* Monitor *accounting reports:* A financial statement consists of:

___ (1) Balance Sheet: Tells where you are on a given date by Assets and Liabilities.

___ (2) Earnings Statement (Profit and Loss): Tells you how you got there by Income less Direct (job) costs, and Indirect (overhead) costs = Profit, or Loss.

___ *e.* *Mark up* for Reimbursable Expenses (travel, printing, etc.): Usually 10%.

___ *f.* Negotiating *contracts*

___ (1) Estimate scope of services.

___ (2) Estimate time, costs, and profit.

___ (3) Determine method of compensation:

___ (*a*) Percent of construction cost

___ (*b*) Lump sum

___ (*c*) Hourly rates

___ (*d*) Hourly rates with maximum "upset"

___ *g.* Contract checklist

___ (1) Detailed scope of work, no interpretation necessary.

___ (2) Responsibilities of both parties.

___ (3) Monthly progress payments.

___ (4) Interest penalty on overdue payments.

___ (5) Limit length of construction administration phase.

___ (6) Construction cost estimating responsibilities.

___ (7) For cost-reimbursable contracts, specify a provisional overhead rate (changes year to year).

___ (8) Retainer, applied to fee but not costs.

___ (9) Date of agreement, and time limit on contract.

___ (10) Approval of work—who, when, where.

___ (11) Ways to terminate contract, by both parties.
___ (12) For changes in scope, bilateral agreement, and an equitable adjustment in fee.
___ (13) Court or arbitration remedies and who pays legal fees.
___ (14) Signature and date by both parties.

(5)

PHASE 1 PRE DESIGN SCHEDULE OF A/E SERVICES	BY ARCHITECT	BY CONSULTANT	BY OWNER				NOT TO BE DONE
1 PROJECT ADMINISTRATION							
2 COORDINATION/CHECKING							
3 COORD. W/ GOVERNMENT							
4 PROGRAMMING							
5 SPACE DIAGRAMS							
6 SURVEY OF EXIST'G. FACILITIES							
7 MARKETING STUDIES							
8 ECONOMIC STUDIES							
9 PROJECT FINANCING							
10 PROJECT BUDGETING							
11 PRESENTATIONS							

PHASE 2 SITE ANALYSIS SCHEDULE OF A/E SERVICES	BY ARCHITECT	BY CONSULTANT	BY OWNER				NOT TO BE DONE
1	PROJECT ADMINISTRATION							
2	COORDINATION / CHECKING							
3	COORD. W/ GOVERNMENT							
4	SURVEYS							
5	SITE ANALYSIS & SELECTION							
6	SITE DEVELOPMENT PLANNING							
7	SITE UTILIZATION STUDIES							
8	UTILITY STUDIES							
9	ENVIRONMENTAL STUDIES							
10	ZONING							
11	PROJECT SCHEDULING							
12	PROJECT BUDGETING							
13	PRESENTATIONS							

PHASE 3 SCHEMATIC DESIGN SCHEDULE OF A/E SERVICES	BY ARCHITECT	BY CONSULTANT	BY OWNER				NOT TO BE DONE
1 PROJECT COORDINATION							
2 COORDINATION / CHECKING							
3 COORD. W/ GOVERNMENT							
4 ARCHITECTURAL DESIGN							
5 STRUCTURAL DESIGN							
6 MECHANICAL DESIGN							
7 ELECTRICAL DESIGN							
8 CIVIL DESIGN							
9 LANDSCAPE DESIGN							
10 INTERIOR DESIGN							
11 MATERIALS RESEARCH / SPEC'S							
12 PROJECT SCHEDULING							
13 COST ESTIMATING							
14 PRESENTATIONS							

PHASE 4 DESIGN DEVELOPMENT SCHEDULE OF A/E SERVICES	BY ARCHITECT	BY CONSULTANT	BY OWNER				NOT TO BE DONE
1 PROJECT ADMINISTRATION							
2 COORDINATION / CHECKING							
3 COORD. W/ GOVERNMENT							
4 ARCHITECTURAL DESIGN							
5 STRUCTURAL DESIGN							
6 MECHANICAL DESIGN							
7 ELECTRICAL DESIGN							
8 CIVIL DESIGN							
9 LANDSCAPE DESIGN							
10 INTERIOR DESIGN							
11 MATERIALS RESEARCH /SPEC'S							
12 PROJECT SCHEDULING							
13 COST ESTIMATING							
14 PRESENTATIONS							

PHASE 5 CONSTRUCTION DOCUMENTS SCHEDULE OF A/E SERVICES	BY ARCHITECT	BY CONSULTANT	BY OWNER				NOT TO BE DONE
1 PROJECT ADMINISTRATION							
2 COORDINATION / CHECKING							
3 COORD. W/ GOVERNMENT							
4 ARCHITECTURAL DOCUMENTS							
5 STRUCTURAL DOCUMENTS							
6 MECHANICAL DOCUMENTS							
7 ELECTRICAL DOCUMENTS							
8 CIVIL DOCUMENTS							
9 LANDSCAPE DOCUMENTS							
10 INTERIORS DOCUMENTS							
11 SPECIFICATIONS							
12 PROJECT SCHEDULING							
13 COST ESTIMATING							
14 PRESENTATIONS							

PHASE 6 BIDDING OR NEGOTIATIONS SCHEDULE OF A/E SERVICES	BY ARCHITECT	BY CONSULTANT	BY OWNER				NOT TO BE DONE
1 PROJECT ADMINISTRATION							
2 COORDINATION / CHECKING							
3 GOVERNMENT PLAN CHECK							
4 PRE-QUALIFICATION OF BIDDERS							
5 BIDDING MATERIALS							
6 ADDENDA							
7 BIDDING / NEGOTIATIONS							
8 ALTERNATES / SUBSTITUTIONS							
9 SPECIAL BIDDING SERVICES							
10 BID EVALUATION							
11 CONST. CONTRACT AGREEMENTS							

PHASE 7 CONSTRUCTION CONTRACT ADM. SCHEDULE OF A/E SERVICES	BY ARCHITECT	BY CONSULTANT	BY OWNER				NOT TO BE DONE
1	PROJECT ADMINISTRATION						
2	COORDINATION / CHECKING						
3	COORD. W/ GOVERNMENT						
4	OFFICE ADMINISTRATION						
5	FIELD OBSERVATION						
6	PROJECT PRESENTATION						
7	INSPECTION COORDINATION						
8	SUPPLEMENTAL DOCUMENTS						
9	CHANGE ORDERS						
10	SCHEDULE MONITORING						
11	CONSTRUCTION COST ACCOUNTING						
12	PROJECT CLOSEOUT						

PHASE 8 POST CONST. SERVICES SCHEDULE OF A/E SERVICES	BY ARCHITECT	BY CONSULTANT	BY OWNER				NOT TO BE DONE
I PROJECT ADMINISTRATION							
2 COORDINATION / CHECKING							
3 COORD. W/ GOVERNMENT							
4 MAINTENANCE AND OPERATIONAL PROGRAMMING							
5 START UP ASSISTANCE							
6 RECORD DRAWINGS							
7 WARRANTY REVIEW							
8 POST CONST. EVALUATION							

PHASE 9 SUPPLEMENTAL SERVICES SCHEDULE OF A/E SERVICES	BY ARCHITECT	BY CONSULTANT	BY OWNER			NOT TO BE DONE
1 SPECIAL STUDIES						
2 RENDERINGS						
3 MODEL CONSTRUCTION						
4 LIFE CYCLE COST ANALYSIS						
5 VALUE ENGINEERING						
6 QUANTITY SURVEYS						
7 DETAILED COST ESTIMATES						
8 ENERGY STUDIES						
9 ENVIRONMENTAL MONITORING						
10 TENANT RELATED SERVICES						
11 GRAPHICS DESIGN						
12 ARTS AND CRAFTS						
13 FURNISHINGS DESIGN						
14 EQUIPMENT						
15 PROJECT PUBLIC RELATIONS						
16 LEASING BROCHURES						
17 EXPERT WITNESS						
18 COMPUTER APPLICATIONS						
19 MATERIALS & SYSTEMS TESTING						

PHASE 9 SUPPLEMENTAL SERVICES — CONTINUED — SCHEDULE OF A/E SERVICES	BY ARCHITECT	BY CONSULTANT	BY OWNER				NOT TO BE DONE
20	DEMOLITION SERVICES							
21	MOCK UPS							
22	PHOTOGRAPHY							
23	MOTION PICTURES							
24	COORD. W/ NON - DESIGN PROFESSIONALS							
25	SPECIAL DISCIPLINES CONSULTANTS							
26	SPECIAL BLD'G. TYPE CONSULTANTS							

NOTES

B. "SYSTEMS" THINKING

In the planning and design of buildings, a helpful, all-inclusive tool is to think in terms of overall "systems" or "flows." For each of the following checklist items, follow from the beginning or "upper end" through to the "lower end" or "outfall":

___ 1. People Functions
    ___ *a.* Follow flow of occupants from one space to another. This includes sources of vertical transportation (stairs, elevators, etc.) including pathways to service equipment.
    ___ *b.* Follow flow of occupants to enter building from off site.
    ___ *c.* Follow flow of occupants to exit building as required by code.
    ___ *d.* Follow flow of accessible route as required by law.
    ___ *e.* Follow flow of materials to supply building (including furniture and off site).
    ___ *f.* Follow flow of trash to leave building (including to off site).
    ___ *g.* Way finding: do graphics or other visual clues aid flow of the above six items?

___ 2. Structural Functions
    ___ *a.* Follow flow of gravity loads from roof down columns, through floors, to foundations and soils.
    ___ *b.* Follow flow of lateral loads:
        ___ (1) Earthquake from ground up through foundations, columns, walls, floors, and roof.
        ___ (2) Wind from side walls to roof and floors, through columns, to foundations and the earth.
        ___ (3) Follow flow of uplift loads from wind and earthquake by imagining the roof being pulled up and that there are positive connections from roof to columns and walls (through floors) down to foundations and the earth.

___ 3. Water, Moisture, and Drainage
    ___ *a.* Follow rainwater from highest point on roof to drain, through the piping system to outfall (storm sewer or site) off site.
    ___ *b.* Follow rainwater from highest points of site, around building, to outfall off site.
    ___ *c.* Follow rain or moisture at exterior walls and windows down building sides or "weeped" through assemblies to outfall.

    ___ *d.* Follow vapor from either inside or outside the building, through the "skin" (roof and walls) to outfall.

    ___ *e.* Follow water supply from source to farthest point of use.

    ___ *f.* Follow contaminated water from farthest point of use to outfall (sewer main or end of septic tank).

    ___ *g.* Follow vapor flow into materials over year and allow for blockage, swelling, or shrinkage.

___ 4. <u>Heat</u>

    ___ *a.* Follow sun paths to and into building to plan for access or blocking.

    ___ *b.* Follow excessive external (or internal) heat through building skin and block if necessary.

    ___ *c.* Follow source of internal heat loads (lights, people, equipment, etc.) to their "outfall" (natural ventilation or AC, etc.).

    ___ *d.* Follow heat flow into materials over a year, a day, etc. and allow for expansion and contraction.

___ 5. <u>Air</u>

    ___ *a.* Follow wind patterns through site to encourage or block natural ventilation through building, as required.

    ___ *b.* Follow air patterns through building. When natural ventilation is used, follow flow from inlets to outlets. When air is still, hot air rises and cold air descends.

    ___ *c.* Follow forced air ventilation patterns through building to address heat (add or dissipate) and odors.

___ 6. <u>Light</u>

    ___ *a.* Follow paths of natural light (direct or indirect sun) to and into building. Encourage or block as needed.

    ___ *b.* Follow paths of circulation and at spaces to provide artificial illumination where necessary. This includes both site and building.

___ 7. <u>Energy and Communications</u>

    ___ *a.* Follow electric or gas supply from off site to transformer, to breakers or panels to each outlet or point of connection.

    ___ *b.* Follow telephone lines from off site to TMB to each phone location.

___ 8. <u>Sound</u>

    ___ *a.* Identify potential sound sources, potential receiver locations, and the potential sound paths between the two.

    ___ *b.* Follow sound through air from source to receiver. Mitigate with distance or barrier.

    ___ *c.* Follow sound through structure from source to receiver. Mitigate by isolation of source or receiver.

NOTES

<u>**NOTES**</u>

__ C. SPECIFICATIONS (CSI FORMAT)

Use this section as a checklist of everything that makes or goes into buildings, to be all-inclusive in the planning and designing of buildings, their contents, and their surroundings:

Bidding Requirements, Contract Forms, and Conditions of the Contract
___ 00010 Pre-bid information
___ 00100 Instructions to bidders
___ 00200 Information available to bidders
___ 00300 Bid forms
___ 00400 Supplements to bid forms
___ 00500 Agreement forms
___ 00600 Bonds and certificates
___ 00700 General conditions
___ 00800 Supplementary conditions
___ 00900 Addenda

Specifications—By Division

Division 1—General Requirements
___ 01010 Summary of work
___ 01020 Allowances
___ 01025 Measurement and payment
___ 01030 Alternates/alternatives
___ 01035 Modification procedures
___ 01040 Coordination
___ 01050 Field engineering
___ 01060 Regulatory requirements
___ 01070 Identification systems
___ 01090 References
___ 01100 Special project procedures
___ 01200 Project meetings
___ 01300 Submittals
___ 01400 Quality controls
___ 01500 Construction facilities and temporary controls
___ 01600 Material and equipment
___ 01650 Starting of systems/commissioning
___ 01700 Contract closeout
___ 01800 Maintenance

Division 2—Sitework
___ 02010 Subsurface investigation
___ 02050 Demolition
___ 02100 Site preparation
___ 02140 Dewatering
___ 02150 Shoring and underpinning

___ 02160 Excavation support systems
___ 02170 Cofferdams
___ 02200 Earthwork
___ 02300 Tunneling
___ 02350 Piles and caissons
___ 02450 Railroad work
___ 02480 Marine work
___ 02500 Paving and surfacing
___ 02600 Utility piping materials
___ 02660 Water distribution
___ 02680 Fuel and steam distribution
___ 02700 Sewerage and drainage
___ 02760 Restoration of underground pipelines
___ 02770 Ponds and reservoirs
___ 02780 Power and communications
___ 02800 Site improvements
___ 02900 Landscaping

Division 3—Concrete
___ 03100 Concrete formwork
___ 03200 Concrete reinforcement
___ 03250 Concrete accessories
___ 03300 Cast-in-place concrete
___ 03370 Concrete curing
___ 03400 Precast concrete
___ 03500 Cementitious decks and toppings
___ 03600 Grout
___ 03700 Concrete restoration and cleaning
___ 03800 Mass concrete

Division 4—Masonry
___ 04100 Mortar and masonry grout
___ 04150 Masonry accessories
___ 04200 Unit masonry
___ 04400 Stone
___ 04500 Masonry restoration and cleaning
___ 04550 Refactories
___ 04600 Corrosion-resistant masonry
___ 04700 Simulated masonry

Division 5—Metals
___ 05010 Metal materials
___ 05030 Metal finishes
___ 05050 Metal fastenings
___ 05100 Structural metal framing
___ 05200 Metal joists
___ 05300 Metal decking

___ 05400 Cold-formed metal framing
___ 05500 Metal fabrications
___ 05580 Sheet metal fabrications
___ 05700 Ornamental metal
___ 05800 Expansion control
___ 05900 Hydraulic structures

Division 6—Wood and Plastic
___ 06050 Fasteners and adhesives
___ 06100 Rough carpentry
___ 06130 Heavy timber construction
___ 06150 Wood-metal systems
___ 06170 Prefabricated structural wood
___ 06200 Finish carpentry
___ 06300 Wood treatment
___ 06400 Architectural woodwork
___ 06500 Structural plastics
___ 06600 Plastic fabrications
___ 06650 Solid polymer fabrications

Division 7—Thermal and Moisture Protection
___ 07100 Waterproofing
___ 07150 Dampproofing
___ 07180 Water repellents
___ 07190 Vapor retarders
___ 07195 Air barriers
___ 07200 Insulation
___ 07240 Exterior and finish systems
___ 07250 Fireproofing
___ 07270 Fire-stopping
___ 07300 Shingles and roofing tiles
___ 07400 Manufactured roofing and siding
___ 07480 Exterior wall assemblies
___ 07500 Membrane roofing
___ 07570 Traffic coatings
___ 07600 Flashing and sheet metal
___ 07700 Roof specialties and accessories
___ 07800 Skylights
___ 07900 Joint sealers

Division 8—Doors and Windows
___ 08100 Metal doors and frames
___ 08200 Wood and plastic doors
___ 08250 Door-opening assemblies
___ 08300 Special doors
___ 08400 Entrances and storefronts
___ 08500 Metal windows

___ 08600 Wood and plastic windows
___ 08650 Special windows
___ 08700 Hardware
___ 08800 Glazing
___ 08900 Glazed curtain walls

Division 9—Finishes
___ 09100 Metal support systems
___ 09200 Lath and plaster
___ 09250 Gypsum board
___ 09300 Tile
___ 09400 Terrazzo
___ 09450 Stone facing
___ 09500 Acoustical treatment
___ 09540 Special wall surfaces
___ 09545 Special ceiling surfaces
___ 09550 Wood flooring
___ 09600 Stone flooring
___ 09630 Unit masonry flooring
___ 09650 Resilient flooring
___ 09680 Carpet
___ 09700 Special flooring
___ 09780 Floor treatment
___ 09800 Special coatings
___ 09900 Painting
___ 09950 Wall covering

Division 10—Specialties
___ 10100 Visual display boards
___ 10150 Compartments and cubicles
___ 10200 Louvers and vents
___ 10240 Grilles and screens
___ 10250 Service wall systems
___ 10260 Wall and corner guards
___ 10270 Access flooring
___ 10290 Pest control
___ 10300 Fireplaces and stoves
___ 10340 Manufactured exterior specialties
___ 10350 Flagpoles
___ 10400 Identifying devices
___ 10450 Pedestrian control devices
___ 10500 Lockers
___ 10520 Fire protection specialties
___ 10530 Protective covers
___ 10550 Postal specialties
___ 10600 Partitions
___ 10650 Operable partitions

___ 10670 Storage shelving
___ 10700 Exterior protection devices for openings
___ 10750 Telephone specialties
___ 10800 Toilet and bath accessories
___ 10880 Scales
___ 10900 Wardrobe and closet specialties

Division 11—Equipment
___ 11010 Maintenance equipment
___ 11020 Security and vault equipment
___ 11030 Teller and service equipment
___ 11040 Ecclesiastical equipment
___ 11050 Library equipment
___ 11060 Theater and stage equipment
___ 11070 Instrumental equipment
___ 11080 Registration equipment
___ 11090 Checkroom equipment
___ 11100 Mercantile equipment
___ 11110 Commercial laundry and dry-cleaning equipment
___ 11120 Vending equipment
___ 11130 Audiovisual equipment
___ 11140 Vehicle service equipment
___ 11150 Parking control equipment
___ 11160 Loading dock equipment
___ 11170 Solid-waste-handling equipment
___ 11190 Detention equipment
___ 11200 Water supply and treatment equipment
___ 11280 Hydraulic gates and valves
___ 11300 Fluid waste treatment and disposal equipment
___ 11400 Food service equipment
___ 11450 Residential equipment
___ 11460 Unit kitchens
___ 11470 Darkroom equipment
___ 11480 Athletic, recreational, and therapeutic equipment
___ 11500 Industrial and process equipment
___ 11600 Laboratory equipment
___ 11650 Planetarium equipment
___ 11660 Observatory equipment
___ 11680 Office equipment
___ 11700 Medical equipment
___ 11780 Mortuary equipment
___ 11850 Navigational equipment
___ 11870 Agricultural equipment

Division 12—Furnishings
___ 12050 Fabrics
___ 12100 Artwork

___ 12300 Manufactured casework
___ 12500 Window treatment
___ 12600 Furniture and accessories
___ 12670 Rugs and mats
___ 12700 Multiple seating
___ 12800 Interior plants and planters

Division 13—Special Construction
___ 13010 Air-supported structures
___ 13020 Integrated assemblies
___ 13030 Special purpose rooms
___ 13080 Sound, vibration, and seismic control
___ 13090 Radiation protection
___ 13100 Nuclear reactors
___ 13120 Preengineered structures
___ 13150 Aquatic facilities
___ 13175 Ice rinks
___ 13180 Site-constructed incinerators
___ 13185 Kennels and animal shelters
___ 13200 Liquid and gas storage tanks
___ 13220 Filter underdrains and media
___ 13230 Digester covers and appurtenances
___ 13240 Oxygenation systems
___ 13260 Sludge-conditioning systems
___ 13300 Utility control systems
___ 13400 Industrial and process control systems
___ 13500 Recording instrumentation
___ 13550 Transportation control instrumentation
___ 13600 Solar energy systems
___ 13700 Wind energy systems
___ 13750 Cogeneration systems
___ 13800 Building automation systems
___ 13900 Fire suppression and supervisory systems
___ 13950 Special security construction

Division 14—Conveying Systems
___ 14100 Dumbwaiters
___ 14200 Elevators
___ 14300 Escalators and moving walks
___ 14400 Lifts
___ 14500 Material-handling systems
___ 14600 Hoists and cranes
___ 14700 Turntables
___ 14800 Scaffolding
___ 14900 Transportation systems

Division 15—Mechanical
___ 15050 Basic mechanical materials and methods
___ 15250 Mechanical insulation
___ 15300 Fire protection
___ 15400 Plumbing
___ 15500 Heating, Ventilation, and Air Conditioning
      (HVAC)
___ 15550 Heat generation
___ 15650 Refrigeration
___ 15750 Heat transfer
___ 15850 Air handling
___ 15880 Air distribution
___ 15950 Controls
___ 15990 Testing, adjusting, and balancing

Division 16—Electrical
___ 16050 Basic electrical materials and methods
___ 16200 Power generation—built-up systems
___ 16300 Medium voltage distribution
___ 16400 Service and distribution
___ 16500 Lighting
___ 16600 Special systems
___ 16700 Communications
___ 16850 Electrical resistance heating
___ 16900 Controls
___ 16950 Testing

NOTES

___ 1. _Programming_ is a process leading to the statement of an architectural problem and the requirements to be met in offering a solution. It is the search for sufficient information to clarify, to understand, to state the problem. Programming is problem seeking and design is problem solving.

___ 2. Use the Information Index on pp. 32–33 as a guide for creating a program for more complex projects.

___ 3. Efficiency Ratios: Use the following numbers to aid in planning the size of buildings in regard to the ratio of net area to gross area:

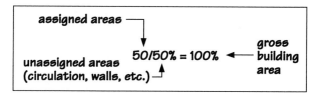

Note: The gross area of a building is the total floor area based on outside dimensions. The net area is based on the interior dimensions. For office or retail space, net leasable area means the area of the primary function of the building excluding such things as stairwells, corridors, mech. rooms, etc.

Common Range		
Automobile analogy	For buildings	Ratios
Super Luxury	Superb	50/50
Luxury	Grand	55/45
Full	Excellent	60/40
Intermediate	Moderate	65/35
Compact	Economical	67/33
Subcompact	Austere	70/30
Uncommon Range		
	Meager	75/25
	Spare	80/20
	Minimal	85/15
	Skeletal	90/10

See App. A, item B, p. 507 for common ratios by building type.

The following table gives common breakdowns of unassigned areas:

Circulation	16.0	20.0	22.0	24.0	25.0
Mechanical	5.0	5.5	7.5	8.0	10.0
Structure and walls	7.0	7.0	8.0	9.5	10.0
Public toilets	1.5	1.5	1.5	2.0	2.5
Janitor closets	0.2	0.5	0.5	0.5	1.0
Unassigned storage	0.3	0.5	0.5	1.0	1.5
	30.0%	35.0%	40.0%	45.0%	50.0%

NOTES

INFORMATION INDEX

	GOALS What does the client want to achieve & why?	FACTS What is it all about?

FUNCTION What's going to happen in the building?
    People
    Activities
    Relationships
	Mission
	Maximum number
	Individual identity
	Interaction/privacy
	Hierarchy of values
	Security
	Progression
	Segregation
	Encounters
	Efficiency
		Statistical data
		Area parameters
		Manpower/workloads
		User characteristics
		Community characteristics
		Value of loss
		Time-motion study
		Traffic analysis
		Behavioral patterns
		Space adequacy

FORM What is there now & what is to be there?
    Site
    Environment
    Quality
	Site elements
	(Trees, water, open space,
	    existing facilities,
	    utilities)
	Efficient land use
	Neighbors
	Individuality
	Direction
	Entry
	Projected image
	Level of quality
		Site analysis
		Climate analysis
		Cope survey
		Soils analysis
		F.A.R. and G.A.C.
		Surroundings
		Psychological implications
		Cost/SF
		Building efficiency
		Functional support

ECONOMY Concerns the initial budget & quality of construction.
    Initial budget
    Operating costs
    Lifecycle costs
	Extent of funds
	Cost effectiveness
	Maximum return
	Return on investment
	Minimize oper. costs
	Maint. & oper. costs
	Reduce life cycle costs
		Cost parameters
		Maximum budget
		Time-use factors
		Market analysis
		Energy source-costs
		Activities & climate
		    factors
		Economic data

TIME Deals with the influences of history, the inevitability of change from the present, & projections into the future.
    Past
    Present
    Future
	Historic preservation
	Static/dynamic
	Change
	Growth
	Occupancy date
		Significance
		Space parameters
		Activities
		Projections
		Linear schedule

CONCEPTS How does the client want to achieve the goals?	NEEDS How much money, space, & quality (as opposed to wants)?	PROBLEM What are the significant conditions & the general directions the design of the building should take?
Service grouping People grouping Activity grouping Priority Security controls Sequential flow Separated flow Mixed flow Relationships	Space requirements Parking requirements Outdoor space req'mts. Building efficiency Functional alternatives	Unique and important performance requirements which will shape building design.

Enhancement
Climate control
Safety
Special
   foundations
Density
Interdependence
Home base
Orientation
Accessibility
Character
Quality control
	Quality (cost/SF)
	Environmental & site
	   influences on costs
		Major form considerations which will affect building design.

Cost control Efficient allocation Multifunction Merchandising Energy conservation Cost control	Cost estimate analysis Entry budget (FRAS) Operating costs Life cycle costs	Attitude toward the initial budget and its influence on the fabric and geometry of the building.
Adaptability Tailored/loose fit Convertibility Expansibility Concurrent scheduling	Phasing Escalation	Implications of change/growth on long-range performance.

NOTES

__ E. CONSTRUCTION COSTS

Note: Most costs throughout this book (and this chapter) are from the following sources:

(11) (16) (17) (33) (34) (40) (40a)

___ 1. This book has rough cost data throughout. Rough costs are **boldface.** Subcontractor's overhead and profit, plus tax, are included. Both material (M) and labor (L) are included, usually with a general idea of percentage of each to the total (100%). Because there is room for only one cost per "element," often an idea of possible variation (higher or lower) of cost is given. Sometimes two numbers are given—the first being for residential and the second for commercial. One must use judgment in this regard to come up with a reasonable but rough cost estimate. As costs change, the user will have to revise costs in this book. The easiest way to do this will be to add historical modifiers, published each year, by various sources. The costs in this book are approx. costs at mid-1997. Over the last few years costs have increased about 2% to 3% per year. Be sure to compound when using this rule of thumb.

EXAMPLE :

A CONSTRUCTION ITEM IN THE BOOK GIVES THE FOLLOWING:
$5.00/SF (40% M & 60% L) (VARIATION OF +100% & -20%)
THIS MEANS THAT AS A GOOD AVERAGE THE COST OF THE ITEM INSTALLED (WITH THE SUBCONTRACTOR'S O.H. & P.) IS $5/SF, THE MATERIAL COST IS APPROX. $5 X .40 = $2/SF. THE LABOR COST IS APPROX. $5 X 0.60 = $3/SF. HOWEVER, A VERY EXPENSIVE VERSION CAN BE ROUGHLY 100% HIGHER ($5 X 2 = $10/SF) OR A CHEAPER VERSION CAN BE ROUGHLY 20% LOWER ($5 X 0.80 = $4/SF. BUT THE APPROX. AVERAGE COST IS $5.00/SF. NOTE: GENERAL CONTRACTOR'S O.H. & P. NOT INCLUDED.

___ 2. <u>Cost Control and Estimating</u>
Cost estimating can be time-consuming. It can also be dangerous in that wrong estimates may require time-consuming and expensive redesign. From the beginning of a project, responsibility for cost control (if any) should clearly be

established. If the architect is responsible for doing estimates, the architect should consider the following points:

___ *a.* Apples to Apples: In discussing costs and budgets with clients and builders, the parties must be sure they are comparing "apples to apples" (i.e., what is included and excluded). Examples of misunderstandings:

___ (1) Cost of land (is usually excluded).

___ (2) Financing costs (are usually excluded).

___ (3) Architectural/Engineering (A/E) fees (are usually excluded).

___ (4) City or government fees (are usually excluded).

___ (5) Is site work included or excluded in a $/SF estimate?

___ (6) Are Furniture, Fixture, and Equipment (FF&E) costs included or excluded (usually excluded)?

EXAMPLE:

AN ARCHITECT IS WORKING FOR A "SPEC" BUILDER. THE ARCHITECT HAS IN MIND A $60/SF BUDGET. THE SPEC. BUILDER HAS IN MIND A $50/SF BUDGET. THE ARCHITECT'S NUMBER HAS A GENERAL CONTRACTOR'S O.H. & P. OF SAY, 20% AS IF THE PROJECT WERE BID OR NEGOTIATED WITH AN INDEPENDENT CONTRACTOR. THE SPEC. BUILDER IS THINKING ABOUT HIS DIRECT COSTS, ONLY. THEY ARE COMPARING "APPLES TO ORANGES", BUT IF THE BUILDER'S NUMBER IS ADJUSTED:

$50/SF × 1.20 = $60/SF

OR IF THE ARCHITECT'S NUMBER IS ADJUSTED:

$60/SF × 0.80 = $50/SF

THEN, THEY ARE TALKING "APPLES TO APPLES".

___ *b.* Variables: The $/SF figures for various building types shown in App. A, item D are for average simple buildings. They (as all other costs in this book) may need to be modified by the following variables:

___ (1) *Location.* Modify costs for actual location. Use modifiers often published or see App. B, item V.

___ (2) *Historical Index.* If cost data is old, modify to current or future time by often-published modifiers.

___ (3) *Building Size.* The $/SF costs may need to be modified due to size of the project (see App. A, item C). Median sizes may be modified roughly as follows:

As size goes down, cost goes up by ratio of *1 to 2.*

As size goes up, cost goes down by ratio of *3 to 1.*

___ (4) *Shape and Perimeter.* Increases in perimeter and more complicated shapes will cause costs to go up. Where single elements are articulated (e.g., rounded corners or different types of coursing and materials in a masonry wall), add 30% to the costs involved.

___ (5) *Height.* As the number of stories goes up the cost goes up due to structure, fire protection, life safety issues, etc. **For each additional story add 1% to 5%.**

___ (6) *Quality of Materials, Construction, and Design.* Use the following rough guidelines to increase or decrease as needed:

Automobile analogy	For buildings	%
Super Luxury	Superb	+120
Luxury	Grand	+60
Full	Excellent	+20
Intermediate	Moderate	100
Compact	Economical	−10
Subcompact	Austere	−20

Note: Quality from lowest to highest can double the cost.

___ c. Costs (and construction scheduling) can be affected by weather, season, materials shortages, labor practices.

   ___ *d.* Beyond a 20-mile radius of cities, extra transportation charges increase material costs slightly. This
may be offset by lower wage rates. In dense urban
areas costs may increase.

   ___ *e.* In doing a total estimate, an allowance for general
conditions should be added. This usually ranges
from 5 to 15%, with *10%* a typical average.

   ___ *f.* At the end of a total estimate, an allowance for the
general contractor's overhead and profit should be
added. This usually ranges from *10 to 20%*. Market
conditions at the time of bidding will often affect
this percentage as well as all items. The market can
swing 10 to 20% from inactive to active times.

   ___ *g.* Contingencies should always be included in estimates as listed below. On alterations or repair
projects, *20%* is not an unreasonable allowance to
make.

   ___ *h.* Use rounding of numbers in all estimating items.

   ___ *i.* Consider using "add alternates" to projects where
the demand is high but the budget tight. These alternates should be things the client would like but does
not have to have and should be clearly denoted in
the drawings.

   ___ *j.* It is often wise for the architect to give estimates in
a range.

   ___ *k.* Because clients often change their minds or things
go wrong that cannot be foreseen in the beginning,
it may pay to advise the client to withhold from his
budget a confidential *5 to 10%* contingency. On the
other hand, clients often do this anyway, without
telling the architect.

   ___ *l.* Costs can further be affected by other things:
Government overhead $\approx$+100%
Award-winning designs are often $\approx$+200 to 300%

___ 3. Cost Control Procedure

   ___ *a.* At the *predesign phase* or beginning of a project,
determine the client's *budget* and what it includes, as
well as anticipated size of the building. Back out all
non construction costs such as cost of land, furniture
and fixtures, design fees, etc. Verify, in a simple format (such as $/SF, $/room, etc.) that this is reasonable. See App. A, item D for average $/SF costs as a
comparison and guideline.

   ___ *b.* At the *schematic design phase,* establish a reasonable $/SF target. Include a *15% to 20% contingency.*

___ *c.* At the *design development phase,* as the design becomes more specific, do a "systems" estimate. See Part 13 as an aid. For small projects a "unit" estimate might be appropriate, especially if basic plans (i.e., framing plans, etc.) not normally done at this time can be quickly sketched up for a "take off." Include a *10% to 15% contingency.*

___ *d.* At the *construction documents phase,* do a full unit "take off." For smaller projects, the estimate in the last phase may be enough, provided nothing has changed or been added to the project. Add a *5% to 10% contingency.*

___ 4. <u>Typical Single Family Residential Costs</u>

The following guidelines may be of use to establish $/SF budgets (site work not included):

___ *a.* Production Homes:

___ (1) For a 4-corner, 1600-SF tract house, wood frame, 1 story, with a 450-SF garage, no basement, and of average quality, use ***$67.00/SF*** (conditioned area only) as a 1997 national average. Break down as follows:

Item	*% of total*
1 General (including O & P)	18.5
2 Sitework (excavation only)	1
3 Concrete	6
4 Masonry (brick hearth and veneer)	.5
5 Metals	
6 Wood	
Rough carpentry	17
Finish carpentry and cabinetry	7.5
7 Thermal and moisture protection (insulation and roofing)	8
8 Doors, windows, and hardware	4
9 Finishes (stucco, wallboard, resilient flooring, carpet, paint)	19
10 Specialties (bath accessories and prefab fireplace)	1.5
11 Equipment (built-in appliances)	1.5
12–14	
15 Mechanical	
Plumbing	8
HVAC (heating only)	3
16 Electrical (lighting and wiring)	4.5
	100%

___ (2) Modify as follows:

  ___ (a) For "tract" or repetitive homes deduct 8% to 12%.

  ___ (b) For perimeter per the following percentages:
For 6 corners, add 2½%. For 8 corners add 5½%. For 10 corners add 7½%.

  ___ (c) Quality of construction:

Low	Average	Good	Best
−15%	100%	+20%	+50%

  ___ (d) Deduct for rural areas: 5%

  ___ (e) Add for 1800-SF house (better quality) 4%

  ___ (f) Add for 2000-SF house (better quality) 3%

  ___ (g) Deduct for over 2400 SF house (same quality) 3%

  ___ (h) Add for second story 4%

  ___ (i) Add for split-level house 3%

  ___ (j) Add for 3-story house 10%

  ___ (k) Add for masonry construction 9%

  ___ (l) Add for finished basement 40%

  ___ (m) Adjust for garage (larger or smaller): use 50% of house area.

  ___ (n) *No site work is included!*

___ b. Custom-designed homes:
The result of the above can be easily increased by ⅓ to ¾ or more. See App. A, p. 518.

___ 5. <u>Typical Commercial Building Cost Percentages</u>

Division	New const.	Remodeling
1. General requirements	6 to 8%	about 30%
2. Sitework	4 to 6%	for general
3. Concrete	15 to 20%	
4. Masonry	8 to 12%	
5. Metals	5 to 7%	
6. Wood	1 to 5%	
7. Thermal and moisture protection	4 to 6%	
8. Doors, windows, and glass	5 to 7%	
9. Finishes	8 to 12%	about 30%

10. Specialties*		for divisions
11. Equipment*		8–12
12. Furnishings*	6 to 10%*	
13. Special construction*		
14. Conveying systems*		about 40%
15. Mechanical	15 to 25%	for mech.
16. Electrical	8 to 12%	and elect.
Total	100%	

Note: FF&E (Furniture, Fixtures, and Equipment) are often excluded from building cost budget.

___ 6. Guidelines for Tenant Improvements (TI) in Office Buildings:
  ___ a. To estimate costs: take full building costs (see App. A, item D) less cost for frame and envelope and less ½ mech. and elect. costs.
  ___ b. **Costs for office building frames and envelopes: $25 to $35/SF.**
  ___ c. **TI costs range from $20 to $50/SF (in extreme cases $100/SF).**
___ 7. Guidelines for Demolition
  ___ a. Total buildings: *$3 to $5/SF*
  ___ b. Separate elements: *10% to 50%* of in-place const. cost of element.
___ 8. Project Budgeting
  ___ a. At the programming phase a total project budget may be worked using the following guidelines:

A. Building cost (net area/efficiency ratio = Gross area, gross area × unit cost = building cost)	$_____
B. Fixed equipment costs (lockers, kit. equip., etc.), percent of line A*	$_____
C. Site development cost, percent of line A*	$_____
D. Total construction cost (A + B + C)	$_____
E. Site acquisition and/or demolition (varies widely)	$_____
F. Movable equipment (such as furnishings) percent of line A* (also see App. A, item F)	$_____
G. Professional fees (vary from 5 to 10%), percent of line D	$_____
H. Contingencies*	$_____

I.	Administrative costs (varies from 1 to 2%), percent of line D[†]	$_____

J.	Total budget required (D, E–J)	$_____

*Percentages: low: 5%; medium: 10–15%; high: 20%; very high: 30%.
[†]For those projects which require financing costs, the following can be added to line J:
  1. Permanent financing (percent of line K):
    Investment banker fee varies, 2.5 to 6%.
    Construction loan fee varies, 1 to 2%.
  2. Interim financing (percent of line D):
    Approximately varies 1.5 to 2% above prime rate per year of construction time.

___ *b.* How to work back from total budget to building cost:

The following formula can be used to reduce line K, total budget required, to line A, building cost:

$$\text{Building cost} = \frac{\text{total budget} - \text{site acquisition}}{X + Y + Z}$$

$X = 1 + ($___% fixed equip.$) + ($___% site dev.$)$
$Y = (X) [($___% contingency$) + ($___% prof. fee$) + ($___% adm. cost$)]$
$Z = $___% movable equipment

Where necessary, interim financing percentage is added to adm. cost. Permanent financing percentage becomes T in $X + Y + Z + T$.

___ 9. <u>Use Architectural Areas</u> of Buildings as an aid in cost-estimating. See Architectural Area Diagram on p. 43. When doing "conceptual" estimating, by comparing your project to already built projects you can come up with an adjusted area by adding or subtracting the ratios shown.

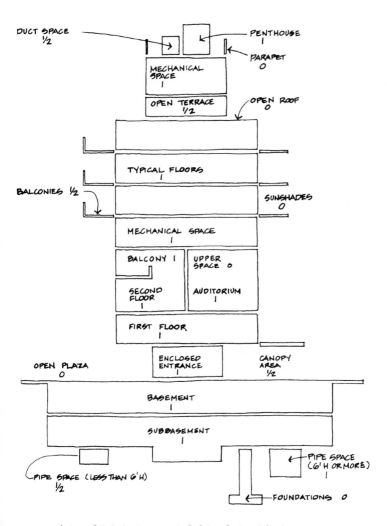

ARCHITECTURAL AREA DIAGRAM

EXAMPLE:

PROBLEM: ESTABLISH A FULL PRELM. BUDGET FOR A PROPOSED 25000 SF OFFICE BUILDING ON A 3 ACRE SITE IN WICHITA, KANSAS. WORK UP A RANGE OF LOW, MEDIUM, & HIGH AND THEN FURTHER DEVELOP THE AVERAGE.

SOLUTION:

	LOW	AVE.	HIGH
A. BASICS			
1. SITE DEV. COSTS (see P.165) THESE ARE $/SF OF SITE LESS BUILDING FOOTPRINT.	2	6	10
2. BUILDING SHELL COSTS (see P. 516, APPEN A, ITEM D), THESE ARE $/SF.	63	82	108.50
3. T.I. COSTS (see p. 41). THESE ARE $/SF	25	30	35
4. F.F. & E. COSTS (see P. 516, APPEN. A, ITEM F). THESE ARE $/SF FOR FURNISHINGS & EQUIP.	20	25	35

B. SPECIFICS	$000		
1. SITE DEV. COSTS 3 AC X 43560 SF/AC LESS 25000 SF BLDG. FOOTPRINT = 105680 SF. MULTIPLY THIS X $/SF IN 1, ABOVE.	211.36	634.08	1056.8
2. BUILDING SHELL COSTS. 25000 SF X $/SF IN 2, ABOVE.	1575	2050	2712.5
S.T. OF G.C. COSTS	$1786.36	$2684.08	$3767.3
SAY:		$2685000	

3. T.I. COSTS
   25000 SF X 75% (see
   P. 516, APP. A, ITEM B) = 18750 SF   – CONTINUED –

LEASE AREA TIMES $/SF   408.75   562.5   656.25
OF 3, ABOVE.
      SAY: $565000

4. F.F. & E. COSTS. MULTIPLY
  NET AREA OF 18750 SF ×   375   468.75   656.25
  $/SF OF 4, ABOVE
      SAY: $470000

5. A/E DESIGN FEES
  (%). SEE P.516, APPEN.   3%   6.5%   10%
  A, ITEM E.
  USE AVE. OF 6.5% × SHELL
  & T.I. COSTS OF $3250000 $212000

C. SUMMARY

SUMMARY OF AVE. COSTS IN LUMP SUM AND $/SF
(GROSS). ADJUST CONST. COSTS FOR WICHITA, KS
BY MULTIPLYING BY 0.81 (SEE P.531, APP. B, ITEM
V). ROUND ALL NUMBERS AS THIS IS JUST A PRELM.
BUDGET.

	LUMP SUM	X 0.81 ADJUSTED FOR WICHITA	$/SF (GROSS)
SITE DEV COSTS:	634000	513500	20.50
BUILD'G. SHELL:	2050000	1660000	66.50
T.I. COSTS:	565000	458000	18.50
S.T., G.C. COSTS		$2631500	$105.50/SF
F.F. & E. COSTS		470000	19.00
A/E FEES		212000	8.50
TOTALS:		$3313500	$133/SF

NOTES

___ 1. Estimate *Scheduling*

Project value	Const. time
Under $1,400,000	10 months
Up to $3,800,000	15 months
Up to $19,000,000	21 months
Over $19,000,000	28 months

  ___ *a.* Design time runs 25 to 40% of construction time (up to 100% for small projects, including government review).

  ___ *b.* Construction time can be affected by building type. Using commercial buildings as a base, modify other building types: industrial: −20%; research and development: +20%; institutional buildings: +30%.

___ 2. Site Observation Visits

  ___ *a.* Take:
- ___ (1) Plans
- ___ (2) Specifications
- ___ (3) Project files
- ___ (4) Tape
- ___ (5) Chalk
- ___ (6) Camera
- ___ (7) Paper
- ___ (8) Pencil
- ___ (9) Calculator
- ___ (10) Checklist
- ___ (11) Field report forms
- ___ (12) Flashlight
- ___ (13) String line and level

  ___ *b.* List of site visits for small projects:
- ___ (1) After building stake out is complete
- ___ (2) After excavation is complete and rebar is in place
- ___ (3) When foundation is being placed
- ___ (4) When under-slab utilities and stem walls under way
- ___ (5) During placement of concrete slab on grade
- ___ (6) During masonry and/or frame walls and columns and layout of interior walls
- ___ (7) During floor and/or roof framing, wall and roof sheathing (prior to roofing)
- ___ (8) During roofing
- ___ (9) During drywall, plaster, plumbing, electrical, and HVAC
- ___ (10) At end of project (punch list)

NOTES

___ G. PRACTICAL MATH AND TABLES

(13) (29) (45)

___ 1. <u>General:</u> Architects seldom have to be involved in higher mathematics, but they need to continually do simple math *well.*

   ___ *a.* For rough estimating (such as in this book) an accuracy of more than 90% to 95% is seldom required.

   ___ *b.* Try to have a rough idea of what the answer should be, before the calculation (i.e., does the answer make sense?).

   ___ *c.* Round numbers off and don't get bogged down in trivia.

   ___ *d.* For final exact numbers that are important (such as final building areas), go slow, and recheck calculations at least once.

___ 2. <u>Decimals of a Foot</u>   <u>Decimals of an Inch</u>

$1'' = .08'$	$7'' = .58'$	$\frac{1}{8}'' = 0.125''$	$\frac{5}{8}'' = 0.625''$
$2'' = .17'$	$8'' = .67'$	$\frac{1}{4}'' = 0.250''$	$\frac{3}{4}'' = 0.750''$
$3'' = .25'$	$9'' = .75'$	$\frac{3}{8}'' = 0.375''$	$\frac{7}{8}'' = 0.875''$
$4'' = .33'$	$10'' = .83'$	$\frac{1}{2}'' = 0.50''$	$1'' = 1.0''$
$5'' = .42'$	$11'' = .92'$		
$6'' = .50'$	$12'' = 1.0'$		

___ 3. <u>Simple Algebra</u>

One unknown and $A = B/C$ Example: $3 = 15/5$
   two knowns $B = A \times C$ $15 = 3 \times 5$
                     $C = B/A$ $5 = 15/3$

___ 4. <u>Ratios and Proportions</u>

One unknown and three knowns (cross multiplication)

$$\frac{A}{B} = \frac{C}{D} \qquad \text{Example:} \quad \frac{X}{5} \bowtie \frac{10}{20} \qquad 20\,X = 5 \times 10$$

$$A \times C = B \times D \qquad X = \frac{5 \times 10}{20} = 2.5 \qquad X = 2.5$$

___ 5. <u>Exponents and Powers</u>

$10^6 = 10 \times 10 \times 10 \times 10 \times 10 \times 10 = 1,000,000$ [1 + 6 zeros]
$10^0 = 1.0$
$10^{-6} = 0.000001$ [6 places to left or 5 zeros in front of 1]

___ 6. <u>Percent Increases or Decreases</u>

   50% increase = $\frac{1}{2}$ increase, use $\times 1.5$
   100% increase = double, use $\times 2.0$
   200% increase = triple, use $\times 3.0$
   Example: 20 increases to 25
   To find percent increase: 25–20 = 5 [amount of increase]
                               5/20 = 0.25 or 25% increase

___ 7. <u>Slopes, Gradients, and Angles</u>
(see p. 51)

___ *a.* Slope = "rise over run" or

$$\% \text{ slope} = \frac{\text{rise}}{\text{run}} \times 100$$

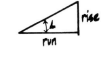

___ *b.* Gradient:
as ratios of rise to run
Example: expressed as 1 in 12
for a ramp or as 4″ in 12″ for
a roof

___ *c.* Angle
Degree angle based on rise
and run (see properties of
right angles)

___ 8. <u>Properties of Right Angles</u>

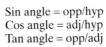

45° angle: $a^2 + b^2 = c^2$

or $c = \sqrt{a^2 + b^2}$

For other right angles use simple
trigonometry:

Sin angle = opp/hyp
Cos angle = adj/hyp
Tan angle = opp/adj

Use calculators with trig. functions
or table on p. 52.

___ 9. <u>Properties of Non-Right Angles</u>
Use law of sines:

a/sin A = b/sin B = c/sin C
a/b = sin A/sin B, etc.

___ 10. <u>Properties of Circles</u>
A circle is divided into 360 equal parts, called *degrees* (°).
One degree is an angle at the center of a circle which cuts
off an arc that is ¹⁄₃₆₀ of the circumference. Degrees are subdivided into 60 minutes (′). Minutes are subdivided into 60
seconds (″). See p. 56.

___ 11. <u>Equivalents of Measure</u>
Use the three bar graphs on p. 56 for quick metric conver-
sions.

___ 12. <u>Geometric Figures</u>
Use the formulas on pp. 57–58 to calculate areas and volumes.

___ 13. <u>Units and Conversions</u>
     Use the formulas on pp. 59–66 to convert units.

Table of Slopes, Grades, Angles

% Slope	Inch/ft	Ratio	Deg. from horiz.
1	⅛	1 in 100	
2	¼	1 in 50	
3	⅜		
4	½	1 in 25	
5	⅝	1 in 20	3
6	¾		
7	⅞		
8	approx. 1	approx. 1 in 12	
9	1⅛		
10	1¼	1 in 10	6
11	1⅜	approx. 1 in 9	
12	1½		
13	1⅝		
14	1¾		
15			8.5
16	1⅞		
17	2	approx. 2 in 12	
18	2⅛		
19	2¼		
20	2⅜	1 in 5	11.5
25	3	3 in 12	14
30	3.6	1 in 3.3	17
35	4.2	approx. 4 in 12	19.25
40	4.8	approx. 5 in 12	21.5
45	5.4	1 in 2.2	24
50	6	6 in 12	26.5
55	6⅝	1 in 1.8	28.5
60	7¼	approx. 7 in 12	31
65	7¾	1 in 1½	33
70	8⅜	1 in 1.4	35
75	9	1 in 1.3	36.75
100	12	1 in 1	45

Trigonometry Tables

Deg	Sin	Cos	Tan	Deg	Sin	Cos	Tan	Deg	Sin	Cos	Tan
1	.0175	.9998	.0175	31	.5150	.8572	.6009	61	.8746	.4848	1.8040
2	.0349	.9994	.0349	32	.5299	.8480	.6249	62	.8829	.4695	1.8807
3	.0523	.9986	.0524	33	.5446	.8387	.6494	63	.8910	.4540	1.9626
4	.0698	.9976	.0699	34	.5592	.8290	.6745	64	.8988	.4384	2.0503
5	.0872	.9962	.0875	35	.5736	.8192	.7002	65	.9063	.4226	2.1445
6	.1045	.9945	.1051	36	.5878	.8090	.7265	66	.9135	.4067	2.2460
7	.1219	.9925	.1228	37	.6018	.7986	.7536	67	.9205	.3907	2.3559
8	.1392	.9903	.1405	38	.6157	.7880	.7813	68	.9272	.3746	2.4751
9	.1564	.9877	.1584	39	.6293	.7771	.8098	69	.9336	.3584	2.6051
10	.1736	.9848	.1763	40	.6428	.7660	.8391	70	.9397	.3420	2.7475
11	.1908	.9816	.1944	41	.6561	.7547	.8693	71	.9455	.3256	2.9042
12	.2079	.9781	.2126	42	.6691	.7431	.9004	72	.9511	.3090	3.0777
13	.2250	.9744	.2309	43	.6820	.7314	.9325	73	.9563	.2924	3.2709
14	.2419	.9703	.2493	44	.6947	.7193	.9657	74	.9613	.2756	3.4874
15	.2588	.9659	.2679	45	.7071	.7071	1.0000	75	.9659	.2588	3.7321
16	.2756	.9613	.2867	46	.7193	.6947	1.0355	76	.9703	.2419	4.0108
17	.2924	.9563	.3057	47	.7314	.6820	1.0724	77	.9744	.2250	4.3315
18	.3090	.9511	.3249	48	.7431	.6691	1.1106	78	.9781	.2079	4.7046
19	.3256	.9455	.3443	49	.7547	.6561	1.1504	79	.9816	.1908	5.1446
20	.3420	.9397	.3640	50	.7660	.6428	1.1918	80	.9848	.1736	5.6713
21	.3584	.9336	.3839	51	.7771	.6293	1.2349	81	.9877	.1564	6.3138
22	.3746	.9272	.4040	52	.7880	.6157	1.2799	82	.9903	.1392	7.1154
23	.3907	.9205	.4245	53	.7986	.6018	1.3270	83	.9925	.1219	8.1443
24	.4067	.9135	.4452	54	.8090	.5878	1.3764	84	.9945	.1045	9.5144
25	.4226	.9063	.4663	55	.8192	.5736	1.4281	85	.9962	.0872	11.4301
26	.4384	.8988	.4877	56	.8290	.5592	1.4826	86	.9976	.0698	14.3007
27	.4540	.8910	.5095	57	.8387	.5446	1.5399	87	.9986	.0523	19.0811
28	.4695	.8829	.5317	58	.8480	.5299	1.6003	88	.9994	.0349	28.6363
29	.4848	.8746	.5543	59	.8572	.5150	1.6643	89	.9998	.0175	57.2900
30	.5000	.8660	.5774	60	.8660	.5000	1.7321	90	1.000	.0000	∞

Note: Deg = degrees of angle; Sin = sine; Cos = cosine; Tan = tangent.

___ 14. Perspective Sketching

Use the following simple techniques of using 10′ cubes and lines
at 5′ with diagonals for quick perspective sketching:

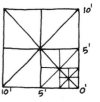

___ a. The sketches shown on p. 54
show two techniques:
The *first* establishes diagonal
Vanishing Points (VP) on the
Horizon Line (HL) at certain distances from the
VPs, also on the HL. 10′ cubes are established by pro-
jecting diagonals to the VPs. The *second* technique
has 10′ cubes and lines at the 5′ half-points. Diagonals through the half-points continue the 5′ and 10′
module to the VPs. The vertical 5′ roughly equals eye
level, and establishes the HL. Half of 5′ or 2.5′ is a
module for furniture height and width.

___ b. The sketch shown on p. 55 illustrates the most common way people view buildings. That is, close up, at
almost a one-point perspective. To produce small
sketches, set right vertical measure at ½″ apart. Then,
about 10½″ to left, set vertical measure at ⅜″ apart.
This will produce a small sketch to fit on 8½ × 11
paper. Larger sketches can be done using these pro-
portions.

PERSPECTIVE SKETCHING

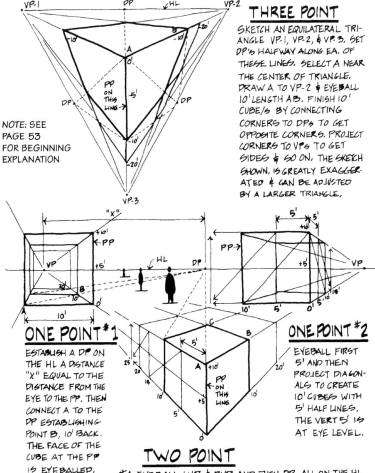

THREE POINT

SKETCH AN EQUILATERAL TRI-
ANGLE VP-1, VP-2, & VP-3, SET
DP's HALFWAY ALONG EA. OF
THESE LINES. SELECT A NEAR
THE CENTER OF TRIANGLE.
DRAW A TO VP-2 & EYEBALL
10' LENGTH AB. FINISH 10'
CUBE/s BY CONNECTING
CORNERS TO DPs TO GET
OPPOSITE CORNERS. PROJECT
CORNERS TO VPs TO GET
SIDES & SO ON. THE SKETCH
SHOWN, IS GREATLY EXAGGER-
ATED & CAN BE ADJUSTED
BY A LARGER TRIANGLE,

NOTE: SEE
PAGE 53
FOR BEGINNING
EXPLANATION

ONE POINT #1

ESTABLISH A DP ON
THE HL A DISTANCE
"X" EQUAL TO THE
DISTANCE FROM THE
EYE TO THE PP. THEN
CONNECT A TO THE
DP ESTABLISHING
POINT B, 10' BACK.
THE FACE OF THE
CUBE AT THE PP
IS EYEBALLED.

ONE POINT #2

EYEBALL FIRST
5' AND THEN
PROJECT DIAGON-
ALS TO CREATE
10' CUBES WITH
5' HALF LINES.
THE VERT 5' IS
AT EYE LEVEL.

TWO POINT

#1 EYEBALL LVP & RVP AND THEN DP, ALL ON THE HL.
CONNECT A TO DP. EYEBALL FIRST 10' ON LINE AB.
CONNECT B TO LVP. THE INTERSECTION ESTABLISH-
ES POINT C, 10' BACK, & SO ON.

#2 5' DIAGONALS CAN ALSO BE USED BY EYEBALLING
THE FIRST 5'.

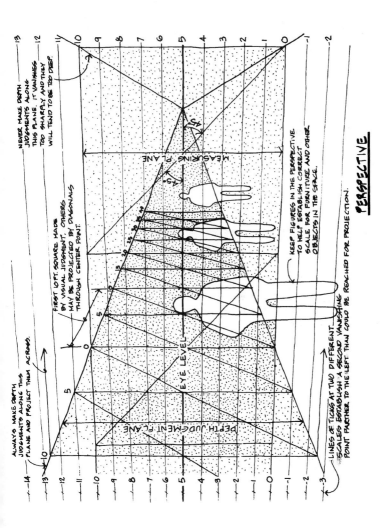

NEVER MAKE DEPTH JUDGMENTS ALONG THIS PLANE. IT VANISHES TOO SHARPLY AND THEY WILL TEND TO BE TOO DEEP.

ALWAYS MAKE DEPTH JUDGMENTS ALONG THIS PLANE AND PROJECT THEM ACROSS.

FIRST LEFT SQUARE MADE BY VISUAL JUDGMENT. OTHERS MAY BE PROJECTED BY DIAGONALS THROUGH CENTER POINT.

KEEP FIGURES IN THE PERSPECTIVE TO HELP ESTABLISH CORRECT SCALE FOR FURNITURE AND OTHER OBJECTS IN THE SPACE.

LINES OF TICKS AT TWO DIFFERENT SCALES ESTABLISH A SECOND VANISHING POINT FURTHER TO THE LEFT THAN COULD BE REACHED FOR PROJECTION.

MEASURING PLANE

DEPTH JUDGEMENT PLANE

EYE LEVEL

PERSPECTIVE

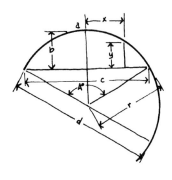

$$\text{Circumference} = 6.28318\,r = 3.14159\,d$$
$$\text{Diameter} = 0.31831 \text{ circumference}$$
$$\text{Area} = 3.14159\,r^2 = \pi r^2$$

$$\text{Arc} \quad a = \frac{\pi r A^\circ}{180^\circ} = 0.017453\,r A^\circ$$

$$\text{Angle} \quad A^\circ = \frac{180^\circ d}{\pi r} = 57.29578\,\frac{a}{r}$$

$$\text{Radius} \quad r = \frac{4 b^2 + c^2}{8 b}$$

$$\text{Chord} \quad c = 2\sqrt{2 b r - b^2} = 2 r \sin\frac{A}{2}$$

$$\text{Rise} \quad b = r - \tfrac{1}{2}\sqrt{4 r^2 - c^2} = \frac{c}{2}\tan\frac{A}{4}$$

$$= 2 r \sin^2\frac{A}{4} = r + y - \sqrt{r^2 - x^2}$$

$$y = b - r + \sqrt{r^2 - x^2}$$

$$x = \sqrt{r^2 - (r + y - b)^2}$$

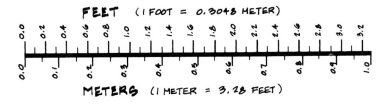

FEET (1 FOOT = 0.3048 METER)

METERS (1 METER = 3.28 FEET)

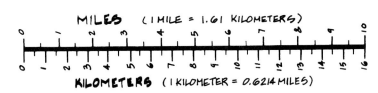

MILES (1 MILE = 1.61 KILOMETERS)

KILOMETERS (1 KILOMETER = 0.6214 MILES)

DEGREES FAHRENHEIT

DEGREES CENTIGRADE

GEOMETRIC FIGURES

PLANE SHAPES (TWO - DIMENSIONAL)

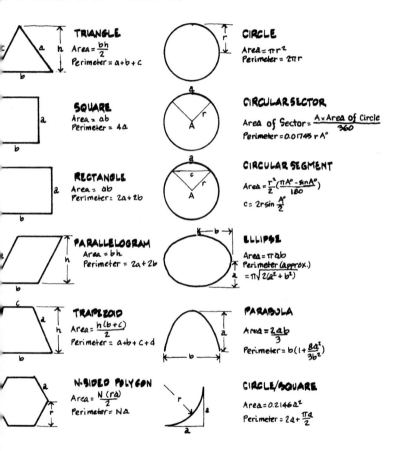

TRIANGLE
Area $= \dfrac{bh}{2}$
Perimeter $= a+b+c$

SQUARE
Area $= ab$
Perimeter $= 4a$

RECTANGLE
Area $= ab$
Perimeter $= 2a+2b$

PARALLELOGRAM
Area $= bh$
Perimeter $= 2a+2b$

TRAPEZOID
Area $= \dfrac{h(b+c)}{2}$
Perimeter $= a+b+c+d$

N-SIDED POLYGON
Area $= \dfrac{N(ra)}{2}$
Perimeter $= Na$

CIRCLE
Area $= \pi r^2$
Perimeter $= 2\pi r$

CIRCULAR SECTOR
Area of Sector $= \dfrac{A \times \text{Area of Circle}}{360}$
Perimeter $= 0.01745\, r\, A°$

CIRCULAR SEGMENT
Area $= \dfrac{r^2}{2}\left(\dfrac{\pi A° - \sin A°}{180}\right)$
$c = 2r \sin \dfrac{A°}{2}$

ELLIPSE
Area $= \pi ab$
Perimeter (approx.)
$= \pi \sqrt{2(a^2 + b^2)}$

PARABOLA
Area $= \dfrac{2ab}{3}$
Perimeter $= b\left(1 + \dfrac{8a^2}{3b^2}\right)$

CIRCLE/SQUARE
Area $= 0.2146 a^2$
Perimeter $= 2a + \dfrac{\pi a}{2}$

GEOMETRIC FIGURES

SOLID BODIES (THREE-DIMENSIONAL)

CUBE

Area = $6a^2$
Volume = a^3

CYLINDER

Area = $2\pi r^2 + 2\pi rh$
Volume = $\pi r^2 h$

RECTANGULAR PRISM

Area = $2ab + 2ac + 2bc$
Volume = abc

CONE

Area = $\pi r \sqrt{r^2 + h^2} + \pi r^2$
Volume = $\dfrac{\pi r^2 h}{3}$

SPHERE

Area = $4\pi r^2$
Volume = $\dfrac{4\pi r^3}{3}$

SPHERICAL SEGMENT

Area = $2\pi ra$
Volume = $\dfrac{\pi a^2 (3r - a)}{3}$

ELLIPSOID

Volume = $\dfrac{\pi abc}{3}$

PARABOLOID

Volume = $\dfrac{\pi r^2 h}{2}$

LENGTH

METERS m	INCHES in.	FEET ft.	YARD yd.	RODS r.	CHAINS ch.	MILES, U.S.		KILO- METERS km
						STATUTE	NAUTICAL	
1	39.37	3.28	1.09	0.199	0.05	$0.^3 6214$	$0.^3 05396$	0.001
0.025	1	0.083	0.028	$0.^2 051$	$0.^2 213$	$0.^4 158$	$0.^4 137$	$0.^4 0254$
0.305	12	1	0.333	0.06	0.015	$0.^3 189$	$0.^3 165$	$0.^3 305$
0.914	36	3	1	0.18	0.045	$0.^3 568$	$0.^3 443$	$0.^3 914$
5.029	198	16.5	5.5	1	0.25	$0.^2 313$	$0.^2 271$	$0.^2 503$
20.117	792	66	22	4	1	0.013	0.0109	0.020
1609.35	63360	5280	1760	320	80	1	0.868	1.609
1853.25	72962.5	6080.2	2026.7	368.5	92.12	1.15	1	1.853
1000	39370	3280.8	1093.6	198.8	49.71	0.621	0.540	1

✻ 1 METER (m) = 10 DECIMETERS (dm.) = 100 CENTIMETERS (cm.) = 1000 MILLIMETERS (mm)

NOTE: NOTATIONS $0.^2, 0.^3, 0.^4$, ETC., INDICATE THE NUMBER OF ZEROS.

EXAMPLE; 1 METER = $0.^3 6214$ = 0.0006214 STATUTE MILES.

AREAS

SQUARE METERS SM	SQUARE INCHES SI	SQUARE FEET SF	SQUARE YARDS SY	SQUARE RODS SR	ACRES AC	HECTARES HA	SQUARE MILES STATUTE	SQUARE KILOMETER SQ KM
1	1550.0	10.76	1.196	0.039	$0.^{3}247$	0.0001	$0.^{6}386$	$0.^{5}1$
$0.^{3}65$	1	$0.^{2}69$	$0.^{3}77$	$0.^{4}26$	$0.^{6}16$	$0.^{7}65$	$0.^{9}25$	$0.^{9}65$
0.093	144	1	0.111	$0.^{2}37$	$0.^{4}23$	$0.^{5}93$	$0.^{7}36$	$0.^{7}93$
0.836	1296	9	1	0.033	$0.^{3}21$	$0.^{4}84$	$0.^{6}32$	$0.^{6}84$
25.293	39204	272.25	30.25	1	0.006	$0.^{2}25$	$0.^{5}98$	$0.^{4}26$
4046.87	6272640	43560	4840	160	1	0.405	$0.^{2}16$	$0.^{2}41$
10000	15499969	107639	11959.9	395.37	2.47104	1	$0.^{2}39$	0.01
2589999		27878400	3097600	1024000	640	259	1	2.59
1000000		10763867	1195985	39536.6	247.104	100	0.386	1

VOLUMES

CUBIC DECI-METER OR LITERS	CUBIC INCHES	CUBIC FEET	CUBIC YARDS	U.S. QUARTS		U.S. GALLONS		U.S. BUSHELS
				LIQUID	DRY	LIQUID	DRY	
1	61.02	0.035	0.²13	1.057	0.908	0.264	0.227	0.028
0.016	1	0.³58	0.⁴21	0.017	0.015	0.²43	0.²72	0.²47
28.32	1728	1	0.037	29.92	25.714	7.481	6.429	0.804
764.56	46656	27	1	807.90	694.28	201.97	173.57	21.70
0.946	57.75	0.033	0.²124	1	0.859	0.25	0.215	0.027
1.1012	67.20	0.039	0.²144	1.1637	1	0.291	0.25	0.031
3.786	231	0.134	0.²495	4	3.437	1	0.859	0.107
4.405	268.8	0.156	0.²576	4.655	4	1.164	1	0.125
35.24	2150.4	1.244	0.0461	37.24	32	9.309	8	1

U.S. DRY MEASURE: 1 BUSHEL = 4 PECKS = 8 GALLONS = 32 QUARTS = 64 PINTS
U.S. LIQUID MEASURE: 1 GALLON = 4 QUARTS = 8 PINTS = 32 GILLS = 128 FLUID OUNCES
1 U.S. GALLON = 0.83268 IMPERIAL GALLON

WEIGHTS

KILO-GRAMS KG	GRAINS	OUNCES TROY	OUNCES AVOIR	POUNDS TROY	POUNDS AVOIR	TONS NET (SHORT) 2000 lbs	TONS GROSS (LONG) 2240 lbs	TONS METRIC 1000 KG
1	15432.4	32.15	35.27	2.679	2.205	$0.0^{2}1102$	$0.0^{3}984$	0.001
$0.0^{4}648$	1	$0.0^{2}208$	$0.0^{3}23$	$0.0^{3}174$	$0.0^{3}143$	$0.0^{7}714$	$0.0^{7}638$	$0.0^{7}648$
0.031	480	1	1.097	0.083	0.069	$0.0^{4}343$	$0.0^{4}306$	$0.0^{4}311$
0.024	437.5	0.911	1	0.076	0.063	$0.0^{4}313$	$0.0^{4}279$	$0.0^{4}284$
0.373	5760	12	13.166	1	0.823	$0.0^{3}411$	$0.0^{3}367$	$0.0^{3}373$
0.454	7000	14.58	16	1.215	1	0.0005	$0.0^{3}446$	$0.0^{3}454$
907.185	14000000	29166.7	32000	2430.56	2000	1	0.893	0.907
1016.05	15680000	32666.7	35840	2722.22	2240	1.12	1	1.016
1000	15432356	32150.7	35274	2679.23	2204.62	1.1102	0.984	1

1 LONG HUNDREDWEIGHT (CWT.) = 1/20 TON = 4 QUARTERS = 8 STONE = 112 LBS = 50.8 KG

DENSITIES

GRAMS PER CU. CENTIMETER g/cm³	POUNDS PER CU. INCH lb/in³	POUNDS PER CU. FOOT lb/ft³	POUNDS PER CU. YARD lb/yd³	KILOGRAMS PER CU. METER kg/m²	POUNDS PER BUSHEL, U.S.	POUNDS PER GALLON, DRY, U.S.	POUNDS PER GALLON, LIQUID, U.S.	KILOGRAMS PER HECTOLITER kg/hl
1	0.036	62.43	1685.56	1000	77.689	9.711	8.345	100
27.68	1	1728	46656	27679.7	2150.4	268.8	231	2767.97
0.016	$0.0^{3}579$	1	27	16.02	1.24	0.156	0.134	1.602
$0.0^{3}59$	$0.0^{4}21$	0.037	1	0.593	0.046	$0.0^{2}576$	$0.0^{2}495$	0.059
0.001	$0.0^{4}36$	0.062	1.686	1	0.078	$0.0^{2}97$	$0.0^{2}83$	0.10
0.013	$0.0^{3}47$	0.804	21.696	12.87	1	0.125	0.107	1.287
0.103	$0.0^{2}37$	6.429	173.57	102.97	8	1	0.859	10.297
0.119	$0.0^{2}43$	7.481	201.97	119.83	9.31	1.164	1	11.98
0.01	$0.0^{3}36$	0.624	16.86	10	0.777	0.097	0.083	1

63

(17a)

PASCALS N/m^2	BARS $10^5 N/m^2$	POUNDS & PER IN^2	ATMOS-PHERES	COLUMNS OF MERCURY (0°C, g = 9.807 m/s²)		COLUMNS OF WATER (15°C, g = 9.807 m/s²)	
				cm	in	cm	in
1	$0.0^4 1$	$0.0^3 145$	$0.0^4 1$	$0.0^3 75$	$0.0^3 295$	0.0102	0.004
100000	1	14.5	0.99	75	29.53	1020.7	401.8
6894.8	0.0689	1	0.068	5.17	2.04	70.37	27.7
101326	1.01	14.696	1	76	29.92	1034	407.1
1333	0.013	0.193	0.013	1	0.39	13.61	5.357
3386	0.034	0.49	0.033	2.54	1	34.56	13.61
97.98	$0.0^3 98$	0.014	$0.0^3 97$	$0.0^3 73$	0.029	1	0.39
248.9	$0.0^2 25$	0.036	$0.0^2 25$	0.187	0.073	2.54	1

POWER

HORSE-POWER	KILO-WATTS	METRIC HORSE-POWER	kgf·m PER SEC.	FT-LBf PER SEC.	KILO-CALORIES PER SEC.	B.T.U. PER SEC.
1	0.746	1.014	76.04	550	0.178	0.707
1.341	1	1.36	102.0	737.6	0.239	0.948
0.986	0.736	1	75	542.5	0.176	0.697
0.013	$0.0^{2}98$	0.013	1	7.23	$0.0^{2}23$	$0.0^{2}93$
$0.0^{2}18$	$0.0^{2}14$	$0.0^{2}18$	0.138	1	$0.0^{3}32$	$0.0^{2}13$
5.615	4.187	5.692	426.9	3088	1	3.968
1.415	1.055	1.434	107.6	778.2	0.252	1

ENERGY OR WORK

JOULES (NEWTON-METER)	KILOGRAM-METERS	FOOT-POUNDS	KILOWATT HOURS	METRIC HORSE POWER-HOURS	HORSE POWER-HOURS	LITER-ATMOS-PHERES	KILO-CALORIES	BRITISH THERMAL UNITS
1	0.102	0.738	0.0^6278	0.0^6378	0.0^637	0.0^2987	0.0^324	0.0^3948
9.807	1	7.233	0.0^6272	0.0^6370	0.0^637	0.0968	0.0^2234	0.0^293
1.356	0.138	1	0.0^6377	0.0^6512	0.0^6505	0.0134	0.0^3324	0.0013
3600000	367100	2655000	1	1.36	1.34	35528	859.9	3412
2648000	270000	1952900	0.736	1	0.986	26131	632.4	2510
2684500	2737500	1980000	0.746	1.014	1	26493	641.2	2544
101.33	10.33	74.74	0.0^428	0.0^438	0.0^438	1	0.024	0.096
4186.8	426.9	3088	0.0^2116	0.0^2158	0.0^2156	41.32	1	3.968
1055	107.6	778.2	0.0^329	0.0^399	0.0^393	10.41	0.252	1

NOTES

NOTES

___ H. BUILDING LAWS

___ 1. _Zoning_ (42)

Zoning laws vary from city to city. The following checklist is typical of items in a zoning ordinance:

___ *a.* Zone
___ *b.* Allowable use
___ *c.* Prohibited uses or special-use permit
___ *d.* Restrictions on operation of facility
___ *e.* Minimum lot size
___ *f.* Maximum building coverage
___ *g.* Floor area ratio
___ *h.* Setbacks for landscaping
___ *i.* Building setbacks: front, side, street, rear
___ *j.* Required open space
___ *k.* Maximum allowable height
___ *l.* Restrictions due to adjacent zone(s)
___ *m.* Required parking
___ *n.* Required loading zone
___ *o.* Parking layout restrictions
___ *p.* Landscape requirements
___ *q.* Environmental impact statements
___ *r.* Signage
___ *s.* Site plan review
___ *t.* "Design review"
___ *u.* Special submittals required for approval and/or hearings:
    ___ (1) Fees
    ___ (2) Applications
    ___ (3) Drawings
    ___ (4) Color presentations
    ___ (5) Sample boards
    ___ (6) List of adjacent land owners
    ___ (7) Other
___ *v.* Although not part of the zoning ordinance, private covenants, conditions, and restrictions (CC&Rs) that "run" with the land should be checked.
___ *w.* Other

NOTES

___ 2. _Code Requirements for Residential_ (26)
     Construction (1997 UBC)

Use the following checklist for single-family residences:
___ *a.* Location on lot
    ___ (1) Openings must be 3′ from property line.
    ___ (2) Walls less than 3′ must be 1-hour construction.
___ *b.* Separation between dwelling units must be a min. of 1-hour construction.
___ *c.* Windows and ventilation
    ___ (1) Habitable rooms must have natural light by exterior windows with area of at least $\frac{1}{10}$ floor area, but min. of 10 SF.
    ___ (2) Bath and laundry-type rooms must have ventilation by operable exterior windows with area of not less than $\frac{1}{20}$ floor area. Min. of 1.5 SF.
    ___ (3) Habitable rooms must have natural ventilation by operable exterior windows with area of not less than $\frac{1}{20}$ floor area. Min. of 5 SF.
    ___ (4) In lieu of natural ventilation, mechanical ventilation may be used:
        ___ (*a*) In habitable rooms, two air changes per hour, $\frac{1}{5}$ of air supply taken from outside.
        ___ (*b*) In bath and laundry-type rooms, five air changes per hour.
        ___ (*c*) The point of discharge must be at least 3 ft from any building opening.
        ___ (*d*) Bathrooms with lavatory and WC only may have circulating fan.
    ___ (5) Any room may be considered as a portion of an adjoining room when $\frac{1}{2}$ of area of the common wall is open and provides an opening of at least $\frac{1}{10}$ of floor area of interior room, or 25 SF, whichever is greater.
    ___ (6) Eaves over windows shall not be less than 30″ from side and rear property lines.
___ *d.* Ceiling heights
    ___ (1) Habitable rooms, 7′6″ min.
    ___ (2) Other rooms, 7′0″ min.
    ___ (3) Where exposed beams are used, height is to bottom when spacing less than 48″; otherwise, it is measured to the top.

___ (4) At sloped ceilings, the min. ceiling height is required at only ½ the area, but never less than 5′ height.

___ (5) At furred ceilings, the min. ceiling height is required at only ⅔ the area, but furred ceiling to be at 7′0″ min.

___ e. Sanitation

___ (1) Room with WC shall be separated from food preparation or storage area by a tight-fitting door.

___ (2) Every Dwelling Unit (DU) shall have a kitchen with a sink.

___ (3) Every DU shall have a bath with a WC, lavatory, bathtub, or shower.

___ (4) Every sink, lavatory, bathtub, or shower shall have hot and cold running water.

___ f. Room dimensions

___ (1) At least one room shall have at least 120 SF.

___ (2) Other habitable rooms, except kitchens, shall have at least 70 SF and shall be not less than 7′ in any dimension.

___ (3) Each WC shall be located in a clear space of 30″ wide and have 24″ clearance in front.

___ g. Fire warning system

___ (1) Each dwelling must have smoke detectors in each sleeping room and the corridor to sleeping rooms, at each story (close proximity to stairways), and basement.

___ (2) In new construction, smoke detectors are to be powered by building wiring but equipped with backup battery.

___ (3) If additions or alterations (exceeding $1000) or sleeping rooms are being added, the entire building shall have smoke detectors.

___ (4) In existing buildings, smoke detectors may be solely battery-operated.

___ h. Exits

___ (1) Doors

___ (a) At least one entry door shall be 3′ wide by 6′8″ high.

___ (b) There must be a floor or landing at each side of each door, not more than 1″ below door and sloped not greater than 2%.

___ (c) At interior stairs, doors may open

at the top step; if door swings away from step and step or landing is not lower than 8″, the landing must be the width of stair or door and 36″ deep.

___ (2) Emergency exits

    ___ (a) Sleeping rooms below 4th floor, and basements shall have at least one operable window.

    ___ (b) The windows shall be operable from the inside and have a min. clear opening of 5.7 SF (24″ high min., 20″ wide min.) and sill shall not be higher than 44″ above floor.

    ___ (c) Bars, grilles, or grates may be installed provided they are operable from inside, and the building has smoke detectors.

___ *i.* Stairs

___ (1) Rise: 4″ min., 7″ max., except stairs serving occupant load of less than 10, rise = 8″ max., tread = 9″ min.

___ (2) Run: 11″ min.

___ (3) Variation in treads and risers = ⅜″ max.

___ (4) Winders: require tread at 12″ out from narrow side, but always no less than 6″ at any point.

___ (5) Spiral stairs limited to 400 SF of area served with 26″ min. clear width. Tread at 12″ from center to be 7½″. Max. riser = 9½″. Min. headroom = 6′6″.

___ (6) Handrails

    ___ (a) At least one, at open side, continuous with 12″ extensions top and bottom, and terminations to posts or walls

    ___ (b) Height: 34″ to 38″ above tread nosing

    ___ (c) Clearance from walls: 1½″

    ___ (d) Width of grip: 1¼″ to 2″

___ (7) Headroom: 6′8″ min.

___ (8) Guardrails at floor or roof openings, more than 30″ above grade. Height = 36″ min. If open, submembers must be spaced so a 4″ dia. sphere cannot pass through.

___ *j.* Garages and carports
      ___ (1) Garage of 1000 SF max. may be attached to dwelling provided ceiling has ½″ type-X gypsum board and separation wall is 1 hr (20 min. for door).
      ___ (2) Open carport does not have the above requirements.
___ *k.* Fireplaces: See p. 360.

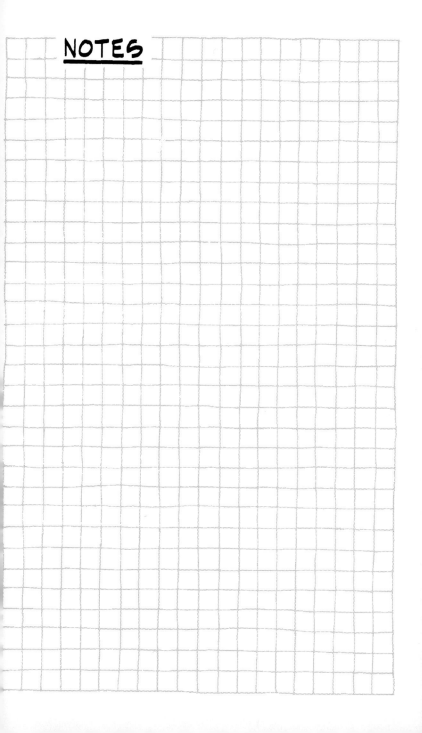

NOTES

NOTES

___ 3. *Building Code (Based on 1997 UBC)* ⑩ ㉔

Note: Generally, the 1994 UBC is the same, except where noted.

Configuring a building that meets fire safety code requirements is one of the architect's primary responsibilities. This handbook uses only the Uniform Building Code (UBC) as a guide. However, all other model codes in the U.S. are similar in approach.

Steps in preliminary code check are:

___ *a.* Establish occupant load (see UBC Table 10-A, p. 105).
___ *b.* Determine occupancy classification (see UBC Table 3-A, p. 91). Also see App. A, item A.
___ *c.* Determine allowable area (see UBC Table 5-B, p.102).
___ *d.* Determine allowable height (see UBC Table 5-B, p. 102).
___ *e.* Determine construction type (see UBC Table 5-B, p. 102).
___ *f.* Determine hourly ratings of construction components for construction type (see UBC Table 6-A, p. 104).
___ *g.* Determine required occupancy separations (see UBC Table 3-B, p. 93).
___ *h.* Determine sprinkler requirements.
___ *i.* Determine if area separation walls are needed.
___ *j.* Determine if exterior walls and windows have adequate fire protection (see UBC Table 5-A, p. 94).
___ *k.* Check exiting.
___ *l.* Other.

___ *a.* *Occupant Load:* Determining the occupant load from UBC Table 10-A (in some cases) will help determine the occupancy classification. When starting a project, a listing of architectural program areas by name, along with their floor area, occupant classification, and occupant load should be compiled. Total the occupant load to help determine the final overall occupancy classification and for design of the exiting.
___ *b.* *Occupancy Classification:* The building code classifies buildings by occupancy in order to group similar life-safety problems together. Table 3-A of the

UBC provides a concise definition of all occupancy classifications.

Because the H (Hazardous) occupancies have become very confusing, here are brief explanations of functions to determine which H to use:

___ H-1: Explosions

___ H-2: Flammable liquids in open use (i.e., dip tanks, spraying).

___ H-3: Closed containers, such as in paint warehouses.

___ H-4: Repair garages with use of flammable liquids (i.e., muffler shops, paint shops, etc.).

___ H-5: Aircraft hangars (much like H-4).

___ H-6: High-tech. plants using hazardous materials (mainly a sprinklered F-1 occupancy).

___ H-7: Health hazards (dip tanks in body shops, etc.).

___ c. *Allowable Floor Area:* UBC Table 5-B on p. 102 coordinates the level of fire hazard (occupancy classification) to the required fire resistance (allowable construction type) by defining the allowable area for a one-story building. High-hazard occupancies (like large assembly) can be built only out of the most fire-resistant construction types. A lower-hazard occupancy (like a small office or a residence) can be built using any of the construction types. The allowable construction types are listed from right to left in approximately decreasing order of fire safety and construction cost. Thus choosing a construction type as far to the right as possible will provide the least expensive construction for the type of occupancy in question.

Allowable areas can be further increased by keeping the building away from property lines, from other buildings (a property line is "assumed" halfway between two buildings for the purposes of "yard separation"), or facing on a wide street. When separations are different widths, the smaller of the two applies.

___ *Separation on two sides,* where public ways or yards exceed 20′ in width on two sides, the floor area can be increased by 1.25% for each foot of excess yard width. The increase cannot exceed 50%.

___ *Separation on three sides,* where public ways or yards exceed 20′ in width on three sides, the floor area can be increased by 2.5% for each foot of excess yard width. The increase cannot exceed 100%.

___ *Separation on all sides,* where public ways or yards exceed 20′ in width on all sides, the floor area can be increased by 5% for each foot of excess yard width. The increase cannot exceed 100%. (See UBC for greater increases to S-2 and 5, F-2, and H-5.)

___ Allowable areas can still be further increased for credit for having *fire sprinklers.* The allowable floor area for a 1-story building can be tripled and for a multistory building doubled. The floor area increase can be taken even if the code requires sprinklers for the occupancy (but cannot be used for H-1 and 2 occupancies or atria, increases in stories, or substitution for 1-hour construction).

___ These area modifications can be compounded on top of the area increases for separation of side yards.

___ *d.* _Allowable building height:_ UBC Table 5-B specifies the maximum number of stories that can be built in a particular construction type. A building that is not otherwise required to be sprinklered can have an additional story if sprinklered. But you cannot take both a height increase and an area increase for sprinklers. You have to choose one or the other.

___ *e.* _Construction type:_ Based on the above, you can now select the construction type. Construction types are based on whether or not the building construction materials are combustible or noncombustible, and on the number of hours that a wall, column, beam, floor, or other structural element can resist fire. Wood is an example of a material that is combustible. Steel and concrete are examples of noncombustible materials. Steel, however, will lose structural strength as it begins to soften in the heat of a fire.

There are two ways that construction can be resistant to fire. First it can be *fire-resistive*—built of a monolithic, noncombustible material like concrete or masonry. Second, it can be *protected*—encased in a noncombustible material such as steel columns or wood studs covered with gypsum plaster, wallboard, etc.

The following are the construction types per the UBC:

___ *Type I and Type II (fire-resistive)* construction is noncombustible, built from concrete, masonry, and/or steel, and is used when substantial hourly ratings (4 to 2 hours) are required.

___ *Type II, 1-hour and unprotected (N)* construction is also of the same materials as above, but the hourly ratings are less. Light steel framing would fit into this category.

___ *Type III, 1-hour and unprotected (N)* has noncombustible exterior walls of masonry or concrete, and interior construction of any allowable material including wood.

___ *Type IV* construction is combustible *heavy timber* framing. It achieves its rating from the large size of the timber (2″ thickness, min., actual). The outer surface chars creating a fire-resistant layer protecting the remaining wood. Exterior walls must be of noncombustible materials.

___ *Type V, 1-hour and unprotected (N)* is of light wood framing.

Note: **As the type number goes up, the cost of construction goes down, so you generally want to use the lowest construction type (highest number) the code allows.**

___ *f.* *Hourly ratings:* See UBC Table 6-A for specific requirements of each construction type. See p. 363 on how to achieve these ratings.

___ *g.* *Required occupancy separations:* For hourly ratings, these are determined from UBC Table 3-B. Most buildings will have some mix of occupancies. If one of the occupancies is a minor area and subservient to the major one, the whole building can often be classified as the major occupancy. It will then have to meet the requirements of the more restrictive occupancy, but no separating walls will be necessary.

Some buildings will have different occupancies, none of which is the dominant one. UBC Table 3-B gives the required fire resistance of the walls and/or floors that separate the occupancies. Openings through separation walls must meet the following criteria:

___ For *4-hour walls,* no opening allowed.

___ For *3-hour walls,* openings must not exceed 25% of the length of the wall and no one opening may be larger than 120 SF.

___ For *2-hour walls,* openings to be 1½-hour protected.

___ For *1-hour walls,* openings to be 1-hour protected.

___ h. *Sprinkler requirements:* A sprinkler system can be used to *substitute for 1-hour construction,* if it is not required by the code and is not used for area or height increases. However, exit access corridors, exit stairs, shafts, area separation walls and similar structures must maintain their required fire protection.

A sprinkler system is the most effective way to provide fire safety in a building. The UBC requires fire sprinklers in the following situations:

___ *A occupancies* that are: drinking establishments greater than 5000 SF; multitheater complexes; amusement buildings (unless small and temporary); and theaters with/legitimate stages, over 1000 SF, and any "smoke protected" assembly seating.

___ *E-1 occupancies,* except for: each classroom that has at least 1 exit door at ground level assembly rooms having ½ of required exits at ground level; or where 2-hour separation walls divide the building into 20,000 SF (or less) compartments.

___ *F occupancies* that are woodworking shops of over 2500 SF that generate combustible dust.

___ *H occupancies,* Division 1, 2, 3, 6, and 7 or Division 4 more than 3000 SF.

___ *I occupancies*

___ *M occupancies* where any floor exceeds 12,000 SF or total area exceeds 24,000 SF, or 3 stories or more in height.

___ *R-1 occupancies* that are:

Apartments, three or more stories with 16 or more DUs.

Congregate residences, three or more stories with 20 or more occupants.

Hotels, three or more stories or with 20 or more DUs.

___ *Basements* for Group A (greater than 1500 SF) or E-1 occupancies, greater than 1500 SF.

___ *Exhibition, display, or retail sales areas:*
Group A or B-2, greater than 12,000 SF.
Group B-2, greater than 24,000 SF on all
floors or more than three stories in height.

___ *Stairs,* at enclosed usable space above and
below for Group A-2, 2.1, 3, 4, and E-1 occupancies.

___ *All occupancies without sufficient fire department access through outside wall at basement
or floor in excess of 1500 SF* (Group R-3 and
Group U excluded). Sufficient access is 20 SF
of openings with a minimum dimension of 30″
per 50 LF of wall. If these openings are only
on one side, the floor dimension cannot
exceed 75′ from the opening. Furthermore,
sprinklers are required in buildings with a
floor level of 30 or more occupants that is
located 55′ above the lowest level of fire truck
access.

___ *Miscellaneous:*   Rubbish and linen chutes;
nitrate film storerooms; and combustible-
fiber storage vaults.

See p. 433 for sprinkler installations.

___ i. *Area separation walls:* One building can be
divided into what the code considers separate buildings through the use of area separation walls. The
allowable floor area criteria is then applied individ-
ually to each of the separate areas. The following criteria apply to area separation walls:

___ Type I and Type II FR require 4 hours.
___ Type II—1 hour and N require 2 hours.
___ Type III—1 hour and N require 4 hours
___ Type IV—Require 4 hours
___ Type V—1 hour and N require 2 hours.

The total width of openings cannot exceed 25%
of the length of the wall and must be protected by a
fire assembly with a 3-hour rating for a 4-hour wall
or a 1½-hour rating for a 2-hour wall. Area separation walls must extend from the foundation to a
point 30″ above the roof, unless the roof has a 1-
hour rating. See p. 314 for fire doors.

___ j. *Fire protection of exterior walls and windows:*
This is a function of location of the building on the
property and the occupancy type. See Table 5-A, p.
94. As buildings get closer together, the requirements become more restrictive.

___ *k.* *Exiting and stairs:* At the conceptual stage of architectural design, the most important aspect of the building code requirements is the number and distribution of exits.

A *means of egress* is a continuous path of travel from any point in a building or structure to the open air outside at ground level. It consists of three separate and distinct parts:

___ 1. Exit access
___ 2. The exit
___ 3. The exit discharge

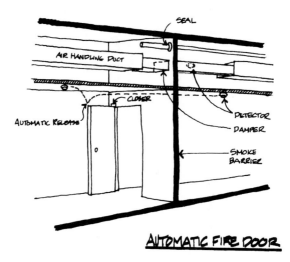

SEAL

AIR HANDLING DUCT

CLOSER

AUTOMATIC RELEASE

DETECTOR

DAMPER

SMOKE BARRIER

AUTOMATIC FIRE DOOR

The *Exit Access* leads to an exit. A minimum of two exits is almost always required (See UBC Table 10-A). Other general requirements:

___ 1. Corridor width is to be no less than 44″ for an occupancy load of 10 or more people. It can be 36″ for fewer than 10 people.
___ 2. Dead-end corridors limited to 20 ft long.
___ 3. When more than one exit is required, the occupant should be able to go toward either exit from any point in the corridor system.
___ 4. Corridors used for exit access require 1-hour construction.
___ 5. Maximum travel distance from any point to an exit is *200 ft* (150 ft in 1994 UBC) for a

nonsprinklered building or *250 ft* (200 ft in 1994 UBC) for a sprinklered building. This distance can be *increased by 100 ft* if the corridor meets all the requirements of this section. Some occupancies require less travel distance.

___ 6. Handrails or fully open doors cannot extend more than 7 inches into the corridor.

___ 7. Doors at their worst extension into the corridor cannot obstruct the required width by more than half.

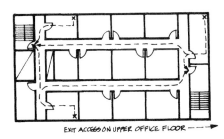

EXIT ACCESS ON UPPER OFFICE FLOOR ‒‒‒➤

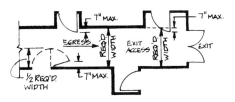

The *exit* is that portion of a means of egress that is separated from the area of the building from which escape is made, by walls, floors, doors, or other means that provide the protected path necessary for the occupants to proceed with safety to a public space. The most common form the exit takes is an enclosed stairway. In a single-story building the exit is the door opening to the outside.

After determining occupant load (Table 10-A, UBC) for spaces, rooms, floors, etc., use the following guidelines:

___ 1. Almost all buildings need 2 exits (see UBC Table 10-A). In more than one story, stairs become part of an exit. Elevators are not exits.

___ 2. An occupant load of 501 to 1000 requires 3 exits.

___ 3. An occupant load of 1001 or more requires 4 exits.

___ 4. In buildings 4 stories and higher and in Types 1 and 2 FR construction, the exit stairs are required to have 2-hour enclosure; otherwise, 1 hour is acceptable.

___ 5. When 2 exits are required, they have to be separated by a distance equal to half the diagonal dimension of the floor and/or room the exits are serving (measured in straight lines). See sketch below.

___ 6. Where more than two exits are required, two of them need to be separated by at least half the diagonal dimension. The others are spaced to provide good access from any direction.

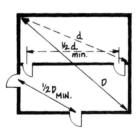

___ 7. May exit from room through one adjoining room only (except rooms with occupant loads of 10 or more), provided adjoining rooms (other than DUs) are not kitchens, storerooms, toilets, closets, etc. Foyers, lobbies, and reception rooms are not considered adjoining rooms and can always be exited through.

___ 8. The total exit width required (in inches) is determined by multiplying the occupant load by *0.3* for *stairs* (0.7 for H-1, 2, 3, 7 and 0.4 for I-2 occupancies) and *0.2* for *other exits* (except 0.4 for H-1, 2, 3, and 7). This width should be divided equally among the required number of exits.

___ 9. Total occupant load for calculating exit stair width is defined as the sum of the occupant load on the floor in question. The maximum exit stair width calculated is maintained for the entire exit. See sketch on p. 87.

___ 10. Minimum exit door width is 36″ with 32″ clear opening. Maximum door width is 48″.

___ 11. The width of exit stairs, and the width of landings between flights of stairs, must all be the same and must meet the minimum exit stair width requirements as calculated or:
44″ minimum width for an occupant load of 50 or more
36″ minimum width for 49 or less, whichever is greater

___ 12. Doors must swing in the direction of travel when serving a hazardous area or when serving an occupant load of 50 or more.

___ A *horizontal exit* is a way of passage through a 2-hour fire wall into another area of the same building or into a different building that will provide refuge from smoke and fire. Horizontal exits cannot provide more than half of the required exit capacity, and any such exit must discharge into an area capable of holding the occupant capacity of the exit. The area is calculated at 3 SF/occupant. In institutional occupancies the area needed is 15 SF/ambulatory person, and 30 SF/nonambulatory person.

___ *Exit discharge* is that portion of a means of egress between the termination of an exit and a public way. The most common form this takes is the door out of an exit stairway opening onto a public street. Exits can discharge through a courtyard with 1-hr. walls that connects the exit with a public way. In type B occupancy office buildings (and I-1.1 hospitals and nursing homes), 50% of the exits can discharge through a street floor lobby area if the entire street floor is sprinklered and the path through the lobby is unobstructed and obvious.

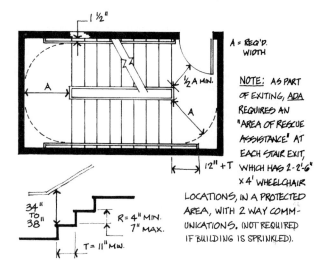

A = REQ'D. WIDTH

NOTE: AS PART OF EXITING, ADA REQUIRES AN "AREA OF RESCUE ASSISTANCE" AT EACH STAIR EXIT, WHICH HAS 2-2'-6" X 4' WHEELCHAIR LOCATIONS, IN A PROTECTED AREA, WITH 2 WAY COMMUNICATIONS. (NOT REQUIRED IF BUILDING IS SPRINKLED).

1 ½"

½ A MIN.

A

12" + T

34" TO 38"

R = 4" MIN.
7" MAX.

T = 11" MIN.

___ *Smokeproof enclosures* for exits are required in any tall building with floors 75′ above the lowest ground level where fire trucks have access. A smokeproof enclosure is an exit stair that is entered through a vestibule that is ventilated by either natural or mechanical means such that products of combustion from a fire will be limited in their penetration of the exit-stair enclosure. Smokeproof enclosures are required to be 2-hour construction. They must discharge directly to the outside, or directly through a 2-hour exit passageway to the outside. In a *sprinklered* building, mechanically pressurized and vented stairways can be substituted for smokeproof enclosures.

Code Requirements for Stairs

UBC requirements	Tread min.	Riser Min.	Riser Max.
General (including HC)	11″	4″	7″
Private Stairways (occ. <10)	9″		8″
Winding—Min. required T at 12″			
from narrow side*	6″ at any pt.		
Spiral—at 12″ from column*	7½″		
Only permitted in R-3 dwellings and R-1 private apartments*			
Rules of thumb for stairs:			
Interior	2R + T = 25		
Exterior	2R + T = 26		

*Requires handrails for ramps >1:15.

Code Requirements for Ramp Slopes

Type	Max. slope	Max. rise	Max. run
UBC, required for accessible			
access	1:12*	5′	
UBC others	1:8*	5′	
Assembly with fixed seats	1:5		
HC, new facilities	1:12*	2.5′	30′
HC, existing facilities	1:10*	6″	5′
	1:8*	3″	2′
HC, curb ramps	1:10	6″	5′

*Requires handrails for ramps >1:15.

NOTES

NOTES

TABLE 3-A—DESCRIPTION OF OCCUPANCIES BY GROUP AND DIVISION[1]

GROUP AND DIVISION	SECTION	DESCRIPTION OF OCCUPANCY
A-1	303.1.1	A building or portion of a building having an assembly room with an occupant load of 1,000 or more and a legitimate stage.
A-2		A building or portion of a building having an assembly room with an occupant load of less than 1,000 and a legitimate stage.
A-2.1		A building or portion of a building having an assembly room with an occupant load of 300 or more without a legitimate stage, including such buildings used for educational purposes and not classed as a Group E or Group B Occupancy.
A-3		Any building or portion of a building having an assembly room with an occupant load of less than 300 without a legitimate stage, including such buildings used for educational purposes and not classed as a Group E or Group B Occupancy.
A-4		Stadiums, reviewing stands and amusement park structures not included within other Group A Occupancies.
B	304.1	A building or structure, or a portion thereof, for office, professional or service-type transactions, including storage of records and accounts; eating and drinking establishments with an occupant load of less than 50.
E-1	305.1	Any building used for educational purposes through the 12th grade by 50 or more persons for more than 12 hours per week or four hours in any one day.
E-2		Any building used for educational purposes through the 12th grade by less than 50 persons for more than 12 hours per week or four hours in any one day.
E-3		Any building or portion thereof used for day-care purposes for more than six persons.
F-1	306.1	Moderate-hazard factory and industrial occupancies include factory and industrial uses not classified as Group F, Division 2 Occupancies.
F-2		Low-hazard factory and industrial occupancies include facilities producing noncombustible or nonexplosive materials that during finishing, packing or processing do not involve a significant fire hazard.
H-1	307.1	Occupancies with a quantity of material in the building in excess of those listed in Table 3-D that present a high explosion hazard as listed in Section 307.1.1.
H-2		Occupancies with a quantity of material in the building in excess of those listed in Table 3-D that present a moderate explosion hazard or a hazard from accelerated burning as listed in Section 307.1.1.
H-3		Occupancies with a quantity of material in the building in excess of those listed in Table 3-D that present a high fire or physical hazard as listed in Section 307.1.1.

(Continued)

91

TABLE 3-A—DESCRIPTION OF OCCUPANCIES BY GROUP AND DIVISION[1] *(Continued)*

H-4		Repair garages not classified as Group S, Division 3 Occupancies.
H-5		Aircraft repair hangars not classified as Group S, Division 5 Occupancies and heliports.
H-6	307.1 and 307.11	Semiconductor fabrication facilities and comparable research and development areas when the facilities in which hazardous production materials are used, and the aggregate quantity of material is in excess of those listed in Table 3-D or 3-E.
H-7	307.1	Occupancies having quantities of materials in excess of those listed in Table 3-E that are health hazards as listed in Section 307.1.1.
I-1.1		Nurseries for the full-time care of children under the age of six (each accommodating more than five children), hospitals, sanitariums, nursing homes with nonambulatory patients and similar buildings (each accommodating more than five patients).
I-1.2	308.1	Health-care centers for ambulatory patients receiving outpatient medical care which may render the patient incapable of unassisted self-preservation (each tenant space accommodating more than five such patients).
I-2		Nursing homes for ambulatory patients, homes for children six years of age or over (each accommodating more than five persons).
I-3		Mental hospitals, mental sanitariums, jails, prisons, reformatories and buildings where personal liberties of inmates are similarly restrained.
M	309.1	A building or structure, or a portion thereof, for the display and sale of merchandise, and involving stocks of goods, wares or merchandise, incidental to such purposes and accessible to the public.
R-1	310.1	Hotels and apartment houses, congregate residences (each accommodating more than 10 persons).
R-3		Dwellings, lodging houses, congregate residences (each accommodating 10 or fewer persons).
S-1		Moderate hazard storage occupancies including buildings or portions of buildings used for storage of combustible materials not classified as Group S, Division 2 or Group H Occupancies.
S-2	311.1	Low-hazard storage occupancies including buildings or portions of buildings used for storage of noncombustible materials.
S-3		Repair garages where work is limited to exchange of parts and maintenance not.requiring open flame or welding, and parking garages not classified as Group S, Division 4 Occupancies.
S-4		Open parking garages.
S-5		Aircraft hangars and helistops.
U-1	312.1	Private garages, carports, sheds and agricultural buildings.
U-2		Fences over 6 feet (1829 mm) high, tanks and towers

TABLE 3-B—REQUIRED SEPARATION IN BUILDINGS OF MIXED OCCUPANCY (HOURS)

	A-1	A-2	A-2.1	A-3	A-4	B	E	F-1	F-2	H-2	H-3	H-4,5	H-6,7[2]	I	M	R-1	R-3	S-1	S-2	S-3	S-5	U-1[3]
A-1		N	N	N	N	3	N	3	3	4	4	4	4	3	3	1	1	3	3	4	3	1
A-2			N	N	N	1	N	1	1	4	4	4	4	3	1	1	1	1	1	3	1	1
A-2.1				N	N	1	N	1	1	4	4	4	4	3	1	1	1	1	1	3	1	1
A-3					N	N	N	N	N	4	4	4	3	2	N	1	1	N	N	3	1	1
A-4						1	N	1	1	4	4	4	4	3	1	1	1	1	1	3	1	1
B							1	N[5]	N	2	1	1	1	1	N	1	1	1	N	1	1	1
E								1	1	4	4	1	3	1	1	1	1	1	1	3	1	1
F-1									1	2	1	1	1	3	N[5]	1	1	N	N	1	1	1
F-2										2	1	1	1	2	1	1	1	N	N	1	1	1
H-1	NOT PERMITTED IN MIXED OCCUPANCIES. SEE SECTION 307.2.9																					
H-2											1	1	2	4	2	4	4	2	2	2	2	1
H-3												1	1	4	1	3	3	1	1	1	1	1
H-4,5													1	4	1	3	3	1	1	1	1	1
H-6,7[2]														4	1	4	4	1	1	1	1	3
I															2	1	1	2	2	4	3	1
M																1	1	1[4]	1[4]	1	1	1
R-1																	N	3	1	3	1	1
R-3																		1	1	1	1	1
S-1																			1	1	1	1
S-2																				1	1	N
S-3																					1	1
S-4	OPEN PARKING GARAGES ARE EXCLUDED EXCEPT AS PROVIDED IN SECTION 311.2																					
S-5																						N

N—No requirements for fire resistance.

[1]For detailed requirements and exceptions, see Section 302.4.

[2]For special provisions on highly toxic materials, see the Fire Code.

[3]For agricultural buildings, see also Appendix Chapter 3.

[4]See Section 309.2.2 for exception.

[5]For Group F, Division 1 woodworking establishments with more than 2,500 square feet (232.3 m²), the occupancy separation shall be one hour.

TABLE 5-A—EXTERIOR WALL AND OPENING PROTECTION BASED ON LOCATION ON PROPERTY FOR ALL CONSTRUCTION TYPES[1,2,3]
For exceptions, see Section 503.4.

OCCUPANCY GROUP[4]	CONSTRUCTION TYPE	EXTERIOR WALLS		OPENINGS[5]
		Bearing	Nonbearing	
		Distances are measured to property lines (see Section 503).		
			× 304.8 for mm	
A-1	I-F.R. II-F.R.	Four-hour N/C	Four-hour N/C less than 5 feet Two-hour N/C less than 20 feet One-hour N/C less than 40 feet NR, N/C elsewhere	Not permitted less than 5 feet Protected less than 20 feet
	II One-hour II-N III One-hour III-N IV-H.T. V One-hour V-N	Group A, Division 1 Occupancies are not allowed in these construction types.		
A-2 A-2.1 A-3 A-4	I-F.R. II-F.R. III One-hour IV-H.T.	Four-hour N/C	Four-hour N/C less than 5 feet Two-hour N/C less than 20 feet One-hour N/C less than 40 feet NR, N/C elsewhere	Not permitted less than 5 feet Protected less than 20 feet
	II One-hour	Two-hour N/C less than 10 feet One-hour N/C elsewhere	Same as bearing except NR, N/C 40 feet or greater	Not permitted less than 5 feet Protected less than 10 feet
A-2 A-2.1[2]	II-N III-N V-N	Group A, Divisions 2 and 2.1 Occupancies are not allowed in these construction types.		
	V One-hour	Two-hour less than 10 feet One-hour elsewhere	Same as bearing	Not permitted less than 5 feet Protected less than 10 feet
A-3	II One-hour	Two-hour N/C less than 5 feet One-hour N/C elsewhere	Same as bearing except NR, N/C 40 feet or greater	Not permitted less than 5 feet Protected less than 10 feet
	II-N	Two-hour N/C less than 5 feet One-hour N/C less than 20 feet NR, N/C elsewhere	Same as bearing	Not permitted less than 5 feet Protected less than 10 feet

Occupancy	Type			Openings
A-3	III-N	Four-hour N/C	Four-hour N/C less than 5 feet Two-hour N/C less than 20 feet One-hour N/C less than 40 feet NR, N/C elsewhere	Not permitted less than 5 feet Protected less than 20 feet
	V One-hour	Two-hour less than 5 feet One-hour elsewhere	Same as bearing	Not permitted less than 5 feet Protected less than 10 feet
	V-N	Two-hour less than 5 feet One-hour less than 20 feet NR elsewhere	Same as bearing	Not permitted less than 5 feet Protected less than 10 feet
	II One-hour	One-hour N/C	Same as bearing except NR, N/C 40 feet or greater	Protected less than 10 feet
	II-N	One-hour N/C less than 10 feet NR, N/C elsewhere	Same as bearing	Protected less than 10 feet
A-4	III-N	Four-hour N/C	Four-hour N/C less than 5 feet Two-hour N/C less than 20 feet One-hour N/C less than 40 feet NR, N/C elsewhere	Not permitted less than 5 feet Protected less than 10 feet
	V One-hour	One-hour	Same as bearing	Protected less than 10 feet
	V-N	One-hour less than 10 feet NR elsewhere	Same as bearing	Protected less than 10 feet
B, F-1, M, S-1, S-3	I-F.R. II-F.R. III One-hour III-N IV-H.T.	Four-hour N/C less than 5 feet Two-hour N/C elsewhere	Four-hour N/C less than 5 feet Two-hour N/C less than 20 feet One-hour N/C less than 40 feet NR, N/C elsewhere	Not permitted less than 5 feet Protected less than 20 feet
	II One-hour	One-hour N/C	Same as bearing except NR, N/C 40 feet or greater	Not permitted less than 5 feet Protected less than 10 feet
B F-1 M S-1, S-3	II-N[3]	One-hour N/C less than 20 feet NR, N/C elsewhere	Same as bearing	Not permitted less than 5 feet Protected less than 10 feet
	V One-hour	One-hour	Same as bearing	Not permitted less than 5 feet Protected less than 10 feet
	V-N	One-hour less than 20 feet NR elsewhere	Same as bearing	Not permitted less than 5 feet Protected less than 10 feet

(Continued)

TABLE 5-A—EXTERIOR WALL AND OPENING PROTECTION BASED ON LOCATION ON PROPERTY FOR ALL CONSTRUCTION TYPES[1,2,3]—(Continued)

OCCUPANCY GROUP[4]	CONSTRUCTION TYPE	EXTERIOR WALLS			OPENINGS[5]
		Bearing	Nonbearing		
		Distances are measured to property lines (see Section 503).			
			× 304.8 for mm		
E-1 E-2[6] E-3[6]	I-F.R. II-F.R. III One-hour III-N IV-H.T.	Four-hour N/C	Four-hour N/C less than 5 feet Two-hour N/C less than 20 feet One-hour N/C less than 40 feet NR, N/C elsewhere		Not permitted less than 5 feet Protected less than 20 feet
	II One-hour	Two-hour N/C less than 5 feet One-hour N/C elsewhere	Same as bearing except NR, N/C 40 feet or greater		Not permitted less than 5 feet Protected less than 10 feet
	II-N	Two-hour N/C less than 5 feet One-hour N/C less than 10 feet NR, N/C elsewhere	Same as bearing		Not permitted less than 5 feet Protected less than 10 feet
	V One-hour	Two-hour less than 5 feet One-hour elsewhere	Same as bearing		Not permitted less than 5 feet Protected less than 10 feet
	V-N	Two-hour less than 5 feet One-hour less than 10 feet NR elsewhere	Same as bearing		Not permitted less than 5 feet Protected less than 10 feet
F-2 S-2	I-F.R. II-F.R. III One-hour III-N IV-H.T.	Four-hour N/C less than 5 feet Two-hour N/C elsewhere	Four-hour N/C less than 5 feet Two-hour N/C less than 20 feet One-hour N/C less than 40 feet NR, N/C elsewhere		Not permitted less than 3 feet Protected less than 20 feet
	II One-hour	One-hour N/C	Same as bearing NR, N/C 40 feet or greater		Not permitted less than 5 feet Protected less than 10 feet
	II-N[3]	One-hour N/C less than 5 feet NR, N/C elsewhere	Same as bearing		Not permitted less than 5 feet Protected less than 10 feet
	V One-hour	One-hour	Same as bearing		Not permitted less than 5 feet Protected less than 10 feet
	V-N	One-hour less than 5 feet NR elsewhere	Same as bearing		Not permitted less than 5 feet Protected less than 10 feet

H-1²,³	I-F.R. II-F.R.	Four-hour N/C	NR N/C	Not restricted³
	II One-hour	One-hour N/C	NR N/C	Not restricted³
	II-N	NR N/C	Same as bearing	Not restricted³
	III One-hour III-N IV-H.T. V One-hour V-N	Group H, Division 1 Occupancies are not allowed in buildings of these construction types.		
H-2²,³ H-3²,³ H-4³ H-6 H-7	I-F.R. II-F.R. III One-hour III-N IV-H.T.	Four-hour N/C	Four-hour N/C less than 5 feet Two-hour N/C less than 10 feet One-hour N/C less than 40 feet NR, N/C elsewhere	Not permitted less than 5 feet Protected less than 20 feet
	II One-hour	Four-hour N/C less than 5 feet Two-hour N/C less than 10 feet One-hour N/C elsewhere	Four-hour N/C less than 5 feet Two-hour N/C less than 10 feet One-hour N/C less than 20 feet NR, N/C elsewhere	Not permitted less than 5 feet Protected less than 20 feet
	II-N	Four-hour N/C less than 5 feet Two-hour N/C less than 10 feet One-hour N/C less than 20 feet NR, N/C elsewhere	Same as bearing	Not permitted less than 5 feet Protected less than 20 feet
	V One-hour	Four-hour less than 5 feet Two-hour less than 10 feet One-hour elsewhere	Same as bearing	Not permitted less than 5 feet Protected less than 20 feet
	V-N	Four-hour less than 5 feet Two-hour less than 10 feet One-hour less than 20 feet NR elsewhere	Same as bearing	Not permitted less than 5 feet Protected less than 20 feet

(Continued)

TABLE 5-A—EXTERIOR WALL AND OPENING PROTECTION BASED ON LOCATION ON PROPERTY FOR ALL CONSTRUCTION TYPES[1,2,3]—(Continued)

OCCUPANCY GROUP[4]	CONSTRUCTION TYPE	EXTERIOR WALLS		OPENINGS[5]
		Bearing	Nonbearing	
		Distances are measured to property lines (see Section 503).		
		× 304.8 for mm		
H-5[2]	I-F.R. II-F.R. III One-hour III-N IV-H.T.	Four-hour N/C	Four-hour N/C less than 40 feet One-hour N/C less than 60 feet NR, N/C elsewhere	Protected less than 60 feet
	II One-hour	One-hour N/C	Same as bearing, except NR, N/C 60 feet or greater	Protected less than 60 feet
	II-N	One-hour N/C less than 60 feet NR, N/C elsewhere	Same as bearing	Protected less than 60 feet
	V One-hour	One-hour	Same as bearing	Protected less than 60 feet
	V-N	One-hour less than 60 feet NR elsewhere	Same as bearing	Protected less than 60 feet
I-1.1 I-1.2 I-2 I-3	I-F.R. II-F.R.	Four-hour N/C	Four-hour N/C less than 5 feet Two-hour N/C less than 20 feet One-hour N/C less than 40 feet NR, N/C elsewhere	Not permitted less than 5 feet Protected less than 20 feet
I-1.1 I-1.2 I-3[2]	II One-hour	Two-hour N/C less than 5 feet One-hour N/C elsewhere	Same as bearing except NR, N/C 40 feet or greater	Not permitted less than 5 feet Protected less than 10 feet
	V One-hour	Two-hour less than 5 feet One-hour elsewhere	Same as bearing	Not permitted less than 5 feet Protected less than 10 feet
I-1.1 I-1.2 I-2 I-3	II-N III-N V-N	These occupancies are not allowed in buildings of these construction types.[7]		
I-3	IV-H.T.	Group I, Division 3 Occupancies are not allowed in buildings of this construction type.		
I-1.1 I-1.2 I-2 I-3	III One-hour	Four-hour N/C	Same as bearing except NR, N/C 40 feet or greater	Not permitted less than 5 feet Protected less than 20 feet

I-1.1 I-1.2 I-2	IV-H.T.	Four-hour N/C	Same as bearing NR, N/C 40 feet or greater	Not permitted less than 5 feet Protected less than 20 feet
I-2	II One-hour	One-hour N/C	Same as bearing except NR, N/C 40 feet or greater	Not permitted less than 5 feet Protected less than 10 feet
	V One-hour	One-hour	Same as bearing	Not permitted less than 5 feet Protected less than 10 feet
	I-F.R. II-F.R. III One-hour III-N IV-H.T.	Four-hour N/C less than 3 feet Two-hour N/C elsewhere	Four-hour N/C less than 3 feet Two-hour N/C less than 20 feet One-hour N/C less than 40 feet NR, N/C elsewhere	Not permitted less than 3 feet Protected less than 20 feet
R-1	II One-hour	One-hour N/C	Same as bearing except NR, N/C 40 feet or greater	Not permitted less than 5 feet
	II-N	One-hour N/C less than 5 feet NR, N/C elsewhere	Same as bearing	Not permitted less than 5 feet
	V One-hour	One-hour	Same as bearing	Not permitted less than 5 feet
	V-N	One-hour less than 5 feet NR elsewhere	Same as bearing	Not permitted less than 5 feet
	I-F.R. II-F.R. III One-hour III-N IV-H.T.	Four-hour N/C	Four-hour N/C less than 3 feet Two-hour N/C less than 20 feet One-hour N/C less than 40 feet NR, N/C elsewhere	Not permitted less than 3 feet Protected less than 20 feet
R-3	II One-hour	One-hour N/C	Same as bearing except NR, N/C 40 feet or greater	Not permitted less than 3 feet
	II-N	One-hour N/C less than 3 feet NR, N/C elsewhere	Same as bearing	Not permitted less than 3 feet
	V One-hour	One-hour	Same as bearing	Not permitted less than 3 feet
	V-N	One-hour less than 3 feet NR elsewhere	Same as bearing	Not permitted less than 3 feet

(Continued)

TABLE 5-A—EXTERIOR WALL AND OPENING PROTECTION BASED ON LOCATION ON PROPERTY FOR ALL CONSTRUCTION TYPES[1,2,3]—(Continued)

OCCUPANCY GROUP[4]	CONSTRUCTION TYPE	EXTERIOR WALLS		OPENINGS[5]
		Bearing	Nonbearing	
		Distances are measured to property lines (see Section 503).		
			× 304.8 for mm	
S-4	I-F.R. II-F.R. II One-hour II-N[3]	One-hour N/C less than 10 feet NR, N/C elsewhere	Same as bearing	Not permitted less than 5 feet Protected less than 10 feet
	III One-hour III-N IV-H.T. V One-hour V-N	Group S, Division 4 open parking garages are not permitted in these types of construction.		
S-5	I-F.R. II-F.R. III One-hour III-N IV-H.T.	Four-hour N/C less than 5 feet Two-hour N/C elsewhere	Four-hour N/C less than 5 feet Two-hour N/C less than 20 feet One-hour N/C less than 40 feet NR, N/C elsewhere	Not permitted less than 5 feet Protected less than 20 feet
	II One-hour	One-hour N/C	Same as bearing except NR, N/C 40 feet or greater	Not permitted less than 5 feet Protected less than 20 feet
	II-N[3]	One-hour N/C less than 20 feet NR, N/C elsewhere	Same as bearing	Not permitted less than 5 feet Protected less than 20 feet
	V One-hour	One-hour	Same as bearing	Not permitted less than 5 feet Protected less than 20 feet
	V-N[3]	One-hour less than 20 feet NR elsewhere	Same as bearing	Not permitted less than 5 feet Protected less than 20 feet

U-1³	I-F.R. II-F.R. III One-hour IV-H.T.	Four-hour N/C	Four-hour N/C less than 3 feet Two-hour N/C less than 20 feet One-hour N/C less than 40 feet NR, N/C elsewhere	Not permitted less than 3 feet Protected less than 20 feet
	II One-hour	One-hour N/C	Same as bearing except NR, N/C 40 feet or greater	Not permitted less than 3 feet
	V One-hour	One-hour	Same as bearing	Not permitted less than 3 feet
	II-N²	One-hour N/C less than 3 feet³ NR, N/C elsewhere	Same as bearing	Not permitted less than 3 feet
	V-N	One-hour less than 3 feet³ NR elsewhere	Same as bearing	Not permitted less than 3 feet
U-2	All	Not regulated		

N/C — Noncombustible.
NR — Nonrated.
H.T. — Heavy timber.
F.R. — Fire resistive.

[1]See Section 503 for types of walls affected and requirements covering percentage of openings permitted in exterior walls. For walls facing streets, yards and public ways, see also Section 601.5.

[2]For additional restrictions, see Chapters 3 and 6.

[3]For special provisions and exceptions, see also Section 503.4.

[4]See Table 3-A for a description of each occupancy type.

[5]Openings requiring protection in exterior walls shall be protected by a fire assembly having at least a three-fourths-hour fire-protection rating.

[6]Group E, Divisions 2 and 3 Occupancies having an occupant load of not more than 20 may have exterior wall and opening protection as required for Group R, Division 3 Occupancies.

[7]See Section 308.2.1, Exception 3.

TABLE 5-B—BASIC ALLOWABLE BUILDING HEIGHTS AND BASIC ALLOWABLE FLOOR AREA FOR BUILDINGS ONE STORY IN HEIGHT[1]

		I	II			III		IV	V	
		F.R.	F.R.	One-hour	N	One-hour	N	H.T.	One-hour	N
TYPE OF CONSTRUCTION						**Maximum Height (feet)**				
		UL	160 (48 768 mm)	65 (19 812 mm)	55 (16 764 mm)	65 (19 812 mm)	55 (16 764 mm)	65 (19 812 mm)	50 (15 240 mm)	40 (12 192 mm)
Use Group	**Height/Area**			Maximum Height (stories) and Maximum Area (sq. ft.) ($\times$ 0.0929 for m²)						
A-1	H	UL	4	Not Permitted	Not Permitted	Not Permitted	Not Permitted	Not Permitted	Not Permitted	Not Permitted
	A	UL	29,900	Not Permitted	Not Permitted	Not Permitted	Not Permitted	Not Permitted	Not Permitted	Not Permitted
A-2, 2.1[2]	H	UL	4	2	NP	2	NP	2	2	NP
	A	UL	29,900	13,500	NP	13,500	NP	13,500	10,500	NP
A-3, 4[2]	H	UL	12	2	1	2	1	2	2	1
	A	UL	29,900	13,500	9,100	13,500	9,100	13,500	10,500	6,000
B, F-1, M, S-1, S-3, S-5	H	UL	12	4	2	4	2	4	3	2
	A	UL	39,900	18,000	12,000	18,000	12,000	18,000	14,000	8,000
E-1, 2, 3[4]	H	UL	4	2	1	2	1	2	2	1
	A	UL	45,200	20,200	13,500	20,200	13,500	20,200	15,700	9,100
F-2, S-2	H	UL	12	4	2	4	2	4	3	2
	A	UL	59,900	27,000	18,000	27,000	18,000	27,000	21,000	12,000
H-1[5]	H	1	1	1	1	1	1	Not Permitted	Not Permitted	Not Permitted
	A	15,000	12,400	5,600	3,700	5,600	3,700	Not Permitted	Not Permitted	Not Permitted
H-2[5]	H	UL	2	1	1	1	1	1	1	1
	A	15,000	12,400	5,600	3,700	5,600	3,700	5,600	4,400	2,500
H-3, 4, 5[5]	H	UL	5	2	1	2	1	2	2	1
	A	UL	24,800	11,200	7,500	11,200	7,500	11,200	8,800	5,100
H-6, 7	H	3	3	3	2	3	2	3	3	1
	A	UL	39,900	18,000	12,000	18,000	12,000	18,000	14,000	8,000

		1	2	3	4	5	6	7	8	9
I-1, 1.2⁶,¹⁰	H	UL	3	1	NP	1	NP	1	1	NP
	A	UL	15,100	6,800	NP	6,800	NP	6,800	5,200	NP
I-2	H	UL	3	2	NP	2	NP	2	2	NP
	A	UL	15,100	6,800	NP	6,800	NP	6,800	5,200	NP
I-3	H	UL	2				Not Permitted⁷				
	A	UL	15,100								
R-1	H	UL	12	4	2⁹	4	2⁹	4	3	2⁹
	A	UL	29,900	13,500	9,100⁹	13,500	9,100⁹	13,500	10,500	6,000⁹
R-3	H	UL	3	3	3	3	3	3	3	3
	A					Unlimited					
S-4³	H					See Table 3-H					
	A										
U⁸	H					See Chapter 3					
	A										

A—Building area in square feet.
H—Building height in number of stories.
H.T.—Heavy timber.
NP—Not permitted.

N—No requirements for fire resistance.
F.R.—Fire resistive.
UL—Unlimited.

[1]For multistory buildings, see Section 504.2.
[2]For limitations and exceptions, see Section 303.2.
[3]For open parking garages, see Section 311.9.
[4]See Section 305.2.3.
[5]See Section 307.
[6]See Section 308.2.1 for exception to the allowable area and number of stories in hospitals, nursing homes and health-care centers.
[7]See Section 308.2.2.2.
[8]For agricultural buildings, see also Appendix Chapter 3.
[9]For limitations and exceptions, see Section 310.2.
[10]For Type II F.R., the maximum height of Group I, Division 1.1 Occupancies is limited to 75 feet (22 860 mm). For Type II, One-hour construction, the maximum height of Group I, Division 1.1 Occupancies is limited to 45 feet (13 716 mm).

TABLE 6-A—TYPES OF CONSTRUCTION—FIRE-RESISTIVE REQUIREMENTS (In Hours)

For details, see occupancy section in Chapter 3, type of construction sections in this chapter and sections referenced in this table.

BUILDING ELEMENT	TYPE I	TYPE II			TYPE III		TYPE IV	TYPE V	
		Noncombustible					Combustible		
	Fire-resistive	Fire-resistive	1-Hr.	N	1-Hr.	N	H.T.	1-Hr.	N
1. Bearing walls—exterior	4 Sec. 602.3.1	4 Sec. 603.3.1	1	N	4 Sec. 604.3.1	4 Sec. 604.3.1	4 Sec. 605.3.1	1	N
2. Bearing walls—interior	3	2	1	N	1	N	1	1	N
3. Nonbearing walls—exterior	4 Sec. 602.3.1	4 Sec. 603.3.1	1 Sec. 603.3.1	N	4 Sec. 604.3.1	4 Sec. 604.3.1	4 Sec. 605.3.1	1	N
4. Structural frame[1]	3 Sec. 602.5	2	1	N	1	N	1 or H.T.	1	N
5. Partitions—permanent	1[2] Sec. 602.3.2	1[2] Sec. 603.3.2	1[2]	N	1	N	1 or H.T.	1	N
6. Shaft enclosures[3]	2	2	1	1	1	1	1	1	1
7. Floors and floor-ceilings	2	2	1	N	1	N	H.T.	1	N
8. Roofs and roof-ceilings	2 Sec. 602.4	1 Sec. 603.5	1 Sec. 603.5	N	1	N	H.T.	1	N
9. Exterior doors and windows	Sec. 602.3.2	Sec. 603.3.2	Sec. 603.3.2	Sec. 603.3.2	Sec. 604.3.2	Sec. 604.3.2	Sec. 605.3.2	Sec. 606.3	Sec. 606.3
10. Stairway construction	Sec. 602.4	Sec. 603.4	Sec. 603.4	Sec. 603.4	Sec. 604.4	Sec. 604.4	Sec. 605.4	Sec. 606.4	Sec. 606.4

N—No general requirements for fire resistance.

H.T.—Heavy timber.

[1] Structural frame elements in an exterior wall that is located where openings are not permitted, or where protection of openings is required, shall be protected against external fire exposure as required for exterior-bearing walls or the structural frame, whichever is greater.

[2] Fire-retardant-treated wood (see Section 207) may be used in the assembly, provided fire-resistance requirements are maintained. See Sections 602 and 603.

[3] For special provisions, see Sections 304.6, 306.6 and 711.

TABLE 10-A—MINIMUM EGRESS REQUIREMENTS[1]

USE[2]	MINIMUM OF TWO MEANS OF EGRESS ARE REQUIRED WHERE NUMBER OF OCCUPANTS IS AT LEAST	OCCUPANT LOAD FACTOR[3] (square feet) × 0.0929 for m²
1. Aircraft hangars (no repair)	10	500
2. Auction rooms	30	7
3. Assembly areas, concentrated use (without fixed seats) Auditoriums Churches and chapels Dance floors Lobby accessory to assembly occupancy Lodge rooms Reviewing stands Stadiums Waiting area	50 50	7 3
4. Assembly areas, less-concentrated use Conference rooms Dining rooms Drinking establishments Exhibit rooms Gymnasiums Lounges Stages Gaming: keno, slot machine and live games area	50	15
5. Bowling alley (assume no occupant load for bowling lanes)	50	11
6. Children's homes and homes for the aged	6	4
7. Classrooms	50	80
8. Congregate residences	10	20
9. Courtrooms	50	200
10. Dormitories	10	40
11. Dwellings	10	50
12. Exercising rooms	50	300
13. Garage, parking	30	50
		200

(Continued)

TABLE 10-A—MINIMUM EGRESS REQUIREMENTS[1] (Continued)

14. Health care facilities—		
Sleeping rooms	8	120
Treatment rooms	10	240
15. Hotels and apartments	10	200
16. Kitchen—commercial	30	200
17. Library—		
Reading rooms	50	50
Stack areas	30	100
18. Locker rooms	30	50
19. Malls (see Chapter 4)	—	—
20. Manufacturing areas	30	200
21. Mechanical equipment room	30	300
22. Nurseries for children (day care)	7	35
23. Offices	30	100
24. School shops and vocational rooms	50	50
25. Skating rinks	50	50 on the skating area; 15 on the deck
26. Storage and stock rooms	30	300
27. Stores—retail sales rooms		
Basements and ground floor	50	30
Upper floors	50	60
28. Swimming pools	50	50 for the pool area; 15 on the deck
29. Warehouses[5]	30	500
30. All others	50	100

[1]Access to, and egress from, buildings for persons with disabilities shall be provided as specified in Chapter 11.

[2]For additional provisions on number of exits from Groups H and I Occupancies and from rooms containing fuel-fired equipment or cellulose nitrate, see Sections 1018, 1019 and 1020, respectively.

[3]This table shall not be used to determine working space requirements per person.

[4]Occupant load based on five persons for each alley, including 15 feet (4572 mm) of runway.

[5]Occupant load for warehouses containing approved high rack storage systems designed for mechanical handling may be based on the floor area exclusive of the

NOTES

NOTES

___ 4. *Accessibility (ADA requirements)*   ⟨20⟩

___ *a.* *General:* This section concerns accessibility for the disabled as required by *ADA,* the Americans with Disabilities Act (Title 3, the national civil rights law), in nongovernment buildings (Title 2 applies to government buildings). Local or state laws may (in part) be more restrictive regarding alterations and new buildings. For each item under consideration, *the more restrictive law applies.*

___ *b.* *ADA* applies to:

    ___ (1) *Places of public accommodation* (excluding private homes, and clubs, as well as churches). Often buildings will have space for both the general public and space for employees only.

    ___ (2) *Commercial facilities* (employees only) requirements are less restrictive requiring only an accessible entry, exit, and route through each type of facility function. Only when a disabled employee is hired (under Title 1) do more restrictive standards apply.

___ *c.* *Existing buildings* are to comply by removing "architectural barriers," as much as possible, when this is "readily achievable" (not requiring undue expense, hardship, or loss of space). This effort, in theory, is to be ever on-going until all barriers are removed. When barriers can't be readily removed, "equivalent facilitation" is allowed. Priorities of removal are:

    ___ (1) Entry to places of public accommodation

    ___ (2) Access to areas where goods and services are made available to the public

    ___ (3) Access to restroom facilities

    ___ (4) Removal of all other barriers

___ *d.* *Alterations* to existing buildings require a higher standard. To the maximum extent possible, the altered portions are to be made accessible. If the altered area is a "primary function" of the building, then an accessible "path of travel" must be provided from the entry to the area (including public restrooms, telephones, and drinking fountains) with exemption only possible when cost of the path exceeds 20% of the cost to alter the primary function.

___ *e.* *New buildings or facilities* must totally comply, with only exceptions being situations of "structural impracticability."

___ *f.* See *Index,* p. 549, for a complete list of *ADA* requirements.

ACCESSIBLE ROUTE PER A.D.A.
(INTERIOR AND EXTERIOR)

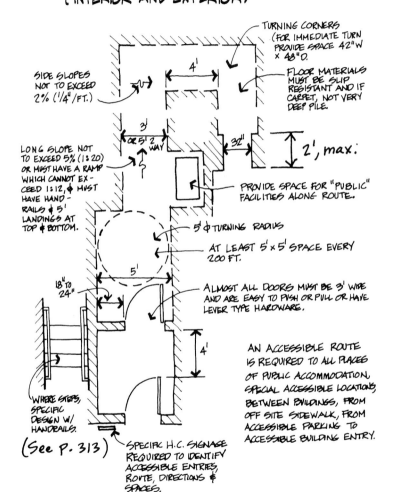

TURNING CORNERS
(FOR IMMEDIATE TURN
PROVIDE SPACE 42"W
X 48"D.

FLOOR MATERIALS
MUST BE SLIP
RESISTANT AND IF
CARPET, NOT VERY
DEEP PILE.

SIDE SLOPES
NOT TO EXCEED
2% (¼"/FT.)

4'

3'
OR 5'½
WAY

32"

2', max.

LONG SLOPE NOT
TO EXCEED 5% (1:20)
OR MUST HAVE A RAMP
WHICH CANNOT EX-
CEED 1:12, ¢ MUST
HAVE HAND-
RAILS ¢ 5'
LANDINGS AT
TOP ¢ BOTTOM.

PROVIDE SPACE FOR "PUBLIC"
FACILITIES ALONG ROUTE.

5' ⌀ TURNING RADIUS

AT LEAST 5' x 5' SPACE EVERY
200 FT.

5'

18" TO
24"

5'

ALMOST ALL DOORS MUST BE 3' WIDE
AND ARE EASY TO PUSH OR PULL OR HAVE
LEVER TYPE HARDWARE.

4'

AN ACCESSIBLE ROUTE
IS REQUIRED TO ALL PLACES
OF PUBLIC ACCOMMODATION,
SPECIAL ACCESSIBLE LOCATIONS,
BETWEEN BUILDINGS, FROM
OFF SITE SIDEWALK, FROM
ACCESSIBLE PARKING TO
ACCESSIBLE BUILDING ENTRY.

WHERE STEPS,
SPECIFIC
DESIGN W/
HANDRAILS.

(See P. 313)

SPECIFIC H.C. SIGNAGE
REQUIRED TO IDENTIFY
ACCESSIBLE ENTRIES,
ROUTE, DIRECTIONS ¢
SPACES.

NOTES

NOTES

__ I. STRUCTURAL SYSTEMS

(1) (2) (7) (10) (19) (24) (38)

Deciding which structural system to use is one of the most prominent choices the architect will have to make. Factors affecting the choice:

___ 1. Construction type by code
___ 2. Long vs. short spans
___ 3. Live loads
___ 4. Low vs. high rise
___ 5. Lateral and uplift
___ 6. Rules of thumb for estimating structural sizes

___ 1. <u>Construction Type by Code</u> (also see p. 79)

    ___ *a. Type I and Type II FR Construction*—require non-combustible materials (concrete, masonry, and steel) and substantial fire-resistive ratings (2, 3, and 4 hours). Both these construction types can be used to build large, tall buildings. The difference is that Type I has no height or area limits for most occupancies. Type I construction requires 3- and 4-hour fire resistance for structural members. Type II has a maximum height limit of 160′ as well as floor area and maximum story limitations as a function of occupancy. Type II requires 3- and 2-hour ratings and thus is less expensive. Typical systems are:

Concrete solid slabs	10′–25′ spans
Concrete slabs win drop panels	20′–35′
Concrete 2-way slab on beam	20′–35′
Concrete waffle slabs	30′–40′
Concrete joists	25′–45′
Concrete beams	15′–40′
Concrete girders	20′–60′
Concrete tees	20′–120′
Concrete arches	60′–150′
Concrete thin shell roofs	50′–70′
Steel decking	5′–15′
Steel beams	15′–60′
Steel plate girders	40′–100′

    ___ *b. Type II 1-Hour and NR Construction*—uses structural members of noncombustible construction materials for exterior walls, interior bearing walls, columns, floors, and roof. This is usually steel framing combined with concrete or masonry walls. Typical systems are:

Steel decking	5′–15′ spans
Steel beams	15′–60′

Steel joists	15′–60′
Steel plate girders	40′–100′
Steel trusses	40′–80′

___ *c.* *Type III 1-Hour and NR Construction*—has exterior walls of noncombustible construction material, usually masonry or concrete; interior columns, beams, floors, and roofs can be constructed of any material, including wood. Typical systems are:

Wood joists	10′–25′ spans
Wood beams	15′–30′
Wood girders	20′–35′
Glu-lam beams	15′–120′
Wood trusses	30′–100′

___ *d.* *Type IV Heavy Timber Construction*—achieves its fire resistance from the large size of the timber members used to frame it (2″ actual +). Exterior walls must be noncombustible. Typical systems are:

Wood planks, T and G, 3″	2′–6′ spans
Wood beams, 6 × 10, min.	15′–30′
Wood girders, 6 × 10, min.	20′–35′
Wood trusses supporting floors 8″ oc. min. and roofs 6″ × 8″	30′–100′
Wood arches supporting floors 8′ oc. min. and roofs 6″ × 8″ min.	30′–120′
Wood glu-lam beams	15′–120′

___ *e.* *Type V 1-Hour and N Construction*—is essentially light wood-frame construction. Typical systems are:

Plywood	2′–4′ spans
Wood planks	2′–6′
Wood joists	10′–25′
Wood beams	15′–30′
Wood girders	20′–35′
Glu-lam beams	15′–150′
Wood trusses	30′–100′

Note: When tentative structural system selected, see Part 13 for details and **costs.**

___ 2. Long vs. Short Spans

Select shortest span for required functional use of the space. *Short spans* (10′, 20′, or 30′) suggest beams, girders, and slabs in bending. This method encloses the space economically with a minimum of structural depth.

Long spans (50′ to 100′ and beyond) suggest the use of shape to aid the structural material. Arches, shells, domes, space frames trusses, and similar structures use their shape to help the structural material span the long distance.

Extra-long spans (such as stadiums) involve roofs spanning great distances. The economics suggest tension and inflatable membrane structures.

___ 3. Loads

    ___ *a.* Roof

        ___ (1) *Live loads* are determined by occupancy use. See p. 120.

        ___ (2) *Snow loads* should be considered when required (especially when loads are 20 lb/SF or more). See App. B, item T. Take into account:

            ___ (*a*) Heavier loads at drift locations

            ___ (*b*) Pitch of roof

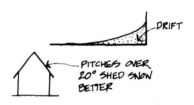

___ *b.* Floor: see p. 116.

___ 4. Low- vs. High-Rise

Low-rise (1 to 6 stories) structural design is dominated by the collection of dead and live loads through slabs, beams, and girders onto the walls and columns where the load is taken down to the foundation and onto the earth below.

High-rise (above 6 stories)design is dominated by the need to withstand the lateral loading of wind and earthquake on the building. This domination of lateral loading forces a building to become more symmetrical as it gets taller. There is substantial additional cost involved in a high-rise solution because of this increased need to resist lateral loads.

Costs: For each added story, add 1% to 5%.

TABLE 16-A—UNIFORM AND CONCENTRATED LOADS

	USE OR OCCUPANCY		UNIFORM LOAD[1] (psf)	CONCENTRATED LOAD (pounds)
	Category	Description	× 0.0479 for kN/m²	× 0.004 48 for kN
1.	Access floor systems	Office use	50	2,000[2]
		Computer use	100	2,000[2]
2.	Armories		150	0
3.	Assembly areas[3] and auditoriums and balconies therewith	Fixed seating areas	50	0
		Movable seating and other areas	100	0
		Stage areas and enclosed platforms	125	0
4.	Cornices and marquees		60[4]	0
5.	Exit facilities[5]		100	0[6]
6.	Garages	General storage and/or repair	100	7
		Private or pleasure-type motor vehicle storage	50	7
7.	Hospitals	Wards and rooms	40	1,000[2]
8.	Libraries	Reading rooms	60	1,000[2]
		Stack rooms	125	1,500[2]
9.	Manufacturing	Light	75	2,000[2]
		Heavy	125	3,000[2]
10.	Offices		50	2,000[2]
11.	Printing plants	Press rooms	150	2,500[2]
		Composing and linotype rooms	100	2,000[2]

12. Residential[8]	Basic floor area	40	0[6]
	Exterior balconies	60[4]	0
	Decks	40[4]	0
	Storage	40	0
13. Restrooms[9]			
14. Reviewing stands, grandstands, bleachers, and folding and telescoping seating		100	0
15. Roof decks	Same as area served or for the type of occupancy accommodated		
16. Schools	Classrooms	40	1,000[2]
17. Sidewalks and driveways	Public access	250	7
18. Storage	Light	125	
	Heavy	250	
19. Stores		100	3,000[2]
20. Pedestrian bridges and walkways		100	

[1]See Section 1607 for live load reductions.
[2]See Section 1607.3.3, first paragraph, for area of load application.
[3]Assembly areas include such occupancies as dance halls, drill rooms, gymnasiums, playgrounds, plazas, terraces and similar occupancies that are generally accessible to the public.
[4]When snow loads occur that are in excess of the design conditions, the structure shall be designed to support the loads due to the increased loads caused by drift buildup or a greater snow design as determined by the building official. See Section 1614. For special-purpose roofs, see Section 1607.4.4.
[5]Exit facilities shall include such uses as corridors serving an occupant load of 10 or more persons, exterior exit balconies, stairways, fire escapes and similar uses.
[6]Individual stair treads shall be designed to support a 300-pound (1.33 kN) concentrated load placed in a position that would cause maximum stress. Stair stringers may be designed for the uniform load set forth in the table.
[7]See Section 1607.3.3, second paragraph, for concentrated loads. See Table 16-B for vehicle barriers.
[8]Residential occupancies include private dwellings, apartments and hotel guest rooms.
[9]Restroom loads shall not be less than the load for the occupancy with which they are associated, but need not exceed 50 pounds per square foot (2.4 kN/m^2).

TABLE 16-B—SPECIAL LOADS[1]

USE		VERTICAL LOAD	LATERAL LOAD
Category	Description	(pounds per square foot unless otherwise noted)	
		× 0.0479 for kN/m²	
1. Construction, public access at site (live load)	Walkway, see Section 3303.6	150	
	Canopy, see Section 3303.7	150	
2. Grandstands, reviewing stands, bleachers, and folding and telescoping seating (live load)	Seats and footboards	120[2]	See Footnote 3
3. Stage accessories (live load)	Catwalks	40	
	Followspot, projection and control rooms	50	
4. Ceiling framing (live load)	Over stages	20	
	All uses except over stages	10[4]	
5. Partitions and interior walls, see Sec. 1611.5 (live load)			5
6. Elevators and dumbwaiters (dead and live loads)		2 × total loads[5]	
7. Mechanical and electrical equipment (dead load)		Total loads	
8. Cranes (dead and live loads)	Total load including impact increase	1.25 × total load[6]	0.10 × total load[7]
9. Balcony railings and guardrails	Exit facilities serving an occupant load greater than 50		50[8]
	Other than exit facilities		20[8]
	Components		25[9]
10. Vehicle barriers	See Section 311.2.3.5		6,000[10]

		See Footnote 11	See Footnote 11
11. Handrails			
12. Storage racks	Over 8 feet (2438 mm) high	Total loads[12]	See Table 16-O
13. Fire sprinkler structural support		250 pounds (1112 N) plus weight of water-filled pipe[13]	See Table 16-O
14. Explosion exposure	Hazardous occupancies, see Section 307.10		

[1]The tabulated loads are minimum loads. Where other vertical loads required by this code or required by the design would cause greater stresses, they shall be used.

[2]Pounds per lineal foot (× 14.6 for N/m).

[3]Lateral sway bracing loads of 24 pounds per foot (350 N/m) parallel and 10 pounds per foot (145.9 N/m) perpendicular to seat and footboards.

[4]Does not apply to ceilings that have sufficient total access from below, such that access is not required within the space above the ceiling. Does not apply to ceilings if the attic areas above the ceiling are not provided with access. This live load need not be considered as acting simultaneously with other live loads imposed upon the ceiling framing or its supporting structure.

[5]Where Appendix Chapter 30 has been adopted, see reference standard cited therein for additional design requirements.

[6]The impact factors included are for cranes with steel wheels riding on steel rails. They may be modified if substantiating technical data acceptable to the building official is submitted. Live loads on crane support girders and their connections shall be taken as the maximum crane wheel loads. For pendant-operated traveling crane support girders and their connections, the impact factors shall be 1.10.

[7]This applies in the direction parallel to the runway rails (longitudinal). The factor for forces perpendicular to the rail is $0.20 \times$ the transverse traveling loads (trolley, cab, hooks and lifted loads). Forces shall be applied at top of rail and may be distributed among rails of multiple rail cranes and shall be distributed with due regard for lateral stiffness of the structures supporting these rails.

[8]A load per lineal foot (× 14.6 for N/m) to be applied horizontally at right angles to the top rail.

[9]Intermediate rails, panel fillers and their connections shall be capable of withstanding a load of 25 pounds per square foot (1.2 kN/m²) applied horizontally at right angles over the entire tributary area, including openings and spaces between rails. Reactions due to this loading need not be combined with those of Footnote 8.

[10]A horizontal load in pounds (N) applied at right angles to the vehicle barrier at a height of 18 inches (457 mm) above the parking surface. The force may be distributed over a 1-foot-square (304.8-millimeter-square) area.

[11]The mounting of handrails shall be such that the completed handrail and supporting structure are capable of withstanding a load of at least 200 pounds (890 N) applied in any direction at any point on the rail. These loads shall not be assumed to act cumulatively with Item 9.

[12]Vertical members of storage racks shall be protected from impact forces of operating equipment, or racks shall be designed so that failure of one vertical member will not cause collapse of more than the bay or bays directly supported by that member.

[13]The 250-pound (1.11 kN) load is to be applied to any single fire sprinkler support point but not simultaneously to all support joints.

TABLE 16-C—MINIMUM ROOF LIVE LOADS[1]

ROOF SLOPE	METHOD 1			METHOD 2		
	Tributary Loaded Area in Square Feet for Any Structural Member					
	× 0.0929 for m²					
	0 to 200	201 to 600	Over 600	Uniform Load[2] (psf)	Rate of Reduction r (percentage)	Maximum Reduction R (percentage)
	Uniform Load (psf)					
	× 0.0479 for kN/m²					
1. Flat[3] or rise less than 4 units vertical in 12 units horizontal (33.3% slope). Arch or dome with rise less than one eighth of span	20	16	12	20	.08	40
2. Rise 4 units vertical to less than 12 units vertical in 12 units horizontal (33% to less than 100% slope). Arch or dome with rise one eighth of span to less than three eighths of span	16	14	12	16	.06	25
3. Rise 12 units vertical in 12 units horizontal (100% slope) and greater. Arch or dome with rise three eighths of span or greater	12	12	12	12	No reductions permitted	
4. Awnings except cloth covered[4]	5	5	5	5		
5. Greenhouses, lath houses and agricultural buildings[5]	10	10	10	10		

[1]Where snow loads occur, the roof structure shall be designed for such loads as determined by the building official. See Section 1614. For special-purpose roofs, see Section 1607.4.4.

[2]See Sections 1607.5 and 1607.6 for live load reductions. The rate of reduction r in Section 1607.5 Formula (7-1) shall be as indicated in the table. The maximum reduction R shall not exceed the value indicated in the table.

[3]A flat roof is any roof with a slope of less than 1/4 unit vertical in 12 units horizontal (2% slope). The live load for flat roofs is in addition to the ponding load required by Section 1611.7.

[4]As defined in Section 3206.

[5]See Section 1607.4.4 for concentrated load requirements for greenhouse roof members.

___ 5. <u>Lateral and Uplift:</u> Beyond vertical loads, consideration should always be given to horizontal and uplift forces. For these, the UBC factors in the *importance* of the occupancies ("essential occupancy with higher safety factor") such as hospitals, police and fire stations, emergency structures, hazardous-materials facilities, etc.

   ___ a. *Wind forces* are based on known *wind speeds.* Minimum is usually 70 mph (13 lb/SF) and maximum usually 130 mph (44 lb/SF) for hurricanes (with the range between being 4 lb to 7 lb/SF added for each additional 10 mph). See App. B, item S. Added to this are *factors for height* of the building. Also, see p. 298 for shingles.

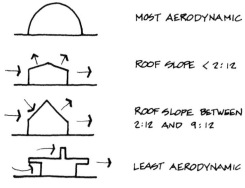

MOST AERODYNAMIC

ROOF SLOPE < 2:12

ROOF SLOPE BETWEEN 2:12 AND 9:12

LEAST AERODYNAMIC

   ___ b. *Seismic forces* are caused by ground waves due to earthquake shock, causing vertical and horizontal movement.

The weight of the building usually absorbs the vertical element, leaving the horizontal force transmitted through the building foundations to the structure above. The weight of the building resists side movement. Present engineering procedure is to design the building for a side force, like wind.

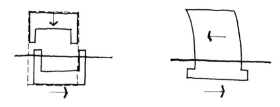

Seismic forces grow in proportion to the weight of the building and the square of its height. The total seismic force the building must withstand is a percent of its total weight. This force is usually 10 to 50% of the total weight of the building. In determining the required force, the UBC considers:

___ (1) *Risk:* based on location. Zones 4 and 3 are the most hazardous. Zones 0 and 1 are the least hazardous. See App. B, item E.

Costs increase about 1% to 2% for every increase in zone (2% to 5% for high-rise, and 5% to 8% for long-span, heavy construction).

___ (2) Importance of *occupancy:* See p. 121.

___ (3) *Soils* and site geology: Rock-like materials are best. Soft clays are poor.

___ (4) *Resistance* of the structure:

    ___ (*a*) The less weight the better

    ___ (*b*) The more flexible the better, or

    ___ (*c*) The stiffer the better

_____ *c.* Lateral design and overall building shape

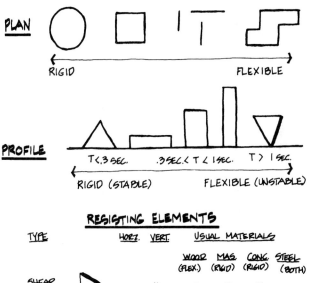

PLAN

RIGID ←——————————————→ FLEXIBLE

PROFILE

T < .3 SEC.   .3 SEC.< T < 1 SEC.   T > 1 SEC.

RIGID (STABLE) ←——————→ FLEXIBLE (UNSTABLE)

RESISTING ELEMENTS

TYPE		HORZ.	VERT.	USUAL MATERIALS			
				WOOD (FLEX.)	MAS. (RIGID)	CONC. (RIGID)	STEEL (BOTH)
SHEAR WALL			X	X	X	X	
BRACED FRAME		X	X				X
RIGID FRAME *		X	X				X
DIAPHRAM		X		X		X	X

*ALSO TERMED "MOMENT RESISTING FRAME" IS ACTUALLY VERY FLEXIBLE W/ POSSIBLE SWAY AND NON-STRUCTURAL DAMAGE.

DESIGNS CAN MIX VARIOUS ELEMENTS. THE AMOUNT NEEDED IS BASED ON THE AMOUNT OF FORCE TO BE RESISTED. THESE ELEMENTS MUST BE FACED BOTH WAYS, IDEALLY IN EQUAL AMOUNTS OR THE BUILDING WILL BE SUBJECT TO TORSION.

LATERAL DESIGN STRATEGIES

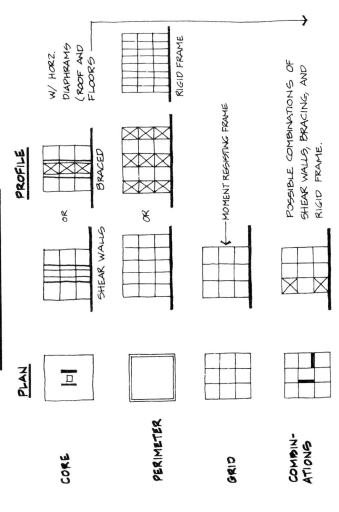

PLAN

PROFILE

CORE

SHEAR WALLS

OR

BRACED

W/ HORZ. DIAPHRAMS (ROOF AND FLOORS)

RIGID FRAME

PERIMETER

OR

GRID

← MOMENT RESISTING FRAME

COMBIN-ATIONS

POSSIBLE COMBINATIONS OF SHEAR WALLS, BRACING, AND RIGID FRAME.

124

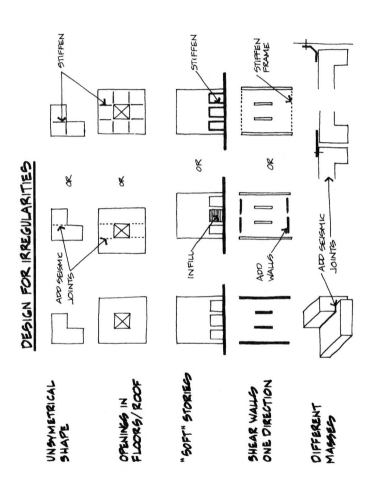

DESIGN FOR IRREGULARITIES

UNSYMMETRICAL SHAPE — ADD SEISMIC JOINTS — OR — STIFFEN

OPENINGS IN FLOORS/ROOF — ADD SEISMIC JOINTS — OR — STIFFEN

"SOFT" STORIES — INFILL — OR — STIFFEN

SHEAR WALLS ONE DIRECTION — ADD WALLS — OR — STIFFEN FRAME

DIFFERENT MASSES — ADD SEISMIC JOINTS

125

___ *d.* Nonstructural seismic considerations
In seismic zones 3 and 4, the following things should be considered:

___ (1) Overhead utility lines, antennae, poles, and large signs pose a hazard.

___ (2) Secure and brace roof-mounted and floor-mounted equipment for lateral load and uplift. This would include AC equipment, hot water heaters, and electrical service sections.

___ (3) Brace structure-supported piping and ducts for side sway. Avoid long, straight runs.

___ (4) Brace structure-supported suspended ceilings for side sway. Allow for movement where wall occurs.

___ (5) Sleeve piping through foundation walls.

___ (6) Locate building exits to avoid falling elements such as power poles or signs.

___ (7) Anchor veneers to allow for movement.

___ (8) Partitions should be constructed to assume the added seismic lateral load caused by the furniture or equipment.

___ (9) Seismic joints should include partition construction details to provide a continuous separation through the roof, floor, walls, and ceiling.

___ (10) Interior partitions and fire-rated walls that are floor-to-floor need to be designed for lateral movement. Also, consider corners, tee-junctions of walls, and junctions of walls and columns.

___ (11) Brace suspended light fixtures. Consider plastic rather than glass lenses.

___ (12) Battery-powered emergency lighting needs positive attachment.

___ (13) Use tempered or laminated glass, or plastic, at large-glass areas that could cause damage. Use resilient mountings.

___ (14) Laterally secure tall furniture and shelving.

___ 6. *Structural Components (A Primer):* Many of today's engineering courses have become so cluttered with theory and mathematics that even graduate engineers sometimes lose sight of the simple basic principles. Use this section to remind you of basic structural principles.

___ *a.* <u>Types of forces</u>
    ___ (1) Tension
    ___ (2) Compression
    ___ (3) Bending

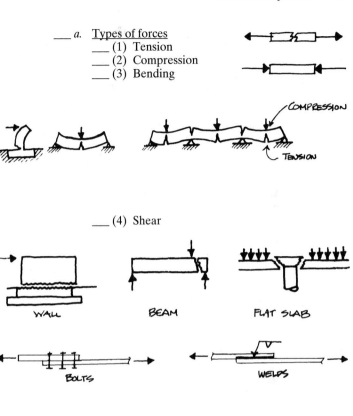

    ___ (4) Shear

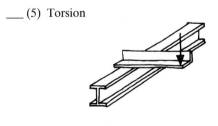

    ___ (5) Torsion

    ___ (6) Buckling

___ *b.* <u>Beams</u>

    ___ (1) Simple beams have tension at the bottom and compression at the top.

    ___ (2) If the beam is made deeper, "d" (the moment arm) is increased and the compressive and tensile forces decreased. The deeper the beam, the stronger.

    ___ (3) Within limits, small holes can often be cut through the beams at center, middepth, without harm. But notches or holes at top or bottom will reduce strength.

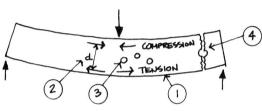

    ___ (4) Since shear is usually greatest close to the supports, judgment must be used regarding cutting holes or notches in the web close to the support. Also, see p. 271.

    ___ (5) Continuous beams can often carry more load than simple span beams.

    ___ (6) A point to watch for in cantilever and continuous beams is possible uplift at a rear support.

    ___ (7) Beams may be fixed or restrained. The bending stress at midspan is less (so beam depth is less) but connections become more involved.

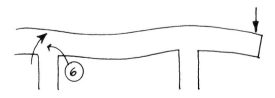

___ *c.* <u>Slabs</u>
    ___ (1) Are nothing more than wide, flat beams.
    ___ (2) Generally, by far, the greatest stress in flat slabs occurs where the columns try to punch through the slab. Slab openings next to columns can trigger failures!

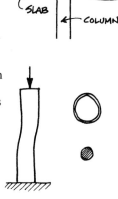

___ *d.* <u>Columns:</u> Because of the tendency for columns to buckle, fatter ones carry more load than thinner ones (with same cross-sectional area and length).

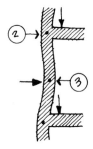

___ *e.* <u>Walls</u>
    ___ (1) Bearing walls act as wide, flat columns, carrying their loads in compression.
    ___ (2) Walls must be tied to the floor and roof.
    ___ (3) Bond beams tie the wall together, so more of it will act to resist any specific load.
    ___ (4) Shear walls fail by:

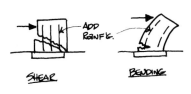

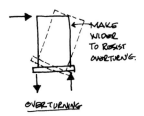

_____ _f._ <u>Trusses</u>

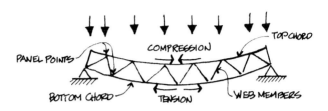

_____ (1) Are usually lighter and more efficient than solid beams carrying the same load, but take more vertical space.

_____ (2) Are made by a series of triangles supporting load at panel points. Patterns other than triangles can change shape easily and must be avoided or specially treated.

_____ (3) Connections of web and chords become very important. The center of gravity of intersecting web members should meet at or very close to the center of gravity of the chord.

_____ (4) Loads should be carried at the panel points, not between. This is probably the most common problem with trusses.

_____ (5) Field shifting or removal of web members to allow passage of ducts or other items may be dangerous.

_____ (6) If trusses cantilever over a support or are continuous over a support, the bottom chords must often be

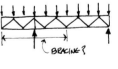

braced against sideways buckling where they are in compression.

___ *g.* <u>Arches</u> (or sloped roofs) Need resistance to lateral thrust by either of the following:

   ___ (1) Strengthening or thickening the supports

   ___ (2) Tension members added

___ *h.* <u>Connections</u>

   ___ (1) Connections are usually the most critical elements of any structure. Statistically, failures are much more apt to occur at a connection than anywhere else. When connections fail, they often fail suddenly, not giving the warnings of deflection and cracking inherent in, say, a bending failure of a beam. Thus a connection failure is apt to be more hazardous to life and limb than are some other types of failures.

   ___ (2) Connections are often more sensitive to construction tolerances or errors than are the structural members themselves.

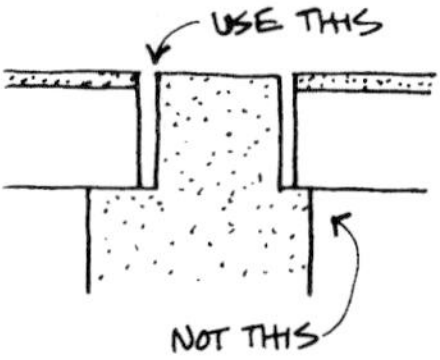

   ___ (3) In cases where a strong material (such as steel or prestressed concrete) must be connected to a weaker material (such as concrete blocks), the stronger material may carry a load that is not easily carried by the weaker. The connection must spread the load over a large area of the weaker material and must also not cause undue bending.

   ___ (4) Don't pare connection designs to the bone! Estimate the maximum amount of probable field error and design the connection for it. If possible, provide a second line of defense. Try to make connections as fool-proof as possible. Allow as much room as possible for field tolerances.

___ (5) Where possible, locate construction joints at a point of low beam shear and locate connections where loads transmitted through the connection are a minimum.

___ (6) Consider the prying, levering, or twisting action in connections. Consider the effects of connection eccentricities on the members themselves.

___ (7) Consider the effects of shrinkage or other lateral movement.

___ (8) Use care in stacking beams and girders on top of columns, particularly deep beams and girders that want to overturn. Provide bracing.

___ (9) Consider using shop over field connections, when possible, because they are done under more favorable conditions.

___ 7. *Rules of Thumb for Estimating Structural Sizes (Span-to-Depth Ratios):* Most rules of thumb for structural estimating are based on *span-to-depth ratios.* First select likely spans from structural systems (page 113). Then, *the span in feet or inches is divided by the ratio to get the depth in either feet or inches.* The higher the number the better.

Example: If ratio is 8 and span is 8 ft, then depth is 1 ft.

Ratios for Typical Elements:

Beams and joists of all kinds range from 10 to 24. Use lower ratios for heavy or concentrated loads. The ratio of *20* is a good all-purpose average for steel, wood, and concrete.

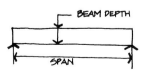

Cantilevered beams: In general, the optimal length of a cantilever is *one-third* the supported span.

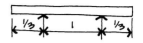

Columns: The ratios of unbraced length to least thickness of most column types range from 10 to 30, with *20* being a good average.

Slabs: Reinforced concrete slabs of various types have ratios ranging from 20 to 35, with *24* being a good average.

SEE BEAM, P. 132.

Trusses of various types and materials have ratios ranging from 4 to 12. The lower ratio is appropriate for trusses carrying heavy floor loads or concentrated loads. The ratio *8* is a good average for estimating roof trusses.

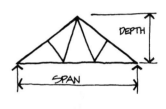

For more specific ratios based on materials and specific types of structural elements, see pp. 215, 235, 257, and 277.

NOTES

__ J. ENERGY "Passive" and "Active" Approaches to Conservation: (30) (44)

__ 1. Building Type

All buildings produce internal heat. All buildings are affected by external loads (heating or cooling) based on the climate and internal loads (heat from equipment, lights, people, etc.). Large commercial buildings tend to be internally dominated. Residences or small commercial buildings tend to be the exact opposite.

__ 2. Human Comfort

The comfort zone may be roughly defined as follows: Most people in the temperate zone, sitting indoors in the shade in light clothing, will feel tolerably comfortable at temperatures ranging from *70° to 80°F* as long as the relative humidity lies between *20% and 50%*. As humidity increases, they will begin to become uncomfortable at lower and lower temperatures until the relative humidity reaches *75% to 80%,* when discomfort at any temperature sets in. But if they are sitting in a draft, the range of tolerable temperature shifts upward, so that temperatures of *85°F* may be quite comfortable in the *20% to 50%* relative humidity range, if local air is moving at *200 ft/min.* Indoor air moving more slowly than *50 ft/min* is generally unnoticed, while flows of *50 to 100 ft/min* are pleasant and hardly noticed. Breezes from *100 to 200 ft/min* are pleasant but one is constantly aware of them, while those from *200 to 300 ft/min* are first slightly unpleasant, then annoying and drafty. See psychrometric chart on p. 143 for "passive" strategies.

__ 3. Climate

In response to a climate, if a building is to be designed for "passive" (natural) strategies, it is important to determine the demands of the climate. Is the climate severe (for either heating or cooling, as well as humidity) or temperate? Which predominates, heating or cooling? Is the climate wet or dry? Once the climatic demands are determined, what climatic elements are available to offer comfort relief? Is sun available for winter heating? Are breezes available for summer cooling?

In determining passive and energy conservation strategies for a building in an unfamiliar climate consult App. B to make the following determinations:

__ *a.* If two-thirds of the heating degree days (HDD) exceed the cooling degree days, *winter heating* will need to be the predominant strategy or a major consideration.

___ *b.* If cooling degree days (CDD) are greater than two-thirds of the heating degree days, *summer cooling* should be the major strategy or consideration.

___ *c.* If two-thirds of the heating degree days roughly equals the cooling degree days, both winter heating and summer cooling will be needed strategies though these will be likely *temperate* climates.

___ *d.* When heating degree days exceed 6000, a *severely cold climate* will have to be designed for.

___ *e.* When cooling degree days exceed 2000, a *severely hot climate* will have to be designed for.

___ *f.* When annual average evening relative humidity exceeds 80% and rainfall averages 40″/yr, or more, an *extremely humid climate* will have to be designed for.

___ *g.* When annual average evening relative humidity is less than 65% and rainfall averages 15″/yr, or less, an *extremely dry climate* will have to be designed for.

___ *h.* When annual winter sunshine exceeds 50%, *passive winter heating* may be a good strategy, if needed. Summer shading will be an important factor in a hot climate.

___ *i.* Most locations in the United States have annual average daily wind exceeding 5 mph, so *natural ventilation* as a means of cooling may be a good strategy, if needed. But this may also be a problem if in a cold climate.

___ *j.* *Microclimates* at specific sites can vary from the overall climate due to:

   ___ (1) Large bodies of water (10°F milder).

   ___ (2) Built-up area (5°F warmer).

   ___ (3) Elevation (5°F cooler for each 1000 ft rise).

   ___ (4) Land forms: Tops of hills receive wind. Valleys get cool in evenings. Breezes rise up slopes in day and descend in evenings: South slopes receive most year-around sun; north, the least, with east and west slopes the most summer morning and afternoon sun.

EXAMPLE:

PROBLEM: DETERMINE LIKELY "PASSIVE" & ENERGY
CONSERVATION STRATEGIES FOR A BUILD'G.
SITE IN ALBUQUERQUE, NEW MEXICO.

SOLUTION:

1. <u>CLIMATE STRATEGIES</u>:
   CHECK STRATEGIES STARTING ON P. 135 AGAINST
   CLIMATE DATA IN APP. B ON PAGE 533
   (LINE 26 FOR ALBUQUERQUE).

   a. <u>WINTER HEATING</u> (APP. B, ITEMS L & M)
      (.66 × 4414 HDD = 2913 HDD > 1254 CDD)
   b. THRU f. DO NOT APPLY FOR ALBUQUERQUE.
   g. <u>DRY CLIMATE</u> (APP. B, ITEMS I & O).
   h. <u>SUNSHINE</u> FOR WINTER HEATING (APP. B,
      ITEM K).
   i. <u>USE BREEZES</u> FOR COOLING IN MILD SUMMERS.

   SUMMARY:
   EVEN THOUGH ALBUQUERQUE IS A DESERT WITH ONLY
   8 INCHES OF RAIN PER YEAR (ITEM I), DUE TO ITS
   ELEVATION OF 5310 FEET (ITEM B), IT HAS MILD
   SUMMERS WHERE NATURAL BREEZES MAY HELP COOL.
   ITS WINTERS REQUIRE HEATING. BECAUSE OF THE
   LARGE AMOUNT OF YEARLY SUNSHINE OF 76 % (ITEM
   K), PASSIVE SOLAR HEATING IS A VERY LIKELY STRAT-
   AGY TO USE.

2. <u>DESIGN STRATEGIES</u> (USING CHECKLIST ON P.138):
   FOR WINTER HEATING CONSIDER PASSIVE SOLAR
   (8) & (9), + (14) THRU (21)

   FOR SUMMER COOLING CONSIDER NATURAL BREEZE
   (45) THRU (54).

___ 4. <u>Checklist for Passive Building Design</u> (Strategies for Energy Conservation):

Note: Many of the following items conflict, so it is impossible to choose all.

   _X_   Cold climate or winter
     _X_   Hot climate or summer

Windbreaks

___   (1) Use neighboring land forms, structures, or vegetation for winter wind protection.

___   (2) Shape and orient building shell to minimize wind turbulence.

Plants and water

   ___   (3) Use ground cover and planting for site cooling.

   ___   (4) Maximize on-site evaporative cooling; ocean or water zones, such as fountains, modify climate 10°F.

   ___   (5) Use planting next to building skin.

   ___   (6) Use roof spray or roof ponds for evaporative cooling.

Indoor/outdoor rooms

___ ___   (7) Provide outdoor semiprotected areas for year-round climate moderation.

___   (8) Provide solar-oriented interior zone for maximizing heat.

___ ___   (9) Plan specific rooms or functions to coincide with solar orientation (i.e., storage on "bad" orient such as west, living on "good" such as south).

Earth sheltering

___ ___   (10) Recess structure below grade or raise existing grade for earth-sheltering effort.

___ ___   (11) Use slab-on-grade construction for ground temperature heat exchange. See p. 292 for perimeter insulation.

___ ___   (12) Use sod roofs (12″ of earth will give about a 9-hour time lag).

   ___   (13) Use high-capacitance materials at interiors to store "coolth." Works best with night ventilation.

Solar walls and windows

___   (14) Maximize reflectivity of ground and building surfaces outside windows facing winter sun.

Cold   Hot

___   (15) Shape and orient building shell to maxi-
                   mize exposure to winter sun. Glass needs
                   to face to within 15 degrees of due south.

___   (16) Use high-capacitance materials to store
                   solar heat gain. Best results are by distrib-
                   uting "mass" locations throughout interior.
                   On average, provide 1 to 1¼ CF of concrete
                   or masonry per each SF of south-facing
                   glass. For an equivalent effect, 4 times more
                   mass is needed when not exposed to sun.
                   Do not place carpeting on these floor
                   areas.

___   (17) This same "mass effect" (see 16) can be
                   used in reverse in hot, dry (clear sky) cli-
                   mates. "Flush" building during cool night
                   to precool for next day. Be sure to shade
                   the mass.

___ ___   (18) Use solar wall and/or roof collectors on
                   south-oriented surfaces (also hot-water
                   heating). Optimum tilt angle for roof
                   solar collectors is equal to latitude of site
                   (+/– 15°). See p. 523.

___   (19) Maximize south-facing glazing (with over-
                   hangs as needed). On average, south-fac-
                   ing glass should be 10 to 25% of floor
                   area. For north latitude/cold climates this
                   can go up to 50%. For south latitude/hot
                   climates this strategy may not be appro-
                   priate.

___   (20) Provide reflective panels outside of glaz-
                   ing to increase winter irradiation.

___   (21) Use skylights for winter solar gain and
                   natural illumination. See p. 473.

Thermal envelope

___ ___   (22) Minimize the outside wall and roof areas
                   (ratio of exterior surface to enclosed vol-
                   ume). Best ratios:
                         2-story dome—12%; 2-story cylin-
                              der—14%
                         2-story square—15%; 3-story
                              square—16%
                         1-story square—17%

___ ___   (23) Use attic space as buffer zone between
                   interior and outside climate. Vent above
                   ceiling insulation. See pp. 287 and 292.

Cold Hot

___   (24) Use basement or crawl space as buffer zone between interior and ground. See p. 292 for insulation.

___ ___ (25) Provide air shafts for natural or mechanically assisted house-heat recovery. This can be recirculated warm at high ceilings or recovered heat from chimneys.

___   (26) Centralize heat sources within building interior. (Fireplaces, furnaces, hot water heater, cooking, laundry, etc.) Lower level for these most desirable.

     ___ (27) Put heat sources (HW, laundry, etc.) outside building.

___ ___ (28) Use vestibule or exterior "wind shield" at entryways. Orient away from undesirable winds.

___ ___ (29) Locate low-use spaces, storage, utility, and garage areas to provide buffers. Locate at "bad" orientations (i.e., on north side in cold climate or west side in hot climate).

___ ___ (30) Subdivide interior to create separate heating and cooling zones. One example is separate living and sleeping zones.

___ ___ (31) Select insulating materials for resistance to heat flow through building envelope. For minimum insulation recommendations, see p. 144 and/or guidelines by *ASHRAE* 90A-80. If walls are masonry, insulation is best on outside.

___ ___ (32) Apply vapor barriers to control moisture migration. See p. 289.

     ___ (33) Use of radiant barriers. See p. 291.

___ ___ (34) Develop construction details to minimize air infiltration and exfiltration. See p. 309.

___ ___ (35) Provide insulating controls at glazing. See p. 331.

___ ___ (36) Minimize window and door openings (usually N, E, and W).

___ ___ (37) Detail window and door construction to prevent undesired air infiltration. See p. 315 for doors and 319 for windows.

___ ___ (38) Provide ventilation openings for air flow to and from specific spaces and appliances. See p. 360 for fireplaces.

<u>Cold</u> <u>Hot</u>

Sun shading

    ___   (39) Minimize reflectivity of ground and building faces outside windows facing summer sun.

    ___   (40) Use neighboring land forms, structures, or vegetation for summer shading.

    ___   (41) Shape and orient building shell to minimize solar exposure. Best rectangular proportions are 1 (east and west) to between 1.5 and 2 (north and south).

    ___   (42) Provide shading for walls exposed to summer sun. For landscaping, see p. 201.

    ___   (43) Use heat-reflective materials on solar-oriented surfaces. White or light colors are best.

    ___   (44) Provide shading for glazing exposed to sun. See p. 367.

Natural ventilation

    ___   (45) Use neighboring land forms, structures, or vegetation to increase exposure to breezes.

    ___   (46) Shape and orient building shell to maximize exposure to breezes. Long side should face prevailing breeze within 20 to 30 degrees.

    ___   (47) Use "open plan" interior to promote air flow.

    ___   (48) Provide vertical air shafts to promote interior air flow.

    ___   (49) Use double roof and wall construction for ventilation within the building shell.

    ___   (50) Orient door and window openings to facilitate natural ventilation from prevailing breezes. For best results:

            Windows on opposite sides of rooms.
            Inlets and outlets of equal size giving maximum air change.
            A smaller inlet increases air speed.

    ___   (51) Use wing walls, overhangs, and louvers to direct summer wind flow into interior.

    ___   (52) Use louvered wall for maximum ventilation control.

    ___   (53) Use roof monitors for "stack effect ventilation."

Cold   Hot

       ___   (54) Often fan power is needed to help ventilation cooling. See 5a (below).

___ 5. Checklist for Active Building Design (Strategies for Energy Conservation)

  ___ *a.* Whenever possible, use fans in lieu of compressors, as they use about 80% less energy. In residential, this may take the form of "whole-house" fans. See *o*, below.

  ___ *b.* Design for natural lighting in lieu of artificial lighting. In hot climates or summers, avoid direct sun. See p. 473.

  ___ *c.* Use high-efficiency lighting (50–100 lumens per watt). See Part 16A. Provide switches or controls to light only areas needed and to take advantage of daylighting. See Part 16B.

  ___ *d.* Use gas rather than electric when possible, as this can be up to 75% less expensive.

  ___ *e.* Use efficient equipment and appliances
     ___ (1) Microwave rather than convection ovens.
     ___ (2) Refrigerators rated 5–10 kBtu/day or 535–1070 kwh/yr.

  ___ *f.* If fireplaces, use high-efficiency type with tight-fitting high-temperature glass, insulated and radiant-inducing boxed with outside combustion air. See p. 360.

  ___ *g.* Use night setback and load-control devices.

  ___ *h.* Use multizone HVAC.

  ___ *i.* Locate ducts in conditioned space or tightly seal and insulate.

  ___ *j.* Insulate hot and cold water pipes (R = 1 to 3).

  ___ *k.* Locate air handlers in conditioned space.

  ___ *l.* Install thermostats away from direct sun and supply grilles.

  ___ *m.* Use heating equipment with efficiencies of 70% for gas and 175% for electric, or higher.

  ___ *n.* Use cooling equipment with efficiencies of SEER = 10, COP = 2.5 or higher.

  ___ *o.* Use "economizers" on commercial HVAC to take advantage of good outside temperatures.

  ___ *p.* At dry, hot climates, use evaporative cooling.

  ___ *q.* Use gas or solar in lieu of electric hot water heating. Insulate hot water heaters. For solar hot water, see p. 437.

  ___ *r.* For solar electric (photovoltaic), see p. 503.

___ *s.* For some building types and at some locations, utilities have peak load rates, such as on summer afternoons. These peak rates should be identified and designed for. Therefore, designing for peak loads may be more important than yearly energy savings. In some cases saving energy and saving energy cost may not be the same.

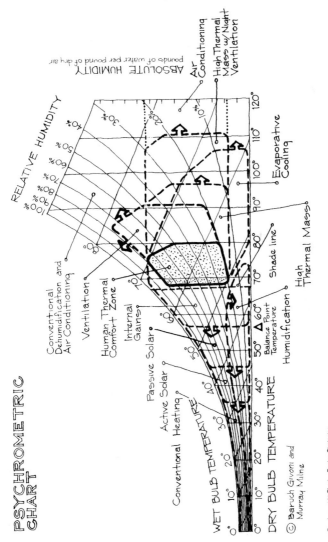

Psychrometric Chart—Design Strategies

___ 6. <u>Energy Code</u> (ASHRAE 90A—1980). For U values, see p. 292.

    ___ *a.* Although there are more current national energy codes, these envelope guidelines, based on the old ASHRAE 90A, should help the designer determine if a preliminary design is in the "ballpark." These rules of thumb are for building envelope only. Should the walls fail to meet code requirements, the roof can be made to compensate, and vice versa. Should these rough preliminary calculations fail, this may indicate that either the design is poor from an energy conservation standpoint or that other features (such as passive heating) need to be considered by more stringent calculation or computer modeling.

    Use the following steps to roughly check for compliance:

    ___ *b.* Approximate compliance can be checked by using the following formulas:

        ___ (1) For Walls, Winter Heating:

$$Uw = \frac{(Uw_1 \times Aw_1) + (Ug_1 \times Ag_1) + (Ud_1 \times Ad_1)}{Aw}$$

        ___ (2) For Walls, Summer Cooling:

$$OTTVw = \frac{(Uw_1 \times Aw_1 \times Tdeg) + (Ag_1 \times SF_1 \times SC_1) + (Ug_1 \times Ag_1 \times \Delta t)}{Aw}$$

        ___ (3) For Roofs, Winter Heating:

$$Ur = \frac{(Ur_1 \times Ar_1) + (Ug_1 \times Ag_1)}{A_{Total\ Roof}}$$

        ___ (4) For Roofs, Summer Cooling:

$$OTTVr = \frac{(Ur_1 \times Ar_1 \times Tdeg) + (138 \times Ag_1 \times Sc_1) + (Ug_1 \times Ag_1 \times \Delta t)}{A_{Total\ Roof}}$$

where:

    Uw, Ur are the overall wall and roof U values.

    $OTTVw$ and r are the overall wall and roof cooling thermal transfer values.

    Uw_1, Ur_1 are the U values of the wall and roof components.

    Aw_1, Ar_1 are the areas of the *solid* wall and roof components.

Ug$_1$, Ag$_1$ are the U values and areas for glass.

Ud$_1$, Ad$_1$ are the U values and areas for doors.

HDD = Heating degree days.

TDEQ = Temp. difference factor for thermal mass. See p. 293 for wt. of materials. See Figure 4 for values.

SF = Solar factor. See Figure 5.

SC = Shading coefficient of glass. See pp. 331 and 334.

Δt is the difference between summer dry-bulb temperature found in App. B, item Q and 78°F indoor temperature.

Note: Where more than one type of wall, roof, window (or skylight) is used, each U and A term in formulas must be expanded (i.e., U$_2$, A$_2$, etc.) and totaled.

___ *c.* Determine building type

    ___ (1) Type A-1 is 1- and 2-family residential dwellings.

    ___ (2) Type A-2 is all other residential buildings of 3 stories and under, including hotels and motels.

    ___ (3) Type B is all other buildings.

___ *d.* The values determined in *b,* above, must equal or be less than <u>*one-half*</u> the values in the graphs on pp. 146 and 147. The one-half factors in because current codes are more stringent than the old ASHRAE 90-A. For HDD and CDD, see App. A, items L and M.

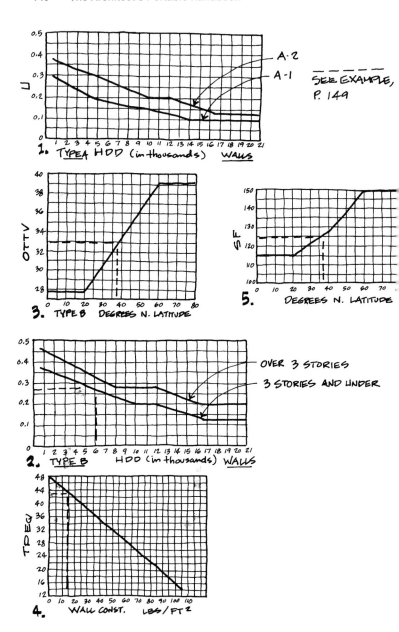

1. TYPE A HDD (in thousands) WALLS

A·2
A-1

SEE EXAMPLE, P. 149

3. TYPE B DEGREES N. LATITUDE

5. DEGREES N. LATITUDE

2. TYPE B HDD (in thousands) WALLS

OVER 3 STORIES

3 STORIES AND UNDER

4. WALL CONST. LBS/FT²

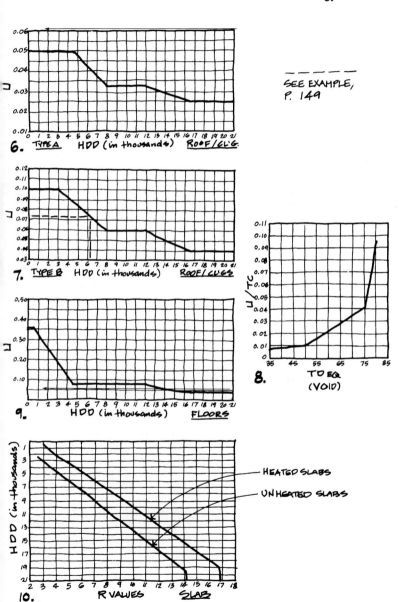

SEE EXAMPLE,
P. 149

6. <u>TYPE A</u>   HDD (in thousands)   <u>ROOF/CL'G</u>

7. <u>TYPE B</u>   HDD (in thousands)   <u>ROOF/CL'GS</u>

8.   TD EQ   (VOID)

9.   HDD (in thousands)   <u>FLOORS</u>

10.   R VALUES   <u>SLAB</u>

HEATED SLABS

UNHEATED SLABS

HDD (in thousands)

___ *e.* Check compliance:
    ___ (1) Type A-1 and 2 buildings:
        ___ (*a*) Heating, walls:
                Calculate, using Formula (1), to insure that designed value is ½ or less of the value in Figure 1.
        ___ (*b*) Heating, roof:
                Calculate, using Formula (3), to insure that designed value is ½ or less of the value in Figure 2.
        ___ (*c*) Heating, floors over underheated spaces:
                Calculate, using Formula (2), to insure that designed value is ½ or less of the value in Figure 9.
        ___ (*d*) Slabs on grade must conform to value shown in Figure 10 for perimeter insulation.
                Note: ASHRAE 90-A never required A-1 and 2 buildings to check for summer cooling, but you can check for cooling by using (*c*) and (*d*) below.
    ___ (2) Type B buildings:
        ___ (*a*) Heating, walls:
                Calculate, using Formula (1), to insure that designed value is ½ or less of the value in Figure 2.
        ___ (*b*) Heating, roof:
                Calculate, using Formula (3), to insure that designed value is ½ or less of the value in Figure 7.
        ___ (*c*) Cooling, walls:
                Calculate, using Formula (2), to insure that designed value is ½ or less of the value in Figure 3.
        ___ (*d*) Cooling, roof:
                Calculate, using Formula (4), to insure that designed value is 4.25 or less.
        ___ (*e*) Same as 1(*c*) above.
        ___ (*f*) Same as 1(*d*) above.

EXAMPLE:

PROBLEM: A LODGE BUILDING OF A RESORT IS BEING DESIGNED FOR A MOUNTAIN SITE IN COLORADO SPRINGS, CO. CHECK TO SEE IF THE PRELIMINARY DESIGN, SHOWN BELOW, APPEARS TO BE ENERGY EFFICIENT.

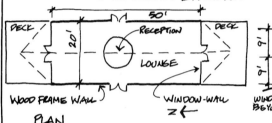

PLAN   SECTION

DATA:

LATITUDE: 38°-5 (p.526)   **NOTE:**
HDD = 6346 (p.527)   DISREGARD DOORS.
WALL: $U = 0.11$, AREA = 900 SF   ASSUME A
WINDOW-WALL (D.G.): $U = 0.5$,   TYPE B
                    AREA = 720 SF BUILDING.
ROOF: $U = 0.025$, AREA = 1273 SF

SOLUTION: (TYPE B BUILDINGS, P. 148)

a. HEATING, WALLS:

DESIGNED: (FORMULA (1) ON P. 144)

$$U_w = \frac{(U_w \times A_w) + (U_g \times A_g)}{A \text{ OF TOTAL WALL}}$$

$$= \frac{(0.11 \times 900) + (0.5 \times 720)}{900 + 720} = 0.28$$

REQUIRED: FIGURE 2 (P. 146) = $0.28 \div 2 = 0.14$

PROBLEM ! ∴ DESIGNED IS HIGHER THAN REQ'D.

b. HEATING, ROOF:

DESIGNED: (FORMULA 3 ON P. 144)

$$U_r = \frac{U_{r_i} \times A_{r_i}}{A \text{ TOTAL ROOF}} = \frac{0.025 \times 1273}{1273} = 0.025$$

-CONTINUED-

REQUIRED: FIGURE 7 (P.147) = 0.072 ÷ 2 = 0.0375
OK, DESIGNED IS LESS THAN REQUIRED

C. COOLING, WALLS:
DESIGNED: (FORMULA 2 ON P.144)

$$OTTV_W = \frac{(U_{w_i} \times A_{W_i} \times TD_{EQ}) + (A_g \times SF \times SC) + (U_g \times A_g \times \Delta t)}{\text{AREA OF TOTAL WALL}}$$

WHERE: TD_{EQ} = 43 (FIG. 4), ASSUMING 15#/SF WT.
SF = 125 FOR 38°-5 N. LAT. (FIG. 5)
SC = 0 FOR N. GLASS & 0.5 FOR S. GLASS
(SEE P. 331), AS AN AVERAGE ≈ 0.25
Δt = 91°F (SEE APP. B, ITEM Q, P.527)
LESS 78°F (INDOOR TEMP) = 13°

$$= \frac{(0.025 \times 900 \times 43) + (720 \times 125 \times 0.25) + 0.025 \times 720 \times 13}{900 + 720}$$

= 14.6

REQUIRED: (FIGURE 3, P. 146) = 33 ÷ 2 = 16.5
OK: DESIGNED IS LESS THAN REQ'D.

d. COOLING, ROOF:
DESIGNED: (FORMULA 4, P. 144), NO GLASS!

$$OTTV_r = \frac{(U_r \times A_r \times TD_{EQ})}{\text{AREA OF ROOF}} = \frac{0.025 \times 1273 \times 43}{1273}$$

= 1.075

REQUIRED: 8.5 ÷ 2 = 4.25
OK: DESIGNED IS LESS THAN REQUIRED

e. N/A (NO FLOOR ABOVE AIR).
f. UNHEATED SLAB: FROM FIGURE 10 (P.147), SLAB
IS REQ'D. TO HAVE R = 5.25
PERIMETER INSULATION.

CONCLUSION:
EVERY ELEMENT HAS PASSED EXCEPT FOR THE WALLS
DURING WINTER HEATING. THIS SHOULD NOT BE SURPRIS-
ING GIVEN ALL THE GLASS IN SUCH A COLD CLIMATE.
— CONTINUED —

POSSIBLE OPTIONS:

1. LOWER U VALUE OF GLASS:

   USE LOW E, DOUBLE GLAZED W/ R = 3.12 (P. 334)

   $$U = \frac{1}{R} = \frac{1}{3.12} = 0.32$$

   REWORK FORMULA 1:

   $$U_W = \frac{(0.11)(900) + (0.32)(720)}{900 + 720} = 0.2 > 0.14$$

   <u>STILL FAILS</u>

2. LOWER U VALUE STILL FURTHER (SEE P. 292)
3. REDUCE GLASS AREA
4. UPGRADE ROOF AND/OR OPAQUE WALL U'S TO MAKE UP FOR GLASS.
5. ACCOUNT FOR OTHER FACTORS, SUCH AS 'PASSIVE' SOLAR HEATING (CALCULATING THIS IS BEYOND THE SCOPE OF THIS BOOK). THIS MAY BE REALISTIC CONSIDERING THE SITE GETS 68% SUN (SEE APP. B, ITEM K, P. 526) WHICH IS ABOVE 50% (SEE ITEM 19, P. 139) AND THE SLAB ON GRADE (ASSUMING NO CARPET) ABSORBING THE SUN'S HEAT (SEE ITEM 16, P. 139). BUT THIS APPROACH WOULD PROBABLY REQUIRE A COMPUTER SIMULATION TO PROVE COMPLIANCE IF AN ENERGY CODE WERE IN EFFECT AT THIS LOCATION.

NOTES

__ **K. ACOUSTICS** (2a) (3) (4) (10)

There is both a positive function and a negative function to consider in acoustic design.

The positive function is to ensure that the reverberation characteristics of a building are appropriate to their function. See 1 below.

On the negative side, the task is to make certain that unwanted outside noises are kept out of quiet areas of the building. See 2 below.

__ 1. *Room Acoustics*
Sound can be likened to light. *Sound control* uses reflection and diffusion to enhance acoustics in such spaces as auditoriums and sound studios, and absorption for noise control in more typical spaces such as offices.

__ *a.* Reflection: The geometry of the room is important in effective sound control. Large concave surfaces concentrate sound and should usually be avoided, while convex surfaces disperse sound.

__ *b.* Diffusion promotes uniform distribution of continuous sound and improves "liveness" (very important in performing arts). It is increased by objects and surface irregularities. Ideal diffusing surfaces neither absorb nor reflect sound but scatter it.

__ *c.* Absorption (see table on p. 160) provides the most effective form of noise control. Sound pressure waves travel at the speed of sound (1100 fps), which is a slow enough velocity that reflections of the original sound-wave form can interfere with perception of the original, intended signal. *Reverberation time* is the measure of this problem.

Sound of any kind emitted in a room will be absorbed or reflected off the room surfaces. Soft materials absorb sound energy. Hard materials reflect sound energy back into the space. The reflected sound can reinforce the direct sound and enhance communication if the room size and room surfaces are configured appropriately. Annoying reverberation (echoes) occur in rooms more than *30*

feet long. Echoes are stronger when the reflection surface is highly reflective and is concave toward the listener.

The room volume and surface characteristics will determine the reverberation time for the room. Reverberation time is the time in seconds that it takes for a sound to decay through 60 decibels. It is calculated as follows:

$$RT = \frac{0.05 \times \text{Room Volume (cf)}}{\text{Average Absorption of Room}}$$

Desirable room reverberation times are:

Office and commercial spaces	0.5 seconds
Rooms for speech	1.0 seconds
Rooms for music	1.5 seconds
Sports arenas	2.0 seconds

The *absorption,* also called noise reduction coefficient (NRC), of a surface is the product of the acoustic coefficient for the surface multiplied by the area of the surface. The sound absorption of a room is the sum of the sound absorptions of all the surfaces in the room. The higher the coefficient, the more sound absorbed, with *1.0* (complete absorption) being the highest possible. Generally, a material with a coefficient below *0.2* is considered to be reflective and above *0.2* to be absorbing. Some common acoustic coefficients are:

1½″ glass fiber clg. panels	1.0
Carpet and pad	0.6
Acoustic tile (no paint)	0.8
Cloth-upholstered seats	0.6
An audience	0.8
Concrete	0.02
Gypsum board	0.05
Glass	0.09
Tile	0.01
Fabric	0.30

The average absorption coefficient of a room should be at least *0.2.* Average absorption above *0.5* is usually not desirable, nor is it economically justified. A lower value is suitable for large rooms; and larger values for controlling sound in small or noisy rooms. Although absorptive materials can be placed anywhere, ceiling treatment is more effective in large rooms, while wall treatment is more effective in small rooms. If additional absorptive material is being added to a room to improve it, the total absorption should be increased at least *3 times* to bring absorption to between *0.2 and 0.5*. An increase of *10 times* is about the practical limit. Each doubling of the absorption in a room reduces RT by ½.

EXAMPLE:

WHAT IS THE ABSORPTION COEFFICIENT AND REV. TIME FOR A 20' × 10' × 9' H OFFICE WITH CARPET FLOOR, A.T.C., & GYPB'D. WALL (BUT ⅓ OF WHICH HAS SOUND ABSORPTION MATERIAL)?

ABSORPTION COEFFICIENT:

FLOOR	0.6 × 200 =	120
⅔ WALL	0.05 × 356 =	18
⅓ WALL	0.8 × 178 =	142
CEILING	0.8 × 200 =	160
		440

$$\text{AVER. COEF. OF ABSORPTION} = \frac{\text{TOTAL ABSORP.}}{\text{TOTAL RM. SURF.}} = \frac{440}{20 \times 9 \times 2 + 10 \times 9 \times 2 + 10 \times 20 \times 2}$$

$$= \frac{440}{940 \ SF} \approx .47 \ o.k.$$

$$\text{REVERBERATION TIME} = \frac{0.05 \times (10 \times 20 \times 9)}{440} = 0.2 < 0.5, \ so \ o.k.$$

____ *d.* Other factors affecting acoustics:

____ If a corridor is appreciably higher than it is wide, some absorptive material should be placed on the walls as well as the ceiling, especially if the floor is hard. If the corridor is wider than its height, ceiling treatment is usually enough.

____ Acoustically critical rooms require an appropriate volume of space. Rooms for speech require 120 CF per audience seat. Rooms for music require 270 CF per audience seat.

____ "Ray diagramming" can be a useful tool in sound control. As with light, the reflective angle of a sound wave equals its incident angle. In like manner, concave shapes focus sound and convex shapes disperse sound.

___ 2. *Sound Isolation*

Sound travels through walls and floors by causing building materials to vibrate and then broadcast the noise into the quiet space. There are two methods of setting up the vibration: through structure-borne sound, and air-borne sound.

Structure-borne sound is the vibration of building materials by vibrating pieces of equipment, or caused by walking on hard floors.

Air-borne sound is a pressure vibration in the air. When it hits a wall, the wall materials are forced to vibrate. The vibration passes through the materials of the wall. The far side of the wall then passes the vibration back into the air.

Noise Reduction and Sound Isolation Guidelines

___ *a.* Choose a quiet, protected site. Orient building with doors and windows away from noise.

___ *b.* Use site barriers such as walls or landscape (dense tree lines or hedges).

___ *c.* Avoid placing noisy areas near quiet areas. Areas with similar noise characteristics should be placed next to each other. Place bedrooms next to bedrooms and living rooms next to living rooms.

___ *d.* As the distance from the sound source increases, pressure at the listener's ear will decrease by the inverse square law (as with light). Therefore, separate sound sources by distance.

___ *e.* Orient spaces to minimize transmission problems. Space windows of adjoining apartments max. distance apart. Place noisy areas back to back. Place closets between noisy and quiet areas.

___ *f.* Massive materials (concrete or masonry) are the best noise-isolation materials.

___ *g.* Choose quiet mechanical equipment. Use vibration isolation, sound-absorbing duct lining, resilient pipe connections. Design for low flow velocities in pipes and ducts.

   ___ *h.* Reducing structure-borne sound from walking on floors is achieved by carpet (with padding, improves greatly).

   ___ *i.* Avoid flanking of sound over ceilings.

   ___ *j.* Avoid flanking of sound at wall and floor intersections.

   ___ *k.* Wall and floor penetrations (such as elect. boxes) can be a source of sound leakage. A 1-square-inch wall opening in a 100-SF gypsumboard partition can transmit as much sound as the entire partition.

   ___ *l.* Many sound leaks can be plugged in the same manner as is done for air leaks, by caulking.

   ___ *m.* Walls and floors are classified by Sound Transmission Class (*STC*), which is a measure of the reduction of loudness provided by various barriers. The higher the number, the better. In determining the required STC rating of a barrier, the following rough guidelines may be used:

STC Effect on Hearing

25	Normal speech clearly heard through barrier.
30	Loud speech can be heard and understood fairly well. Normal speech can be heard but barely understood.
35	Loud speech is unintelligible but can be heard.
42–45	Loud speech can be heard only faintly. Normal speech cannot be heard.
46–50	Loud speech not audible. Loud sounds other than speech can be heard only faintly, if at all.

See p. 161 for recommended STC room barriers.

Rough Estimating of STC Ratings

When the wall or floor assembly is less than that desired, the following modifications can be made. Select the appropriate wall or floor assembly. To improve the rating, select modifications (largest number, + ½ next largest, + ½ next largest, etc):

a. Light frame walls

Base design	*STC Rating*
Wood studs W/ ½″ gyp'bd.	32
Metal studs W/ ⅝″ gyp'bd.	39

Modification	*Added STC*
Staggered Studs	+9
Double surface skin	+3 to +5
Absorption insulation	+5

b. Heavy walls

The greater the density, the higher the rating. Density goes up in the following order: CMU, brick, concrete.

Base Design	*STC Rating*
4-inch CMU, brick, concrete	37–41, 42
6-inch	42, 46
8-inch	47, 49, 51
12-inch	52, 54, 56

Modification	*Added STC*
Furred-out surface	+7 to +10
Add plaster, $\frac{1}{2}''$	+2 to +4
Sand-filled cores	+3

c. Wood floors

Base Design	*STC Rating*
$\frac{1}{2}$-in plyw'd, subfloor with oak floor, no ceiling	25

Modification	*Added STC*
Add carpet	+10
$\frac{5}{8}$-inch gyp'bd. ceiling	+10
Add resilient damping board	+7
Add absorbtion insul.	+3

d. Concrete floors

Base Design	*STC Rating*
4-, 6-, 8-inch thick concrete	41, 46, 51

Modification	*Added STC*
Resil. Susp. Ceiling	+12
Add sleepers	+7
Add absorption insul.	+3

e. Glass

$\frac{1}{4}''$ float	26
double glaze	32

f. Doors

wood HC	26
SC	29
metal	30
special acoustical	35 to 38

Costs: Sound attenuation blankets: 1″ thick = $3.75 (10% L and 90% M). Add $2 per added inch up to 3″.

EXAMPLE:

ROUGHLY ESTIMATE HOW TO GET S.T.C. = 45 FOR AN OFFICE WALL PARTITION MADE OF WOOD STUDS AND GYPB'D.

FROM ABOVE, A WOOD STUD PARTITION W/ ½" GYPB'D. IS ...... S.T.C. = 32

ADD STAGGERED STUDS FOR FULL CREDIT	+9
ADD DOUBLE GYPB'D. FOR ½ CREDIT, BOTH SIDES: ½ × 5 =	+2.5
ADD ABSORPTION BATTS BETWEEN STUDS: ½ × 5 =	+2.5
TOTAL =	46.0

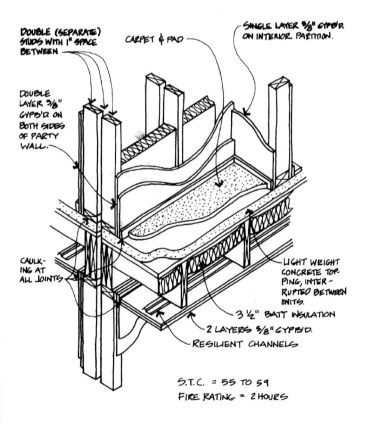

DOUBLE (SEPARATE) STUDS WITH 1" SPACE BETWEEN

CARPET & PAD

SINGLE LAYER ⅝" GYPB'D. ON INTERIOR PARTITION.

DOUBLE LAYER ⅝" GYPB'D ON BOTH SIDES OF PARTY WALL.

CAULKING AT ALL JOINTS

LIGHT WEIGHT CONCRETE TOPPING, INTERRUPTED BETWEEN UNITS.

3 ½" BATT INSULATION

2 LAYERS ⅝" GYPB'D.

RESILIENT CHANNELS

S.T.C. = 55 TO 59
FIRE RATING = 2 HOURS

PARTY WALL DETAIL

(4)

USE OF ABSORPTION IN COMMON OCCUPANCIES

ROOM OCCUPANCY	CEILING TREATMENT	WALL TREATMENT	SPECIAL
AUDITORIUMS, CHURCHES, THEATERS, CONCERT HALLS, RADIO, RECORDING AND T.V. STUDIOS, SPEECH & MUSIC ROOMS			●
BOARDROOMS, TELECONFERENCING	●	●	
CLASSROOMS	●	○	
COMMERCIAL KITCHENS	●		
COMPUTER AND BUSINESS MACHINE ROOMS	●		
CORRIDORS AND LOBBIES	○		
GYMNASIUMS, ARENAS, & RECREATIONAL SPACES	●	●	
HEALTH CARE PATIENT ROOMS	●		
LABORATORIES	●		
LIBRARIES	●		
MECHANICAL EQUIPMENT ROOMS			●
MEETING AND CONFERENCE ROOMS	●	○	
OPEN OFFICE PLAN	●	●	
PRIVATE OFFICES	●		
RESTAURANTS	●	○	
SCHOOLS & INDUSTRIAL SHOPS, FACTORIES	●	●	
STORES AND COMMERCIAL SHOPS	●		

● STRONGLY RECOMMENDED
○ ADVISABLE

SOUND ISOLATION CRITERIA (4)

SOURCE ROOM OCCUPANCY	RECEIVER ROOM ADJACENT	SOUND ISOLATION REQUIREMENT (MINIMUM) FOR ALL PATHS BETWEEN SOURCE AND RECEIVER
EXECUTIVE AREAS, DOCTOR'S SUITES, PERSONNEL OFFICES, LARGE CONFERENCE ROOMS, CONFIDENTIAL PRIVACY REQUIREMENTS	ADJACENT OFFICES AND RELATED SPACES	STC 50-55
NORMAL OFFICES, REGULAR CONFERENCE ROOMS FOR GROUP MEETINGS, NORMAL PRIVACY REQUIRED	ADJACENT OFFICES & SIMILAR ACTIVITIES	STC 45-50
LARGE GENERAL BUSINESS OFFICES, DRAFTING AREAS, BANKING FLOORS	CORRIDORS, LOBBIES, DATA PROCESSING, SIMILAR ACTIVITIES	STC 40-45
SHOP AND LABORATORY OFFICES IN MANUFACTURING LABORATORY OR TEST AREAS, NORM. PRIV.	ADJACENT OFFICES, TEST AREAS, CORRIP.	STC 40-45
MECHANICAL EQUIPMENT ROOMS	ANY SPACE	STC 50-60+
MULTIFAMILY DWELLINGS	NEIGHBORS (SEPARATE OCCUPANCY)	
(a) BEDROOMS	BEDROOMS	STC 48-55
	BATHROOMS	STC 52-58
	KITCHENS	STC 52-58
	LIVING ROOMS	STC 50-57
	CORRIDORS	STC 52-58
(b) LIVING ROOMS	LIVING ROOMS	STC 48-55
	BATHROOMS	STC 50-57
	KITCHENS	STC 48-50
SCHOOL BUILDINGS		
(a) CLASSROOMS	ADJACENT CLASS ROOMS	STC 50
	LABORATORIES	STC 50
	CORRIDORS	STC 45
(b) LARGE MUSIC OR DRAMA AREA	ADJACENT MUSIC OR DRAMA AREA	STC 60
(c) MUSIC PRACTICE ROOMS	MUSIC PRACTICE RMS.	STC 55
INTERIOR OCCUPIED SPACES	EXTERIOR OF BLDG.	STC 35-60
THEATERS, CONCERT HALLS, LECTURE HALLS, RADIO AND T.V. STUDIOS	ANY AND ALL ADJACENT	USE QUALIFIED ACOUSTICAL CONSULTANT.

NOTES

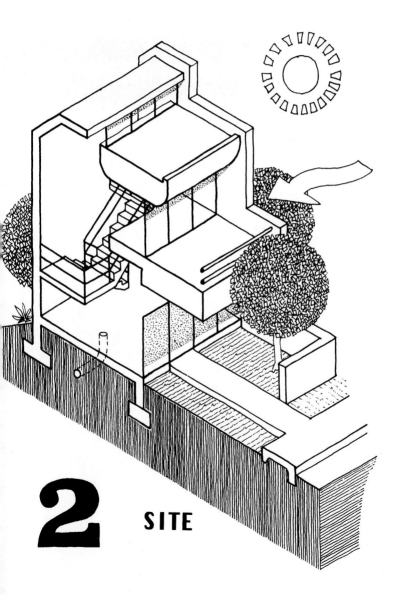

2 SITE

NOTES

___ A. LAND PLANNING (7) (30)

___ 1. *Costs:* **Site work and development costs roughly range from $2 to $10/SF of site area, exclusive of building footprint. This includes parking lot, sidewalks, landscaping, and utilities.**

___ 2. *Slopes:* Use the following guidelines for land selection:
  ___ *a.* Slopes under 1% do not drain well.
  ___ *b.* Slopes under 4% seem flat and are usable for all kinds of activity.
  ___ *c.* Slopes of 4 to 10% are easy grades.
  ___ *d.* Slopes over 10% are steep.
  ___ *e.* Slopes at 15% approach limit of an ordinary loaded vehicle.
  ___ *f.* Slopes at 25% are the limit of mowed surfaces.
  ___ *g.* Slopes over 50% may have erosion problems.

___ 3. *Site Selection* (For Temperate Climates)
  Avoid or make special provision for steep north slopes; west slopes facing water; hilltops; frost pockets or positions at the foot of long, open slopes; bare, dry ground; nearby sources of noise or air pollution. Best sites are well-planted middle slopes facing south, near water.

___ 4. *Streets* (Typical Widths)

Type	Width	R.O.W.
One-way	18′	25′
Minor road	20′	35′
Minor residential street	26′	
Major street	52′	80′
Highway	12′/lane + 8′ shoulder	up to 400′

___ 5. *Parking*
  ___ *a.* In general, estimate *400 SF/car* for parking, drives, and walks.
  ___ *b.* For very efficient double-bay aisle parking, estimate *300 SF/car* for parking and drives only.
  ___ *c.* Typical parking stall: $9' \times 19'$.
  ___ *d.* Parking structure stall: $8.5' \times 19'$.
  ___ *e.* Compact parking stall: $7.5' \times 15'$.
  ___ *f.* ADA-required. HC parking: To be located as close to the accessible entry as possible. One HC stall for ea. 25 up to 100, then 1 per 50 up to 200, then 1 per 100 up to 500. From 501 to 1000: 2%. Over 1001: 20 + 1 for ea. 100 over 1000. First, plus 1 in every 8 HC stalls shall have 8-ft side aisle (for van parking). All other HC spaces shall have 5-ft side aisle (but may be shared). Stalls to be at least 8 feet wide. Grade at these locations cannot exceed 2%.

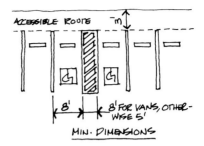

_____ g. Loading dock parking: $10' \times 35' \times 14'$ high.
_____ h. One-way drive, no parking: 12′ wide.
_____ i. Two-way drive, no parking: 18′ to 24′ wide.
_____ j. Recommended pavement slope: 1 to 5%.
_____ k. Primary walks: 6′ to 10′ wide.
_____ l. Secondary walks: 3′ to 6′ wide.
_____ m. Walks adjacent to parking areas with overhanging car bumpers: 2.5′ minimum.
_____ n. Above are for rough estimating; always verify local zoning ordinance.
_____ o. See following diagram and table for typical parking lot sizes:

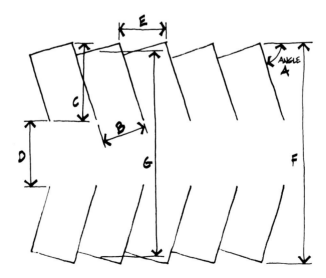

A	B	C	D	E	F	G
					Center-to-center width of two parking rows with access btw'n.	
					Curb to curb	Overlap center line to center line
Parking angle	Stall width	Stall to curb	Aisle width	Curb length		
0°	7'6"	7.5*	11.0	19.0	26.0	26.0
	8'0"	8.0	12.0	23.0	28.0	—
	8'6"	8.5	12.0	23.0	29.0	—
	9'0"	9.0	12.0	23.0	30.0	—
	9'6"	9.5	12.0	23.0	31.0	—
30°	7'6"	14.0*	11.0	15.0	39.0	32.5
	8'0"	16.5	11.0	16.0	44.0	37.1
	8'6"	16.9	11.0	17.0	44.8	37.4
	9'0"	17.3	11.0	18.0	45.6	37.8
	9'6"	17.8	11.0	19.0	46.6	38.4
40°	8'0"	18.3	13.0	12.4	49.6	43.5
	8'6"	18.7	12.0	13.2	49.4	42.9
	9'0"	19.1	12.0	14.0	50.2	43.3
	9'6"	19.5	12.0	14.8	51.0	43.7
45°	7'6"	15.9*	11.0	10.6	42.8	37.9
	8'0"	19.1	14.0	11.3	52.2	46.5
	8'6"	19.4	13.5	12.0	52.3	46.3
	9'0"	20.1	13.0	13.4	53.2	46.2
	9'6"	20.1	13.0	13.4	53.2	46.5
50°	8'0"	19.7	14.0	10.5	53.4	48.3
	8'6"	20.0	12.5	11.1	52.5	47.0
	9'0"	20.4	12.0	11.7	52.8	47.0
	9'6"	20.7	12.0	12.4	53.4	47.3
60°	7'6"	16.7*	14.0	8.7	47.5	40.4
	8'0"	20.4	19.0	9.2	59.8	55.8
	8'6"	20.7	18.5	9.8	59.9	55.6
	9'0"	21.0	18.0	10.4	60.0	55.5
	9'6"	21.2	18.0	11.0	60.4	55.6
90°	7'6"	15.0*	18.0	7.5	48.0	48.0
	8'0"	19.0	26.0†	8.0	64.0	—
	8'6"	19.0	25.0†	8.5	63.0	—
	9'0"	19.0	24.0†	9.0	62.0	—
	9'6"	19.0	24.0†	9.5	62.0	—

* Based on 15'0" stall length for compact cars; all others based on 19'0" stall length.
† Two-way circulation.

6. *Open-Space Proportions*

AN OBJECT (BUILDING) WHOSE MAJOR DIMENSION (VERTICAL OR HORIZONTAL EQUALS IT'S DISTANCE FROM THE EYE IS DIFFICULT TO SEE AS A WHOLE BUT TENDS TO BE ANALYSED IN DETAIL.

WHEN IT IS TWICE AS FAR, IT APPEARS CLEARLY AS A WHOLE.

WHEN IT IS 3 TIMES AS FAR, IT STILL DOMINATES, BUT IS ALSO SEEN IN RELATION TO OTHER OBJECTS.

WHEN IT IS 4 TIMES, OR MORE, IT BECOMES PART OF THE GENERAL SCENE.

AN EXTERNAL ENCLOSURE IS MOST COMFORTABLE WHEN IT'S WALLS ARE ½ TO ⅓ AS HIGH AS THE WIDTH OF THE SPACE ENCLOSED.

IF THE RATIO FALLS BELOW ¼, THE SPACE CEASES TO SEEM ENCLOSED.

NOTES

NOTES

__ B. GRADING AND DRAINAGE

$\textcircled{4}$ $\textcircled{14}$ $\textcircled{18}$ $\textcircled{24}$ $\textcircled{39}$

__ 1. _Grading for Economy_
     __ a. Keep finished grades as close to the natural as possible.
     __ b. Amounts of cut and fill should balance over the site.

__ 2. _Maximum Slopes_
     __ a. Solid rock   ¼:1
     __ b. Loose rock   ½:1 (1:1 for round rock)
     __ c. Loose gravel   1½:1
     __ d. Firm earth   1½:1
     __ e. Soft earth   2:1
     __ f. Mowing grass   4:1

__ 3. _Desirable Grades_

Situation	% of slopes	
	Max.	Min.
__ a. Paved areas		
__ (1) AC	5	1
__ (2) Concrete	5	0.5
__ b. Streets		
__ (1) Length	6–10	0.5
__ (2) Cross	4	2
__ c. Walks		
__ (1) Cross slope	2	2
__ (2) Long slope		
__ (3) (Subj. to freeze and accessible)	5	
__ (4) (Not subj. to above)	14	
__ d. Ramps		
__ (1) HC-accessible (ADA)	8.33	
__ (2) Nonaccessible	12.5	
__ e. At buildings		
__ (1) Grade away 10′		2
__ (2) Impervious materials	21	
__ f. Outdoor areas		
__ (1) Impervious surface	5	0.5
__ (2) Pervious		
__ (a) Ground frost	5	2
__ (b) No ground frost	5	1
__ g. Swales and gutters (concrete)		.3
__ h. Stairs		
__ (1) Landings and treads	2	1

___ 4. *Grades at Buildings*

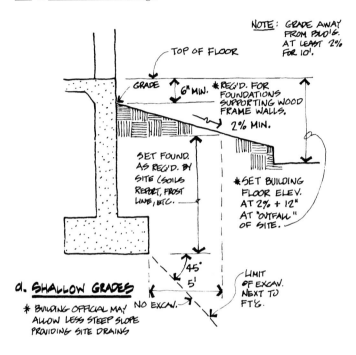

NOTE: GRADE AWAY FROM BLD'G. AT LEAST 2% FOR 10'.

TOP OF FLOOR

GRADE

6" MIN.

* REQ'D. FOR FOUNDATIONS SUPPORTING WOOD FRAME WALLS.

2% MIN.

SET FOUND. AS REQ'D. BY SITE (SOILS REPORT, FROST LINE, ETC.

* SET BUILDING FLOOR ELEV. AT 2% + 12" AT "OUTFALL" OF SITE.

45°

5'

LIMIT OF EXCAV. NEXT TO FT'G.

NO EXCAV.

d. SHALLOW GRADES

* BUILDING OFFICIAL MAY ALLOW LESS STEEP SLOPE PROVIDING SITE DRAINS

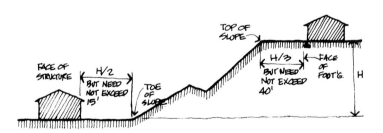

TOP OF SLOPE

FACE OF STRUCTURE

H/2 BUT NEED NOT EXCEED 15'

TOE OF SLOPE

H/3 BUT NEED NOT EXCEED 40'

FACE OF FOOT'G.

H

b. STEEP GRADES FOR SLOPES STEEPER THAN 3 TO 1.

* BUILDING OFFICIAL MAY APPROVE ALTERNATE SETBACKS & CLEARANCES.

___ 5. *Retaining Walls*
     ___ COSTS ≈ $250/CY, all sizes, not including cut, backfill, or compaction.

H	B	d	b	c
3'	2.08 (2.67)	.67 (.75)	1.0 (1.5)	.58 (.5)
6'	3.75 (5.33)	.67 (.83)	2.47 (2.93)	.67 (1.58)
9'	5.17 (7.5)	1.0 (1.0)	3.17 (4.17)	1.0 (2.33)
12'	7.25 (12)	1.17 (1.17)	4.58 (7.83)	1.5 (3)
15'	9 (15)	1.33 (1.5)	5.75 (9.75)	1.93 (3.75)
18'	10.83 (18)	1.5 (1.83)	7.08 (11.67)	2.25 (4.5)
21'	12.58 (21)	1.75 (2.17)	8.17 (13.58)	2.67 (5.25)

LEVEL ↑ SURCHARGE ↑

CANTILEVER RETAINING WALL

1. REINFORCING NOT SHOWN.
2. CONTROL JOINTS @ 25' & EXPAN. JOINTS @ 100'.

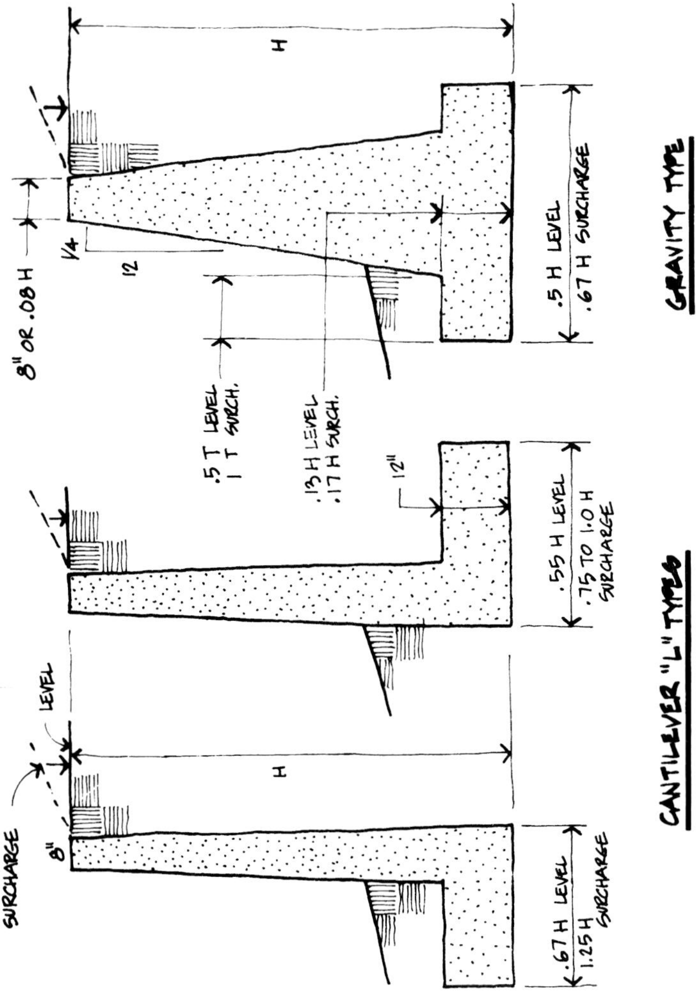

SURCHARGE

8"

LEVEL

H

.67 H LEVEL
1.25 H SURCHARGE

CANTILEVER "L" TYPES

.5 T LEVEL
1 T SURCH.

.13 H LEVEL
.17 H SURCH.

12"

.55 H LEVEL
.75 TO 1.0 H SURCHARGE

8" OR .08 H

1/4

12

H

.5 H LEVEL
.67 H SURCHARGE

GRAVITY TYPE

___ 6. *Earthwork Conversion Factors*
Native, in-place soils can be compacted for greater density. When dug up the density decreases and the volume increases. Use the following to estimate earthwork volumes:

Soil	In place	Loose	Compacted
Sand	1.00	1.10	.95
Earth	1.00	1.25	.80
Clay	1.00	1.40	.90
Rock (blasted)	1.00	1.5	1.30

___ **7. *Earthwork Costs***
The costs given below are based on machinery-moved and compacted earthwork, normal soils, suburban sites, of medium size (2000–15,000 CY):

___ **On site**
    ___ **Cut**   **$3.00/CY**
    ___ **Fill and compaction**   **$2.25/CY**
    (Compaction 20% of total)
___ **Off site**
    ___ **Import**   **$5/CY (5 miles or less) to $10/CY**
    ___ **Export**   **$4/CY (5 miles or less) to $7/CY**

Modifiers:
___ **Difficult soils (soft clays or hard,**
    cementitious soils)   **+100%**
___ **Hand-compacted**   **+400 to 500%**
___ **Volume**
    ___ **Smaller**   **+50 to 200%**
    ___ **Larger**   **−0 to 35%**
___ **Location**
    ___ **Urban sites**   **+100 to 300%**
    ___ **Rural sites**   **−0 to 25%**
    ___ **Situations of severe weather**
        (rain or freezing)   **+5 to 10%**

Other materials:
___ **Sand**   **$6 to $10/CY**
___ **Gravel**   **$15 to $25/CY**
___ **Rock (blasting only)**
    ___ **Rural sites**   **$6 to $8/CY**
    ___ **Urban sites**   **$120/CY**
___ **Jackhammering**   **$1350/CY**

EXAMPLE:

PROBLEM: A SLOPING SITE IN PORTLAND, OR.
IS TO HAVE A BUILDING PAD 90' X 30'.
SOILS ARE NOT UNUSUAL OR DIFFICULT.
ROUGHLY ESTIMATE EARTHWORK COSTS.

SOLUTION:

NATURAL GRADE

IMPORTED COMPACTED FILL

FILL (COMPACTED)

CUT (100 SF/LF)

CUT: 100 SF/LF X 90 LF ÷ 27 = 333 CY @ $3/CY = $1000

FILL: 333 CY X 0.8 (COMPACTED) = 266 CY
@ $2.25 = $ 600

IMPORTED FILL (COMPACTED):
5' HIGH X 30' X 90' ÷ 27 X 1.25 (LOOSE)
= 625 CY @ $8/CY = $5000

TOTAL: $6300

___ 8. *Drainage*

    ___ *a.* General: Rainwater that falls on the surface of a property either evaporates, percolates into the soil (see p. 187), flows off the site, or drains to some point or points on the site. That portion that does not enter the soil is called the *runoff* and provision must be made for this excess water. The grading must be so designed that surface water will flow away from the building. This may sheet-flow across the property line or out driveways to the street. Or, this may necessitate drainage channels with catch basins and storm drains (see p. 193). Each community should be checked for its requirements by contacting the city (or county) engineering or public works department.

    ___ *b.* Rainfall: For small drainage systems, the maximum rainfall in any *2-year* period is generally used. For a more conservative design, the *5- to 10-year* period may be employed. For establishing floor elevations, *100-year* floods, are often used. Lacking more specific data, see App. B, item J, and divide the quantity by half. One inch of rain per hour is equal to approximately one CF of water falling on one acre of ground per second.

___ *c.* Runoff: Volume may be estimated by:

Q = C × I × A, where:
    Q = Quantity of runoff in CF/sec
    C = Coefficient of runoff:

Roofs	0.95
Concrete or asphalt	0.95
Gravel areas	
Loose	0.30
Compact	0.70
Vacant land, unpaved streets	
Light plant growth	0.60
No plants	0.75
Lawns	0.35
Wooded areas	0.20

    I = Intensity of rainfall in inches per hour
    A = Area to be drained, in acres

___ *d.* Storm drains
The following nomograph can be used to estimate storm drain sizes. It is for rough concrete. Materials of smoother surfaces will have smaller sizes. Also, see pp. 193 and 431.

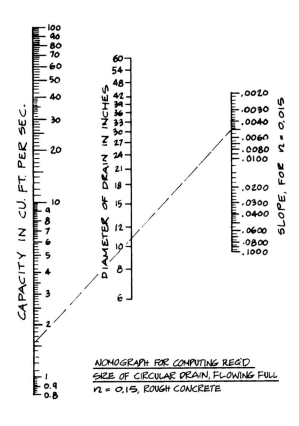

NOMOGRAPH FOR COMPUTING REQ'D
SIZE OF CIRCULAR DRAIN, FLOWING FULL
n = 0.15, ROUGH CONCRETE

EXAMPLE:

PROBLEM: FIND RUN OFF & PRELM. SIZE OF STORM
DRAIN FOR BUILDING SITE IN CHICAGO,
IL. WITH A LAWN AREA OF 22215 SF &
HARD SURFACE AREAS (PAVING, ROOF, WALKS)
OF 13500 SF.

SOLUTION:

1. FIND I FOR CHICAGO (APP. B, ITEM J, P.528) IS
6.3"/hr. BY THE ABOVE RULE OF THUMB, DIVIDE
THIS IN HALF OR 3,2"/hr.

2. $Q_1 = CIA$ (LAWN) = (.35)(3.2)(22215 ÷ 43560) =   0.57
$Q_2 = CIA$ (HARD) = (.95)(3.2)(13500 ÷ 43560) =   0.94
─────
1.6 CF/SEC.

> NOTE: C LAWN = .35
> C HARD = .95
> CONVESION OF SF TO AC IS
> 43560 SF/AC

3. ESTIMATE UNDERGROUND PIPE SIZE WITH A
5% SLOPE. SEE DASHED LINE IN ABOVE NOMO-
GRAPH FOR 11 INCH PIPE. MAKE THIS A 12"
& CONC. PIPE.

NOTES

__ C. SOILS ②④⑱㉚㊴㊺

___ 1. <u>Danger "Flags"</u>
    ___ *a.* High water table.
    ___ *b.* Presence of trouble soils: Peat, other organic materials, or soft clay, loose silt, or fine water-bearing sand.
    ___ *c.* Rock close to surface.
    ___ *d.* Dumps or fills.
    ___ *e.* Evidence of slides or subsidence.
___ 2. <u>Ranking of Soil for Foundations</u>
    ___ *a.* *Best:* Sand and gravel
    ___ *b.* *Good:* Medium to hard clays
    ___ *c.* *Poor:* Silts and soft clays
    ___ *d.* *Undesirable:* Organic silts and clays
    ___ *e.* *Unsuitable:* Peat
___ 3. <u>Basic Soil Types (Identification)</u>
    ___ *a.* *Inorganic* (for foundations)
        ___ (1) Rock: good bearing but hard to excavate
        ___ (2) Course grain
            ___ (*a*) Gravel: 3″ to 2 mm. Well-drained, stable material.
            ___ (*b*) Sand: 0.05 to 2 mm. Gritty to touch and taste. Good, well-drained material if confined, but "quick" if saturated.
        ___ (3) Fine grain
            ___ (*a*) Silt: 0.005 to 0.05 mm. Feels smooth to touch. Grains barely visible. Stable when dry but may creep under load. Unstable when wet. Frost heave problems.
            ___ (*b*) Clays: Under 0.005 mm. Cannot see grains. Sticks to teeth (or hand, when moist). Wide variety in clays, some suitable and some not. Can become expansive when wet.
    ___ *b.* *Organic* (not suitable for foundations). Fibrous texture with dark brown or black color.
___ 4. <u>Most Soils Combine Types</u>
    ___ *a.* Consist of air, water, and solids
    ___ *b.* Size variation of solids a factor

WELL GRADED

UNIFORMLY GRADED (POORLY GRADED)

___ 5. <u>Amounts of types of solids vary, giving different characteristics per following table:</u>

Unified Soil Classification

Soil type	Description	Allow. bearing (lb/SF) (1)	Drain-age (2)	Frost heave potent	Expan. potent (3)
___ BR	Bedrock	30,000	Poor	Low	Low
Gravels					
Clean gravels					
___ GW	Well-graded gravel-sand mixtures, little or no sands	8000	Good	Low	Low
___ GP	Poorly graded gravels or gravel-sand mixtures, little or no fine	8000	Good	Low	Low
Gravels with fines					
___ GM	Silty gravels, gravel-sand-silt mixtures	4000	Good	Med.	Low
___ GC	Clayey gravels, gravel-clay-sand mixtures	4000	Med.	Med.	Low
Sand					
Clean sands					
___ SW	Well-graded sands, gravelly sands, little or no fines	6000	Good	Low	Low
___ SP	Poorly graded sands or gravelly sands, little or no fines	5000	Good	Low	Low
Sands with fines					
___ SM	Silty sand, sand-silt mixtures	4000	Good	Med.	Low
___ SC	Clayey sands, sand-clay mixture	4000	Med.	Med.	Low
Fine grained					
Silts					
___ ML	Inorganic silts and very fine sands, rock flour, silty or clayey fine sands w/slight plasticity	2000	Med.	High	Low
___ MH	Inorganic silts, mica-ceous or diatoma-ceous fine sandy or silty soils, elastic silts	2000	Poor	High	High

Clays

___ CL	Inorganic clays of low to med. plasticity, gravelly, sandy, silty, or lean clays	2000	Med.	Med.	Med.
___ CH	Inorganic clays of high plasticity, fat clays	2000	Poor	Med.	High

Organic

___ OL	Organic silts and organic silty clays	400	Poor	Med.	Med.
___ OH	Organic clays of medium to high plasticity	0	Unsat.	Med.	High
___ PT	Peat and other highly organic soils	0	Unsat.	Med.	High

Notes:

1. Allowable bearing value may be increased 25% for very compact, coarse-grained, gravelly or sandy soils, or for very stiff, fine-grained, clayey or silty soils. Allowable bearing value should be decreased 25% for loose, coarse-grained, gravelly or sandy soils or soft, fine-grained, clayey or silty soils.
2. Percolation rate for good drainage is over 4″/hr; medium drainage is 2–4″/hr; poor is less than 2″/hr. Also, see page 141.
3. Dangerous expansion might occur if these soil types are dry but subject to future wetting.
4. UBC allows 1000 to 1500 psf for nonexpansive soils and small buildings.

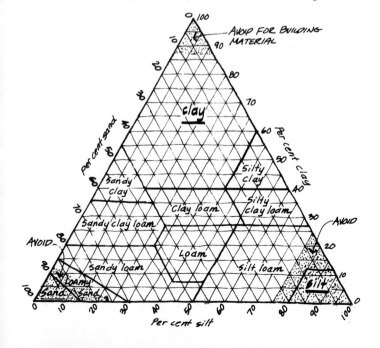

___ 6. *Clays:* Usually give greatest problems for foundations.
    ___ *a.* Measure expansiveness:

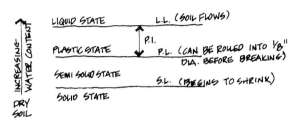

The greater the PI (Plasticity Index), the greater the potential for shrinkage and swelling. Some clays swell up to 20-fold with pressures of several tons/SF. Problems of upheaval vs. settlement usually are 2 to 1.

    ___ *b.* Strength of clays

Consistency	Shear (ton/SF)	Compression (ton/SF)	Rule of thumb
___ Soft	0.25–0.5	<0.5	¼" pencil makes 1" penetration with med. effort.
___ Medium stiff	0.5–1.0	0.5–1.0 1.0–2.0	¼" pencil makes ½" penetration with med. effort.
___ Very stiff	1.0–3.0	2.0–4.0	¼" pencil makes ¼" penetration with much effort.
___ Hard	3.0>	4.0>	¼" steel rod can penetrate less than ⅛". Can hardly scratch.

    ___ 7. *Testing*
        ___ *a.* Simple field tests
            ___ (1) Separation of gravel
                ___ (*a*) Remove from sample all particles larger than ⅛" diameter.
                ___ (*b*) Estimate percent gravel.
            ___ (2) Sedimentation test
                ___ (*a*) Place sample (less gravel) in canteen cup and fill with water.
                ___ (*b*) Shake mixture vigorously.
                ___ (*c*) Allow mixture to stand for 30 seconds to settle out.
                ___ (*d*) Pour off water and save.

___ (*e*) Repeat (b) through (d) above until water poured off is clear.

___ (*f*) Evaporate water from (d) above.

___ (*g*) Estimate percent fines.

___ (3) Comparison of gravel and sand

    ___ (*a*) Gravels have been removed in test (1).

    ___ (*b*) Fines have been removed in test (2).

    ___ (*c*) Dry soil remaining in cup.

    ___ (*d*) Soil remaining in cup will be sand.

    ___ (*e*) Compare dry sand in cup with gravel.

___ (4) Dry strength

    ___ (*a*) Form moist pat 2″ in diameter by ½″ thick.

    ___ (*b*) Allow to dry with low heat.

    ___ (*c*) Place dry pat between thumb and index finger only and attempt to break.

    ___ (*d*) Breakage easy—silt.
            Breakage difficult—CL.
            Breakage impossible—CH.
            (see p. 182, Typical)

___ (5) Powder test

    ___ (*a*) Rub portion of broken pat with thumb and attempt to flake particles off.

    ___ (*b*) Pat powders—silt (M).
            Pat does not powder—clay (C).

___ (6) Thread test (toughness test)

    ___ (*a*) Form ball of moist soil (marble size).

    ___ (*b*) Attempt to roll ball into ⅛″-diameter thread (wooden match size).

    ___ (*c*) Thread easily obtained—clay (C).
            Thread cannot be obtained—silt (M).

___ (7) Ribbon test

    ___ (*a*) Form cylinder of soil approximately cigar-shaped in size.

    ___ (*b*) Flatten cylinder over index finger with thumb; attempting to form ribbon 8″ to 9″ long, ⅛″ to ¼″ thick, and 1″ wide.

    ___ (*c*) 8″ to 9″ ribbon obtained—CH.
            Less than 8″ ribbon—CL.

___ (8) Wet shaking test
     ___ (*a*) Place pat of moist (not sticky) soil in palm of hand (vol. about ½ cu. in.).
     ___ (*b*) Shake hand vigorously and strike against other hand.
     ___ (*c*) Observe rapidity of water rising to the surface.
     ___ (*d*) If fast, sample is silty (M).
            If no reaction, sample is clayey (C).

___ (9) Grit, or bite test
     ___ (*a*) Place pinch of sample between teeth and bite.
     ___ (*b*) If sample feels gritty, sample is silt (M).
     ___ (*c*) If sample feels floury, sample is clay (C).

___ (10) Feel test
     ___ (*a*) Rub portion of dry soil over a sensitive portion of skin, such as inside of wrist.
     ___ (*b*) If feel is harsh and irritating, sample is silt (M).
     ___ (*c*) If feel is smooth and floury, sample is clay (C).

___ (11) Shine test
     ___ (*a*) Draw smooth surface, such as knife blade or thumbnail, over pat of slightly moist soil.
     ___ (*b*) If surface becomes shiny and lighter in texture, sample is a high-compressible clay (CH).
     ___ (*c*) If surface remains dull, sample is a low-compressible clay (CL).

___ (12) Odor test
     ___ (*a*) Heat sample with match or open flame.
     ___ (*b*) If odor becomes musty or foul-smelling, this is a strong indication that organic material is present.

___ (13) Cast test
     ___ (*a*) Compress a handful of moist soil into a ball.
     ___ (*b*) Crumbles with handling—GW, SW, GP or SP.

___ (*c*) Withstands careful handling—SM or SC.

___ (*d*) Handled freely—ML or MH.

___ (*e*) Withstands rough handling—CL or CH.

___ (14) Slaking test

    ___ (*a*) Place soil or rock in sun to dry.

    ___ (*b*) Soak in water for 24 hours.

    ___ (*c*) Repeat (a) and (b) above several times.

    ___ (*d*) If soil or rock disintegrates, it is poor material.

___ (15) Amounts of soil

	Sieve	Jar of water
___ Gravel	Remains on #10	Settles immediately
___ Sand	Remains on #200	Settles in 30 sec
___ Silt	Goes to bottom	Settles in 15–60 min
___ Clay	Goes to bottom	Settles in several hrs

Measure each amount to get approximate percent of each soil type.

___ (16) Testing for percolation: Absorption capacity of soil for sanitary septic systems (see p. 431) may be checked by digging a test pit at the drain field site in the wet season to the depth that the field will lie. Fill the pit with 2′ of water, let fall to a 6″ depth, and time the drop from 6″ to 5″. Repeat until it takes same time to make the 1″ drop in two tests running. The allowable absorption rate of soil, in gallons per SF of drain field per day, is:

Time for 1″ fall, minutes	Approx. absorption rate, gals per SF per day
___ 5 or less	2.5
___ 8	2.0
___ 10	1.7
___ 12	1.5
___ 15	1.3
___ 22	1.0

Total sewage flow = 100 gal per person per day.

___ *b.* Soils reports and data
    ___ (1) Geotechnical or *soils report recommendations* are based on lab tests of materials obtained from on-site borings. Request the following info:
        ___ (*a*) Bearing capacity of soil and settlement
        ___ (*b*) Foundation design recommendations
        ___ (*c*) Paving design recommendations
        ___ (*d*) Compaction recommendations
        ___ (*e*) Lateral strength (active and passive pressure, and coef. of friction)
        ___ (*f*) Permeability
        ___ (*g*) Frost depth
    ___ (2) Typical investigations require *borings* at the center and each corner of the "footprint" of the building, or one per 3000 to 5000 SF.
    ___ (3) **Costs: Under 10,000 SF: $1500 to $3000. Thereafter: $.10 to $.30/SF up to 100,000 SF. Very large or high-rise projects have large negotiated fees.**
    ___ (4) Typical soils report strength characteristics:

___ Noncohesive (granular) soils

Relative density	Blows per foot (N)
___ Very loose	0–4
___ Loose	5–10
___ Firm	11–30
___ Dense	31–50
___ Very dense	51+

___ Cohesive (claylike) soils

Comparative consistency	Blows per foot	Unconfined compressed strength (T/SF)
___ Very soft	0–2	0–0.25
___ Soft	3–4	0.25–0.50
___ Med. stiff	5–8	0.50–1.00
___ Stiff	9–15	1.00–2.00
___ Very stiff	16–30	2.00–4.00
___ Hard	31+	4.00+

Degree of plasticity	PI	Degree of expan. pot.	PI
___ None to slight	0–4	Low	0–15
___ Slight	5–10	Medium	15–25
___ Medium	11–30	High	25+
___ High	31+		

___ (5) For small projects, especially in rural areas, *soils surveys* by USDA Soils Conservation Service are available (free of charge) through the local soil and water conservation district office.

___ 8. Soil Preparation for Foundations

   ___ *a.* Soils may or may not have to be prepared for foundations, based on the specific foundation loads and type and nature of the soil.

   ___ *b.* Problem soils

      ___ (1) Collapsing soils undergo large reductions in volume as they become wet. This magnifies when foundation loads are applied. These soils are found most extensively as wind- or water-deposited sands and silts, sometimes called loess. Man-made fills can have the same effect. The soils exist as loose deposits, with large void spaces between soil particles.

      ___ (2) Expansive soils are usually clays. See 6, above.

   ___ *c.* Compaction is a procedure that increases the density of soil (decreasing the void space and thereby increasing the strength) by either rolling, tamping, or vibrating the surface. Adding moisture increases the density until the optimum moisture at maximum density is obtained. This is given as a percent (usually 90% to 95% desired). Past this, the density decreases.

      ___ (1) Typical procedure lays down a 6″ to 8″ layer ("lift") of soil, which is watered and compacted. For sand, vibratory compaction equip. is used. Sand cannot be over-compacted. For clay, heavy rollers are best. Clay can be over-compacted.

      ___ (2) Problem soils may need:

         ___ (*a*) "Engineered fill" is standard compaction, but with usually a predetermined fill material brought on site, placed, and tested under the supervision of a soils engineer. This may require removing the native problem soil to a predetermined depth.

___ (*b*) <u>Prewetting</u> (causing moisture to penetrate several feet) and then compacting or loading a "<u>surcharge</u>" of soil stockpiled above the native.

___ (*c*) Other:

___ "Dynamic" compaction by dropping heavy weights. This can compact 60′ deep.

___ Deep vibration by a steel shaft driven into the ground. Water may be forced down the shaft. Compaction can occur at depths of 60′ to 100′. This is economical only when used for large sites.

___ Blasting.

___ Compaction piles.

___ Compaction grouting.

___ Stabilization by chemical grouting such as lime (for expansive soils).

___ 9. <u>Foundations</u>

___ *a.* Differential settlement of foundations: ¼″ to ½″, maximum.

___ *b.* Depth of foundations should be at or below the local frost line. See App. B, item C.

___ *c.* For more on foundations, see pp. 213 and 215.

___ 10. <u>Radon</u>

___ *a.* See App. B for likely radon locations.

___ *b.* A colorless, odorless, radioactive gas found in soils and underground water.

___ *c.* Is drawn from the soil through the foundation when the indoor pressure is less than the pressure outside, in the soil. This usually occurs in winter.

___ *d.* Reduction approaches:

___ (1) For slab-on-grade construction, a normal uniform rock base course, vapor barrier, and concrete slab may be satisfactory.

___ (2) Basements

      ___ (*a*) Barrier approach, by complete waterproofing.

      ___ (*b*) Suction approach collects the gas outside the foundation and under the slab, and vents it to the outside. Consists of a collection system of underground pipes (or individual suction pipes at 1/500 SF), and discharge system.

___ (3) **Costs: $350 to $500 during home const., but $500 to $2500 for retrofits.**

___ 11. <u>Termite Treatment</u>

    ___ *a.* Wood buildings should usually have termite treatment under slab on grade.

    ___ *b.* Locations where termites are most prevalent are given in App. B, item F.

    ___ *c.* **Costs: $0.30/SF (55% M and 45% L), variation −35%, +65%.**

NOTES

__ D. UTILITIES (30)

The five main utilities are water, sewer, power, gas, and telephone—with storm drains and cable TV as added options.

UTILITY TRENCHES

Typical Costs for Trench, Excavation, and Compacted Backfill:

___ **For 2′ × 2′ trench with 0 to 1 side slope: $0.55/SF sect./LF trench**

___ **Double cost for 2 to 1 side slope. Add 1% for each additional ft depth past 2′.**

___ **Add to above cost of pipe or conduit listed below.**

___ 1. <u>Storm Drains</u>
    ___ *a.* Most expensive, avoid where possible.
    ___ *b.* Separate from sanitary sewer.
    ___ *c.* Manholes at ends, at each change of horizontal or vertical direction, and each 300′ to 500′.
    ___ *d.* Surface drain no more than 800′ to 1000′ to catch basins, or 500′ if coming from two directions.
    ___ *e.* 4′ deep in cold climates.
    ___ *f.* Minimum slope of 0.3% for a minimum velocity of 2′/sec (never exceed 10′/sec)
    ___ *g.* 12″ minimum diameter in 3″ increments up to 36″.
    ___ *h.* See p. 176 for sizing.

See below for Costs.

___ 2. <u>Sanitary Sewer</u>
    ___ *a.* CO at ends, branchings, turns (less than 90°).
    ___ *b.* Typically, 4″ for house branch up to 8″ diameter for mains and laterals. 6″ for most commercial.
    ___ *c.* Street mains often at –6′, or greater.
    ___ *d.* Slopes of from ⅟₁₆″ to ¼″/ft.
    ___ *e.* Place below water lines or 10′ away.
    ___ *f.* Also see p. 430.

Typical Costs for Drainage and Sewage Piping: (per LF)
___ **Reinforced concrete: 12″ to 84″ diameter = $1.25 to $4.40/inch dia.**
___ **Corrugated metal: 8″ to 72″ diameter = $1.15 to $3.10/inch dia.**
___ **Plain metal: 8″ to 72″ diameter = $1.00 to $2.95/inch dia.**
___ **PVC: 4″ to 15″ diameter = $1.05 to $1.20/inch dia.**
___ **Clay: 4″ to 36″ diameter = $1.40 to $4.25/inch dia.**

Typical Costs for MH and Catch Basins:
___ For 4′ × 4′ deep, C.M.U. or P.C.C. = $1550
___ Adjust: +10% for brick, +15% for C.I.P. conc.
___ Add: $400 each ft down to 14′.

___ 3. Water
    ___ *a.* Flexible in layout.
    ___ *b.* Best located in Right-of-Way (ROW) for mains.
    ___ *c.* Layouts: branch or loop (best).
    ___ *d.* Affected by frost. Must be at −5′ in cold climates.
    ___ *e.* Valves at each branch and at each 1000′ max.
    ___ *f.* FHs layed out to reach 300′ to buildings but no closer than 25′ to 50′. Sometimes high pressure fire lines installed.
    ___ *g.* Typical size: 8″ dia., min., mains
                    6″ dia., min., branch
    ___ *h.* Typical city pressure 60 psi
    ___ *i.* Where city water not available, wells can be put in (keep 100′ from newest sewer, drain field, or stream bed).
    ___ *j.* Also, see p. 429.

Typical Costs for Piping (per LF):
___ Iron: 4″ dia. to 18″ dia. = $3.60/inch dia.
___ Copper: ¾″ dia. to 6″ dia. = $6.70 to $21/inch dia.
___ PVC: 1½″ dia. to 8″ dia. = $2.30/inch dia.

___ 4. Power and Telephone
    ___ *a.* Brought in on primary high-voltage lines, either overhead or underground.
    ___ *b.* Stepped down at transformers to secondary (lower voltage) lines. Secondary lines should be kept down to 400′ or less to building service-entrance sections.
    ___ *c.* Underground distribution may be 2 to 5 times more expensive but is more reliable, does not interfere with trees, and eliminates pole clutter. Always place in conduit.
    ___ *d.* If overhead, transformers are hung on poles with secondary overhead to building. Guyed poles typically 125′ (max.) apart. Where not in R.O.W., 8′ easement required. For footings, provide 1′ of inbedment per every 10′ of height plus 1 extra foot.
    ___ *e.* See p. 497.

Typical Costs for Conduit: 3″ to 4″: $4 to $6/LF
        PC conc. transformer pad, 5′ sq.: $50/ea.

___ 5. <u>Gas</u>
    ___ *a.* Underground, similar to water.
    ___ *b.* Main problem is danger of leakage or explosion, so lines should be kept away from buildings, except at entry.
    ___ *c.* Lines should not be in same trench as electric cable.
    ___ *d.* Also see p. 437.

Typical Costs for Gas Piping:
    ___ **Plastic: $2.50 for 1¼″ to $7.65/LF for 4″ dia.**
    ___ **Steel: $24/LF for 5″ dia. to $44.40/LF for 8″ dia.**

___ 6. <u>Fire Protection:</u> Generally, fire departments want:
    ___ *a.* Fire hydrants at streets or drives that are located about 300 ft apart and located so that a 300-ft hose can extend around building.
    ___ *b.* Min. of at least 16-ft-wide drives around building, with 30′ to 60′ turning radius for fire truck access.
    ___ *c.* Also see p. 433.

Typical Costs:
    Piping costs, same as water (iron or PVC)
    Hydrants: $1650/ea.
    Siamese: $220 to $330/ea.

EXAMPLE:

PROBLEM: ESTIMATE THE COST OF A NEW 200' LONG UNDERGROUND 1½" PVC WATER LINE FOR A BUILDING SITE IN LOS ANGELES, CA. THIS WILL BE PUT IN DURING ROUGH GRADING, PRIOR TO PAVING & LANDSCAPING.

SOLUTION:

1. 2' SQ TRENCH, EXCAV., & FILL: $0.55 (p. 193) × 4 SF × 200' = $440
2. 1½" PVC LINE: 1.5" × $2.30/"dia (p. 194) × 200'   = $690

   $1130

3. LOS ANGELES COST FACTOR   ×   1.07
   (See APP. B, ITEM V, P. 527) $1209
                          SAY: $1200

NOTES

<u>NOTES</u>

___ E. SITE IMPROVEMENTS

Item	Costs
___ 1. Paving	
___ *a.* Asphalt:	
2″ AC	**$.45 to $1/SF (70%M and 40%L)**
For each added inch:	**Increase 25 to 45%**
4″ base:	**$.40 to .60/SF (60%M and 40%L)**
For each added inch:	**Increase 25%**
___ *b.* Concrete drives, walks, patios:	
½″ score joints at 5′ and expan. joints at 20′ to 30′	
4″ concrete slab:	**$1.65 to 2.20/SF (60%M and 40%L)**
Add:	
For base	**See AC, above**
For each inch more	**Add 15%**
For reinforcing	**5 to 10%**
For special finishes	**Add 100%**
For vapor barriers	**See p. 289.**
___ 2. Miscellaneous Concrete	
___ *a.* Curb	**$8/LF (30%M and 70%L)**
___ *b.* Curb and gutter	**$13/LF**
Add for "rolled"	**+25%**
___ *c.* Conc. parking bumpers	**$45/ea. (65%M and 35%L)**
___ *d.* Paint stripes	**$.30/LF (20%M and 80%L)**
___ 3. Fences and Walls	
___ *a.* Chain link	
4′ high	**$5.55 to $7.55/LF (50%M and 50%L)**
6′ high	**$6 to $8.30/LF**
___ *b.* Wrought iron, 3′ to 4′	**$21/LF (70%M and 30%L)**
___ *c.* Wood fencing	**$1.70 to $8.00/SF (60%M and 40%L) depending on material, type, and height**
___ *d.* Walls	**See Parts 3 and 4.**
___ 4. Site Lighting	
___ *a.* Pole mounted for parking lot, 20′ to 40′ high	**$1500 to $3500/ea.**
___ 5. Carports and Canopies	
(no foundations)	**$1600–$3775/car**

NOTES

___ F. LANDSCAPING AND IRRIGATION

___ 1. General
    ___ a. Landscaping can be one of the greatest aesthetic enhancements for the design of buildings.
    ___ b. Landscaping can be used for energy conservation. See p. 138.
    ___ c. Landscaping can be used for noise reduction. See p. 156.
    ___ d. At locations with expansive soils, be careful about plants and irrigation next to buildings.
    ___ e. Existing: Mature trees will not survive a violent change of habitat. The ground may not be cut away near their roots, nor may more than a few inches be added to grade; though a large well with radial drains and 6″ of crushed stone out to the drip may work. As a rule, though, up to 50% of the root system can be lost without killing a plant, providing the other 50% is completely undisturbed. Trees which grew in a wood must be preserved in a clump, since they have shallow roots, while trees that were originally isolated or in open fence lines should be kept so.
    ___ f. As a general rule, trees should be located no closer to buildings than the extent of the mature "drip line." When closer, deeper foundations may be needed, especially in expansive soils.
    ___ g. For interior plants and pots, see p. 377.
    ___ h. Trees are often selected by profile for aesthetics and function:

CANOPY   TALL   ROUND   FOCAL

___ 2. Materials
    ___ a. Select material based on USDA Plant Zones, shown below. See App. B, item H, for various zones.

Zone	Approx. range of ave. annual min. temp.
2	−50 to −40°F
3	−40 to −30°F
4	−30 to −20°F
5	−20 to −10°F
6	−10 to 10°F
7	0 to −30°F
8	10 to 20°F
9	20 to 30°F
10	30 to 40°F

___ b. Next, select plants for microclimate of site (see p. 136) and location around building, as follows:
    ___ (1) Shaded locations and north sides
    ___ (2) Semi-shaded locations and east sides
    ___ (3) Sunny locations and south and west sides
___ c. Select material by the following types:
    ___ (1) Large trees (over 20′, often up to 50′ high)
    ___ (2) Small trees (under 20′ high)
    ___ (3) High shrubs (over 8′ high)
    ___ (4) Moderate shrubs (4′ to 8′ high)
    ___ (5) Low shrubs (under 4′ high)
    ___ (6) Ground covers (spreading plants under 24″ high)
___ d. Select material based on growing season, including:
    ___ (1) Evergreen versus deciduous
    ___ (2) Annuals (put in seasonally, not returning) versus perennials (die in winter but return in spring)
___ e. Selection based on aesthetics:
    ___ (1) Shape (see item 1-*h*, above) and texture
    ___ (2) Color, often dependent on blooming season

Rule of Thumb: Costs of overall landscaping = $1 to $5/SF of landscape area.

Costs shown below: 50%M and 50%L, variation of +/−25%, depending on soil and growing season. For *commercial jobs, add 20%* due to warranties and maintenance.

Trees	15 gal $95/ea.	**Shrubs 1 gal $6 to 8/ea.**
	24″ box $235/ea.	**5 gal $32/ea.**
	specimens $375 to $2500/ea.	**specimens $60/ea.**

Vines	1 gal	$8.50/ea.	Ground covers	
	5 gal	$36/ea.	plants 1 gal	$5/ea.
			lawn sod (incl. topsoil)	$.55 to $1.00/SF
			lawn seed	$.25/SF

Other
Brick border	$7.50/LF to $12.50
Rock	$2.50 to $6.50/SY
Preemergent	$.06/SF
Pots, 14″ ceramic with saucer	$100/ea.

___ 3. <u>Irrigation</u>

    ___ *a.* Can be in the following forms:

Type	Material	Costs
Bubbler	Plants and trees	$3/SF
Spray	Lawn	$3–$5/SF
Drip	Plants and trees	$2.50/SF

    ___ *b.* System should "tee" off water line before entering building. The tee size usually ranges between ¾″ and 2″.

    ___ *c.* Controls usually require a 110V outlet.

<u>NOTES</u>

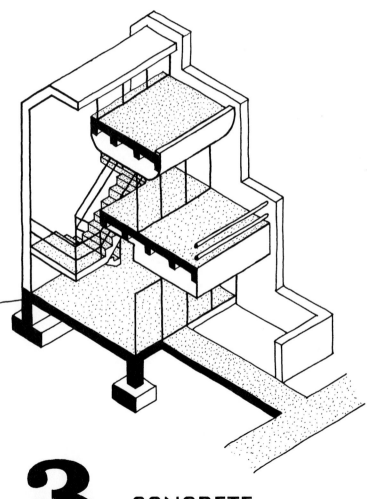

3 CONCRETE

NOTES

__ A. CONCRETE MATERIALS

(4) (19) (38) (43) (45) (46)

___ **1. General Cast-in-Place Costs**
  ___ *a.* **Substructure: $150 to $350/CY (40%M and 60%L)**
  ___ *b.* **Superstructure: $500 to $1000/CY (30%M and 70%L)**

___ 2. Concrete: Consists of (using the general 1-2-3 mix, 1 part cement, 2 parts sand, and 3 parts rock, plus water):
  ___ *a.* Portland cement
        ___ (1) Type I: Normal for general construction.
        ___ (2) Type II: Modified for a lower heat of hydration, for large structures or warm weather.
        ___ (3) Type III: Modified for high, early strength, where forms must be removed as soon as possible, such as high-rise construction or cold weather.
        ___ (4) Type IV: Modified for low heat for very large structures.
        ___ (5) Type V: Modified for sulfate resistance.
        ___ (6) Types IA, IIA, or IIIA: Air-entrained to resist frost.
  ___ *b.* Fine aggregate (sand): ¼″ or smaller.
  ___ *c.* Course aggregate (rock and gravel): ¼″ to 2″.
  ___ *d.* Clean water: Just enough to permit ready working of mix into forms. Mix should not slide or run off a shovel. Major factor effecting strength and durability is the *water-cement ratio,* expressed as gallons of water per sack of cement (usually ranging from 5 to 8). Slump is a measure of this:

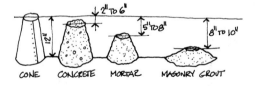

CONE   CONCRETE   MORTAR   MASONRY GROUT

___ 3. Structural Characteristics (Primer)
  ___ *a.* Strength

AVERAGE PHYSICAL PROPERTIES

MATERIAL	ELASTIC LIMIT (PSI)		ULTIMATE STRENGTH (PSI)			ALLOWABLE WORKING UNIT STRESS (PSI)				MODULUS OF ELASTICITY (PSI)	WT. (#/CF.)
	TEN-SION	COM-PRESSION	TEN-SION	COM-PRESSION	SHEAR	TEN-SION	COM-PRESSION	SHEAR	EXTREME FIBER BENDING		
CONCRETE				2500			1125	75		3,000,000	150

207

___ *b.* Bending

___ (1) Concrete is strong in compression but has little dependable tensile strength. Steel is strong in tension. When they are combined in a reinforced concrete bending member, such as a beam or slab, the concrete resists compression and the steel resists the tension. Thus, the reinforcing must be located at the tension face of the member.

Reinforcing splices in continuous-top reinforcing are usually located at midspan. Splices at bottom reinforcing are usually located over supports.

___ (2) Reinforcing: Steel bars start at #2s, which are ¼″ dia. Sizes go up to #11s, with each size an added ⅛″. All bars are deformed except #2s. A common problem is trying to cram too many bars into too small a section.

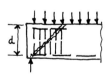

___ (3) Shear

___ (*a*) When concrete fails in shear it is generally due to a tension failure along a diagonal line. Vertical steel "stirrups" or diagonal bars are often used to tie the top and bottom parts together across the potential crack and prevent failure. This steel must be placed accurately in the field.

___ (b) The weakness of concrete in diagonal tension leads to problems with
keys and construction joints.

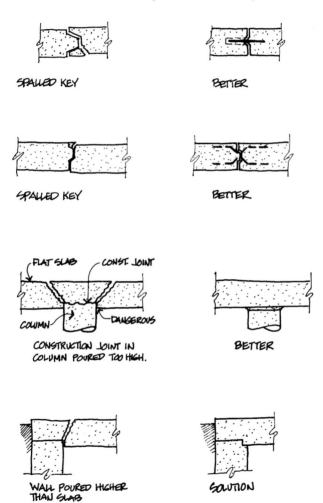

SPALLED KEY   BETTER

SPALLED KEY   BETTER

FLAT SLAB   CONST. JOINT

COLUMN   DANGEROUS

CONSTRUCTION JOINT IN
COLUMN POURED TOO HIGH.   BETTER

WALL POURED HIGHER
THAN SLAB   SOLUTION

___ (4) Bond: Reinforcing lap splices need to be long enough to bond with the concrete. These splices close to the surface are weak, so reinforcing needs to be centered or kept clear of surfaces. In general, bars should not be lap-spliced at points of maximum stress.

___ (5) Columns

135°
Hook

SPIRAL
REINF'G.

___ (a) In columns, both the concrete and the steel can work in compression.

___ (b) Bars need steel ties to keep them from buckling outward. Also, closely spaced ties help confine the concrete against breaking apart.

___ (c) 90° hooks are often used, but should *not* be used in seismic areas. The best anchor for the end of a tie is a 135° hook around the rebar and back into the concrete.

___ (d) The ultimate in tying bars against outward buckling and confining concrete against breaking apart is the spirally reinforced column.

___ (e) Reinforcing is often lap-spliced at floor levels.

___ (6) Concrete shrinks: Details must allow for this. Try to avoid locking fresh concrete between two immovable objects. Pouring sequences should consider this problem.

___ (7) Prestressed Concrete:

SHRINK

BETTER

___ (a) Differs from ordinary, reinforced concrete in that prestressing steel is under a very high tension, compressing the concrete together, before any load is placed on the member. This strengthens the concrete in shear as well as bending. This requires very high-strength steel which is impractical in ordinary reinforced concrete but results in large steel savings.

___ (b) *Posttensioning* involves tightening the rods or cables *after* the concrete is poured and cured. This concentrates a large stress at each end of the cables and requires special care

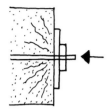

(bearing plates, special hardware, reinforcing, etc.) to prevent failure at these points. If an end connection fails in unbonded posttensioning, there's no reinforcing strength left!

___ (c) *Pretensioning* has none of these "all the eggs in one basket" problems. Pretensioning lends itself to precast, plant-produced members, while posttensioning lends itself to work at the job site.

___ (d) Problems

___ 1. Continuing shrinkage is the most common problem with prestressed concrete. All details must consider long-term shrinkage.

___ 2. Notches in precast tees at bearing may cause problems.

___ 4. <u>Testing:</u> Typical design compressive strengths are $f'c = 2500$ to 3000 psi. To be sure of actual constructed strengths, compressive cylinder tests are made:

7-Day Break	28-Day Break
60 to 70% of final strength	Final strength

The UBC requires average of three tests to meet or exceed $f'c$. No test must fall below $f'c$ by 500 or more psi.

___ 5. <u>Finishes:</u> Different wall finishes can be achieved by:

Type	Cost
___ a. Cast shapes and textures	**$2.50 to $6.00/SF**
___ b. Abrasive treatment (bush hammering, etc.)	**$1.30 to $3.20/SF**
___ c. Chemical retardation (exposed aggregate, etc.)	**$0.70/SF**

 CAST

 BUSH HAMMERED

 EXP. AGG.

NOTES

___ B. FOUNDATIONS

___ 1. <u>Functions</u>
  ___ *a.* Transfers building loads to ground
  ___ *b.* Anchors the building against wind and seismic loads
  ___ *c.* Isolates the building from frost heaving
  ___ *d.* Isolates building from expansive soils
  ___ *e.* Holds building above or from ground moisture
  ___ *f.* Retards heat flow to or from conditioned space
  ___ *g.* Provides storage space (basements)
  ___ *h.* Provides living space (basements)
  ___ *i.* Houses mechanical systems (basements)

___ 2. <u>Types</u>
  ___ *a.* Slab-on-grade ___ *b.* Crawl space ___ *c.* Basement

___ 3. <u>Depths</u> (spread footings) should be at or below frost line (see App. B, item C):

___ *a.*	No Freeze	1′–6″
___ *b.*	+20°F	2′–6″
___ *c.*	+10°F	3′–0″
___ *d.*	0°F	3′–6″
___ *e.*	–10°F	4′–0″
___ *f.*	–20°F	4′–6″

___ 4. <u>Differential Settlement:</u> ¼″ to ½″

NOTES

C. CONCRETE MEMBERS (SIZES AND COSTS)

See p. 132 for span-to-depth ratios.

___ 1. *Concrete Substructure*
    ___ *a.* *Spread footings*

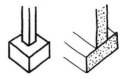

Spread footings located under walls and columns are appropriate for low-rise buildings (one to four stories) where soil conditions are firm enough to support the weight of the building on the area of the spread footings. When needed, footings at columns can be connected together with grade beams to provide more lateral stability in earthquakes. Spread footings are the most widely used type of footing, especially in mild climates, because they are the most economical. Depth of footing should be below topsoil and frost line, on compacted fill (or firm native soil) but should be above water table.

Concrete spread footings are normally 1' thick, but at least as thick as the width of stem wall. Width is normally twice that of stem wall. Typical column footings are 4' square for one-story buildings. Add 1' for each story up to ten stories.

Approximate cost for a column-spread footing (M and L) with excavation, backfill, and reinforcing with 3000 psi concrete, 3' × 3', 12": $116/ea.

Approximate cost for a wall-spread (strip) footing (stem wall not included), 12" × 2' W is $25/LF.

Approximate cost of concrete stem walls: 6" × 4' high is $37.50/LF.

    ___ *b.* *Other foundation systems:* As the weight of the building increases in relation to the bearing capacity (or depth of good bearing) soil, the footings need to expand in size or different systems need to be used.
        ___ (1) For expansive soils with low to medium loads (or high loads with rock not too far

down), _drilled piers (caissons) and grade beams_ can be used. The pier may be straight like a column or "belled" out to spread the load at the bearing level of soil. The grade beam is

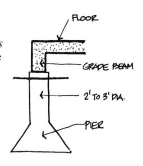

designed to resist expansion or compression of the soil as if it were in the air.

Approximate cost of a 28″ deep × 1′ wide, 8-KLF load _grade beam_ spanning 15′ is $50.25/LF (M and L).

Approximate cost of a 2′ × 50′ concrete caisson (3000 psi concrete) is $2200/each (M and L).

___ (2) _Piles:_   Piles are long columns that are driven into the ground. Piles transfer the loads to a lower, stronger stratum or can transfer the load by friction along the length of the pile (skin friction). Piles are usually grouped together under a footing (pile cap) of reinforced concrete.

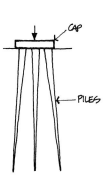

Approximate cost of reinforced concrete (3000 psi) _PILE CAP_ for two piles with a dimension of 6.5′ × 3.5′ by 1′–8′ deep for 45K load is $335/ea. (M & L).

Different types of piles, their loads, and approximate costs (M and L):

___ **CIP concrete, end-bearing, 50k, with 12″ to 14″ steel shell, 25′ long, $610/ea.**

___ **Precast concrete, end-bearing, 50k, 10″ sq., 50′ long, $810/ea.**

___ **Steel pipe, end-bearing, 50k, 12″ dia., 50′ long, $1580/ea.**

___ **Steel H Piles, end-bearing, 100k, 50′ long, $1180/ea.**

___ **Steel-step tapered, end-bearing, 50k, 50′ long, $660/ea.**

___ **Treated wood pile, 3 ea. in cluster, end-bearing, 50k, 25′ long, $1415/ea. group.**

___ **Pressure-injected footings, end-bearing, 50k, 50′ long, $1320/ea.**

H

O

o o
o

O

___ (3) *Mat foundations:* For poor soil conditions and tall buildings (10 to 20 stories) with their overturning moments, a mat foundation is required. A mat foundation is a large mass of concrete laid under the entire building. Mat foundations range from 4′ to 8′ thick.

Approximate cost: See p. 207.

___ 2. *Concrete Superstructure*
   ___ *a.   Concrete slabs*
      ___ (1) *Slab-on-grade:* General rule on paving slabs is that depth should be ½ to ⅓ of average annual frost penetration. Typical thickness:

SLAB
REINF'G.
VAPOR BARRIER
BASE
SUB GRADE

Floors   4″
Garage Floors   5″
Terraces   5″
Driveways   6″ to 8″
Sidewalks   4″ to 6″

Approximate cost of 4″ reinforced slab is $2.30 to $2.70/SF.
For rock base see p. 199.
For vapor barrier see p. 289.
For compacted subgrade see p. 175.
For termite treatment see p. 191.

___ (2) *Reinforced concrete slabs in the air:* For general span-to-depth ratios, see p. 132.
   ___ (*a*) *One-way slab*
      ___ Usual spans: 6′ to 20′
      ___ Typical SDR:
        20 for simple spans
        28 for continuous spans

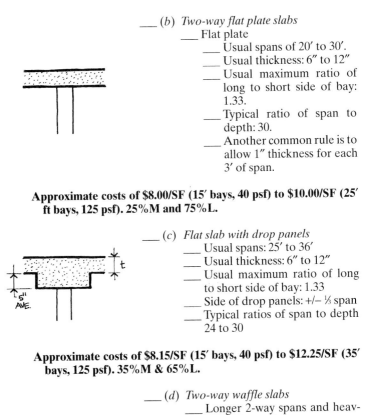

___ (*b*) *Two-way flat plate slabs*
    ___ Flat plate
        ___ Usual spans of 20′ to 30′.
        ___ Usual thickness: 6″ to 12″
        ___ Usual maximum ratio of long to short side of bay: 1.33.
        ___ Typical ratio of span to depth: 30.
        ___ Another common rule is to allow 1″ thickness for each 3′ of span.

Approximate costs of $8.00/SF (15′ bays, 40 psf) to $10.00/SF (25′ ft bays, 125 psf). 25%M and 75%L.

___ (*c*) *Flat slab with drop panels*
    ___ Usual spans: 25′ to 36′
    ___ Usual thickness: 6″ to 12″
    ___ Usual maximum ratio of long to short side of bay: 1.33
    ___ Side of drop panels: +/– ⅓ span
    ___ Typical ratios of span to depth 24 to 30

Approximate costs of $8.15/SF (15′ bays, 40 psf) to $12.25/SF (35′ bays, 125 psf). 35%M & 65%L.

___ (*d*) *Two-way waffle slabs*
    ___ Longer 2-way spans and heavier load capacity.
    ___ Usual spans: 25′ to 40′.
    ___ Standard pan sizes: 20″ to 30″ square with other sizes available. Standard pan depths 8″ to 20″ in 2″ increments.
    ___ Usual maximum ratio of long to short side of bay is 1.33.
    ___ Typical ratio of span to depth: 25–30.

Approximate cost of $11.00/SF (20′ bays, 40 psf) to $14.15/SF (40′ bays, 125 psf). 40%M and 60%L.

___ (*e*) *Precast, prestressed concrete planks*
   ___ Thickness of 6″ to 12″ in 2″ increments.
   ___ Spans of 8′ to 36′.
   ___ Span-to-depth ratio of approximately 30 to 40.
   ___ 1½″ to 2″ conc. topping often used for floors.

Approximate cost of $5.15/SF for 6″ thick (85% M and 15% L) with 35% variation higher or lower. Add $0.20 for each added 2″. Add $1.75/SF for topping.

___ *b.* *Concrete beams and joists*
   ___ (1) Precast concrete I beams (prestressed)
      ___ (*a*) Typical beam thickness of 12″ to 16″.
      ___ (*b*) Spans range from 20′ to 100′.
      ___ (*c*) Approximate ratios of span to depth of 15 to 25.

Approximate cost of $70/LF (90% M and 10% L) with variations of 20% higher or lower.

   ___ (2) Prestressed T beams (single and double tees)
      ___ (*a*) Typical flange widths of ½ to ⅓ the effective depth (8′ to 10′).
      ___ (*b*) Usual spans of 20′ to 120′.
      ___ (*c*) Approximate ratio of span-to-depth ratio: 24 to 32.
      ___ (*d*) Usually has 1½″ to 2″ concrete topping for floors.

Approximate cost of double tee 2′ deep with 35′ to 100′ span is $5.50/SF (90% M and 10% L) with variation of 10% higher or lower.

   ___ (3) Concrete beams and joists. SDR of ≈ 18, or 1″ to 1¼″ for every foot of span. Width should be ½ to ¾ the total depth.

   Approximate cost of P.C. beam, 20′ span is $50.00/LF (70% M and 30% L). Cost can go 3 times higher with 45′ spans and heavy loads.

   ___ *c.* <u>*Concrete columns*</u>
- ___ (1) Round columns usually 12″ minimum.
- ___ (2) Rectangular: 12 in sq. minimum.
- ___ (3) Usual minimum rectangular tied columns 10″ × 12″.
- ___ (4) Square or round spiral columns: 14″; add 2″ for each story.
- ___ (5) Most columns are "short": maximum height *10* times least cross-section dimension. Typical column height is 12.5′ for multistory building.
- ___ (6) Maximum unbraced height for "engineered" long columns: *20* times least cross-section dimension.

Approximate cost of $25 to $100/LF (30% M and 70% L). Use lower number for single-story, min. loads, and min. reinforcing.

   ___ *d.* <u>*Concrete walls*</u>
- ___ (1) <u>Wall Thickness</u>
  - ___ (*a*) Multistory: 8″ top 15′, add 1″ for each successive 25′ down.
  - ___ (*b*) Basements: 8″ minimum.
  - ___ (*c*) Nonbearing: Minimum thickness 6″. Maximum ratio of unsupported height: 25 to 30.
  - ___ (*d*) Precast wall panels: Minimum thickness: $5^{1}/_{2}$″. Maximum ratio of unbraced length to thickness: 45.

Approximate cost of $12.75/SF for 6″, reinf. wall (65% M and 35% L) with variation of 35% higher for special finishes. Add $.40 per each added inch thickness.

- ___ (2) "Tilt-up" (on site precast)
  - ___ (*a*) Height-to-thickness ratio: 40 to 50.
  - ___ (*b*) Typical heights: 22′ to 35′.
  - ___ (*c*) Typical thickness: 5½″ to 8″.
  - ___ (*d*) Typical use: Favorable climate, 20,000 SF size building or larger. Time and material savings can cut cost $\approx \frac{1}{3}$, depending on height and area, compared to masonry.

Costs: $5.20 to $6.60/SF (45% M and 55% L), costs can double for special finishes. Add $\approx$ 30% for concrete columns.

EXAMPLE:

PROBLEM:

SKETCH UP A ROUGH DESIGN & ESTIMATE OF COSTS FOR A 30' x 30' BAY FLOOR SYSM. USING WAFFLE SLAB, CONC, BEAMS AT THE PERIMETER, & CONCRETE COLUMNS.

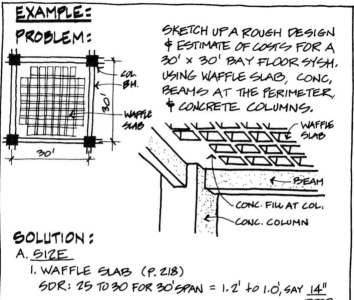

COL. BM.

WAFFLE SLAB

30'

30'

WAFFLE SLAB

BEAM

CONC. FILL AT COL.

CONC. COLUMN

SOLUTION:

A. SIZE

1. WAFFLE SLAB (P. 218)
SDR: 25 TO 30 FOR 30' SPAN = 1.2' to 1.0', SAY <u>14" DEEP</u>

2. BEAM (P. 219)
SDR: 18 FOR 30' SPAN = 1.67' DEEP   SAY <u>12"W</u>
WIDTH: ½ TO ¾ DEPTH = .83' TO 1.25'   <u>x 1'-8" D</u>

3. COLUMN (P. 220)
WIDTH: HEIGHT ÷ 10 = 1.8'   SAY <u>1'-10" SQ.</u>

B. COST

1. WAFFLE SLAB: (½ BETW'N $11 & $14) ≈ $ 12.50/SF
2. BEAM: SAY $65/LF × (30' × 4) ÷ (30'²) ≈ $ 8.65/SF
3. COLUMNS: SAY $80/LF × (18' × 4) ÷ (30'²) ≈ $ 6.40/SF

   $ 27.55/SF

NOTES

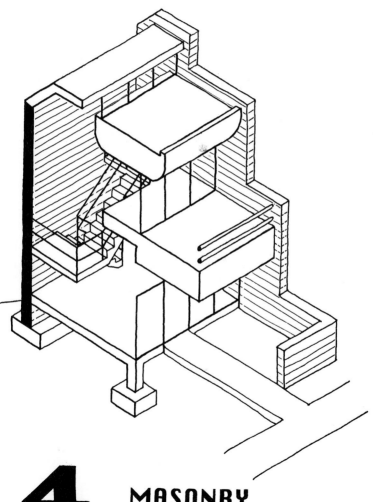

4 MASONRY

NOTES

__ A. MASONRY MATERIALS

$\textcircled{4}$ $\textcircled{19}$ $\textcircled{38}$ $\textcircled{43}$ $\textcircled{45}$

__ 1. <u>General:</u> Masonry consists of:
   __ *a.* Brick
      __ (1) Fired
      __ (2) Unfired ("adobe")
   __ *b.* Concrete block (concrete masonry units or CMU)
   __ *c.* Stone
   __ *d.* Glass block
__ 2. <u>Structural Characteristics</u>
   __ *a.* Strength

AVERAGE PHYSICAL PROPERTIES

	ELASTIC LIMIT (PSI)		ULTIMATE STRENGTH (PSI)			ALLOWABLE WORKING UNIT STRESS (PSI)				MODULUS OF ELASTICITY (PSI)	WT. (#/CF)
	TEN-SION	COM-PRESSION	TEN-SION	f'm COM-PRESSION	SHEAR	TEN-SION	COM-PRESSION	SHEAR	EXTREME FIBER BENDING		
ADOBE				300-500			30	8			110
BRICK				2800		800	100 – 250	50		2,500,000	120
CMU				1500		500	300	38		1,900,000	145
STONE				2500			200-400	8			145

   __ *b.* Reinforcing: Like concrete, masonry is strong in compression, but weak in tension. Therefore, steel reinforcement must usually be added to walls to simulate columns and beams.
      __ (1) Like *columns:* Vertical bars @ 2' to 4' oc.
      __ (2) Like *beams:* "Bond Beams" @ 4' to 8' oc.
      __ (3) Also, added *horizontal wire reinforcement* (ladder or truss type) @ 16" oc. vertically, to help resist lateral forces and cracking.
__ 3. <u>Bonds</u>
   __ *a.* Structural (method of laying units together):
      __ (1) Overlapping units.
      __ (2) *Metal ties* (should be galvanized with zinc coating of 2 oz/SF, or stainless steel). Wire ties usually @ every 3 SF, or . . .
         Metal anchors, usually at 16" oc, vertical and 24" oc, horizontal.
      __ (3) Grout and mortar:
         __ (*a*) *Grout:* A "soup" of sand, cement, water, and often pea gravel that encases reinforcing bars. Usually 2000 psi comp. strength. Always

poured in cavities and high slump. See p. 207.

___ (b) *Mortar:* Stiffer mix of sand, cement, lime, and water, to bond units together by trowel work. Types:

___ N General purpose, medium strength, for above grade.

___ M High strength, for high compression, above-grade.

___ S High strength, for compression and tension.

___ O High lime, low strength, easily workable for veneers not subject to freezing.

___ K Low strength, for interiors.

___ (4) Bond joints

___ (5) Bond patterns

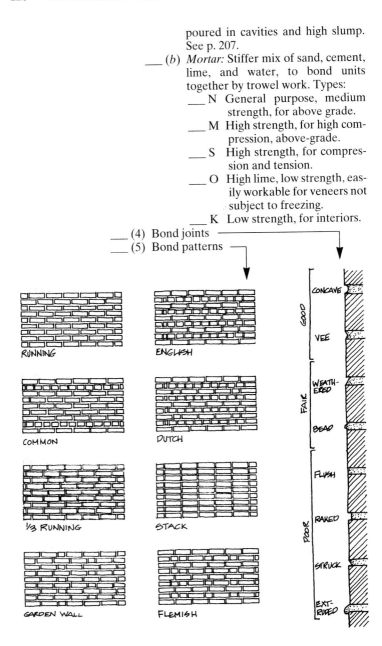

RUNNING

COMMON

⅓ RUNNING

GARDEN WALL

ENGLISH

DUTCH

STACK

FLEMISH

GOOD — CONCAVE, VEE

FAIR — WEATHERED, BEAD

POOR — FLUSH, RAKED, STRUCK, EXTRUDED

___ 4. <u>Control and Expansion Joints</u>
    ___ *a.* Width
       ___ (1) Thermal movement. See p. 306.   = ___
           Plus,
       ___ (2) Movement due to moisture: = ___
           ___ (*a*) Bricks expand; should be
                  laid wet.
           ___ (*b*) Concrete blocks shrink like
                  concrete; should be laid dry.
                  Plus,
       ___ (3) Construction tolerance.   = ___
                     Total width   = ___
    ___ *b.* Locations
       ___ (1) Corners
       ___ (2) Length of walls: 20′ to 25′ oc (double at
           parapets and bond beams.
       ___ (3) Offsets, returns, and intersections.
       ___ (4) Openings:
           ___ (*a*) One side of opening, less than 6′
                  wide.
           ___ (*b*) Two sides of opening, greater than
                  6′ wide.
       ___ (5) Against other materials.
___ 5. <u>Coatings:</u> Must be (see p. 348)
       ___ (1) "Bridgeable" (seal cracks)
       ___ (2) Breathable (do not trap vapor)
___ 6. <u>Brick</u>
    ___ *a.* Types
       ___ (1) Common (building)
       ___ (2) Face
           ___ (*a*) FBX   Select
           ___ (*b*) FBS   Standard
           ___ (*c*) FBA   Architectural
       ___ (3) Clinker
       ___ (4) Glazed
       ___ (5) Fire
       ___ (6) Cored
       ___ (7) Sand-lime (white, yellow)
       ___ (8) Pavers
    ___ *b.* Weatherability
       ___ (1) NW Negligible weathering; for indoor or
           sheltered locations.
       ___ (2) MW Moderate weather locations.
       ___ (3) SW Severe weather locations and/or earth
           contact.

___ *c.* Positions

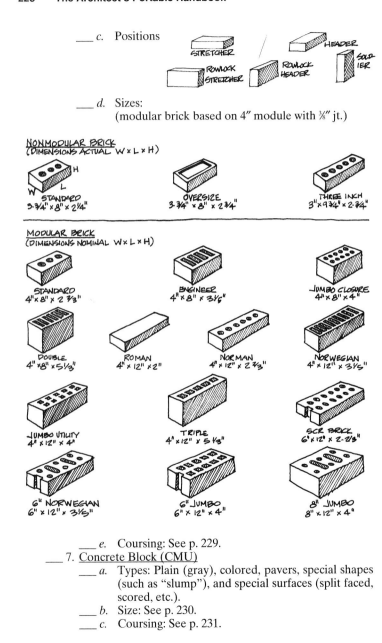

___ *d.* Sizes:
(modular brick based on 4″ module with ⅜″ jt.)

___ *e.* Coursing: See p. 229.
___ 7. Concrete Block (CMU)
    ___ *a.* Types: Plain (gray), colored, pavers, special shapes
       (such as "slump"), and special surfaces (split faced,
       scored, etc.).
    ___ *b.* Size: See p. 230.
    ___ *c.* Coursing: See p. 231.

BRICK COURSING

NONMODULAR columns: **2¼" THICK BRICKS**, **2⅝" THICK BRICKS**, **2¾" THICK BRICKS** (each with ⅜" JOINT and ½" JOINT).
MODULAR columns: **NOMINAL THICKNESS (HEIGHT) OF BRICK** — 2", 2⅔", 3⅕", 4", 5⅓".

COURSE	2¼" ⅜"J	2¼" ½"J	2⅝" ⅜"J	2⅝" ½"J	2¾" ⅜"J	2¾" ½"J	2"	2⅔"	3⅕"	4"	5⅓"
1	2⅝"	2¾"	3"	3⅛"	3⅛"	3¼"	2"	2 11/16"	3 3/16"	4"	5 5/16"
2	5¼"	5½"	6"	6¼"	6¼"	6½"	4"	5 5/16"	6⅜"	8"	10 11/16"
3	7⅞"	8¼"	9"	9⅜"	9⅜"	9¾"	6"	8"	9⅝"	1-0"	1-4"
4	10½"	11"	1-0"	1-0½"	1-0½"	1-1"	8"	10 11/16"	1-0 13/16"	1-4"	1-9 5/16"
5	1-1⅛"	1-1¾"	1-3"	1-3⅝"	1-3⅝"	1-4¼"	10"	1-1 5/16"	1-4"	1-8"	2-2 11/16"
6	1-3¾"	1-4½"	1-6"	1-6¾"	1-6¾"	1-7½"	1-0"	1-4"	1-7 3/16"	2-0"	2-8"
7	1-6⅜"	1-7¼"	1-9"	1-9⅞"	1-9⅞"	1-10¾"	1-2"	1-6 11/16"	1-10⅜"	2-4"	3-1 5/16"
8	1-9"	1-10"	2-0"	2-1"	2-1"	2-2"	1-4"	1-9 5/16"	2-1⅝"	2-8"	3-6 11/16"
9	1-11⅝"	2-0¾"	2-3"	2-4⅛"	2-4⅛"	2-5¼"	1-6"	2-0"	2-4 13/16"	3-0"	4-0"
10	2-2¼"	2-3½"	2-6"	2-7¼"	2-7¼"	2-8½"	1-8"	2-2 11/16"	2-8"	3-4"	4-5 5/16"
11	2-4⅞"	2-6¼"	2-9"	2-10⅜"	2-10⅜"	2-11¾"	1-10"	2-5 5/16"	2-11 3/16"	3-8"	4-10 11/16"
12	2-7½"	2-9"	3-0"	3-1½"	3-1½"	3-3"	2-0"	2-8"	3-2⅜"	4-0"	5-4"
13	2-10⅛"	2-11¾"	3-3"	3-4⅝"	3-4⅝"	3-6¼"	2-2"	2-10 11/16"	3-5⅝"	4-4"	5-9 5/16"
14	3-0¾"	3-2½"	3-6"	3-7¾"	3-7¾"	3-9½"	2-4"	3-1 5/16"	3-8 13/16"	4-8"	6-2 11/16"
15	3-3⅜"	3-5¼"	3-9"	3-10⅞"	3-10⅞"	4-0¾"	2-6"	3-4"	4-0"	5-0"	6-8"
16	3-6"	3-8"	4-0"	4-2"	4-2"	4-4"	2-8"	3-6 11/16"	4-3 3/16"	5-4"	7-1 5/16"
17	3-8⅝"	3-10¾"	4-3"	4-5⅛"	4-5⅛"	4-7¼"	2-10"	3-9 5/16"	4-6⅜"	5-8"	7-6 11/16"
18	3-11¼"	4-1½"	4-6"	4-8¼"	4-8¼"	4-10½"	3-0"	4-0"	4-9⅝"	6-0"	8-0"
19	4-1⅞"	4-4¼"	4-9"	4-11⅜"	4-11⅜"	5-1¾"	3-2"	4-2 11/16"	5-0 13/16"	6-4"	8-5 5/16"
20	4-4½"	4-7"	5-0"	5-2½"	5-2½"	5-5"	3-4"	4-5 5/16"	5-4"	6-8"	8-10 11/16"
21	4-7⅛"	4-9¾"	5-3"	5-5⅝"	5-5⅝"	5-8¼"	3-6"	4-8"	5-7 3/16"	7-0"	9-4"
22	4-9¾"	5-0½"	5-6"	5-8¾"	5-8¾"	5-11½"	3-8"	4-10 11/16"	5-10⅜"	7-4"	9-9 5/16"
23	5-0⅜"	5-3¼"	5-9"	5-11⅞"	5-11⅞"	6-2¾"	3-10"	5-1 5/16"	6-1⅝"	7-8"	10-2 11/16"
24	5-3"	5-6"	6-0"	6-3"	6-3"	6-6"	4-0"	5-4"	6-4 13/16"	8-0"	10-8"

CONCRETE BLOCK TYPES & SIZES

NOMINAL DIMENSIONS W × L × H (ACTUAL DIMENSIONS ARE 3/8" LESS)

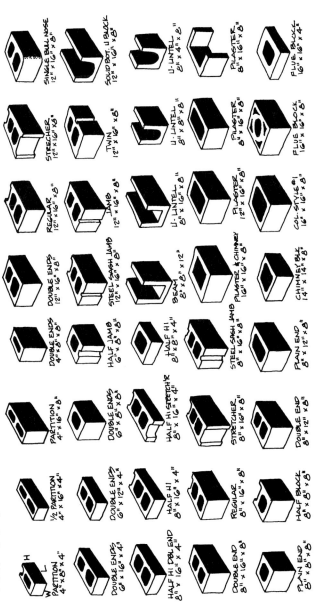

SINGLE BULL NOSE
12" × 16" × 8"

SOLID BOT. U BLOCK
12" × 16" × 8"

U- LINTEL
8" × 4" × 8"

PLASTER
8" × 16" × 8"

FLUE BLOCK
16" × 16" × 4"

STRETCHER
12" × 16" × 8"

TWIN
12" × 16" × 8"

U- LINTEL
8" × 8" × 8"

PLASTER
8" × 16" × 8"

FLUE BLOCK
16" × 16" × 8"

REGULAR
12" × 16" × 8"

JAMB
12" × 16" × 8"

U- LINTEL
8" × 16" × 8"

PLASTER
12" × 16" × 8"

COL. STYLE #1
16" × 16" × 8"

DOUBLE ENDS
12" × 16" × 8"

STEEL SASH JAMB
12" × 16" × 8"

BEAM
8" × 8" × 12"

PLASTER & CHIMNEY
16" × 16" × 8"

CHIMNEY BLK.
14" × 14" × 8"

DOUBLE ENDS
4" × 8" × 8"

HALF JAMB
6" × 8" × 8"

HALF HI
8" × 8" × 4"

STEEL SASH JAMB
8" × 16" × 8"

PLAIN END
8" × 12" × 8"

PARTITION
4" × 16" × 8"

DOUBLE ENDS
6" × 8" × 8"

HALF HI STRETCH'R
8" × 16" × 4"

STRETCHER
8" × 16" × 8"

DOUBLE END
8" × 12" × 8"

1/2 PARTITION
4" × 16" × 4"

DOUBLE ENDS
6" × 12" × 4"

HALF HI
8" × 16" × 4"

REGULAR
8" × 16" × 8"

HALF BLOCK
8" × 8" × 8"

PARTITION
4" × 8" × 4"

W   H
L

DOUBLE ENDS
6" × 16" × 4"

HALF HI DBL END
8" × 16" × 4"

DOUBLE END
8" × 16" × 8"

PLAIN END
8" × 8" × 8"

230

CONCRETE BLOCK COURSING

CSC	4" HIGH BLK.	8" HIGH BLK.	CSC	4" HIGH BLK.	8" HIGH BLK.
1	4"	8"	38	12'-8"	25'-4"
2	8"	1'-4"	39	13'-0"	26'-0"
3	1'-0"	2'-0"	40	13'-4"	26'-8"
4	1'-4"	2'-8"	41	13'-8"	27'-4"
5	1'-8"	3'-4"	42	14'-0"	28'-0"
6	2'-0"	4'-0"	43	14'-4"	28'-8"
7	2'-4"	4'-8"	44	14'-8"	29'-4"
8	2'-8"	5'-4"	45	15'-0"	30'-0"
9	3'-0"	6'-0"	46	15'-4"	30'-8"
10	3'-4"	6'-8"	47	15'-8"	31'-4"
11	3'-8"	7'-4"	48	16'-0"	32'-0"
12	4'-0"	8'-0"	49	16'-4"	32'-8"
13	4'-4"	8'-8"	50	16'-8"	33'-4"
14	4'-8"	9'-4"	51	17'-0"	34'-0"
15	5'-0"	10'-0"	52	17'-4"	34'-8"
16	5'-4"	10'-8"	53	17'-8"	35'-4"
17	5'-8"	11'-4"	54	18'-0"	36'-0"
18	6'-0"	12'-0"	55	18'-4"	36'-8"
19	6'-4"	12'-8"	56	18'-8"	37'-4"
20	6'-8"	13'-4"	57	19'-0"	38'-0"
21	7'-0"	14'-0"	58	19'-4"	38'-8"
22	7'-4"	14'-8"	59	19'-8"	39'-4"
23	7'-8"	15'-4"	60	20'-0"	40'-0"
24	8'-0"	16'-0"	61	20'-4"	40'-8"
25	8'-4"	16'-8"	62	20'-8"	41'-4"
26	8'-8"	17'-4"	63	21'-0"	42'-0"
27	9'-0"	18'-0"	64	21'-4"	42'-8"
28	9'-4"	18'-8"	65	21'-8"	43'-4"
29	9'-8"	19'-4"	66	22'-0"	44'-0"
30	10'-0"	20'-0"	67	22'-4"	44'-8"
31	10'-4"	20'-8"	68	22'-8"	45'-4"
32	10'-8"	21'-4"	69	23'-0"	46'-0"
33	11'-0"	22'-0"	70	23'-4"	46'-8"
34	11'-4"	22'-8"	71	23'-8"	47'-4"
35	11'-8"	23'-4"	72	24'-0"	48'-0"
36	12'-0"	24'-0"	73	24'-4"	48'-8"
37	12'-4"	24'-8"	74	24'-8"	49'-4"

___ 8. <u>Stone</u>
    ___ *a.* Type unit
        ___ (1) *Ashlar:* Best for strength and stability; is square-cut on level beds. Joints of ½″ to ¾″.
        ___ (2) *Squared stone* (coursed rubble): Next-best for strength and stability; is fitted less carefully than ashlar, but more carefully than rubble.
        ___ (3) *Rubble:* Built with a minimum of dressing, with joints unevenly coursed, or in a completely irregular pattern. Stones are lapped for bond and many stones extend through wall (when full-width wall) to bond it transversely. If built carefully, with all interstices completely filled with good cement mortar, has ample durability for ordinary structures.
    ___ *b.* Typical materials
        ___ (1) Limestone
        ___ (2) Sandstone
        ___ (3) Quartzite
        ___ (4) Granite
    ___ *c.* Wall types
        ___ (1) Full width
        ___ (2) Solid veneer (metal ties to structural wall)
        ___ (3) Thin veneer (set against mortar bed against structural wall)
    ___ *d.* Pattern types (see p. 237)

NOTES

NOTES

___ B. MASONRY MEMBERS (SIZES AND COSTS)

See p. 132 for span-to-depth ratios.

___ 1. <u>Concrete Block (CMU)</u>
  ___ *a.* CMU columns
    See p. 133 for general rule
    of thumb. Max. ht. to
    thickness ratio = *20*. Min.
    size = 12″ × 12″.
  ___ *b.* CMU walls
    ___ (1) Nominal min.
      thickness: 6″
    ___ (2) Ratio of unsup-
      ported length or
      ht. to thickness: *25
      to 35*

Costs: CMU (Reg. wt., gray, running bond, typ. reinf'g. and grout)

4″ walls:	**$5.00/SF**	**(Typical 25 to 30%M and 75 to**
6″ walls:	**$5.50/SF**	**70%L)**
8″ walls:	**$6.50/SF**	**(Variations for special block, such as**
12″ walls:	**$8.25/SF**	**glazed, decorative, screen, etc. + 15%**
		to 150%)

Deduct 30 to 40% for residential work.

___ 2. <u>Brick Masonry</u>
  ___ *a.* <u>Columns</u>
    ___ (1) See p. 133 for general
      rule of thumb.
    ___ (2) Usual min. dimension
      of 12″ (sometimes 8″).
    ___ (3) Maximum height = 20 ×
      least dimensions.
    ___ (4) If unreinforced = 10 × least dimensions.

Costs: 12″ × 12″, standard brick: $30.00/VLF (20%M and 80%L).

  ___ *b.* <u>Pilasters</u>
    ___ (1) Usually consid-
      ered when wall
      is 20′ high or
      more.

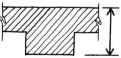

___ (2) Typically needed under beams or heavy trusses.

___ (3) Depth of pilaster: ¹⁄₁₂ of wall height.

___ *c.* <u>Brick walls</u>

    ___ (1) Maximum ratio of unsupported length or height to thickness: 20.

    ___ (2) Reinforced bearing walls: Nominal minimum thickness: 6″.

    ___ (3) Unreinforced bearing wall:
1 story: 6″ min. thickness
2 stories: 12″ thick
+ 35′: 12″ upper 35′ and + 4″ added to each 35′ below

    ___ (4) Cavity walls: Typical nominal minimum dimensions of 10″ (including 2″ air space).

Costs: Standard brick, running bond w/reinforcing (25%M & 75%L) (Variations of +5%, −20%):

4″, single wythe, veneer:	$9.50/SF
8″, double wythe, cavity-filled:	$20.00/SF
12″, triple wythe, cavity-filled:	$30.00/SF

For other bonds, add 15% to 30%

___ *d.* <u>Brick arches</u>

    ___ (1) Minor arches:

        ___ (*a*) Span: Less than 6′

        ___ (*b*) Configuration: All

        ___ (*c*) Load: Less than 1000 PLF

        ___ (*d*) Span-to-depth: *0.15 max.*

    ___ (2) Major arches:

        ___ (*a*) Span: Over 6′

        ___ (*b*) Configuration: Semicircular & parabolic

        ___ (*c*) Load: Over 1000 PLF

        ___ (*d*) Span-to-depth: greater than *0.15*

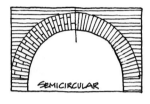

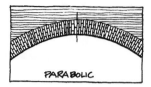

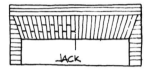

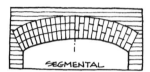

___ 3. <u>Stone Masonry</u>
    ___ *a.*   <u>Bearing walls</u>
        ___ (1) Nominal minimum thick-
             ness = 16″.
        ___ (2) Maximum ratio of unsup-
             ported length or height to
             thickness = 14.
    ___ *b.*   <u>Nonbearing walls</u>
        ___ (1) Nominal minimum thick-
             ness = 16″, veneer = 1½″
             cut stone, 4″ rough.
        ___ (2) Maximum ratio of unsupported length or
             height to thickness = 18.

Costs: 4″ veneer (most common): \$12.00 to \$14.50/SF (40%M and 60%L) (Variation: + 50%)
18″ rough stone wall (dry): \$40/CF (40% and 60%L)

RANDOM RUBBLE

COURSE RUBBLE

MOSAIC

COURSED ASHLER

RANDOM ASHLER

3 HT. RANDOM ASHLER

EXAMPLE:

PROBLEM: A WALL OF BRICK VENEER AND C.M.U. BACKUP IS TO BE 6'-4" HIGH. FIGURE THE COURSING FOR BOTH BRICK VENEER AND CONCRETE BLOCK.

SOLUTION:

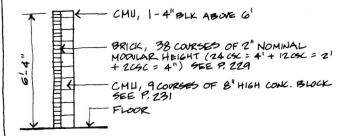

CMU, 1-4" BLK ABOVE 6'

BRICK, 38 COURSES OF 2" NOMINAL MODULAR HEIGHT (24 CSC = 4' + 12 CSC = 2' + 2 CSC = 4") SEE P. 229

CMU, 9 COURSES OF 8" HIGH CONC. BLOCK SEE P. 231

FLOOR

6'-4"

NOTES

NOTES

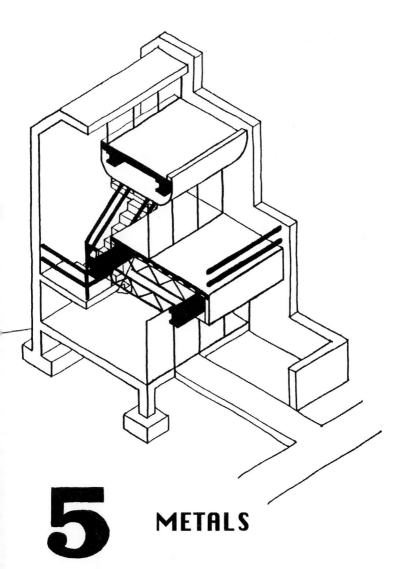

5 METALS

NOTES

___ A. METAL MATERIALS

$\textcircled{4}$ $\textcircled{19}$ $\textcircled{32}$ $\textcircled{38}$ $\textcircled{45}$

___ 1. General
    ___ *a.* Ferrous metals (contains iron)
        ___ (1) Iron: Soft, easily worked, oxidizes rapidly, susceptible to acid.
        ___ (2) Cast iron: Brittle, corrosion-resistant, high-compressive strength. Used for gratings, stairs, etc.
        ___ (3) Malleable iron: Same as above, but better workability.
        ___ (4) Wrought iron: Soft, corrosion- and fatigue-resistant, machinable. Used for railings, grilles, screws, and ornamental items.
        ___ (5) Steel: Iron with carbon. Strongest metal. Used for structural purposes. See p. 244.
        ___ (6) Stainless steel: An alloy for max. corrosion resistance. Used for flashing, handrails, hardware, connections, and equipment.
    ___ *b.* Nonferrous metals (not containing iron)
        ___ (1) Aluminum: Soft, ductile, high corrosion resistance, low strength.
        ___ (2) Lead: Dense, workable, toxic, corrosion-resistant. Improved with alloys for hardness and strength. Used as waterproofing, sound isolation, and radiation shielding.
        ___ (3) Zinc: Corrosion-resistant, brittle, low-strength. Used in "galvanizing" of other metals for corrosion resistance for roofing, flashing, hardware, connections, etc.
        ___ (4) Chromium and nickel: Used as alloy for corrosion-resistant bright "plating."
        ___ (5) Monel: High corrosion resistance. Used for fasteners and anchors.
        ___ (6) Copper: Resistant to corrosion, impact, and fatigue. Ductile. Used for wiring, roofing, flashing, and piping.
        ___ (7) Bronze: An alloy for "plating."
        ___ (8) Brass: Copper with zinc. Used for hardware, handrails, grilles, etc.
___ 2. Corrosion to Metals
    ___ *a.* Galvanic action, or corrosion, occurs between dissimilar metals or metals and other metals when sufficient moisture is present to carry an electric

current. The farther apart two metals are on the following list, the greater the corrosion of the more susceptible one:

> Anodic (+): Most susceptible to corrosion
> > Magnesium
> > Zinc
> > Aluminum
> > Cadmium
> > Iron/steel
> > Stainless steel (active)
> > Soft solders
> > Tin
> > Lead
> > Nickel
> > Brass
> > Bronzes
> > Nickel-copper alloys
> > Copper
> > Stainless steel (passive)
> > Silver solder
>
> Cathodic (−): Least susceptible to corrosion

___ *b.* Metals deteriorate also when in contact with chemically active materials, particularly when water is present. Examples include aluminum in contact with concrete or mortar, and steel in contact with treated wood.

___ 3. <u>Gauges:</u> See pp. 245 and 246.

___ 4. <u>Structural Steel</u>

___ *a.* General: The most commonly used strength grade of steel is 36,000 psi yield strength (A-36). For heavily loaded members such as columns, girders, or trusses—where buckling, lateral stability, deflection, or vibration does not control member selection—higher-yield strength steels may be economically used. A 50,000 psi yield strength is most frequently used among high-strength, low-alloy steels.

High-strength, low-alloy steels are available in several grades and some possess corrosion resistance to such a degree that they are classified as "weathering steel."

Concrete and masonry reinforcing steel (rebar) are 40,000 psi and 60,000 psi. Wire mesh is 60 to 70 ksi.

METAL GAUGES

| GAUGE NO. | GRAPHIC SIZES | U.S. STD. REVISED | | GRAPHIC SIZES |
		DECIMAL	FRACTION	
000	■	.3750"	3/8"	●
00	■	.3437"	11/32"	●
0	■	.3125"	5/16"	●
I.	■	.2812"	9/32"	●
2.	■	.2656"	17/64"	●
3.	■	.2391"	15/64"	●
4.	■	.2242"	7/32°	●
5.	■	.2092"	13/64"	●
6.	■	.1943"	3/18"	●

7	■	.1793"	¹¹/₆₄" +	●
8	■	.1644"	¹¹/₆₄" −	●
9	■	.1495"	⁶/₃₂" −	●
10	■	.1345"	⁹/₆₄" −	●
11	■	.1196"	¹/₈" −	●
12	■	.1046"	⁷/₆₄" −	●
13	■	.0897"	³/₃₂" −	●
14	■	.0747"	⁵/₆₄" −	●
15	■	.0673"	¹/₁₆" +	●
16	■	.0598"	¹/₁₆" −	●
17	■	.0538"	³/₆₄" +	●
18	■	.0478"	³/₆₄" +	●
19	■	.0418"	³/₆₄" −	●
20	■	.0359"	¹/₃₂" +	●
21	■	.0329"	¹/₃₂" +	●
22	■	.0299"	¹/₃₂" −	●
23	▪	.0269"	¹/₃₂" −	●
24	■	.0239"	¹/₃₂" −	●
25	•	.0209"	¹/₆₄" +	●
26	•	.0179"	¹/₆₄" +	●
27	•	.0164"	¹/₆₄" +	•
28	•	.0149"	¹/₆₄" −	•
29	•	.0135"	¹/₆₄" −	•
30	•	.0120"	¹/₆₄" −	•

AVERAGE PHYSICAL PROPERTIES

MATERIAL	ELASTIC LIMIT (psi)		ULTIMATE STRENGTH (psi)			ALLOW. WORKING UNIT STRESS (psi)				MODULUS OF ELASTICITY (psi)	WT. (#/C.F.)
	TEN-SION	COM-PRESSION	TEN-SION	COM-PRESSION	SHEAR	TEN-SION	COM-PRESSION	SHEAR	EXTREME FIBER BENDING		
CAST IRON			25000	75000	20000		9000			12 000 000	450
WROUGHT IRON	25000	25000	48 000	48 000	40000	12000	12000	8000	12000	28 000 000	485
STEEL A-36	36000	36000	70 000	70 000	55 000	22000	20000	14500	24000	29 000 000	490
ALUM. ALLOY 6061-T6	35000		38 000			30000	15000			12000	10 000 000	170

___ b. Economy: The weight of structural steel per SF of floor area increases with bay size, as does the depth of the structure. Cost of steel may not rise as rapidly as weight, if savings can be realized by reducing the number of pieces to be fabricated and erected. Improved space utilization afforded by larger bay sizes is offset by increases in wall area and building volume resulting from increased structure depth.

Steel frame economy can be improved by incorporating as many of the following cost-reducing factors into the structure layout and design as architectural requirements permit.

___ (1) Keep columns in line in both directions and avoid offsets or omission of columns.

___ (2) Design for maximum repetition of member sizes within each level and from floor to floor.

___ (3) Reduce the number of beams and girders per level to reduce fabrication and erection time and cost.

___ (4) Maximize the use of simple beam connections by bracing the structure at a limited number of moment-resisting bents or by the most efficient method, cross-bracing.

___ (5) Utilize high-strength steels for columns and floor members where studies indicate that cost can be reduced while meeting other design parameters.

___ (6) Use composite design, but consider effect of in-slab electric raceways or other discontinuities.

___ (7) Consider open-web steel joists, especially for large roofs of one-story structures, and for floor framing in many applications.

The weight of steel for roofs or lightly loaded floors is generally least when long beams and short girders are used. For heavier loadings, long girders and short filler beams should result in less steel weight. The most economical framing type (composite; noncomposite, continuous simple spans, etc.) and arrangement must be determined for each structure, considering such factors as structure depth, building volume, wall area, mechanical system requirements, deflection or vibration limitations, wind or seismic load interaction between floor system, and columns or shear walls.

___ *c. Composite construction* combines two different materials or two different grades of a material to form a structural member that utilizes the most desirable properties of each materials.

   ___ (1) Composite systems currently used in building construction include:
      ___ (*a*) Concrete-topped composite steel decks
      ___ (*b*) Steel beams acting compositely with concrete slabs
      ___ (*c*) Steel columns encased by or filled with concrete
      ___ (*d*) Open-web joists of wood and steel or joists with plywood webs and wood chords
      ___ (*e*) Trusses combining wood and steel
      ___ (*f*) Hybrid girders utilizing steel of different strengths
      ___ (*g*) Cast-in-place concrete slabs on precast concrete joists or beams

   ___ (2) To make two different materials act compositely as one unit, they must be joined at their interface by one or a combination of these means:
      ___ (*a*) Chemical bonding (concrete)
      ___ (*b*) Gluing (plywood, glulam)
      ___ (*c*) Welding (steel, aluminum)
      ___ (*d*) Screws (sheet metal, wood)
      ___ (*e*) Bolts (steel, wood)
      ___ (*f*) Shear studs (steel to concrete)

___ (g) Keys or embossments (steel deck to concrete, concrete to concrete)
___ (h) Dowels (concrete to concrete)
___ (i) Friction (positive clamping force must be present)

Individual elements of the composite unit must be securely fastened to prevent slippage with respect to one another.

___ d. Shapes and designations

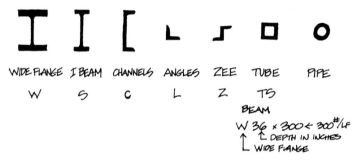

WIDE FLANGE	I BEAM	CHANNELS	ANGLES	ZEE	TUBE	PIPE
W	S	C	L	Z	TS	

BEAM
W 36 × 300 ← 300 #/LF
↑ ↑ DEPTH IN INCHES
L WIDE FLANGE

___ e. Open-web steel joists
___ (1) Types

TYPE	DES-IGNATION	DEPTHS	SPANS	BEARINGS			
				MASONRY	CONC.	STEEL	DEPTH
ECONOMY	K SERIES	8" TO 30"	8' - 60'	4-6"	4"	2½"	2½"
LONG SPAN	LH SERIES	18" TO 48"	25' - 96'	6-12"	6-9"	4"	5"
DEEP LONG SPAN	DLH SERIES	52" TO 72"	89' - 144'				

___ (2) Joist designation

25 LH 10 ← CHORD
↑ ↑↑ TYPE OF STEEL
     LONG SPAN
   NOMINAL DEPTH

___ (3) Use K Series for roofs, short spans, or light loads.

___ (4) Use LH Series for floors, longer spans, or heavier loads. Use DHL Series for longer spans.

___ (5) Horizontal or diagonal bridging is required to prevent lateral movement of top and bottom chords, usually from 10 to 15 oc.

___ (6) Overhangs can be created by extending top chords (up to 5'6").

___ *f.* Steel decking

___ (1) Thickness

Total w/conc.	Deck	Span
2½" to 5"	1½"	2' to 6'
4" to 6"	1½"	6' to 12'
5½" to 7½"	3"	9' to 16'

___ (2) Gauges: 16, 18, 20, 22

___ (3) For shorter spans, usually 4', plain deck with rigid insulation on top is often used. For this type:

___ (*a*) Small openings up to 6" sq. may be cut without reinforcing. Larger openings require steel framing.

___ (*b*) Roof-mounted equipment cannot be placed directly on deck, but must be supported on structure below.

___ *g.* Structural connections

___ (1) Rivets (hardly used anymore)

___ (2) Bolts

___ (3) Welds

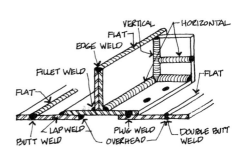

BASIC WELD SYMBOLS									
BEAD	FILLET	PLUG OR SLOT	SQUARE	V	BEVEL	U	J	FLARE V	FLARE BEVEL
⌒	△	▽	‖	∨	⋁	Y	Ϸ	⋎	⋏

SUPPLEMENTARY WELD SYMBOLS				
	WELD ALL AROUND	FIELD WELD	CONTOUR	
			FLUSH	CONVEX
	○	●	—	⌒

STANDARD LOCATION OF ELEMENTS OF WELD SYMBOL

FINISH SYMBOL

CONTOUR SYMBOL

ROOT OPENING, DEPTH OF FILLING FOR PLUG AND SLOT WELDS

SIZE IN INCHES

REFERENCE LINE

SPECIFICATION, PROCESS OR OTHER REFERENCE

TAIL (MAY BE OMITTED WHEN REFERENCE NOT USED)

BASIC WELD SYMBOL OR DETAIL REFERENCE

GROOVE ANGLE OR INCLUDED ANGLE OF COUNTERSINK FOR PLUG WELDS

LENGTH OF WELD IN INCHES

PITCH (C. TO C. SPACING OF WELDS IN INCHES)

WELD ALL AROUND SYMBOL

FIELD WELD SYMBOL

ARROW CONNECTING REFERENCE LINE TO ARROW SIDE OF JOINT (ALSO POINTS TO GROOVED MEMBER IN BEVEL & J GROOVED JOINTS)

____ 5. Light Metal Framing

    ____ *a.* Joists

        ____ (1) Makes an economical floor system for light loading and spans up to 32′

        ____ (2) Depths: 6″, 8″, 9″, 10″, 12″

        ____ (3) Spacings: 16″, 24″, 48″ oc

        ____ (4) Gauges: 12 through 18 (light = 20–25 GA; structural = 18–12 GA)

        ____ (5) Bridging, usually 5′ to 8′ oc

    ____ *b.* Studs

        ____ (1) Sizes

            ____ (*a*) Widths: ¾″, 1″, 1⅜″, 1⅝″, 2″

            ____ (*b*) Depths: 2½″, 3⅝″, 4″, 6″, 8″

___ (2) Gauges: 14, 15, 16, 18, 20
___ (3) Spacings: 12″, 16″, 24″ oc
___ 6. <u>Miscellaneous Metals</u>
   ___ *a.* Nails
      ___ (1) Size: Penny designated as d. A 2-penny nail
             is 1″ long. Each additional "penny" adds ¼″
             length, to:
                   12-penny = 3¼″ long
                   16-penny = 3½″
                   20-penny = 4″
                   30-penny = 4½″
                   40-penny = 5″
                   50-penny = 5½″
                   60-penny = 6″
             Rule of thumb: Use nail with length 3×
             thickness of board being secured.
      ___ (2) Types

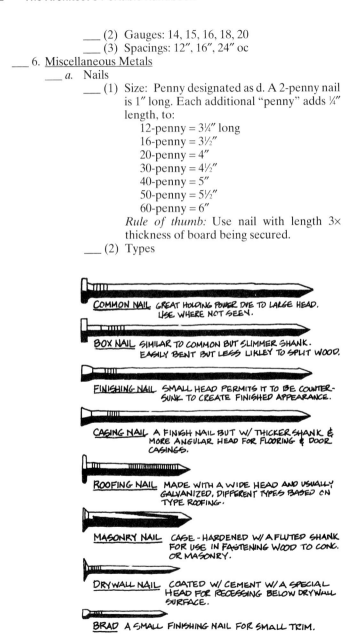

COMMON NAIL GREAT HOLDING POWER DUE TO LARGE HEAD. USE WHERE NOT SEEN.

BOX NAIL SIMILAR TO COMMON BUT SLIMMER SHANK. EASILY BENT BUT LESS LIKLEY TO SPLIT WOOD.

FINISHING NAIL SMALL HEAD PERMITS IT TO BE COUNTERSUNK TO CREATE FINISHED APPEARANCE.

CASING NAIL A FINISH NAIL BUT W/ THICKER SHANK & MORE ANGULAR HEAD FOR FLOORING & DOOR CASINGS.

ROOFING NAIL MADE WITH A WIDE HEAD AND USUALLY GALVANIZED, DIFFERENT TYPES BASED ON TYPE ROOFING.

MASONRY NAIL CASE-HARDENED W/ A FLUTED SHANK FOR USE IN FASTENING WOOD TO CONC. OR MASONRY.

DRYWALL NAIL COATED W/ CEMENT W/ A SPECIAL HEAD FOR RECESSING BELOW DRYWALL SURFACE.

BRAD A SMALL FINISHING NAIL FOR SMALL TRIM.

___ *b.* Screws and bolts

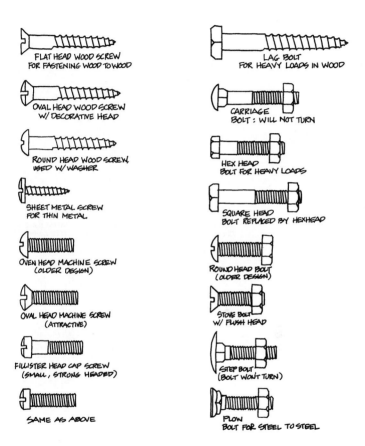

FLAT HEAD WOOD SCREW
FOR FASTENING WOOD TO WOOD

OVAL HEAD WOOD SCREW
W/ DECORATIVE HEAD

ROUND HEAD WOOD SCREW,
USED W/ WASHER

SHEET METAL SCREW
FOR THIN METAL

OVEN HEAD MACHINE SCREW
(OLDER DESIGN)

OVAL HEAD MACHINE SCREW
(ATTRACTIVE)

FILLISTER HEAD CAP SCREW
(SMALL, STRONG HEADED)

SAME AS ABOVE

LAG BOLT
FOR HEAVY LOADS IN WOOD

CARRIAGE
BOLT : WILL NOT TURN

HEX HEAD
BOLT FOR HEAVY LOADS

SQUARE HEAD
BOLT REPLACED BY HEXHEAD

ROUND HEAD BOLT
(OLDER DESIGN)

STOVE BOLT
W/ FLUSH HEAD

STEP BOLT
(BOLT WON'T TURN)

PLOW
BOLT FOR STEEL TO STEEL

___ *c.*   Timber connectors (see p. 268 for **costs**)

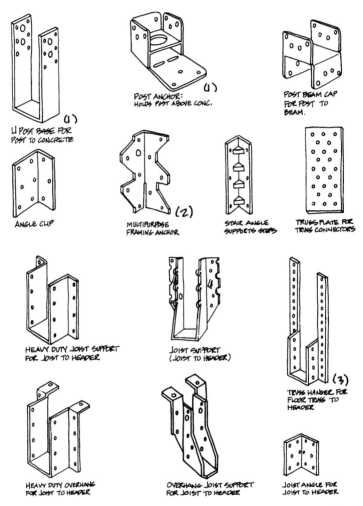

U POST BASE FOR
POST TO CONCRETE (1)

POST ANCHOR: (1)
HOLDS POST ABOVE CONC.

POST BEAM CAP
FOR POST TO
BEAM.

ANGLE CLIP

MULTIPURPOSE (2)
FRAMING ANCHOR

STAIR ANGLE
SUPPORTS STEPS

TRUSS PLATE FOR
TRUSS CONNECTORS

HEAVY DUTY JOIST SUPPORT
FOR JOIST TO HEADER

JOIST SUPPORT
(JOIST TO HEADER)

TRUSS HANGER FOR (3)
FLOOR TRUSS TO
HEADER

HEAVY DUTY OVERHANG
FOR JOIST TO HEADER

OVERHANG JOIST SUPPORT
FOR JOIST TO HEADER

JOIST ANGLE FOR
JOIST TO HEADER

Notes: Numbers in parentheses below, with corresponding uses, refer to connectors illustrated above.
  (1) Individual post base supports in concrete foundations.
  (2) Truss or joist to plate and stud to plate, every other member (every member in high-wind regions).
  (3) For hanging a beam from a truss or deep beam, above.

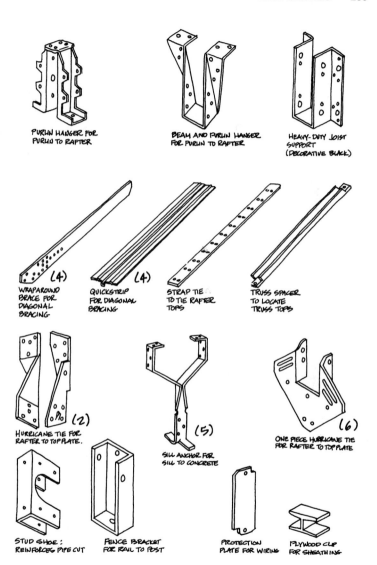

PURLIN HANGER FOR
PURLIN TO RAFTER

BEAM AND PURLIN HANGER
FOR PURLIN TO RAFTER

HEAVY-DUTY JOIST
SUPPORT
(DECORATIVE BLACK)

WRAPAROUND
BRACE FOR
DIAGONAL
BRACING (4)

QUICKSTRIP
FOR DIAGONAL
BRACING (4)

STRAP TIE
TO TIE RAFTER
TOPS

TRUSS SPACER
TO LOCATE
TRUSS TOPS

HURRICANE TIE FOR
RAFTER TO TOP PLATE. (2)

SILL ANCHOR FOR
SILL TO CONCRETE (5)

ONE PIECE HURRICANE TIE
FOR RAFTER TO TOP PLATE (6)

STUD SHOE:
REINFORCES PIPE CUT

FENCE BRACKET
FOR RAIL TO POST

PROTECTION
PLATE FOR WIRING

PLYWOOD CLIP
FOR SHEATHING

(4) High lateral wall braces used mainly for erection bracing at each
    corner.
(5) To hold sill in place at each corner and every 4' to 6' o.c.
(6) Can be used for pitched joist to wall or plate.

NOTES

__ B. STEEL MEMBERS (SIZE AND COSTS)

(1) (10) (23) (26)

See p. 132 for span-to-depth ratios.

__ 1. **General Costs:** **Steel framing for 1-story building:**
20′ × 20′ bays: $9.00/SF
For each added 10′ of bay, up to 40′: +30%
For 2- to 6-story: +$1.00/SF

__ 2. Light Steel Construction
__ a. Stud walls
__ (1) Widths of 1⅝″, 2½″, 3⅝″, 4″, and 6″.
__ (2) Maximum heights range from 9′ to 16′.
__ (3) Available in load-bearing (LB), 14 GA to 20 GA, and non-load-bearing (NLB), 26 GA to 14 GA.

Costs: 3⅝″ studs, LB, 16″ oc: $2.80 /SF wall area (20%M and 80%L)

Deduct or add 10% for each increment of size.
For 24″ oc: −15%
For 12″ oc: +70%
For NLB (25 GA): −30%

__ b. Joists
__ (1) Span 15′ to 30′.
__ (2) See p. 132 for rule of thumb on span-to-depth ratio.
__ (3) Typical savings of 16″ to 24″ oc.

Costs: 8″ deep, 16″ oc, 40 psf, 15′ span: $3.20/SF floor

Add 15% for each added 5′ span up to 25′.
For 30′ span, add 75%.
24″ oc, about same cost.

__ c. Steel pipe and tube columns
__ (1) Minimum pipe diameter: 3½″. Minimum tube size: 3″ sq.
__ (2) In general, assuming normal load conditions, the minimum diameter in inches can be estimated by multiplying the height in feet by *0.33*.

Costs: 3″ dia. or 3″ sq., 10′ unsupported height: $15/LF (55%M and 45%L). Cost can go up to double as load, height, and size (up to 8″) increase.

257

___ 3. Heavy Steel Construction
    ___ *a.* Steel decking
        ___ (1) For roofs, depths range from 1½″ to 3″, for spans of 6′ to 18′.
        ___ (2) For floors, depths range from 1½″ to 3″ for spans of 7′ to 12′.
        ___ (3) For cellular steel floors:
                Thickness: 4″ to 7½″
                Spans: 8′ to 16′
        ___ (4) Gauges range from 24 to 18 in increments of 2.

Costs: 1½″, 22 GA, galvanized, non-composite roof deck: $1.60/SF (60%M and 40%L). Add $0.30 for each jump in heavier gauge to 16 GA.

1½″, 18 GA, galvanized, cellular floor deck: $5.00/SF (85%M and 15%L). $6.00 for 3″. $8.85 for 4½″.

4″ concrete on 1½″, 22 GA deck, 6′ span, 125 psf: $3.10/SF (45%M and 55%L). Add 4% for each added foot in span up to 10′.

    ___ *b.* Open-web joists
        ___ (1) Span range: 8′ to 48′, up to 145′ for long-span joist.
        ___ (2) Spacings: 4′ to 8′ at floors, 8′ at roofs.
        ___ (3) Manufactured in 2″ increments from 8″ to 30″ deep and 18″ to 72″ for long-span type.
        ___ (4) Range of span-to-depth ratios: 19 to 24.
        ___ (5) Designations: Economy K Series, long-span LH Series, and deep, long-span DLH Series.

Costs: K Series: $7.00 to $10.50/LF (50%M and 50%L)
      LH Series: $9.25 to $21.50/LF
      DLH Series: $14.75 to $27.50/LF

    ___ *c.* Steel beams
        ___ (1) Usual spans of 10′ to 60′.
        ___ (2) Typical bay sizes of 30′ to 40′.
        ___ (3) For roof beams, depth of beam in inches can be estimated at 0.5 times the span in feet.
        ___ (4) For floor beams, depth of beam in inches

can be estimated at *0.6* times the span in feet.

___ (5) Steel plate girders: Spans range from 60′ to 100′, with approximate span-to-depth ratio of 14.

Typical costs for steel beams: *$1600* to *$2000* per ton (50% M and 50% L). For small projects use larger costs. For large projects (over 4 stories) use smaller costs.

Use the following table to help estimate weight from depth estimated in item 3 or 4, above.

Beam depth (″)	Roof (lb/LF)	Floor (lb/LF)
8	18	24
10	22	26
12	26	30
14	30	38
16	36	45
18	40	50
21	55	62
24	62	76
27	84	94

Table based on minimum roof live load of 20 psf. Add 15–25% more weight for snow, etc. For girders, add 25%.

___ *d.* Steel columns
  ___ (1) See p. 133 for span-to-depth ratio.
  ___ (2) In general, the 6 and 8 W columns carry most lightweight, low-rise construction. The 10, 12, and 14 W columns have capacities in various weights, to handle a large variation of extremes in lengths and loads.
  ___ (3) Maximum stock size in length is 40′. Column length in high-rise is 25′.
  ___ (4) Safe loads for normal single-story heights can be related to the weights of steel sections. For lightweight sections, the safe load in kips equals approximately 4 times the weight of the section per foot. For heavy-

weight sections the safe load equals approximately 5 times the weight of the steel section per foot.

Costs: See floor beams, above, and increase weight by 30%.

___ *e.* Steel trusses
___ (1) Flat or arched steel trusses
Spans: 30′ to 220′
Span-to-depth ratio: 10 to 12
Spacings: 12′ to 20′.
___ (2) Triangular steel trusses
Spans: 30′ to 150′
Span-to-depth ratios: 2.5 to 4.5
Spacings: 12′ to 20′.

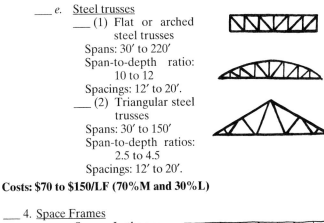

Costs: $70 to $150/LF (70%M and 30%L)

___ 4. Space Frames
___ *a.* Spans: In theory are unlimited, with cantilevers of 15% to 30% of span.
___ *b.* Span-to-depth ratios:
Roof
Column support: *18*
Edge support: *20* to *25*
Floor: *16* to *20*
___ *c.* Modules: Depth to width of 1:3 to 7:10.

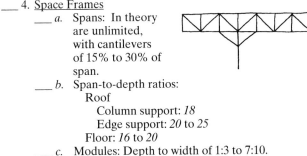

Costs: $25/SF (65%M and 35%L)

EXAMPLE:

PROBLEM:

SKETCH UP A ROUGH DESIGN & ESTIMATE OF COSTS FOR A 36' x 36' BAY FLOOR SYSTEM FOR STEEL CONSTRUCTION.

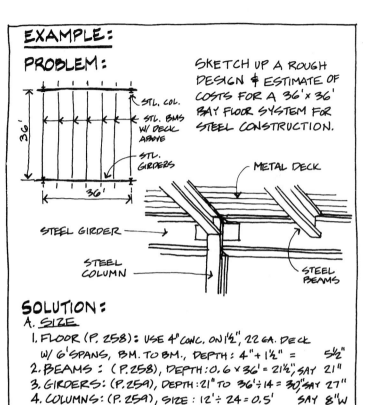

STL. COL.

STL. BMS W/ DECK ABOVE

STL. GIRDERS

36'

36'

METAL DECK

STEEL GIRDER

STEEL COLUMN

STEEL BEAMS

SOLUTION:

A. SIZE

1. FLOOR (P. 258): USE 4" CONC. ON 1½", 22 GA. DECK
   W/ 6' SPANS, BM. TO BM., DEPTH: 4" + 1½" =   5½"
2. BEAMS: (P. 258), DEPTH: 0.6 × 36' = 21½", SAY 21"
3. GIRDERS: (P. 259), DEPTH: 21" TO 36' ÷ 14 = 30", SAY 27"
4. COLUMNS: (P. 259), SIZE: 12' ÷ 24 = 0.5'   SAY 8"W

B. COSTS

1. FLOOR: 4" CONC. ON 1½" MET. DECK W/ 6' SPAN ≑ $3^{10}
2. BEAMS:
   21" = 62$^\#$/LF × 7 EA × 36' SPAN = 15624$^\#$
   15624$^\#$ ÷ 2000$^\#$/TON × $2000/TON ÷ 36' × 36' ≑ $12^{05}
3. GIRDERS:
   27" = 84$^\#$ × 1.25 (P. 259) × 4 EA × 36' =
   15120$^\#$ ÷ 2000$^\#$/TON × $2000/TON ÷ 36' × 36' ≑ $11^{65}
4. COLUMNS:
   8" = 24$^\#$/LF × 1.3 (P. 260) × 4 EA × 12' =
   1498$^\#$ ÷ 2000$^\#$/TON × $2000/TON ÷ 36' × 36' ≑ $1^{15}
                                                        $27^{95}/SF

NOTES

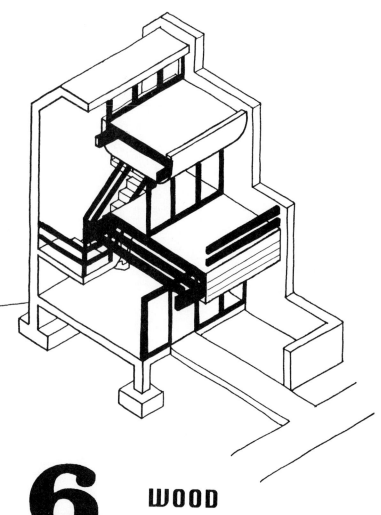

6 WOOD

NOTES

__ A. WOOD MATERIALS

$\quad$ (4) (11) (12) (19) (31) (38) (43) (45)

___ 1. <u>General</u> (*Note:* See p. 274 for species table. See pp. 252–255 for nails and connectors.)

$\quad$ ___ *a.* *Two general types of wood* are used in buildings:

$\qquad$ ___ (1) Softwood (from evergreen trees) for general construction

$\qquad$ ___ (2) Hardwood (from deciduous trees) for furnishings and finishes

$\quad$ ___ *b.* *Moisture and shrinkage:* The amount of water in wood is expressed as a percentage of its oven-dry (dry as possible) weight. As wood dries, it first loses moisture from within the cells without shrinking; after reaching the fiber saturation point (dry cell), further drying results in shrinkage. Eventually wood comes to dynamic equilibrium with the relative humidity of the surrounding air. Interior wood typically shrinks in winter and swells in summer. Average equilibrium moisture content ranges from 6% to 11%, but wood is considered dry enough for use at 12% to 15%. The loss of moisture during seasoning causes wood to become harder, stronger, stiffer, and lighter in weight. Wood is most decay-resistant when moisture content is under 20%.

___ 2. <u>Lumber</u>

$\quad$ ___ *a.* *Sizes*

$\qquad$ ___ (1) Sectional

Nominal sizes	To get actual sizes
2×'s up to 8×'s	deduct ½″
8×'s and larger	deduct ¾″

$\qquad$ ___ (2) Lengths

$\qquad\qquad$ ___ (*a*) Softwoods: cut to lengths of 6′ to 24′, in 2′ increments

$\qquad\qquad$ ___ (*b*) Hardwoods: cut to 1′-long increments

$\quad$ ___ *b.* *Economy:* best achieved when layouts are within a 2′- or 4′-module, with subdivisions of 4″, 16″, 24″, and 48″

$\quad$ ___ *c.* *Defects*

DEFECT	END VIEW	LONG VIEW
BOW		

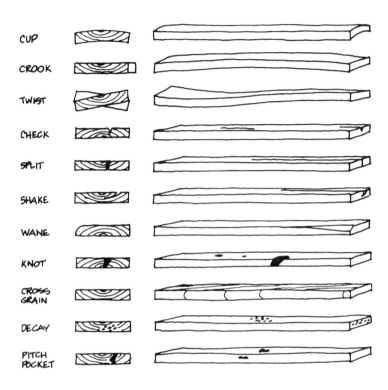

CUP

CROOK

TWIST

CHECK

SPLIT

SHAKE

WANE

KNOT

CROSS GRAIN

DECAY

PITCH POCKET

___ *d. Grades*
   ___ (1) *Factory or shop-type lumber:* used primarily
            for remanufacturing purposes (doors, win-
            dows, millwork, etc.).
   ___ (2) *Yard-type lumber*
       ___ (*a*) Boards:
               ___ 1″ to 1½″ thick, 2″ and wider
               ___ Graded for appearance only
               ___ Used as siding, subflooring,
                   trim
       ___ (*b*) Dimensioned lumber:
               ___ 2″ to 4″ thick, 2″ and wider
               ___ Graded for strength (stress gr.)
               ___ Used for general construction
               ___ Light framing: 2″ to 4″ wide

___ Joists and planks: 6″ and wider
___ Decking: 4″ and wider (*select and commercial*).
___ (*c*) Timbers:
___ 5″ × 5″ and larger
___ Graded for strength and serviceability
___ May be classified as "structural."
___ (3) *Structural grades* (in descending order, according to stress grade):
___ (*a*) Light framing: *Construction, Standard,* and *Utility*
___ (*b*) Structural light framing (joists, planks): *Select Structural, No. 1, 2, or 3* (some species may also be appearance-graded for exposed work).
___ (*c*) Timber: *Select Structural No. 1.*
Note: Working stress values can be assigned to each of the grades according to the species of wood.
___ (4) *Appearance grades*
___ (*a*) For natural finishes: *Select A or B.*
___ (*b*) For paint finishes: *Select C or D.*
___ (*c*) For general construction and utility: *Common, Nos. 1 thru 5.*
___ *e.* *Pressure-treated wood:* Softwood lumber treated by a process that forces preservative chemicals into the cells of the wood. The result is a material that is immune to decay. This should not generally be used for interiors. Where required:
___ (1) In direct contact with earth
___ (2) Floor joists less than 18″ (or girders less than 12″) from the ground
___ (3) Plates, sills, or sleepers in contact with concrete or masonry
___ (4) Posts exposed to weather or in basements
___ (5) Ends of beams entering concrete or masonry, without ½″ air space
___ (6) Wood located less than 6″ from earth
___ (7) Wood structural members supporting moisture-permeable floors or roofs, exposed to weather, unless separated by an impervious moisture barrier

___ (8) Wood retaining walls or crib walls

___ (9) For exterior construction such as stairs and railings, in geographic areas where experience has demonstrated the need

___ *f. Framing-estimating rules of thumb:* For 16-inch oc stud partitions, estimate one stud for every LF of wall, then add for top and bottom plates. For any type of framing, the quantity of basic framing members (in LF) can be determined based on spacing and surface area (SF):

12 inches oc	1.2 LF/SF
16 inches oc	1.0 LF/SF
24 inches oc	0.8 LF/SF

(Doubled-up members, bands, plates, framed openings, etc., must be added.) Framing accessories, nails, joist hangers, connectors, etc., may be roughly estimated by adding **0.5% to 1.5% of the cost of lumber.** Estimating lumber can be done in *board feet* where one BF is the amount of lumber in a rough-sawed board one foot long, one foot wide, and one inch thick (144 cubic inches) or the equivalent volume in any other shape. As an example, one hundred one-inch by 12-inch dressed boards, 16 feet long, contain:

$$100 \times 1 \times 12 \times 16/12 = 1600 \text{ BF}$$

Use the following table to help estimate board feet:

BF per SF of surface

	12-inch oc	16-inch oc	24-inch oc
2×4s	0.8	0.67	0.54
2×6s	1.2	1.0	0.8
2×8s	1.6	1.33	1.06
2×10s	2.0	1.67	1.34
2×12s	2.4	2.0	1.6

___ 3. <u>Details</u>

WINDOW ROUGH OPENING

INSIDE WALL TO
OUTSIDE WALL.

INSIDE WALL TO
OUTSIDE WALL

WALL TO CL'G.

WALL TO CL'G.

OUTSIDE CORNER

OUTSIDE CORNER

OUTSIDE CORNER

___ 4. <u>Laminated Lumber</u>

   ___ *a.* *Laminated timber* (glu-lam beams): For large structural members, these are preferable to solid timber in terms of finished dressed appearance, weather resistance, controlled moisture content, and size availability. See p. 278.

   ___ *b.* *Sheathing Panels*

      ___ (1) *Composites:* veneer faces bonded to reconstituted wood cores

      ___ (2) *Nonveneered panels:*

         ___ (*a*) Oriented Strand Board (OSB).

         ___ (*b*) Particle Board

___ (3) Plywood
    ___ (*a*) Two main types
        ___ *Exterior grade*
           __ Made with waterproof adhesive
           __ C-grade face or better
           __ For permanent exterior use
        ___ *Interior grade*
           __ Made with water-resistant adhesives
           __ D-grade face or better

THICKNESS
ODD NUMBER OF PLIES.
GRAIN DIRECTION SAME.
FOR FACE & BACK
PLIES (LONGITUDINAL).

    ___ (*b*) Grading according to face veneers
        ___ N All heartwood or all sapwood (for natural finish)
        ___ A Smooth paint grade
        ___ B Solid smooth surface
        ___ C Sheathing grade (lowest grade for exterior use)
        ___ D Lowest grade of interior plywood
    ___ (*c*) Engineered grades:
        ___ *Structural I and II, Standard, and C-C Exterior*
        ___ Span identification index

32/16 ———LEFT HAND NUMBER FOR ROOF SUPPORTS
       ———RIGHT HAND NUMBER FOR FLOOR SUPPORTS

    ___ (*d*) Thickness: 3 ply = ¼, ⅜
                   5 ply = ½, ⅝, ¾
                   7 ply = ⅞, 1, 1⅛, and 1¼ inch
    ___ (*e*) Size sheets: 4′ (or 5′) × 8′ (or 12′)
___ 5. <u>Structural Wood</u>
    ___ *a.* Strengths

AVERAGE PHYSICAL PROPERTIES

MATERIAL	ELASTIC LIMIT (psi)		ULTIMATE STRENGTH (psi)			ALLOWABLE WORKING UNIT STRESS (psi)				MODULUS OF ELAST. (psi)	WT. (LB/ C.F.)
	TEN-SION	COM-PRESS.	TEN-SION	COM-PRESS.	SHEAR	TEN-SION	COM-PRESS.	SHEAR	EXTR. FIBER BEND'G.		
TIMBER PARALLEL TO GRAIN	3000	3000	10000	8000	500	1200	1000	100	1200	1200000	40
PERPENDICULAR TO GRAIN					3000		300	400			

___ *b.* Wood shrinks across grain much more than parallel to grain. Avoid locking nonshrinking materials to wood.

___ *c.* Wood is much weaker across grain than parallel to grain in both tension and compression. A cross-grain angle greater than 1 in 10 seriously weakens the wood in bending.

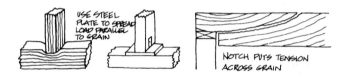

___ *d.* Wood beams deflect or sag more under long-term loads than they do at the beginning. Long-term sag is about 1½ to twice beginning sag.

___ *e.* Wood beams may be weak in resistance to horizontal shear. Since this shear is closest to beam supports, *holes through wood* beams should be avoided near supports. Notches on the ends of joists should not exceed ¼ the depth. Holes bored in joists should not be within 2″ of top or bottom and their diameter should not be greater than ⅓ *depth*. Notches at top and bottom should not exceed ⅙ *depth* and should not be in middle ⅓ *of span*. Holes bored in studs should not be greater than *40%* (60% if studs doubled) and should not be closer to the edge than ⅝″.

___ 6. <u>Finish Wood (Interior Hardwood Plywoods)</u>
    ___ *a. Sizes*
        ___ (1) Thicknesses: ⅛″ to 1″ in 1/16″ and ⅛″ increments
        ___ (2) Widths: 18, 24, 32, 36, 48 inches
        ___ (3) Lengths: 4, 5, 6, 7, 8, 10 feet
    ___ *b. Types*
        ___ (1) Technical: fully waterproof bond
        ___ (2) Type I (exterior): fully waterproof bond/weather- and fungus-resistant

   ___ (3) Type II (interior): water-resistant bond
   ___ (4) Type III (interior): moisture-resistant bond
___ *c. Grades*
   ___ (1) Premium 1: very slight imperfections
   ___ (2) Good 1: suitable for natural finishes
   ___ (3) Sound 2: suitable for painted finishes
   ___ (4) Utility 3: may have open defects
   ___ (5) Backing 4: may have many flaws
___ *d. Grains and patterns*

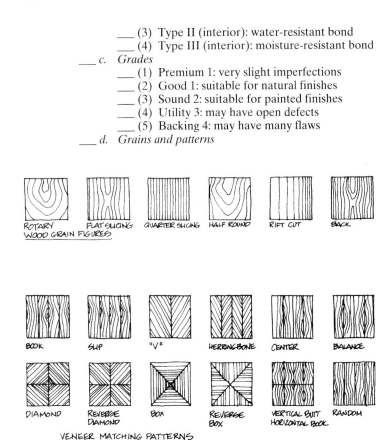

ROTARY   FLAT SLICING   QUARTER SLICING   HALF ROUND   RIFT CUT   BACK
WOOD GRAIN FIGURES

BOOK   SLIP   "V"   HERRINGBONE   CENTER   BALANCE

DIAMOND   REVERSE DIAMOND   BOX   REVERSE BOX   VERTICAL BUTT HORIZONTAL BOOK   RANDOM

VENEER MATCHING PATTERNS

Costs: Prefinished plywood paneling: $2.00 to $6.00/SF
Trim: $2.50 to $5.30/LF
Cabinetry: See p. 371

<u>NOTES</u>

7. SPECIES

● DENOTES COMMON USES AND PROPERTIES
O POSSIBLE OR LIMITED USAGE
□ TREATED WOOD ONLY
✳ FLAME SPREAD RATING
SCALE OF 1 TO 10 WHERE 1 IS LOWEST & 10 HIGHEST

#	SPECIES	COLOR	VENEERS	BOARDS/PLANKS	DIMENSION	STRIPS/BLOCKS	POSTS	FRAMING	SHEATHING	SIDING	FRAMING	PANELING
	SOFTWOODS											
1	CEDAR, WESTERN RED	RED BROWN TO WHITE SAPWOOD	O	●	●		●	●	●	●	●	●
2	CYPRESS, BALD	YELLOWISH BROWN					●	●	●	●	●	●
3	FIR, DOUGLAS (COAST)	REDDISH TAN		●	●	●	●	●	●	●	●	O
4	HEMLOCK, WESTERN	PALE BROWN		●	●		●	●	●	●	●	
5	LARCH, WESTERN	BROWN					●	●	●	●	●	
6	PINE - LEDGEPOLE			●	●		O	●	O	O	O	
7	– PONDEROSA	WHITE TO PALE YELLOW		●	●		O	●	O	●	●	●
8	– RED	LIGHT BROWN		●	●		O	●	O	●	●	●
9	– SOUTHERN	WHITE TO PALE YELLOW		●	●	●	O	●	●	●	●	●
10	– SUGAR	CREAMY WHITE					●	●	●	●	●	●
11	REDWOOD - OLD GROWTH	DEEP RED TO DARK BROWN	O	●	●		●	O	O	●	O	●
12	SPRUCE - BLACK						O	O	O	O	O	
13	– ENGLEMAN	CREAMY WHITE		●	●		O	O	O	O	O	
14	– RED						O	●	O	O	O	
15	– SITKA	LIGHT YELLOWISH TAN		●	●		O	●	O	O	O	
	HARDWOODS											
1	ASH, WHITE	CREAMY WHITE TO LIGHT BROWN	●			O						O
2	BEECH	WHITE TO REDDISH BROWN	●			●						●
3	BIRCH, YELLOW	LIGHT BROWN	●			●						●
4	CHERRY	REDDISH BROWN	●			●						●
5	ELM, AMERICAN	BROWN	●									●
6	LOCUST, BLACK	GOLDEN BROWN					O					O
7	MAHOGANY	REDDISH BROWN	●			●						●
8	MAPLE (HARD) SUGAR	WHITE TO REDDISH BROWN	●			●						●
9	OAK, RED	REDDISH TAN TO BROWN	●			●						●
10	POPLAR, YELLOW	WHT. TO BROWN W/GREEN CAST	●							O		●
11	ROSEWOOD	MIXED REDS, BROWNS & BLACKS	●									●
12	TEAK	TAWNY YELLOW TO DARK BRN.	●			●						●
13	WALNUT, BLACK	DARK BROWN	●	O								●

USES													PROPERTIES									NOTES	
FLOORS			ROOFS		FOUNDATION/OUTDOOR						EQUIP.												
JOISTS	ROUGH	FINISH	RAFTERS	DECKING	PILES	WD. FOUND.	RET. WALLS	POSTS	DECKS	FURNITURE	CABINETS	FURNITURE	SHRINKAGE	BENDG STRENG.	COMPRESSION =	COMPRESSION ⊥	HARDNESS SIDE	IMPACT, BENDING	RESIST. TO DECAY	WEATHERING	PAINTABILITY		
																						SOFTWOODS	
O			●	●				●	●	●	O	O	2	4	5	4	3	4	8	7	7	*70	1
O			●	●					●	●	O	O	5	6	6	6	6	6	8	7	7	*145-150	2
●	●	●	●	●	■	■	■	■	■				7	7	7	6	7	6	6	5	4	*70-100	3
●			●	●		■	■	■	■				7	6	6	5	6	7	5	5	5	*60-70	4
●			●	●	□				●				8	3	7	6	7	6	6	5	4		5
O			●						■				5	4	5	4	4	5	5	5	5	*93	6
O			●	●		■	■		■		O	O	4	3	4	5	4	5	5	5	6	*105-200	7
O			●	●		■			●		O	O	5	5	5	5	5	6	5	5	4	*142	8
O	●	●	●	●	■	■	■	■	■				7	7	7	6	7	6	5	5	5	*130-190	9
O			●	●					■		O	O	3	3	4	3	3	4	5	5	6		10
O			O	●				●	■	●	O	O	2	5	6	5	5	4	8	7	7	*70	11
O			O	O					□				5	4	5	3	5	5	5	5	5		12
O			O	O					□				5	3	3	3	3	4	5	5	5		13
O			O	O					□				6	5	5	5	5	4	5	5	5		14
O			●	●					□				6	5	5	5	5	5	5	5	5		15
																						HARDWOODS	
		O										●	5	6	6	6	6	6	4	5	5		1
											●	●	8	5	5	5	5	5	5	5	6		2
		O									●	●	7	5	4	4	5	6	5	5	6	*105-110	3
		O									●	●	3	4	5	3	4	3	6	5	5		4
												●	6	3	3	8	4	4	5	5	5		5
							O	O	O				2	8	8	8	8	5	8	5	5		6
				●							O	O											7
				●							O	●	6	6	6	6	6	5	5	5	6	*104	8
				●							O	O	7	3	3	5	5	3	5	5	5	*100	9
											O	O	4	3	3	2	3	3	5	5	7	*170-185	10
											●	●											11
		O		O							O	●	●										12
		O									●	●	4	6	6	4	6	4	7	6	5	*130-140	13

NOTES

__ B. WOOD MEMBERS (SIZE AND COSTS)

$\textcircled{1}$ $\textcircled{10}$ $\textcircled{23}$

___ 1. <u>General:</u> See p. 132 for span-to-depth ratios.
Rough lumber costs by board feet:

Studs	**$0.80/BF**
Posts	**$0.90/BF**
Joists	**$0.85/BF**
Beams (Doug. Fir)	**$1.00/BF**

Note: The above are material costs only. Total in-place cost may be estimated by *doubling* the above numbers.

___ 2. <u>Light-Frame Construction</u>
    ___ *a.* <u>Stud walls:</u> Usually 2 × 4s or 2 × 6s at 16″ oc or 24″ oc with one bottom and two 2× top plates.

Costs: 2 × 4s at 24″oc: $0.95/SF (50% M and 50% L) with variation of ±10%. Add 20% for each spacing jump (i.e., 16″ and 12″ oc).

2 × 6s at 24″oc: $1.15/SF (M, L, variation, and spacing, same as above).

    ___ *b.* <u>Roof joists and rafters:</u>
Rule of thumb for roof joists, rafters, and ceiling joists:
Quick estimates of joist depths in inches can be made by multiplying span in feet by:
   0.45 for ceiling joists
   0.5 for roof joists
Usual spacing: 24″ oc.

For more precise sizing, see p. 281.

Costs: 2 × 6s at 24″oc: $1.15/SF (50% M and 50% L), variation of + 10%. Add 20% for each spacing increase (i.e., 16″ and 12″oc. 2 × 8s: $1.40/SF. 2 × 10s: $1.90/SF. 2 × 12s: $2.45/SF.

Ceiling joists: $1.00 to $1.70/SF

    ___ *c.* <u>Floor joists</u>
      ___ (1) See p. 132 for general rule span-to-depth ratio.

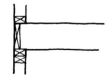

___ (2) Usual span range: 8′ to 24′.
___ (3) Usual spacing: 16″ oc.
___ (4) For more precise sizing, see p. 281.

Costs: 2 × 6s at 24″ oc: $0.85/SF (50%M and 50%L).
16″ oc: $0.90/SF.   12″ oc: $1.20/SF. Add 20% for each 2″
size increase up to 2 × 12s.

___ 3. Heavy Timber Construction
   ___ *a.* Wood beams
      ___ (1) Solid wood beams
         ___ (*a*) Thickness range: 2″ to 14″
         ___ (*b*) Spacing range: 4′ to 20′.
         ___ (*c*) Approximate span-to-
            depth ratios: *16 to 20.*
      ___ (2) Solid wood girders: Commonly
used span-to-depth ratio for gird-
ers with concentrated load is *12.* Width will
be *3/4* to *1/2* of depth. To estimate depth in
inches, multiply span in feet by *1.*

Approximate cost range from $8.00/LF for 4 × 8s to 4 × 12s.
$13.70/LF for 6 × 8s to 6 × 12s (65% M and 35% L).

   ___ *b.* Glu-lam beams
      ___ (1) Usual span range: 16′ to 50′.
      ___ (2) Spacing: 8′ to 30′.
      ___ (3) Thickness range from 3⅛″ to
         10¾″.
      ___ (4) Approximate span-to-depth
         ratio: *16 to 20.*
      ___ (5) Ratio of depth to width is
         about 2 to 1 for light beams
         and 3 to 1 for large members.
      ___ (6) Depth varies in 1½″ increments.

Approximate costs: Douglas fir, industrial grade:

3⅛″ × 6″: $10.20/LF (45%M and 55%L). Add $2.25 for each
3″ depth to 18″.

5⅛″ × 6″: $12.70/LF (50%M and 50%L). Add $3.40 for each
3″ depth to 24″.

6¾″ × 12″: $23.90/LF (75%M and 25%L). Add $4.80 for each
3″ depth to 24″.

For architectural grade, add 20%.
For prestain, add 10%.

___ *c.* <u>Columns and posts:</u> The ratios of unbraced length to least thickness of most types range from 10 to 30 with *20* a good average.

Approximate costs of *$5.30/LF* for 4 × 4 to *$9.40/LF* for 6 × 6 (same M and L ratios as beams).

___ *d.* <u>Wood decking</u>
    ___ (1) Thickness: 2″ to 4″
    ___ (2) Span-to-depth ratio: *25 to 48*
    ___ (3) Spans: 4′ to 8′

Approximate costs of $3.30/SF for 3″ fir to $8.00/SF for 4″ cedar (70% to 90% M, 30% to 10% L).

___ 4. <u>Trusses</u>
    ___ *a.* <u>Light frame trusses</u>
        ___ (1) Usually 2′ oc
        ___ (2) Roof span-to-depth ratio: *15–20*
        ___ (3) Floor span-to-depth ratio: *12 to 15*
        ___ (4) Usual spans 30′ to 60′

Approximate cost range: Fink truss, 2 × 4s, 3 to 12 slope, 24′ span: $84.00/each (55% M and 45% L).

King post, 2 × 4s, 4 to 12 slope, 42′ span: $152.00/each (75% M and 25% L).

    ___ *b.* <u>Heavy wood trusses</u>
        ___ (1) Flat trusses
            ___ (*a*) Typical range of spans: 40′ to 160′
            ___ (*b*) Spacing 12′ to 20′
            ___ (*c*) Usual ratio of truss depth to span ranges from *1 to 8* to *1 to 10.*
        ___ (2) Bowstring trusses
            ___ (*a*) Typical range of spans: 40′ to 200′
            ___ (*b*) Spacing: 12′ to 20′
            ___ (*c*) Usual span-to-depth ratio of *6 to 8*

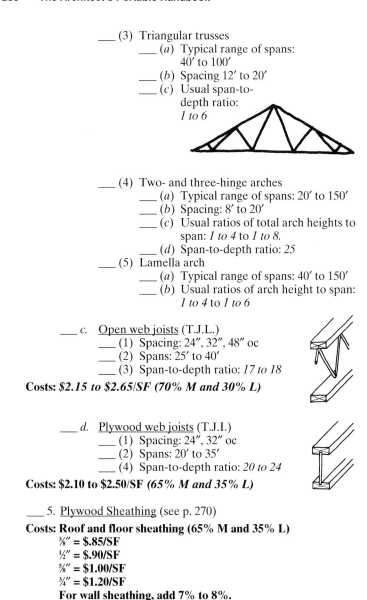

___ (3) Triangular trusses
  ___ (*a*) Typical range of spans:
    40′ to 100′
  ___ (*b*) Spacing 12′ to 20′
  ___ (*c*) Usual span-to-
    depth ratio:
    1 to 6

___ (4) Two- and three-hinge arches
  ___ (*a*) Typical range of spans: 20′ to 150′
  ___ (*b*) Spacing: 8′ to 20′
  ___ (*c*) Usual ratios of total arch heights to
    span: *1 to 4* to *1 to 8.*
  ___ (*d*) Span-to-depth ratio: *25*
___ (5) Lamella arch
  ___ (*a*) Typical range of spans: 40′ to 150′
  ___ (*b*) Usual ratios of arch height to span:
    1 to 4 to *1 to 6*

___ *c.* <u>Open web joists</u> (T.J.L.)
 ___ (1) Spacing: 24″, 32″, 48″ oc
 ___ (2) Spans: 25′ to 40′
 ___ (3) Span-to-depth ratio: *17 to 18*
Costs: *$2.15 to $2.65/SF (70% M and 30% L)*

___ *d.* <u>Plywood web joists</u> (T.J.I.)
 ___ (1) Spacing: 24″, 32″ oc
 ___ (2) Spans: 20′ to 35′
 ___ (4) Span-to-depth ratio: *20 to 24*
Costs: $2.10 to $2.50/SF *(65% M and 35% L)*

___ 5. <u>Plywood Sheathing</u> (see p. 270)
Costs: Roof and floor sheathing (65% M and 35% L)
 ⅜″ = $.85/SF
 ½″ = $.90/SF
 ⅝″ = $1.00/SF
 ¾″ = $1.20/SF
 For wall sheathing, add 7% to 8%.

TABLE FOR ALLOWABLE SPANS FOR WOOD FLOOR JOISTS & ROOF RAFTERS

This table based on Douglas Fir/Larch No.2 or better. Reduce allowable span by 5% for southern pine and by 15% for hem-fir No.2.

*High- or low-slope roofs

MEMBER SIZE →	2 x 6			2 x 8			2 x 10			2 x 12		
ON CENTER SPACING IN INCHES →	12"	16"	24"	12"	16"	24"	12"	16"	24"	12"	16"	24"
ALLOWABLE MAX. SPAN IN FT. & IN. →												
CONDITIONS & LOADS ↓												
FLOOR JOISTS, 40#/SF LIVE LOAD, 10#/SF DEADLOAD	10-9	9-9	8-6	14-2	12-10	11-3	18-0	16-5	14-4	21-11	19-11	17-5
CEILING JOISTS, 10#/SF LIVE LOAD, 5#/SF DEADLOAD	19-6	17-8	15-6	25-8	23-4	20-5		26-0				
*ROOF RAFTERS OR JOISTS												
NO CEILING (10#/SF DEAD LOAD)												
(L/180) 20#/SF L.L. (Fb=1200 psi)	14-2	12-4	10-0	18-9	16-3	13-3	23-11	20-8	16-11			
30#/SF L.L. (Fb=1200 psi)	12-4	10-8	8-8	16-3	14-0	11-6	20-8	17-11	14-8			
DRYWALL CLG (15#/SF DEAD LOAD)												
(L/240) 20#/SF L.L.	13-2	11-5	9-4	17-4	15-0	12-3	22-1	19-2	15-8		23-3	19-0
30#/SF L.L.	11-7	10-0	8-2	15-3	13-3	10-10	19-6	16-11	13-9	23-9	20-6	16-9
*HEAVY ROOF (20#/SF DEAD LOAD)												
(L/240) 20#/SF L.L.	12-4	10-8	8-8	16-3	14-0	11-6	20-8	17-11	14-8	25-2	21-9	17-9
30#/SF L.L.	11-0	9-6	7-9	14-6	12-7	10-3	19-6	16-0	13-1	22-6	19-6	15-11

281

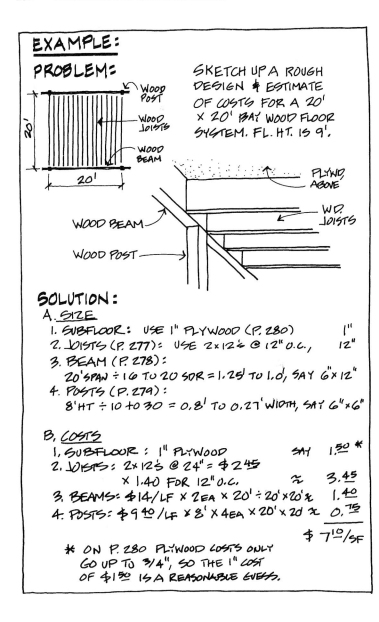

EXAMPLE:

PROBLEM:

SKETCH UP A ROUGH DESIGN & ESTIMATE OF COSTS FOR A 20' X 20' BAY WOOD FLOOR SYSTEM. FL. HT. IS 9'.

WOOD POST

WOOD JOISTS

WOOD BEAM

20'

20'

PLYWD. ABOVE

WD. JOISTS

WOOD BEAM

WOOD POST

SOLUTION:

A. SIZE
1. SUBFLOOR: USE 1" PLYWOOD (P. 280)   1"
2. JOISTS (P. 277): USE 2×12's @ 12" O.C.,   12"
3. BEAM (P. 278):
   20' SPAN ÷ 16 TO 20 SDR = 1.25' TO 1.0', SAY 6"×12"
4. POSTS (P. 279):
   8' HT ÷ 10 TO 30 = 0.8' TO 0.27' WIDTH, SAY 6"×6"

B. COSTS
1. SUBFLOOR: 1" PLYWOOD   SAY   1.$\frac{50}{}$ *
2. JOISTS: 2×12's @ 24" = \$2.45
           × 1.40 FOR 12" O.C.   ≈   3.45
3. BEAMS: \$14/LF × 2 EA × 20' ÷ 20'×20'   1.$\frac{40}{}$
4. POSTS: \$9.$\frac{40}{}$/LF × 8' × 4 EA × 20'×20' ≈ 0.$\frac{75}{}$
                                           \$ 7.$\frac{10}{}$/SF

   * ON P. 280 PLYWOOD COSTS ONLY
     GO UP TO 3/4", SO THE 1" COST
     OF \$1.$\frac{50}{}$ IS A REASONABLE GUESS.

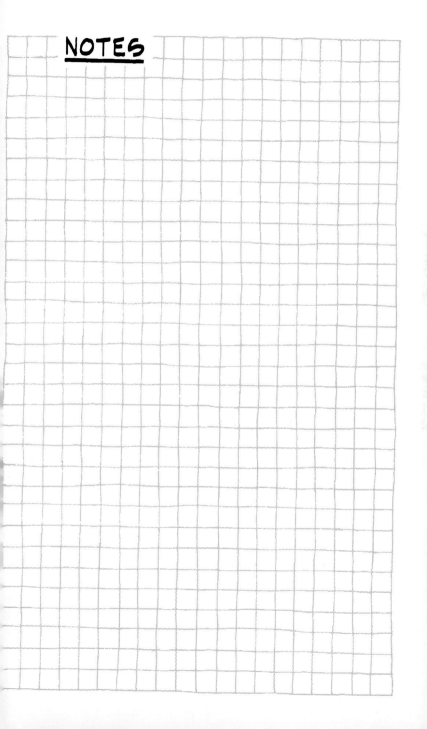

NOTES

NOTES

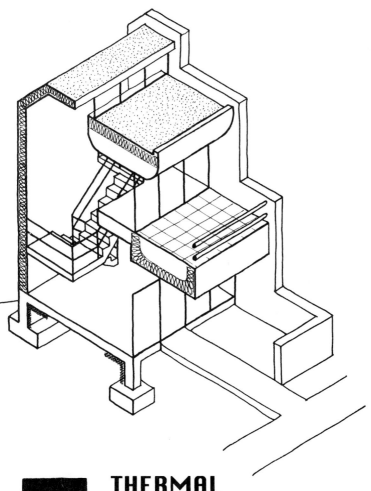

7 THERMAL AND MOISTURE PROTECTION

NOTES

__ A. ATTIC VENTILATION

__ 1. When there is attic space under roof, *venting of attic will:*
   __ *a.* Reduce heat buildup.
   __ *b.* Provide escape route for moisture.
   __ *c.* In cold climates, help prevent ice dams from forming.

__ 2. Even when there is *no attic,* the venting effect can still be achieved with at least a *1″* air space above the insulation.

__ 3. In some cases, the argument can be made for having *no venting* at all. This can be done in dry climates and building types where vapor is less of a problem or if the "wet" side of the roof is sealed against vapor migration. Because the codes require venting but often are not enforced, this needs to be checked with building officials.

__ 4. Venting can be done by:
   __ *a.* Cross-ventilation
   __ *b.* Stack effect
   __ *c.* Fans

__ 5. The UBC requires that where climatic conditions warrant, attics or enclosed rafters should have net free ventilating area of at least $\frac{1}{150}$ of the plan area. This can be reduced to $\frac{1}{300}$ if *50%* of the vent area is at upper portion, at least *3′* above eave, or if a vapor barrier is on warm side of attic insulation.

__ 6. Area required to provide 1 SF vent:

¼″ Screen	1 SF
¼″ Screen w/louvers	2 SF
⅛″ Screen	1.25 SF
⅛″ Screen w/louvers	2.25 SF
¹⁄₁₆″ Screen	2 SF
¹⁄₁₆″ Screen w/louvers	3 SF

HIP ROOF

GABLE ROOF W/ RIDGE VENT

SHED ROOF

GABLE ROOF W/ WALL VENTS

Costs: Louvers with screens: $25 to $45/SF (35% M and 65% L)

___ B. WATER AND DAMPPROOFING

___ 1. *Waterproofing* is the prevention of water flow (usually under hydrostatic pressure such as saturated soil) into the building. This is usually basement walls or decks. This can be by:

    ___ *a.* Membranes: Layers of asphalt with plies of saturated felt or woven fabric

    ___ *b.* Hydrolithic: Coatings of asphalt or plastics (elastomeric)

    ___ *c.* Admixtures: To concrete

Typical costs:
Elastomeric, ½″ neoprene: $2.00/SF (50% M and 50% L)
Bit. membrane, 2-ply felt: $1.20/SF (35% M and 65% L)

___ 2. *Dampproofing* is preventing dampness (from earth or surface water without hydrostatic pressure) from penetrating into the building. This can be:

    ___ *a.* Below grade: 2 coats asphalt paint, dense cement plaster, silicons, and plastics.

    ___ *b.* Above grade: See paints and coatings, p. 348.

Typical costs:
Asphalt paint, per coat: $0.55/SF (50% M and 50% L)

__ C. VAPOR BARRIERS

___ 1. <u>General</u>
    ___ *a.* Vapor can penetrate walls and roof by:
        ___ (1) Diffusion—vapor passes through materials due to:
            ___ (*a*) Difference in vapor pressure between inside and outside.
            ___ (*b*) Permeability of construction materials.
        ___ (2) Air leakage by:
            ___ (*a*) Stack effect
            ___ (*b*) Wind pressure
            ___ (*c*) Building pressure
    ___ *b.* Vapor is not a problem until it reaches its *dew point* and condenses into moisture, causing deterioration in the building materials of wall, roof, and floor assemblies.

___ 2. <u>Vapor Barriers:</u> Should be placed on the warm or humid side of the assembly. For *cold* climates this will be toward the inside. For warm, humid climates, this will be toward the outside. Barriers are also often put under slabs-on-grade to protect flooring from ground moisture.

    Vapor barriers are measured by *perms* (grains/SF/hr/inch mercury vapor pressure difference). One grain equals about one drop of water. For a material to qualify as a vapor barrier, its perm rate must be *1.0* or less. A good perm rate for foil laminates, polyethylene sheets, etc. equals *0.1* or less (avoid aluminum foil against mortar). See p. 293 for perms of various materials. Care must be taken against puncturing the barrier.

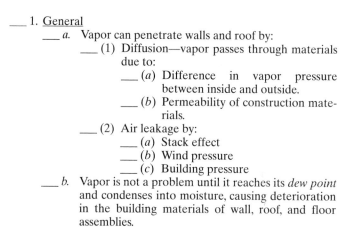

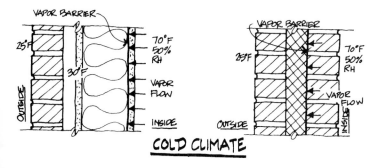

COLD CLIMATE

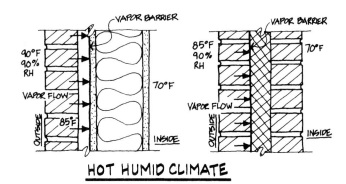

HOT HUMID CLIMATE

Other methods are elastomeric coatings on interior wallboard in cold climates and at exterior masonry or stucco walls in hot, wet climates. See p. 348 for coatings. Care must be taken to caulk all joints and cracks (see p. 306).

___ 3. Roof Vapor Retarders

   ___ *a.* As a general guide, vapor retarders should be considered for use when:

      ___ (1) The outside, mean, average January temperature is below 40°F.

      ___ (2) The expected winter, interior, RH is 45% or greater.

   ___ *b.* Vapor retarders generally fall into two classes:

      ___ (1) Bituminous membranes: A typical 2-ply installation using 3 moppings of steep asphalt rates at less than .005 perms.

      ___ (2) Sheet systems, with sealed laps, such as PVC films, kraft paper, or alum. foil, with perm ratings ranging from 0.10 to 0.50.

   ___ *c.* When vapor is a concern in top of deck insulation, moisture relief vents (preferably one-way) at a min. of one per 1000 SF should be considered.

___ 4. Asphalt Saturated Felts: See p. 302.

Typical costs: Polyethylene sheets, 2–10 mill. $.15 to $.20/SF

__ D. RADIANT BARRIERS

__ 1. Radiant barriers *reflect* long-
wave (invisible) radiation created by the sun heating the
exterior skin of the building.

__ 2. Use for *hot climates or summer*
conditions only. Effective for
retarding the penetration of
exterior summer heat into
building, but not the other way
in winter.

__ 3. Most critical *locations:*
    __ *a.* The roof is most critical because it faces the sun.
    __ *b.* Use at walls can be effective when:
        __ (1) On east and west sides.
        __ (2) Climate is less than 2000 HDD and greater
            than 2500 CDD. See p. 523.
        __ (3) On south walls when climate is greater than
            3500 CDD.
      Note: For HDD and CDD, see App. B, items L
      and M.

__ 4. Radiation is blocked by a *reflective surface* next to an air
space. The barrier can be on either side of the air space, or
on both sides.

__ 5. The reflective surface can be *foil-faced batting, reflective
aluminum foil sheets,* or *reflective paint.*

__ 6. *Emissivity* is a measure of radiant-barrier effectiveness (the
lower the e-number the better):
    __ *a.* Minimum for foils should be e = 0.06.
    __ *b.* Minimum for paints should be e = 0.23

__ 7. *Added R* value can be approximated for summer at e = 0.05:
    __ *a.* Horizontal air space: Reflectance up, R = 5.3
        Reflectance both sides, R = 6.0
    __ *b.* Vertical air space: Reflectance out, R = 3.6
        Reflectance both sides, R = 4.6

__ 8. Must guard against dust reducing barrier effectiveness.

Costs: Aluminum foil barrier: $.20/SF (70% M and 30% L)

__ E. INSULATION ⑦

__ 1. Insulation is the entrapment of air within modern light-weight materials, to resist heat flow.

__ 2. For minimum total resistance (ΣR) for building elements, find Insulation Zone from App. B, item U., then refer to below:

	Min. insulation, R		
Zone	Cl'g.	Wall	Floor
1	19	11	11
2	26	13	11
3	26	19	13
4	30	19	19
5	33	19	22
6	38	19	22

__ 3. In the design of a building, design the different elements (roof, wall, floor) to be at the minimum ΣR. Each piece of construction has some resistance, with lightweight insulations doing the bulk of the resistance of heat flow.

$$\Sigma R = R1 + R2 + R3 + R4 + R5, \text{etc.} \qquad *(\text{air films})$$

See p. 293 for resistance (r) of elements to be added.

Another common term is U Value, the coefficient of heat transmission.

$$U = \text{Btuh/ft}^2/°F = \frac{1}{\Sigma R}$$

__ 4. Other factors in control of heat flow

__ a. The *mass* (density or weight) of building elements (such as walls) will delay and store heat. Time lag in hours is related to thermal conductivity, heat capacity, and thickness. This increases as weight of construction goes up with about ½% *per lb/CF.* Desirable time lags in temperate climates are: Roof—12 hrs; north and east walls—0 hrs; west and south walls—8 hrs. This effect can also be used to increase R values, at the approximate rate of *+0.4%* for every added lb/CF of weight.

__ b. *Light colors* will reflect and *dark colors* will absorb the sun's heat. Cold climates will favor dark surfaces, and the opposite for hot climates. For summer roofs, the overall effect can be 20% between light and dark.

__ c. See page 291 for radiant barriers.

___ 5. Typical Batts:

    R = 11   3½″ thick
    R = 19   6″
    R = 22   6½″
    R = 26   8¼″
    R = 30   9″

Typical Costs:

    C.L. 'G. batt, 6″ R = 19: $.80/SF (60% M and 40% L)
                9″ R = 30: $1.10/SF
    Wall batt,   4″ R = 11: $.50/SF (50% M and 50% L)
                6″ R = 19: $.60/SF
    Add $.05/SF for foil backs.
    Rigid: $.60/SF, ¾″, R = 2.8 to $1.15/SF, 2¼″, R = 8.3.

___ 6. Insulating Properties of Building Materials:

Material	Wt. #/CF	r value (per in)	Perm
Water	60		
Earth dry	75 to 95	.33	
saturated		.05	
Sand/gravel dry	100–120		
wet			
Concrete req.	150	.11	
lt. wt.	120	.59	
Masonry			
Mortar	130	.2	
Brick, common	120	.2	1 (4″)
8″ CMU, reg. wt.	85	1.11	.4
lt. wt.	55	2	
Stone	±170	.08	
Metals			
Aluminum	165	.0007	0 (1 mil)
Steel	490	.0032	
Copper	555	.0004	
Wood			
Plywood	36	1.25	½″ = .4 to 1
Hardwood	40	.91	
Softwood	30	1.25	2.9 (¾″)
Waterproofing			.05
Vapor barrier			.05

Material	Wt. #/CF	r value (per in)	Perm
Insulations			
Min. wool batt	4	±3.2	>50
Fill		3.7	>50
Perlite	11	2.78	
Board polystyrene		4	1–6
fiber		2.94	
glass fiber		4.17	
urethane		8.5	
Air			
Betwn. nonrefl.		1.34	
One side refl.		4.64	
Two sides refl.			
Inside film		.77 (ave)	
Outside film			
winter		.17	
summer		.25	
Roofing (see p. 302)			
Doors			
Metal			
Fiber core		1.69	
Urethane core		5.56	
Wood, solid 1¾″		3.13	
HC 1⅜″		2.22	
Glass, single	160	(see p. 334)	
Plaster (stucco)	110	.2	
Gypsum	48	.6	
CT	145		
Terrazzo			
Acoustical CLGs			
Resilient flooring		.05	
Carpet and pad		2.08	
Paint			.3 to 1 (see p. 348)

EXAMPLE:

PROBLEM: USING ROOF ASSEMBLY C (P.394), ADD ROOFING, INSULATION, AND CEILING. ESTIMATE TOTAL U VALUE & COSTS. THE BUILDING IS IN PHOENIX, AZ.

SOLUTION:

MT'L.	R		$/SF	
AIR	0.25	①	—	②
B.U. ROOF	0.88	③	1³⁰ ₃	④
½" PLYWD.	0.63	⑤	⑥	⑦
AIR	4.64	①	—	⑧
INSULATION	26.0		1⁰⁰	⑧
STRUCTURE	—		2⁰⁰	⑥
½" GYP'BD	0.3		0.60	⑨
AIR	0.77		—	

$$\Sigma R = \overline{33.47} \qquad \overline{\$4^{90}/SF}$$

$$U = 0.30 \qquad \times 0.89 \text{ PHX,}$$
$$\textcircled{10} \qquad \overline{\$4 \, \frac{35}{}} \, \text{AZ}$$

SEE P. 527

NOTES:
① SEE P. 294.
② ASSUME SUMMER.
③ SEE P. 303.
④ WITH CAP SHEET.
⑤ SEE P. 293.
⑥ STRUCTURE COST, SEE P. 394, ASSUME $2⁰⁰/SF.
⑦ ½ OF R OF 1.25 FOR ½" PLYWOOD
⑧ BATT W/ ALUM. FOIL FACE UP. ASSUME $⁰⁰/SF. SEE P. 293.
⑨ GYPB'D : ½ × .6R = .3R (SEE P. 294 & P. 340)
⑩ COULD ADD ANOTHER R = 5.3 FOR RADIANT BARRIER EFFECT IN SUMMER. SEE P. 291.

__ F. EXTERIOR INSULATION AND FINISHING SYSTEMS (EIFS)

__ 1. Exterior Insulation and Finishing Systems (EIFS) provide a stucco appearance using exterior insulation. They involve a combination of exterior-applied synthetic stucco on rigid insulation on a substrate (see item 31 on p. 140). Substrate can be masonry, gypsum board, plywood, etc.

__ 2. Rigid insulation is typically expanded polystyrene (R/in. = 4.17) of 1″ up to 4″ thickness, and is usually applied by adhesive.

__ 3. Synthetic stucco is applied after a fiber mesh is embedded in an adhesive.

Costs: For 1″ board $5.50/SF (30% M and 70% L), + 30% variation. Add $0.20/SF for each added 1″ of insulation.

___ G. ROOFING   ㊲ ㊺

For costs, see p. 302.
   ___ 1. <u>General</u>
       ___ *a.* Shape (see p. 287)
          ___ (1) Flat
          ___ (2) Hip
          ___ (3) Gable
          ___ (4) Shed
       ___ *b.* Pitch: See p. 51 for slopes. Use the following graphic as a guide for roofing selection:

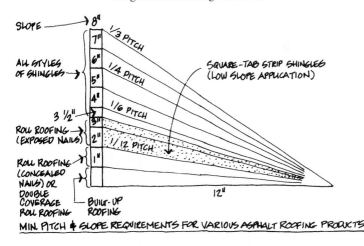

MIN. PITCH & SLOPE REQUIREMENTS FOR VARIOUS ASPHALT ROOFING PRODUCTS

       ___ *c.* Drainage: See p. 431.
       ___ *d.* Fire resistance: Per the UBC (see page 301), roofing is designated as either nonrated or rated. When rated, roofing must be not readily flammable, provide a degree of fire protection to the deck, not slip from position, and not produce flying brands during a fire. Rated roofs are broken down as follows:
          ___ (1) Class A: Resists severe fires, flames on top do not spread more than 6′, and no burn through roof.
          ___ (2) Class B: Resists moderate fires, flames on top do not spread more than 8′, and no burn through roof.
          ___ (3) Class C: Resists light fires, flames on top do not spread more than 13′, and some burn through roof.

___ 2. Basic Roofing Types
    ___ *a.* Shingles and tiles
        ___ (1) Normally have felt underlayment.
        ___ (2) Laid on pitched roofs of greater than 3 in 12 (or 2 in 12 with special underlayment).
        ___ (3) At high-wind locations, shingles have tendency to blow off roof edges, unless special attachment.
    ___ *b.* Single ply
        ___ (1) Modified bitumen
            ___ (*a*) APP: rubber-like sheets, can be dead-level, often with underlayment.
            ___ (*b*) SBS: same as above, but more flexible sheets.
        ___ (2) Single ply (without underlayment), can be dead-level.
            ___ (*a*) EPDM: single rubberized sheets, sealed at seams, unattached or adheared to substrate. Can be rock ballasted. Normally black.
            ___ (*b*) CSPE ("Hypalon"): Like above, but using a synthetic rubber that is normally white.
            ___ (*c*) PVC: Like above, but using plastic-like sheets that are normally white.
    ___ *c.* Coal tar pitch
        ___ (1) Like a built-up roof, of asphaltic products, except coal tar has a lower melt point and is better at self-sealing punctures.
        ___ (2) Use on very low slopes (1% to 2%).
        ___ (3) Coal tar can be hazardous to work with.

Coal tar is normally 50% more expensive than built-up roofing.

    ___ *d.* Metal roofing
    ___ *e.* Urethane
        ___ (1) Sprayed-on insulation with sprayed-on waterproof coating
        ___ (2) Very good for irregular-shaped roofs
        ___ (3) Weak point is delicate coating on top, which is susceptible to puncture
    ___ *f.* Built-up: Plies of asphalt-impregnated sheets (often fiberglass) that are adhered together with hot asphalt moppings. (See Design Checklist which follows.)

DESIGN CHECKLIST

___ 1. Roof leaks are often associated with edges and penetrations. Therefore, these require the greatest amount of care.

___ 2. "Flat" roofs should never be dead-level. Design substrate or structure for minimum of 2% ($\frac{1}{4}''$ per ft) to 4% ($\frac{1}{2}''$ per ft) slope for drainage.

___ 3. Place drains at midspans, where deflection of structure is greatest.

___ 4. When drains must be placed at columns or bearing walls, add another $\frac{1}{2}$% (approx. $\frac{1}{240}$ the span) to allow for deck or structure deflection.

___ 5. Where camber is designed into structural members, this must also be calculated into the required slope.

___ 6. Provide drainage "crickets" ("saddles") to allow water flow around equipment platforms or against parapets.

___ 7. To prevent ponding, roof drains are best recessed. Drains should be cast iron.

___ 8. For roof drains, scuppers, gutters, downspouts, etc., see p. 431.

___ 9. The drainage system should be laid out to accommodate any required building expansion joints. See p. 306.

___ 10. Roof expansion joints should be provided at structural joints; where steel frame or deck changes direction; where separate wings of L, U, or T shapes; where different types of deck materials meet; where additions meet existing buildings; where unheated areas meet heated areas; and where movement between vertical walls and roof may occur.

___ 11. Where expansion joints are not used, provide area dividers at *150* to *200* ft, laid out in square or rectangular areas, not restricting the flow of water.

___ 12. All horizontal-to-vertical intersections, such as walls and equipment platforms, should have 45° cants, crickets, flashing, and counter-flashing. Curbs should be 8″ to 14″ high so that there is at least 8″ between top of curb and roof. Premanufactured metal curbs should be 16 GA (or 18 GA with bracing).

___ 13. Roof penetrations of pipes and conduits should be grouped and housed. Keep minimum of 18″ between curbs, pipes, and edges of roof. If pitch pockets must be used, reduce size so that no more than 2″ separate edge of metal and edge of penetration.

___ 14. If substrate is preformed rigid insulation, two layers (with offset joints) are best, with top layer installed with long dimension of boards perpendicular to drainage and end joints staggered. Surface must be prepared prior to roofing.

___ 15. Use vapor retarder when needed. See p. 289.

___ 16. Substrate Decks

    ___ *a. Plywood* should be interior type with exterior glue, graded C-D, or better. Joints should be staggered and blocked or ply clipped. Base ply should be mechanically fastened.

    ___ *b. Wood planks* should be min. nominal 1″, T&G, with cracks or knotholes larger than $\frac{1}{2}$″ covered with sheet metal. Edge joints should be staggered. Use separator sheet, mechanically fastened as base ply.

    ___ *c. Steel decks* should be 22 GA or heavier. Rigid insulation should be parallel to flutes, which are perpendicular to slope.

    ___ *d. Cast-in-place concrete* should be dry, then primed, unless rigid insulation used; then use vapor retarder or vent insulation.

    ___ *e. Precast concrete* should have rigid insulation. Do not apply first ply to planks.

    ___ *f. Lightweight concrete or gypsum concrete* must be dry and then have a coated base ply or vented base ply mechanically attached.

OCCUPANCY	TYPES OF CONSTRUCTION								
	I	II			III		IV	V	
	F.R.	F.R.	One-hour	N	One-hour	N	H.T.	One-hour	N
A-1	B	B	—	—	—	—	—	—	—
A) 2-2.1	B	B	B	—	B	—	B	B	—
A-3	B	B	B	B	B[1]	B	B[1]	B[1]	C
A-4	B	B	B	B	B[1]	B	B[1]	B[1]	B[1]
B	B	B	B	B	B	B	B	B	C
E	B	B	B	B	B[1]	B	B[1]	B[1]	B[1]
F	B	B	B	B	B[1]	C	B[1]	B[1]	C
H-1	A	A	A	A	—	—	—	—	—
H) 2-3-4-5-6-7	A	B	B	B	B	B	B	B	B
I) 1.1-1.2-2	A	B	B	—	B	—	B	B	—
I-3	A	B	B[1]	—	B[2]	—	—	B[3]	—
M	B	B	B	B	B[1]	C	B[1]	B[1]	C
R-1	B	B	B	B	B[1,3]	C[3]	B[1,3]	B[1,3]	C[2,3]
R-3	B	B	B	B	NR	NR	NR	NR	NR
S-1, S-3	B	B	B	B	B[1]	C	B[1]	B[1]	C
S-2, S-5	B	B	B	B	B	B	B	B	B[1]
S-4	B	B	B	B	—	—	—	—	—
U	B	B	B	B	NR[4]	NR[4]	NR[4]	NR[4]	NR[4]

A—Class A roofing. B—Class B roofing. C—Class C roof covering. F.R.—Fire resistive.
H.T.—Heavy timber. N—No requirements for fire resistance. NR—Nonrated roof coverings.

[1]Buildings that are not more than two stories in height and have not more than 6,000 square feet (557 m²) of projected roof area and where there is a minimum of 10 feet (3048 mm) from the extremity of the roof to the property line or assumed property line on all sides except for street fronts may have Class C roof coverings that comply with UBC Standard 15-2.

[2]See Section 308.2.2.

[3]Nonrated roof coverings may be used on buildings that are not more than two stories in height and have not more than 3,000 square feet (279 m²) of projected roof area and where there is a minimum of 10 feet (3048 mm) from the extremity of the roof to the property line on all sides except for street fronts.

[4]Unless otherwise required because of location, Group U, Division 1 roof coverings shall consist of not less than one layer of cap sheet; or built-up roofing consisting of two layers of felt and a surfacing material of 300 pounds per roofing square (14.6 kg/m²) of gravel or other approved surfacing material, or 250 pounds (12.2 kg/m²) of crushed slag.

ROOFING COMPARISON (DATA AND COSTS)

TYPE		SLOPE IN./FT. MIN.	SLOPE IN./FT. MAX.	UNDERLAYMENT	FASTENERS	WT. #/SQ	P PER IN²	FIRE CL	LIFE YRS	TYPICAL COSTS (add ± 30% for edge conditions on 'flat' roofs)
UNDERLAYMENT/ ROLL ROOFING	FELT			N/A		15 to 30	.06			$0.12/SF (10%M & 90%L) $0.15/SF
SHINGLES	ASPHALT	4	12	15# FELT	GALV. GT. OR ALUM. ROOF NAILS	300	.44	C	25 TO 40	$95 TO $170/SQ. (55%M & 45%L)
	FIBERGLASS	2				250		A		
	WOOD SHAKES	3		30# FELT OR ON WD. STRIPES	CORR. RESIST. NAILS	150	.87	B	25	$195 TO $470/SQ. (60%M & 40%L)
						300		B*	50	$220 TO $320/SQ. *ADD $100/SQ. FOR FIRE RETARDING
TILE	SLATE	4 TO 6		30# FELT	COPPER WIRE & NAILS	700 TO 4000	.05	A	100	$495 TO $1285/SQ. (70%M & 30%L)
	"SPANISH" CLAY	4		30# FELT	NON-COR. COPPER NAILS / 10d COR. RESIST.	800 TO 1450	.01	A	100	$410 TO $830/SQ. (65%M & 35%L)
	CONC.				GALV.COR. PER., OR S.S. BOX NAILS	950		A		$250 TO $290/SQ.

ROOFING COMPARISON (DATA AND COSTS)

TYPE	SLOPE IN./FT. MIN.	SLOPE IN./FT. MAX.	UNDER-LAYMENT	FASTEN-ERS	WT. #/SQ.	L PER IN.	FIRE CL.	LIFE YRS.	TYPICAL COSTS
METAL — STANDING SEAM, 22 TO 26 GA. PAINTED	3		30# FELT	ANCHOR CLIPS, GALV. NAILS OR SCREWS	130			30 TO 50	$570/SQ. (80%M & 20%L)
"FLAT" — BUILT-UP	1/4		N/A	N/A	550		A TO C	20	$100 TO 150/SQ. (30%M & 70%L). ADD $35/SQ. FOR GRAVEL.
W/ GRAVEL		3							
W/ CAP SHEET		6				.88			ADD $20/SQ. FOR CAP SHT.
SINGLE PLY			40# FIBERGLASS		40				$130 TO 200/SQ.
URETHANE W/ ELAST. COATING					2.5 #/CF	7.2	A TO C		$350 TO 400/SQ. (2" THK.)

NOTES

__ H. FLASHING (4)

___ 1. Purpose: To stop water penetration at joints and intersections of building elements by use of pliable, long-lasting
materials.

___ 2. Materials

    ___ *a.* Stainless steel: *best*

    ___ *b.* Copper

    ___ *c.* Aluminum

    ___ *d.* Galvanized metal (must be painted)

    ___ *e.* Flexible (PVC, EPDM, etc.)

    ___ *f.* Felt: *worst*

___ 3. Locations

    ___ *a.* At *roof*

        ___ (1) Edges

        ___ (2) Where roof meets vertical elements, such as
walls

        ___ (3) Penetrations

    ___ *b.* At *walls*

        ___ (1) Copings at top

        ___ (2) Foundation sills

        ___ (3) Openings (heads/sills)

___ 4. Typical Details

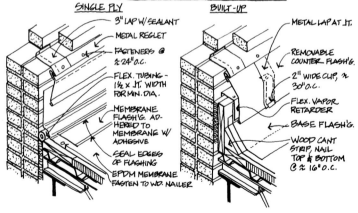

FLASHING FOR NON-WALL SUPPORTED DECK

SINGLE PLY — 3" LAP W/ SEALANT — METAL REGLET — FASTENERS @ ≈ 24" O.C. — FLEX. TUBING – 1½ x JT. WIDTH FOR MIN. DIA. — MEMBRANE FLASH'G. ADHERED TO MEMBRANE W/ ADHESIVE — SEAL EDGES OF FLASHING — EPDM MEMBRANE FASTEN TO WD. NAILER

BUILT-UP — METAL LAP AT JT. — REMOVABLE COUNTER FLASH'G. — 2" WIDE CLIP, ≈ 30" O.C. — FLEX. VAPOR RETARDER — BASE FLASH'G. — WOOD CANT STRIP, NAIL TOP & BOTTOM @ ≈ 16" O.C.

Costs: **Complete roof to parapet assembly: ≈ $17.40/LF**
Complete edge of roof assembly: ≈ $13.30/LF
Metal flashing: $5.70 to $8.60/SF (10% M and 90% L)
Copper flashing: $6.10 to $9.00/SF (45% M and 55% L)

__ I. JOINTS

__ 1. <u>General</u>

    __ *a.* Joints need to be planned because buildings and construction materials move small amounts over time.

        The two greatest sources of joint failure are failure to clean the joint and failure to tool the sealant.

UNTOOLED   TOOLED

    __ *b.* Types

        __ (1) *Expansion joints* allow for movement. These will often go completely through the building structure with columns on each side of joint. See p. 125 for seismic joints.

        __ (2) *Control joints* allow for control of cracking of finish materials by providing an indention to induce the crack in a straight line. See p. 209 for concrete slabs. See p. 227 for masonry. See p. 299 for roofing. See p. 339 for plaster.

        __ (3) *Weather seals* reduce infiltration through building from outside (or vice versa).

    __ *c.* Locations (Expansion Joints)

        __ (1) New building adjoining existing structure

        __ (2) Long, low building abutting higher building

        __ (3) Wings adjoining main structure

        __ (4) Long buildings (125′ for masonry, and 200′ for steel or concrete buildings)

        __ (5) Long, low connecting wings between buildings

        __ (6) Intersections at wings of L-, T-, or U-shaped buildings

        __ (7) Control joints along walls and at openings

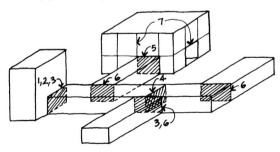

___ *d.* Components
    ___ (1) Sealant
    ___ (2) Joint filler
___ *e.* Widths = thermal expansion + moisture + tolerance.
    ___ (1) Thermal expansion = Ec × Δt × L
        ___ (*a*) Ec, coefficient of thermal expansion of material, as follows:

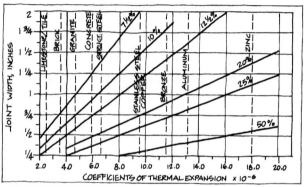

JOINT WIDTHS FOR SEALANTS WITH VARIOUS MOVEMENT CAPABILITIES
FOR 10 FOOT PANELS AT Δt OF 130°F

        ___ (*b*) Δt = max. probable temp. difference the material will experience over time. For ambient conditions, take the difference between items P and Q in App. B. Because materials absorb and/or retain heat, the result should be increased for the type of material (can easily double).
        ___ (*c*) L = Length in inches.
    ___ (2) *Moisture* can add to expansion or to shrinkage, depending on the material. See p. 227.
    ___ (3) *Construction tolerance:* depends on material. For PC concrete panels use ⅛″ for 10′ lengths and ¼″ for 30′ lengths.

EXAMPLE: ASSUME CONC. WALL PANELS, 5′ WIDE. EXPECT CONC.
Δt OF 120°F & A TOLERANCE OF ⅛″. USE A SEALANT
W/ 20% MOVEMENT CAPABILITIES.
FROM CHART ABOVE: ½″ ($\frac{120°F}{130°F}$) + ⅛″ = $^{19}/_{32}$″ OR ⅝″
SINCE PANEL IS 5′ WIDE: ⅝″ ÷ 2 = $^{5}/_{16}$″ OR <u>⅜</u>″

___ *f.* Depths:

Joint width	Depth of sealant	
	Concrete, masonry, stone	Metal, glass, and other nonporous materials
Min. ¼″	¼″	¼″
¼″ to ½″	Same as width	¼″
½″ to 1″	One-half width	One-half width
1″ to 2″	Max. ½″	Max. ½″

___ 2. Sealants

COMPARATIVE PROPERTIES OF SEALANTS

LEGEND: 1=POOR 2=FAIR 3=GOOD 4=VERY GOOD 5=EXCELLENT	BUTYL	ACRYLIC WATER BASE	ACRYLIC SOLVENT BASE	POLYSULFIDE, ONE PART	POLYSULFIDE, TWO PART	POLYURETHANE, ONE PART	POLYURETHANE, TWO PART	SILICONE	NOTES
RECOMMENDED MAX. JOINT MOVEMENT, % ±	7.5	7.5	12.5	25	25	15	25	25	(1)
LIFE EXPECTANCY IN YEARS	10+	10	15-20	20	20	20+	20+	20+	
MAX. JOINT WIDTH (INCHES)	3/4	3/8	3/4	3/4	1	3/4	1-2	3/4	(2)
ADHESION TO: WOOD	●	●	●	●	●	●	●	●	(3)
METAL	●	●	●	●	●	●	●	●	(3)
MASONRY/CONC.	●	●	●	●	●	●	●	●	(3)
GLASS	●	●	●	●	●	●	●	●	(3)
PLASTIC	●	●	●					●	
CURING TIME (DAYS)	120	5	14	14+	7	7+	3-5	2-5	(4,5)
SHORE A HARDNESS	20-40	30-35	20-40	25-35	25-50	25-45	25-45	30-40	
SELF LEVELING AVAILABLE	N/A		●	●	●		●	●	
NON-SAG AVAILAB.	N/A	●	●	●	●	●	●	●	
RESISTANCE TO: (SEE LEGEND) ULTRAVIOLET	2-3	1-3	3-4	2	2-3	3	3	5	
CUT/TEAR	2	1-2	1	3	3	4-5	4-5	1-2	
ABRASION	2	1-2	1-2	1	1	3	3	1	
WEATHERING	2	1-3	3-4	3	3	3-4	3-4	4-5	
OIL/GREASE	1-2	2	3	3	3	3	3	2	
COMPRESSION	2-3	1-2	1	3	3	4	4	4.5	
EXTENSION	1	1-2	1	2-3	2-3	4-5	4-5	4-5	

(1) SOME HIGH PERFORMANCE URETHANES & SILICONES HAVE MOVEMENT CAPABILITIES UP TO 50%.

(2) FIGURES GIVEN ARE CONSERVATIVE. VERIFY W/ MANUFACTURER.

(3) PRIMER MAY BE REQUIRED.

(4) CURE TIME FOR LOW TO MED. MODULES SILICONES IS ABOUT 2 HOURS

(5) SILICONE CAN BE APPLIED OVER A WIDE TEMP. RANGE.

___ 3. <u>Checklist of Infiltration Control</u>

    ___ *a.* Tighten seals around windows and doors, and weather stripping around all openings to the outside or to unconditioned rooms.

    ___ *b.* Caulk around all windows and doors before drywall is hung. Seal all penetrations (plumbing, electrical, etc.).

    ___ *c.* Insulate behind wall outlets and/or plumbing lines in exterior walls.

    ___ *d.* Caulk under headers and sills.

    ___ *e.* Fill spaces between rough openings and millwork with insulation (best application with foam).

    ___ *f.* Install dampers and/or glass doors on fireplaces, combined with outside combustion air intake.

    ___ *g.* Install backdraft dampers on all exhaust fan openings.

    ___ *h.* Close core voids in tops of block foundation walls.

    ___ *i.* Control concrete and masonry cracking.

    ___ *j.* Use airtight drywall methods.

Costs: Exterior joint, ⅜″ × ½″   **$2.25/LF (20% M and 80% L)**
Interior   **$2.00/LF**
For joint fillers and gaskets add 50% to 100%

NOTES

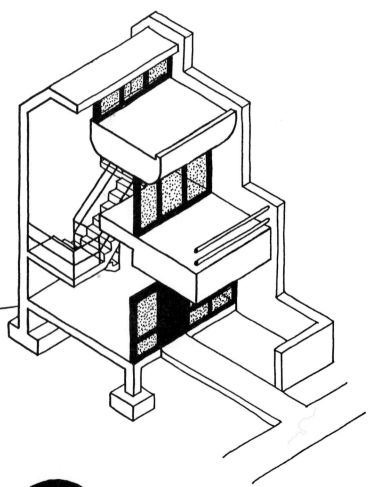

8 DOORS, WINDOWS, AND GLASS

NOTES

___ A. DOORS ④ ⑦ ⑫

___ 1. *Accessible Door Approach* (ADA) ⑳

X = 12" IF DOOR HAS BOTH A CLOSER AND LATCH, OTHERWISE X = 0"

X = 3' MIN. IF Y = 5'
X = 3'-6" MIN. IF Y = 5'-6"

Y = 4' MIN IF DOOR HAS BOTH A CLOSER & LATCH, OTHERWISE
Y = 3'-6"

Y = 4'-6" MIN. IF DOOR HAS A CLOSER, OTHERWISE
V = 4' MIN.

Y = 4' MIN. IF DOOR HAS A CLOSER, OTHERWISE, Y = 3'-6" MIN.

SLIDING & FOLDING DOORS

NOTE: ALL DOORS IN <u>ALCOVES</u> SHALL COMPLY W/ FRONT APPROACHES.

___ 2. *General*

   ___ *a.* Types by operation
       ___ (1) Swinging
       ___ (2) Bypass sliding
       ___ (3) Surface sliding
       ___ (4) Pocket sliding
       ___ (5) Folding

   ___ *b.* Physical types
       (1) Flush   (2) Panelled   (3) French   (4) Glass

       (5) Sash   (6) Jalousie   (7) Louver

       (8) Shutter   (9) Screen   (10) Dutch

___ *c.* Rough openings (door dimensions +)

	Width	Height
In wood stud walls (r.o.)	$+3\frac{1}{2}''$	$+3\frac{1}{2}''$
In masonry walls (m.o)	$+4''$	$+2''$ to $4''$

___ *d.* Fire door classifications

Fire door rating (in hours)	Opening class	Use of wall	Rating of wall (in hours)
3	A	Fire walls	3 or 4
		Fire separations	
$1\frac{1}{2}$	B	Vertical shafts	2
		Exit stairs	
		Fire separations	

Fire door rating (in hours)	Opening class	Use of wall	Rating of wall (in hours)
1	B	Vertical shafts Exit stairs Fire separations	1
¾	C	Fire-resistive partitions Corridors Hazardous areas	1
½		Limited applic. corridors	1 or less
⅓		Corridors	
20 Min.		Smoke barriers	
1½	D	Severe exterior exposure	2 or more
¾	E	Exterior exposure	1 or less

___ e. Energy conservation: Specify doors not to exceed:
   ___ (1) Residential: 0.5 CFM/SF infiltration
   ___ (2) Nonresidential: 11.0 CFM/LF crack infiltration

___ 3. *Hollow Metal Doors and Frames*

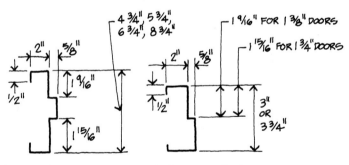

DOUBLE RABBET   SINGLE RABBET

___ a. Material (for gauges, see p. 245). Typical gauges of doors (16, 18, 20) and frames (12, 14, 16, 18)

Use	Frame	Door face
Heavy (entries, stairs public toilets, mech. rms.)	12, 14	16
Medium to low (rooms, closets, etc.)	14, 16, 20	18

___ *b.* Doors (total door construction of 16 to 22 GA)

Thickness	1¾″ and 1⅜″
Widths	2′ to 4′ in 2″ increments
Heights	6′8″, 7′, 7′2″, 7′10″, 8′, 10′

Costs: Frames: 3′ × 7′, 18 GA $5.90/SF (of opening) or 16 GA at $6.65/SF (60% M and 40% L), can vary ±40%.

Doors: 3′ × 7′, 20 GA, 1¾″: $12.70/SF (85% M and 3′ × 6′8″, 20 GA, 1⅜″: $12.25/SF 15% L).

Add: lead lining: $660/ea.,   8″ × 8″ glass, $120/ea., soundproofing $30/ea.,   3-hour $120/ea.,   ¾-hour $25/ea.

___ 4. *Wood Doors*

___ *a.* Types

  ___ (1) Flush
  ___ (2) Hollow core
  ___ (3) Solid core
  ___ (4) Panel (rail and stile)

___ *b.* Sizes

  Thickness: 1¾″ (SC), 1⅜″ (HC)
  Widths: 1′6″ to 3′6″ in 2″ increments
  Heights: 6′, 6′6″, 6′8″, 6′10″, 7′

___ *c.* Materials (birch, lavan, tempered hardboard)

Flush	Panel
Hardwood veneer	#1: hardwood or pine for transp. finish
Premium: for transp. finish	#2: Doug fir plywood for paint
Good #3: For paint.	
Sound: (for paint only)	

___ *d.* Fire doors (with mineral composition cores) B and C labels available, see p. 314.

Typical costs:
  Wood frame: interior, pine: $3.50/SF (of opening)
      exterior, pine: $6.80/SF
      (triple costs for hardwoods)
  Door: H.C. 1⅜″, hardboard $4.60/SF
      S.C. 1¾″, hardboard $9.50/SF (75% M and 25% L)
      Hardwood veneers about same costs.
  For carved solid exterior doors, multiply costs by 4 to 6.

___ 5. *Other Doors*
    ___ *a.* Sliding glass doors

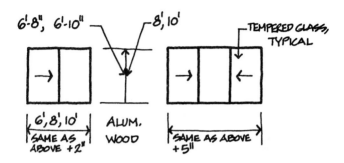

Typical costs (aluminum with ¼″ tempered glass):
    6′ wide: $770 to $870/ea. (85% M and 15% L)
    12′ wide: $1220 to $1690/ea.
    Add 10% for insulated glass.

    ___ *b.* Aluminum "storefront" (7′ ht. typical)
Typical cost with glass: $25/SF (85% M and 15% L). Variation of –25% to +55%.

    ___ *c.* Residential garage doors
        8′ min. width/car (9′ recommended)
        6′6″ min. height (7′2″ min. ceiling).
Costs: $25/SF (75% M and 25% L)

    ___ *d.* Folding doors
        2 panels: 1′6″, 2′0″, 2′6″, 3′0″ openings
        4 panels: 3′0″, 4′0″, 5′0″, 6′0″ openings
        6 panels: 7′6″ opening
        8 panels: 8′0″, 10′0″, 12′0″ openings
Costs: Accordion-folding closet doors with frame and trim: $20.00/SF

NOTES

__ B. WINDOWS ④ ⑫ ㉜ ㊺

For costs, see p. 322.
___ 1. <u>General</u>
    ___ *a.* In common with walls, windows are expected to keep out:

- winter wind
- rain in all seasons
- noise
- winter cold
- winter snow
- bugs and other flying objects
- summer heat

They are expected, at the same time, to let in:

- outside views
- ventilating air
- natural light
- winter solar gain

    ___ *b.* Size designations: 3′ W × 6′ H = 3060
    ___ *c.* For types by operation, see p. 322.
    ___ *d.* For aid to selection of type, see p. 320.
    ___ *e.* Windows come in aluminum, steel and wood. See pp. 324 and 325 for typical sizes.
    ___ *f.* Energy conservation: Specify windows to not exceed 0.34 CFM per LF of operable sash crack for infiltration.

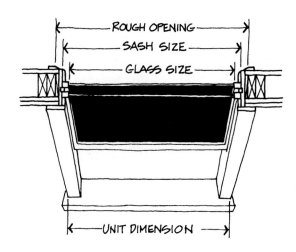

WINDOW TYPES

DISADVANTAGES	DOUBLE HUNG	DOUBLE HUNG, REVERSED	CASEMENT, OUT	CASEMENT, IN	AWNING, CANOPY	PIVOTED, VERTICAL	PIVOTED, HORIZONTAL	TOP HINGED, OUT	BOTTOM HINGED, IN	FIXED SASH	JALOUSIE	MONITOR, CONTINUOUS	PROJECTED	HORIZONTAL SLIDING
ONLY 50% OF AREA OPENABLE	•	•												•
DOESN'T PROTECT FROM RAIN, WHEN OPEN	•	•	•			•								•
INCONVENIENT OPER. IF OVER OBSTRUCTION	•	•												•
HAZ'D. IF LOW VENT NEXT TO WALK			•		•	•	•	•				•	•	
REQUIRES WEATHER STRIPPING	•	•	•	•	•	•	•	•	•					•
HORZ. MEMBERS OBSTRUCT VIEW	•	•		•			•				•			
VERT. MEMBERS OBSTRUCT VIEW	•	•	•	•		•								
WILL SAG IF NOT STRUCTURALLY STRONG			•	•		•					•			
GLASS QUICKLY SOILS WHEN VENT OPEN					•	•	•	•	•		•	•	•	
INFLOWING AIR CANNOT BE DIVERTED DOWN	•	•	•		•		•	•	•		•	•	•	•
EXCESSIVE AIR LEAKAGE											•			
HARD TO WASH											•			
INTERFERES WITH FURNITURE, DRAPES, ETC.				•					•					
SCREENS-STORM SASH DIFFICULT TO PROVIDE						•	•							•
SASH HAS TO BE REMOVED FOR WASHING	•									•		•		•

• INDICATES CHARACTERISTICS

WINDOW TYPES

● INDICATES CHARACTERISTICS

ADVANTAGES	DOUBLE HUNG	DOUBLE HUNG, REVERSED	CASEMENT, OUT	CASEMENT, IN	AWNING, CANOPY	PIVOTED, VERTICAL	PIVOTED, HORIZONTAL	TOP HINGED, OUT	BOTTOM HINGED, IN	FIXED SASH	JALOUSIE	MONITOR, CONTINUOUS	PROJECTED	HORIZONTAL SLIDING
NOT APT TO SAG	●	●			●	●	●	●	●	●		●		●
SCREEN & STORM SASH EASY TO INSTALL	●	●		●	●			●						●
PROVIDED 100% VENT OPENING			●	●	●	●	●	●	●		●	●		
EASY TO WASH W/ PROPER HARDWARE		●				●	●		●					
WILL DEFLECT DRAFTS				●		●	●		●		●	●		
OFFERS RAIN PROTECTION, PARTLY OPEN			●	●	●			●	●		●	●	●	
DIVERTS INFLOWING AIR UPWARD					●		●		●	●	●	●	●	●
ODD SIZES ECONOMICALLY AVAILABLE					●						●			●
LARGE SIZES PRACTICAL														

WINDOW TYPES BY OPERATION AND MATERIAL & COSTS

NOTE: GLASS EXCLUDED IN COSTS   * (90% M & 10% L)

TYPE		VENT	ALUMINUM	STEEL	WOOD
FIXED		0%	$13.30/SF AVE. (70%M & 30%L) VARIATION ±7%	$18/SF AVE.	$25/SF AVE. * VARIATION -10% +20% PICTURE WINDOW
CASEMENT		100%		$20 TO $26/SF AVE. (85%M & 15%L)	$35/SF AVE * VARIATION +70%, -40%
PROJECTED	AWNING	50 TO 100%	$24.25 TO $29.70/SF AVE. (75%M & 25%L)	$26.25 TO $30.30/SF AVE. *	$40/SF AVE. (85%M & 15%L) VARIATION +60%, -40%
	HOPPER				
SLIDING		50 TO 100%	$17 TO $19/SF AVE. (80%M & 20%L)		$26/SF AVE. VARIATION ±60%

DOUBLE-HUNG	50%	$18.50 TO $20.60/ SF AVE. *	$34/SF AVE *	$30/SF AVE. (85%M ¢ 15%L) VARIATION +70%, -45%
JALOUSIE	100%	$20/SF AVE. (80% M ¢ 20%L)		
PIVOTING	100%		$20/SF AVE. (85%M ¢ 15%L)	

TYPICAL WOOD WINDOW SASH SIZES

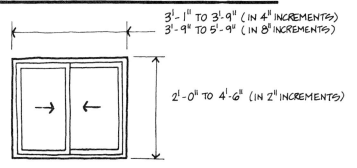

3'-1" TO 3'-9" (IN 4" INCREMENTS)
3'-9" TO 5'-9" (IN 8" INCREMENTS)

2'-0" TO 4'-6" (IN 2" INCREMENTS)

HORIZONTAL SLIDING WINDOWS

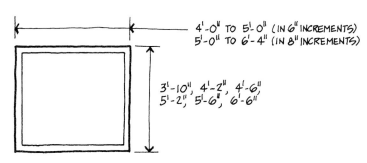

4'-0" TO 5'-0" (IN 6" INCREMENTS)
5'-0" TO 6'-4" (IN 8" INCREMENTS)

3'-10", 4'-2", 4'-6",
5'-2", 5'-6", 6'-6"

PICTURE WINDOWS

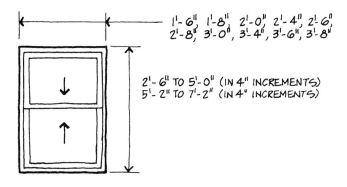

1'-6", 1'-8", 2'-0", 2'-4", 2'-6",
2'-8", 3'-0", 3'-4", 3'-6", 3'-8"

2'-6" TO 5'-0" (IN 4" INCREMENTS)
5'-2" TO 7'-2" (IN 4" INCREMENTS)

DOUBLE HUNG WINDOWS

ALUM. : RESIDENTIAL SIZES
STEEL : NO STD SIZES

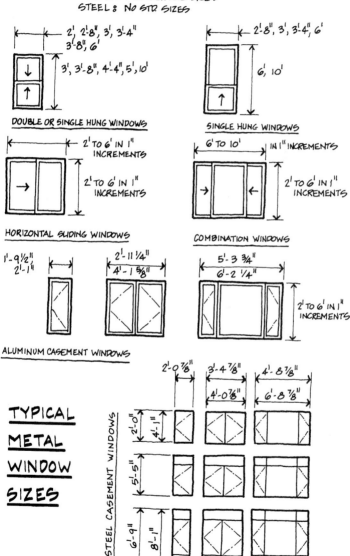

2', 2'-8", 3', 3'-4"
3'-8", 6'

3', 3'-8", 4'-4", 5', 10'

DOUBLE OR SINGLE HUNG WINDOWS

2'-8", 3', 3'-4", 6'

6', 10'

SINGLE HUNG WINDOWS

2' TO 6' IN 1"
INCREMENTS

2' TO 6' IN 1"
INCREMENTS

HORIZONTAL SLIDING WINDOWS

6' TO 10'   IN 1" INCREMENTS

2' TO 6' IN 1"
INCREMENTS

COMBINATION WINDOWS

1'-9½"
2'-1"

2'-11¼"
4'-1⅝"

ALUMINUM CASEMENT WINDOWS

5'-3¾"
6'-2¼"

2' TO 6' IN 1"
INCREMENTS

TYPICAL

METAL

WINDOW

SIZES

STEEL CASEMENT WINDOWS

2'-0⅞"   3'-4⅞"   4'-8⅞"
              4'-0⅞"   6'-8⅞"

2'-0"
4'-1"

5'-5"

6'-9"
8'-1"

NOTES

___ C. HARDWARE ⑫ ⑳

___ 1. <u>General Considerations:</u> How to . . .
    ___ *a.* Hang the door
    ___ *b.* Lock the door
    ___ *c.* Close the door
    ___ *d.* Protect the door
    ___ *e.* Stop the door
    ___ *f.* Seal the door
    ___ *g.* Misc. the door
    ___ *h.* Electrify the door

___ 2. <u>Recommended Locations</u>   ___ 3. <u>Door Hand Conventions</u>

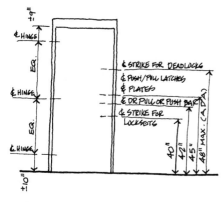

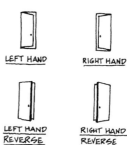

LEFT HAND   RIGHT HAND

LEFT HAND REVERSE   RIGHT HAND REVERSE

⬆ DIRECTION OF TRAVEL ASSUMED TO BE FROM OUTSIDE IN OR FROM KEYED SIDE FOR INTERIOR DOORS.

___ 4. <u>Specific Considerations</u>
    ___ *a.* Function and ease of operation
    ___ *b.* Durability in terms of:
        ___ (1) Frequency of use
            ___ (*a*) Heavy
            ___ (*b*) Medium
            ___ (*c*) Light
        ___ (2) Exposure to weather and climate (aluminum and stainless steel good for humid or coastal conditions)
    ___ *c.* Material, form, surface texture, finish, and color.
___ 5. <u>Typical Hardware</u>
    ___ *a.* Locksets (locks, latches, bolts)
    ___ *b.* Hinges
    ___ *c.* Closers
    ___ *d.* Panic hardware
    ___ *e.* Push/pull bars and plates

  ___ *f.* Kick plates
  ___ *g.* Stops and holders
  ___ *h.* Thresholds
  ___ *i.* Weatherstripping
  ___ *j.* Door tracks and hangers
___ 6. Materials
  ___ *a.* Aluminum
  ___ *b.* Brass
  ___ *c.* Bronze
  ___ *d.* Iron
  ___ *e.* Steel
  ___ *f.* Stainless steel
___ 7. Finishes

BHMA #	US #	Finish
___ 600	US P	Primed for painting
___ 605	US 3	Bright brass, clear coated
___ 606	US 4	Satin brass, clear coated
___ 612	US 10	Satin bronze, clear coated
___ 613	US 10B	Oxidized satin bronze, oil rubbed
___ 618	US 14	Bright nickel plated, clear coated
___ 619	US 15	Satin nickel plated, clear coated
___ 622	US 19	Flat black coated
___ 623	US 20	Light oxidized bright bronze clear C
___ 624	US 20D	Dark oxidized statuary bronze CC
___ 625	US 26	Bright chromium plated
___ 626	US 26D	Satin chromium plated
___ 628	US 28	Satin aluminum, clear anodized
___ 629	US 32	Bright stainless steel
___ 630	US 32D	Satin stainless steel

___ 8. ADA-Accessible Hardware

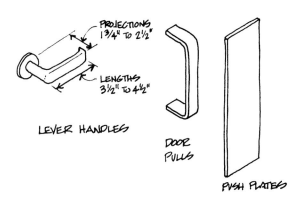

PROJECTIONS
1¾" TO 2½"

LENGTHS
3½" TO 4½"

LEVER HANDLES

DOOR PULLS

PUSH PLATES

___ 9. **Costs:**
    Residential: **$90/door (80% M and 20% L)**
                                Variation −30%, +120%
    Commercial:
     Office:
      Interior: **$180/door (75% M and 25% L)**
      Exterior: **$350/door (add ≈ $425 for exit devices)**
     Note: Special doors, such as for hospitals, can cost up to $570/door

NOTES

___ D. GLASS (24) (45)

___ 1. <u>General:</u> Glass is one of the great modern building materials because it allows the inside of buildings to have a *visual relationship* with the outside. However, there are a number of *problems to be overcome:*

___ 2. <u>Energy:</u> Because more *heat flows through glass than any other building material,* it must be sized and located carefully. See p. 138.

    ___ *a.* Solar: When *heating is needed,* glass can be used on south sides to help. See p. 139. When *heating is to be avoided,* it is best to place glass on north or south sides, avoiding the east and west. The *shading coefficient* is the ratio of the total solar heat gain to that of ⅛″ clear glass. 1.0 is no shade, so the lower the number the better.

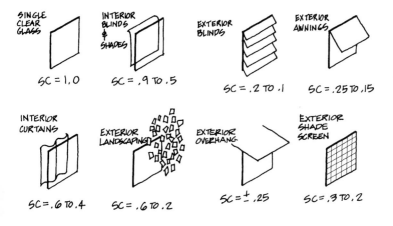

SINGLE CLEAR GLASS — SC = 1.0

INTERIOR BLINDS & SHADES — SC = .9 TO .5

EXTERIOR BLINDS — SC = .2 TO .1

EXTERIOR AWNINGS — SC = .25 TO .15

INTERIOR CURTAINS — SC = .6 TO .4

EXTERIOR LANDSCAPING — SC = .6 TO .2

EXTERIOR OVERHANG — SC = ± .25

EXTERIOR SHADE SCREEN — SC = .3 TO .2

    ___ *b.* Conduction/convection heat flow: Also transfers heat, since glass is a poor insulator. See p. 292.

___ 3. <u>Condensation:</u> As room air comes in contact with cold glass, it drops in temperature, depositing excess water vapor on the surface as liquid condensate. Use the following graph to select glazing to avoid this:

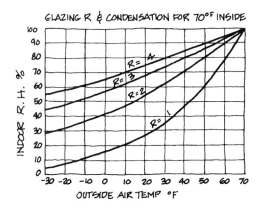

GLAZING R & CONDENSATION FOR 70°F INSIDE

___ 4. <u>Legal Requirements:</u> The UBC requires *safety glazing* at locations hazardous to human impact. Safety glazing is *tempered glass, wired glass,* and *laminated glass.* Hazardous locations are:

  ___ *a.* Ingress and egress doors
  ___ *b.* Sliding glass doors
  ___ *c.* Storm doors
  ___ *d.* Swinging doors
  ___ *e.* Shower and bathtub doors and enclosures
  ___ *f.* Glass in railings
  ___ *g.* Overhead or angled glass and skylights (must be plastic, wired glass, or laminated glass or tempered w/screen below)
  ___ *h.* Glass adjacent to doors and other glass areas within 24″ and less than 60″ high, per below:
  ___ *i.* Glass within 5′ of swimming pool
  ___ *j.* Glass within 5′ of enclosed stairway

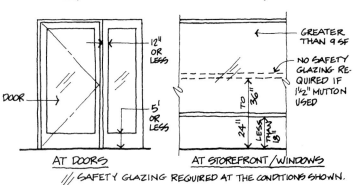

AT DOORS   AT STOREFRONT/WINDOWS

/// SAFETY GLAZING REQUIRED AT THE CONDITIONS SHOWN.

___ 5. Sizing of Glass
___ *a.* Determine wind speeds at site by consulting App. B, item S. Convert to pressure:

Wind pressure at 33′ height

Wind (MPH)	70	80	90	100	110	120	130
Pressure (PSF)	12.6	16.4	20.8	25.6	31.0	36.9	43.3

___ *b.* Multiply results by the following factors:
    ___ (1) For low, normal, open sites: 1.5
    ___ (2) For high, windy, or gusty sites: 3.0
___ *c.* Select glass size from below:

MAXIMUM GLAZING AREA VS. PRESSURE

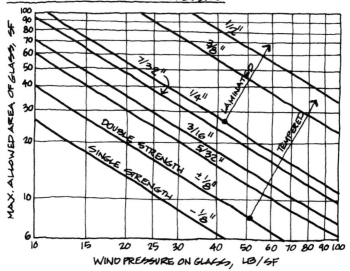

___ 6. **Costs:**
   ¼″ **clear float glass: $7.00 to $9.00/SF (45% M and 55% L)**
   Modifiers:
     Thickness:
       ⅛″ **glass**   **−40%**
       ⅜″ **glass**   **+50%**
       ½″ **glass**   **+150%**
     Structural:
      Tempered   **+20%**
      Laminated **+45%**

Thermal:
    Tinted or reflective   **+20%**
    Double-glazed and/or low E **+100%**

EXAMPLE:

PHOENIX, AZ, S = 75 MPH (SEE APP. B, ITEM 6,
ON P. 527) EQUALS ≈ 13.25 PSF. FOR NORMAL
SITE : 1.5 × 13.25 = 20 PSF.

COULD USE :   55 SF OF ¼" GLASS, OR
               20 SF OF DS GLASS, OR
               15 SF OF SS GLASS

___ 7. <u>Typical Glazing Characteristics</u>

Glazing type	R value	Shade coef.	Vis. trans. (%)	Perf. index
___ Single-Glazed (SG), clear	0.90	1.00	90	0.90
___ SG gray-tinted	"	0.69	43	0.62
___ SG bronze-tinted	"	0.71	52	0.73
___ SG green-tinted	"	0.71	75	1.09
___ SG reflective	"	0.51	27	0.53
___ SG low-E, clear	1.40	0.74	84	1.14
___ SG low-E, gray	"	0.50	41	1.82
___ SG low-E, bronze	"	0.52	49	0.94
___ SG low-E, green	"	0.56	71	1.27
___ Double-Glazed (DG), clear	2.00	0.84	80	0.95
___ DG gray-tinted	"	0.85	39	0.69
___ DG bronze-tinted	"	0.59	47	0.80
___ DG green-tinted	"	0.60	68	1.13
___ DG reflective	"	0.42	26	0.62
___ DG low-E, clear	3.12	0.67	76	1.13
___ DG low-E, gray	"	0.42	37	0.88
___ DG low-E, bronze	"	0.44	44	1.00
___ DG low-E, green	"	0.47	64	1.36
___ DG polyfilm, clear	4.5	0.42	53	1.26
___ DG polyfilm, gray	"	0.27	26	0.96
___ DG polyfilm, bronze	"	0.29	32	1.10
___ DG polyfilm, green	"	0.29	45	1.55

Note: Performance Index ("Coolness Index") = Visual Transmission/Shading Coefficient. The higher the number the better.

<u>NOTES</u>

NOTES

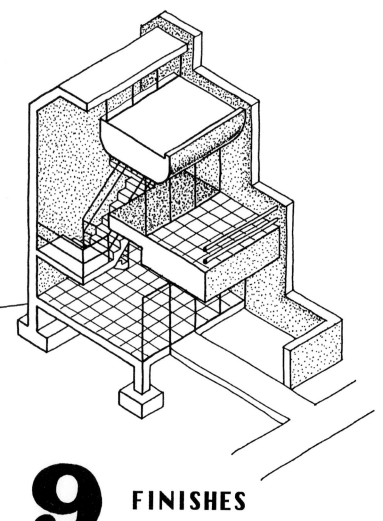

9 FINISHES

NOTES

__ A. PLASTER

Note: For EIFS, see p. 296.

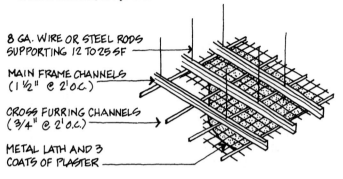

8 GA. WIRE OR STEEL RODS SUPPORTING 12 TO 25 SF

MAIN FRAME CHANNELS (1½" @ 2' O.C.)

CROSS FURRING CHANNELS (¾" @ 2' O.C.)

METAL LATH AND 3 COATS OF PLASTER

TYPICAL CEILING

___ 1. Exterior (stucco) of cement plaster.
___ 2. Interior of gypsum plaster.
___ 3. Wall supports usually studs at between 12″ and 24″ oc. If wood, use 16″ oc min.
___ 4. Full plaster—3 coats (scratch brown, and finish), but walls of masonry can have 1 or 2 coats.
___ 5. Joints: Interior ceilings: 30′ oc max.
   Exterior walls/soffits: 10′ to 20′ oc.
___ 6. Provide vents at dead air spaces (½″/SF).
___ 7. Curing: 48 hrs moist curing, 7 days between coats.

Costs:

Ceilings with paint, plaster, and lath	**$1.50 to $6.50/SF (25% M and 75% L), can vary up to +60% for plaster**
Walls of stucco with paper-backed wire lath	**$2.00/SF for stucco + $.85/SF for lath (50% M and 50% L)**

__ B. GYPSUM WALLBOARD (DRYWALL)

__ 1. Usually in $4' \times 8'$ (or $12'$) sheets from $\frac{1}{4}''$ to $1''$ thick in about $\frac{1}{8}''$ increments.

__ 2. Attach (nail or screw) against wood or metal framing—usually at $16''$ (fire rating) to $24''$ oc.

__ 3. Type "X", $\frac{5}{8}''$ will give 1 hr. fire rating. Roughly each additional $\frac{1}{2}''$ layer will give 1 hr. rating up to 4 hours, depending on backing and application.

__ 4. Water-resistant (green) available for wet areas or exterior.

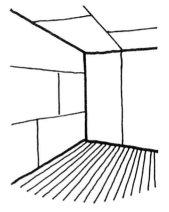

For exterior soffit venting, see p. 287.

Costs:

$\frac{1}{2}''$ **gyp. bd.**	**$.60/SF ceilings**
on wood	**$1.00/SF columns and beams**
frame	**$.60/SF walls**

(Approx. 50% M and 50% L)

Increase 5% for metal frame. Varies about 15% in cost for $\frac{1}{8}'$ ea. thickness. Add $.07/SF for fire resistance. Add $.12/SF for water resistance. Add $.35/SF for joint work and finish.

EXAMPLE:

FIND THE COST OF $\frac{5}{8}''$ GYPB'D. WALL ON FRAME, READY FOR PAINT.

$\frac{1}{2}'' = \$0.60/SF$ (WALL) $+ 9¢$ (15% FOR EXTRA $\frac{1}{8}''$ THICKNESS) $+ \$0.35$ FOR FINISH.

$\therefore \frac{5}{8}'' = \$1.04/SF$, SAY $\$1\frac{05}{}/SF$

__ C. TILE ④ ⑫

___ 1. Settings
   ___ *a.* Thick set (¾″ to 1¼″ mortar bed) for slopes.
   ___ *b.* Thin set (⅛″ mortar or adhesive) for faster and less expensive applications.

___ 2. Joints: ⅛″ to ¼″ (can be epoxy grouted for quarry tile floors).

___ 3. Types
   ___ *a.* Ceramic glazed and unglazed for walls and floors of about ¼″ thick and 4–6″ SQ. Many trim shapes available.
   ___ *b.* Ceramic mosaic for walls and floors of about ¼″ thick and 1″ to 2″ SQ.
   ___ *c.* Quarry tile of earth tones for strong and resistant flooring. Usually ½″ to ¾″ thick by 4″ to 9″ SQ.

Typical Costs:

Note: Costs can vary greatly with special imports of great expense.

Glazed wall tile: $5.35/SF (50% M and 50% L), variation of −25%, +100%

Unglazed floor mosaic: $8.10/SF (65% M and 35% L), variation of +35%, −10%

Unglazed wall tile: $6.00/SF (40% M and 60% L), variation of +35%, −15%

Quarry tile: $8.80/SF (same as above), variation of ±10%

Bases: $8.80/LF (same as above), variation of ±10%

Additions: color variations: +10 to 20%
          abrasive surface: +25 to 50%

___ D. TERRAZZO

___ 1. A poured material (usually ½″ thick) of stone chips in a cement matrix, usually with a polished surface.

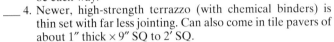

___ 2. Base of sand and concrete.

___ 3. To prevent cracking, exposed metal dividers are set approx. 3′ to 6′ oc each way.

___ 4. Newer, high-strength terrazzo (with chemical binders) is thin set with far less jointing. Can also come in tile pavers of about 1″ thick × 9″ SQ to 2′ SQ.

Costs: $8.00/SF to $13.30/SF (45% M and 55% L)
Tiles: $17.00 to $26.00/SF

___ E. ACOUSTICAL TREATMENT

___ 1. Acoustical Ceilings: Can consist of small (¾″ thick × 1′ SQ) mineral fiber tiles attached to wallboard or concrete (usually glued). Also, acoustical mineral fibers with a binder can be shot on gypsum board or concrete.

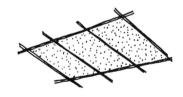

Costs: Small tiles $.85/SF (40% M and 60% L)

___ 2. Suspended Acoustical Tile Ceilings: Can be used to create a plenum space to conceal mechanical and electrical functions. Typical applications are 2′ SQ or 2′ × 4′ tiles in exposed or concealed metal grids that are wire-suspended as in plaster ceilings. The finishes can vary widely.

Costs: Acoustical panels $1.00 to $2.00/SF (70% M and 30% L)
Suspension system $1.00 to $1.25/SF (80% M and 20% L)
When walls do *not* penetrate ceilings, can save $0.10 to $0.20/SF.

__ F. WOOD FLOORING (4) (12)

__ 1. See p. 279 for structural decking.
__ 2. Finished flooring can be of hardwoods or softwoods, of
which oak, southern pine, and Douglas fir are the most
commonly used.
__ 3. All-heartwood grade of redwood is best for porch and exterior flooring.
__ 4. If substrate is concrete, often flooring is placed on small
wood strips (sleepers); otherwise flooring is often nailed to
wood substrates (plywood or wood decking).
__ 5. Because wood is very susceptible to moisture, allowance
must be made for movement and ventilation. Allow expansion at perimeters. Vapor barriers below concrete slabs are
important.
__ 6. Use treated material in hot, humid climates.
__ 7. Three types of wood flooring:
    __ *a.* Strip
    __ *b.* Plank
    __ *c.* Block (such as parque)

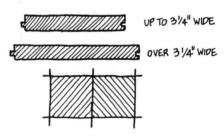

UP TO 3 1/4" WIDE

OVER 3 1/4" WIDE

Typical Costs:
        Wood strip fir $3.40/SF (70% M and 30% L)
        Oak +45% +10% finish
        Maple +45% clean and wax = $0.30/SF

__ G. MASONRY FLOORING (4) (12)

    See Part 4 on materials.

Typical Costs:
        ¾″ × 4″ × 8″ brick: $8.10/SF
        (65% M and 35% L)
        Add 15% for special patterns.

__ H. RESILIENT FLOORING (4) (12)

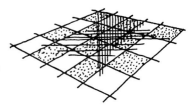

___ 1. Consists of sheets or tiles of vinyl, cork, rubber, linoleum, or asphalt with *vinyl* the most commonly used.

___ 2. Is approx. ¹⁄₁₆″ to ¹⁄₈″ thick with tiles being 9″ SQ to 12″ SQ.

___ 3. Applied to substrate with mastic. Substrate may be plywood flooring, plywood or particleboard over wood deck, or concrete slabs.

___ 4. Vapor barriers often required under slabs.

___ 5. Vinyl base is often applied at walls for this and other floor systems.

A wide range of colors and patterns is available for flooring.

Typical Costs:

Solid vinyl tile ¹⁄₈ × 12 × 12	**$3.00/SF (75% M and 25% L), can go up 20% for various patterns and colors; double for "conductive" type.**
Sheet vinyl	**$2.75/SF (90% M and 10% L), variation of −70% and +100% due to various patterns and colors.**
Vinyl wall base	**$1.75/LF (40% M and 60% L). Can vary +15%.**
Stair treads	**$8.00/LF (60% M and 40% L). Can vary from −10% to +40%.**

___ I. CARPETING (4) (45)

___ 1. Most wall-to-wall carpeting is produced by looping yarns through a coarse-fiber backing, binding the backs of the loops with latex, then applying a second backing for strength and dimensional stability. Finally the loops may be left uncut for a rough, nubby surface or cut for a soft, plush surface.

___ 2. The quality of carpeting is often determined by its *face weight* (ounces of yarn or pile per square yard), not its total weight. Weights run:

    ___ *a.* Low traffic: 20–24 oz/SY
    ___ *b.* Medium traffic: 24–32 oz/SY
    ___ *c.* High-end carpet: 26–70 oz/SY

___ 3. A better measure of comparison:

$$weight\ density\ factor = \frac{face\ weight \times 36}{pile\ height} = oz/CY$$

Ideally, this should be as follows:

    ___ *a.* Residential: 3000 to 3600 oz/CY
    ___ *b.* Commercial: 4200 to 7000 oz/CY

___ 4. There are two basic carpet installation methods:

    ___ *a.* *Padded and stitched* carpeting: Stretched over a separate pad and mechanically fastened at joints and the perimeter. Soft foam pads are inexpensive and give the carpet a soft, luxurious feel. The more expensive jute and felt pads give better support and dimensional stability. Padding adds to foot comfort, helps dampen noise, and some say, adds to the life of the carpet.

    ___ *b.* *Glued-down* carpets: Usually used in commercial areas subject to heavily loaded wheel traffic. They are usually glued down with carpet adhesive with a pad. This minimizes destructive flexing of the backing and prevents rippling.

___ 5. Maintenance Factors

    ___ *a.* Color: Carpets in the midvalue range show less soiling than very dark or very light colors. Consider the typical regional soil color. Specify patterned or multicolored carpets for heavy traffic areas in hotels, hospitals, theaters, and restaurants.

    ___ *b.* Traffic: The heavier the traffic, the heavier the density of carpet construction. If rolling traffic is a factor, carpet may be of maximum density for minimum resistance to rollers. Select only level-loop or dense, low-cut pile.

___ 6. Carpet Materials:

Fiber	Advantages	Disadvantages
Acrylic (rarely used)	Resembles wool	Not very tough; attracts oily dirt
Nylon (most used)	Very tough; resists dirt, resembles wool; low-static buildup	None
Polyester deep pilings	Soft and luxurious	Less resilient; attracts oily dirt
Polypropylene indoor-outdoor	Waterproof; resists fading and stains; easy to clean	Crushes easily
Wool	Durable; easy to clean; feels good; easily dyed	Most expensive

___ 7. **Costs: (90% M and 10% L) (Variation ±100%) See p. 377 for interiors wholesale/retail advice. Figure 10% waste. Repair/level floors: $1.65 to $6.10/SY (45% M and 55% L)**

Padding
    Sponge: $5.60/SY (70% M and 30% L) Variation ±10%
    Jute: −10%
    Urethane: −25%
Carpet
    Acrylic, 24 oz, med. wear: $20.50/SY
    **   28 oz, med./heavy: $25.50/SY**
Residential
    Nylon, 15 oz, light traffic: $15.25/SY
    **   28 oz, med. traffic: $18.00/SY**
Commercial
    Nylon, 28 oz, med. traffic: $19.00/SY
    **   35 oz, heavy: $22.35/SY**
    Wool, 30 oz, med. traffic: $30.00/SY
    **   42 oz, heavy: $41.00/SY**
Carpet tile: $2.50 to $5.00/SY

CARPET TYPES

<u>TYPE OF WEAVE</u>   <u>CHARACTERISTICS AND BEST USES</u>

<u>LEVEL LOOP</u> : EVEN HEIGHT, TIGHTLY SPACED UN-
CUT LOOPS. TEXTURE IS HARD AND PEBBLY.
HARD WEARING AND EASY TO CLEAN. IDEAL
FOR OFFICES AND HIGH TRAFFIC AREAS.

<u>MULTI-LEVEL LOOP</u> : UNEVEN HEIGHT IN PATTERNS,
TIGHTLY SPACED UNCUT LOOPS. TEXTURE IS
HARD & PEBBLY. HARD-WEARING & EASY TO
CLEAN. IDEAL FOR OFFICES AND HIGH TRAFFIC
AREAS.

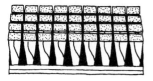

<u>PLUSH 'CUT' PILE</u> : EVENLY CUT YARNS WITH
MINIMAL TWIST. EXTREMELY SOFT, VELVETY
TEXTURE. VACUUMING AND FOOTPRINTS APPEAR
AS DIFFERENT COLORS, DEPENDING ON LIGHT
CONDITIONS. IDEAL FOR FORMAL ROOMS W/
LIGHT TRAFFIC.

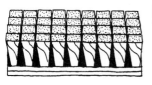

<u>FRIEZE 'CUT' PILE</u> : EVENLY CUT YARNS WITH
TIGHT TWIST. EXTREMELY SOFT, VELVETY
TEXTURE. VACUUMING AND FOOTPRINTS AP-
PEAR AS DIFFERENT COLORS, DEPENDING ON
LIGHT CONDITIONS. IDEAL FOR FORMAL RM'S
WITH LIGHT TRAFFIC.

<u>CUT AND LOOP</u> : COMBINATION OF BOTH PLUSH
AND LEVEL-LOOP. HIDES DIRT FAIRLY WELL.
IDEAL FOR RESIDENTIAL APPLICATIONS.

<u>INDOOR-OUTDOOR</u> : CUT, TIGHTLY TWISTED
YARNS THAT TWIST UPON THEMSELVES. TEXT-
URE IS ROUGH. HIDES DIRT EXTREMELY WELL
AND IS NEARLY AS TOUGH AS LEVEL-LOOP.
IDEAL FOR RESIDENTIAL APPLICATIONS.

__ J. PAINT AND COATINGS

___ 1. <u>General</u>

   ___ *a.* Paints and coatings: are liquids (the "vehicle") with pigments in suspension, to protect and decorate building surfaces.

   ___ *b.* Applications: brushed, rolled, sprayed

   ___ *c.* Failures: 90% are due to either moisture problems or inadequate preparation of surface.

   ___ *d.* Surface Preparation:

      ___ (1) Wood: Sand if required; paint immediately.

      ___ (2) Drywall: Let dry (0 to 7 days). If textured surface is required, prime prior to texturing.

      ___ (3) Masonry and stucco: Wait for cure (28 days).

   ___ *e.* Qualities:

      ___ (1) Thickness

         ___ (*a*) Primers (and "undercoats"): ½ to 1 dry mills/coat.

         ___ (*b*) Finish coats: 1 to 1½ dry mills/coat.

      ___ (2) Breathability: Allowing vapor passage to avoid deterioration of substrate and coating. Required at (see p. 289):

         ___ (*a*) Masonry and stucco: 25 perms

         ___ (*b*) Wood: 15 perms

         ___ (*c*) Metals: 0 perms

   ___ *f.* Paint Surfaces:

      ___ (1) Flat: Softens and distributes illumination evenly. Reduces visibility of substrate defects. Not easily cleaned. Usually used on ceilings.

      ___ (2) Eggshell: Provides most of the advantages of gloss without glare.

      ___ (3) Semigloss

      ___ (4) Gloss: Reflects and can cause glare, but also provides smooth, easily cleanable, nonabsorbtive surface. Increases visibility of substrate defects.

   ___ *g.* Legal Restrictions:

      ___ (1) Check state regulations on paints for use of volatile organic compounds (VOC), use of solvents, and hazardous waste problems.

      ___ (2) Check fire department restrictions on spraying interiors after occupancy or during remodelling.

___ 2. <u>Material Types</u>
    ___ *a.* Water-repellent preservatives: For wood.
    ___ *b.* Stains: Solid (opaque), semitransparent, or clear.
    ___ *c.* Wood coatings: Varnish, shellac, lacquers.
    ___ *d.* Wood primer-sealer: Designed to prevent bleeding through of wood resin contained in knots and pitch pockets, and to seal surface for other coatings. Usually apply 2 coats to knots. Since primer-sealer is white, cannot be used on clear finishes.
    ___ *e.* Latex primer: Best first coat over wallboard, plaster, and concrete. Adheres well to any surface except untreated wood.
    ___ *f.* Alkyd primer: Used on raw wood. Latex "undercoats" can also be used.
    ___ *g.* CMU filler: A special latex primer for reducing voids and to smooth surface on masonry. Does not waterproof.
    ___ *h.* Latex paint: A synthetic, water-based coating, this is the most popular paint because it complies with most environmental requirements, is breathable, and cleans up with water. Use for almost all surfaces including primed (or undercoated) wood. Adheres to latex and flat oils. Avoid gloss oils and alkyds other than primers. Subdivided, as follows:
        ___ (1) Polyvinyl acetate (PVA): Most commonly used. Provides 25+ perms.
        ___ (2) Acrylic: Smoother, more elastic, more durable, often used as a primer. Provides less than 5 perms.
    ___ *i.* Alkyd paint: A synthetic semisolvent-based coating, replacing the old oils. This seems to be going out of use due to environmental laws. Used for exterior metal surfaces. Not breathable.

___ 3. <u>Paint Systems and **Costs**</u> (**30% M and 70% L**):

Material	Finish	Prime	Top coats	**Costs**
Preparation (sanding, etc., if required)				**$0.10/SF up to $5/SF**
Exterior				
Wood				
General	gloss flat stain	alkyd * (same)	ext. alkyd enamel ext. alkyd or latex semitrans. or solid	**$0.60/SF**
Floors				
Clear	gloss		alkyd enamel or latex acrylic	**$0.60/SF**
Redw'd. Doors Windows	stain		semitrans. alkyd	**$1.00 to 2.00/SF**
Masonry, concrete, and stucco				
	clear	prime sealer or CMU filler	water-repellent	**$0.70/SF**
	flat	(same)	exterior latex	
Metals	gloss	galv. iron: zinc oxide steel: zinc chromate	ext. alkyd enamel	**$0.40/SF**
	flat	(same)	ext. latex acrylic	**(same)**
Interiors				
Wood				
General	gloss flat	enamel undercoat (same)	alkyd enamel or latex enamel (same)	**$0.25 to $0.70/SF**
Floors	gloss clear	stain, if req'd. (same)	alkyd floor enamel alkyd base varnish	**(same)** **(same)**
Plaster/drywall				
	gloss flat	latex latex	latex latex	
Brick		latex	latex	**(same)**
CMU		CMU filler	latex	**(same)**
Metals	gloss flat	see exterior	epoxy or alkyd enamel alkyd or latex	**(same)**

*or latex "undercoat"

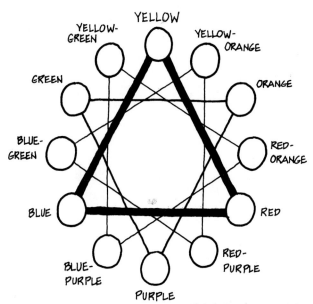

THE COLOR WHEEL
(FOR PIGMENTS)

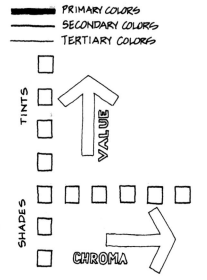

━━━ PRIMARY COLORS
─── SECONDARY COLORS
── TERTIARY COLORS

THINK OF COLOR IN THREE
DIMENSIONS
1. HUE ("COLOR")
2. VALUE (LIGHT TO DARK)
3. CHROMA (SATURATION–
   INTENSITY)

___ 1. <u>Basic Color Schemes</u>

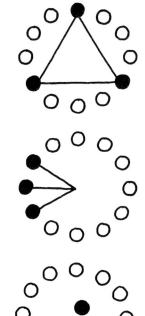

___ *a. Triadic schemes.*
     Made from any three
     hues that are equidis-
     tant on the color
     wheel.

___ *b. Analogous or
     related schemes.*
     Consist of hues that
     are side by side.

___ *c. Monochromatic
     schemes.* Use only
     one color (hue) in a
     range of values and
     intensities, coupled
     with neutral blacks
     or whites.

___ *d. Complementary
     schemes.* Use con-
     trast by drawing
     from exact opposites
     on the color wheel.
     Usually, one of the
     colors is dominant
     while the other is
     used as an accent.
     Usually vary the
     amount and bright-
     ness of contrasting
     colors.

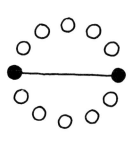

___ *e.* *Split complemen-*
tary schemes. Con-
sist of one hue and the
two hues on each side
of its compliment.

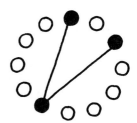

___ *f.* *Double complemen-*
tary schemes. Com-
posed of two adjacent
hues and their respec-
tive hues, directly
opposite on the color
wheel.

___ *g.* *Many-hued schemes.*
Those with more than
three hues. These usu-
ally need a strong
dose of one color as a
base with added col-
ors that are closely
matched in value.

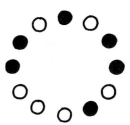

___ 2. <u>Rules of Thumb</u>
    ___ *a.* Your dominant color should cover about ⅔ of the
room's area. Equal areas of color are usually less
pleasing. Typical areas to be covered by the main
color are the walls, ceiling, and part of the floor.
    ___ *b.* The next most important color usually is in the floor
covering, the furniture, or the draperies.
    ___ *c.* The accent colors act as the "spice" for the scheme.
    ___ *d.* Study the proposed colors in the lighting conditions
of where they will be used (natural light, type of
artificial light).
    ___ *e.* The larger the area, the brighter a color will seem.
Usually duller tones are used for large areas.

___ *f.*   Contrast is greater from light to dark than it is from hue to hue or dull to bright saturation.

___ *g.*   Colors that seem identical but are slightly different will seem more divergent when placed together.

___ *h.*   Bold, warm (red/orange) and dark colors will "advance." These can be used to bring in end walls, to lower ceilings, or to create a feeling of closeness in a room.

___ *i.*   Cool (blue/green), dull and light colors "recede." These can be used to heighten ceilings or to widen a room.

___ *j.*   Related colors tend to blend into "harmony."

___ *k.*   From an economic point of view, dark colors absorb more light (and heat) and will require more lighting. Light colors reflect light, requiring less lighting.

___ *l.*   Colors will appear darker and more saturated when reflected from a glossy surface than when reflected from a matte surface.

___ *m.*   A color on a textured surface will appear darker than on a smooth surface.

___ *n.*   Bright colors increase in brilliance when increased in area, and pale colors fade when increased in area.

___ *o.*   Incandescent (warm) lighting normally adds a warming glow to colors. Under this light, consider "cooling" down or graying bright reds, oranges, or yellows.

___ *p.*   Low atmospheric lighting tends to gray down colors.

___ *q.*   Fluorescent lighting changes the hue of colors in varying ways depending on the type used. In some instances it will accent blue tones and make reds look colder. It may make many colors look harsher.

___ *r.*   Southern exposures will bring in warm tones of sunlight.

___ *s.*   Northern exposures will bring in cool light.

___ 3. <u>Percent Light Reflected from Typical Walls and Ceilings</u>

Class	Surface	Color	% Light reflected
Light	Paint	white	81
		ivory	79
		cream	74
	Stone	cream	69
Medium	Paint	buff	63
		lt. green	63
		lt. grey	58
	Stone	grey	56
Dark	Paint	tan	48
		dk. grey	26
		olive green	17
		lt. oak	32
		mohogany	8
	Cement	natural	25
	Brick	red	13

___ 4. <u>Typical Reflectance</u> %
    ___ *a.* Commercial
       Ceiling   80%
       Walls   50%
       Floors   20%
    ___ *b.* Industrial
       Ceiling   50%
       Walls   50%
       Floor   20%
    ___ *c.* Classrooms
       Ceiling   70–90%
       Walls   40–60%
       Floor   30–50%
       Desk top   35–50%
       Blackboard 20%

<u>NOTES</u>

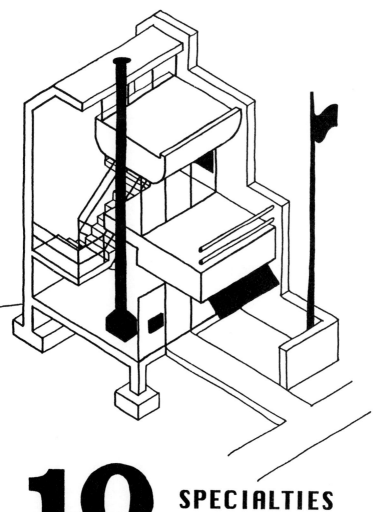

10 SPECIALTIES

NOTES

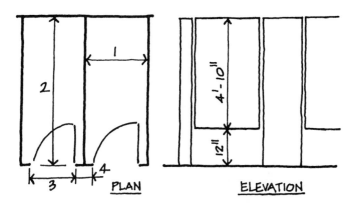

PLAN   ELEVATION

___ 1. Typical widths: 2′6″, 2′8″, 2′10″ (most-used), and 3′0″
___ 2. Typical depths:
    ___ *a.* Open front: 2′6″ to 4′0″
    ___ *b.* Closed front (door): 4′6″ to 4′9″
___ 3. Typical doors: 1′8″, 1′10″, 2′0″, 2′4″, and 2′6″
___ 4. Typical pilasters: 3, 4, 5, 6, 8, or 10 inches
___ 5. For HC-accessible, see pp. 426–428.

Costs: $600 to $800/each compartment

Ceiling-mounted partitions, with plastic-laminate finish, are the least expensive.

___ B. FIREPLACES ④

___ 1. Typical Opening Sizes (see drawings below):

W	H	D	S
2′	1.5′ to 1.75′	1.33′ to 1.5′	
3′	2′	1.67′	6½″
4′	2.12′	1.75′	6″
5′	2.5′ to 2.75′	2′ to 2.17′	9″
6′	2.75′ to 3′	2.17′ to 2.33′	9″

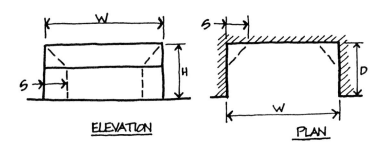

ELEVATION   PLAN

___ 2. For energy conservation, provide:
    ___ *a.* Outside combustion air ducted to firebox
    ___ *b.* Glass doors
    ___ *c.* Blower
___ 3. Per UBC:
    ___ *a.* Hearth extension to front must be 16″ (or 20″ if opening greater than 6 SF).
    ___ *b.* Hearth extension to side must be 8″ (or 12″ if opening greater than 6 SF).
    ___ *c.* Thickness of wall of firebox must be 10″ brick (or 8″ firebrick).
    ___ *d.* Top of chimney must be 2′ above any roof element within 10′.

Costs: Fabricated metal: $500 to $1500 (75% M and 25% L)

__ C. GRAPHICS (4)

___ 1. General: Visual identification and direction by signage is very important for "wayfinding" to, between, around, in, and through buildings. Signage is enhanced by:

    ___ *a.* Size
    ___ *b.* Contrast
    ___ *c.* Design of letter character and graphics.

CONTRAST!

___ 2. Road Signage: Can be roughly estimated as follows:

| SPEED | VIEWING | | SIGN SIZE | COPY SIZE |
MPH	DISTANCE	ANGLE	SF	INCH HT.
15	220'		8	
30	310'		40	5
40	450'	35°		7
45	660'		90	
50	545'	30°		8½
60	610 - 880'	20°	150	9½

___ 3. Building Signage
    ___ *a.* Site directional/warning signs should be:
        ___ (1) 6' from curb
        ___ (2) 7' from grade to bottom
        ___ (3) 100'–200' from intersections
        ___ (4) 1 to 2.5 FT SQ
    ___ *b.* Effective pedestrian viewing distance 20' to 155'
    ___ *c.* Effective sign size: ≈10'/inch height (10' max. viewing distance per inch of height of sign).
    ___ *d.* Effective letter size: ≈50'/inch height.
    ___ *e.* As a rule, letters should constitute about 40% of sign and should not exceed 30 letters in width.
    ___ *f.* Materials
        ___ (1) Exterior
            ___ (*a*) Building: fabricated aluminum, illuminated plastic face, back-lighted, cast aluminum, applied letter, die-raised, engraved, and hot-stamped.
            ___ (*b*) Plaque and sign: cast bronze or aluminum, plastic/acrylic, stone, masonry, and wood.

___ (2) Interior
    ___ (*a*) Permanent mounting: vinyl tape/ adhesive backing, silastic adhesive, or mechanical attachment.
    ___ (*b*) Semipermanent: vinyl tape square on inserts.
    ___ (*c*) Changeable: dual-lock mating fasteners, magnets, magnetic tape or tracks.

___ *g.* Mounting heights

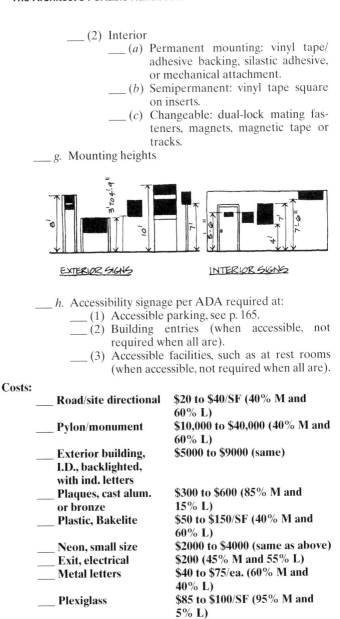

EXTERIOR SIGNS   INTERIOR SIGNS

___ *h.* Accessibility signage per ADA required at:
    ___ (1) Accessible parking, see p. 165.
    ___ (2) Building entries (when accessible, not required when all are).
    ___ (3) Accessible facilities, such as at rest rooms (when accessible, not required when all are).

Costs:

___ **Road/site directional**	**$20 to $40/SF (40% M and 60% L)**
___ **Pylon/monument**	**$10,000 to $40,000 (40% M and 60% L)**
___ **Exterior building, I.D., backlighted, with ind. letters**	**$5000 to $9000 (same)**
___ **Plaques, cast alum. or bronze**	**$300 to $600 (85% M and 15% L)**
___ **Plastic, Bakelite**	**$50 to $150/SF (40% M and 60% L)**
___ **Neon, small size**	**$2000 to $4000 (same as above)**
___ **Exit, electrical**	**$200 (45% M and 55% L)**
___ **Metal letters**	**$40 to $75/ea. (60% M and 40% L)**
___ **Plexiglass**	**$85 to $100/SF (95% M and 5% L)**
___ **Vinyl**	**$20 to $30/SF (75% M and 25% L)**

__ D. FIREPROOFING (1) (4) (24)

___ 1. See p. 80 for requirements.
___ 2. Thicknesses (in inches) of fire resistance structural materials will give hourly ratings, as follows:

ITEM	NON-COMBUSTIBLE						HEAVY TIMBER	LIGHT WOOD FRAME
	4 HR.	3 HR.	2 HR.	1½ HR.	1 HR.	O HR.		
STEEL, STRUCTURAL* LT. GA. JOISTS STUDS	←	SEE NOTE 3, BELOW			SEE NOTE 3c			→
CONCRETE, COLUMNS	6-8"	14"	12"	10"	8"			
WALLS		6½"	6"	5"	3½"			
SLABS		6.2"	5"	4.3"	3½"			
POST TENSION FLOOR		6.2"	5"	4.25"	3½"			
PRE-CAST CONC.COL		12"	10"	8"	6"			
BEAMS		9½"	7"	7"	4"			
WALLS		6½"	6"	5"	3.5"			
SLABS		6.2"	5"	4.3"	3.5"			
PLANKS		8"+2" TOPPING	8"	8"	8"			
TEE BMS			3.25"	2.75"	1.75"	← TOPPINGS		
BRICK, MASONRY WALLS VAULTS & DOMES (RISE NOT LESS THAN 1/12 SPAN)	6-8"	8" 8"	6" 8"	6" 6"	4" 4"			SEE NOTE 3, BELOW
C.M.U. MASONRY WALLS	8"SOLID	8"	8"	6"	4"			
WOOD: COLUMNS, FLOOR ROOF BEAMS, FLOOR ROOF TRUSSES, FLOOR ROOF							8×8 6×8 6×10 4×6 8×8 4×6	
WOOD DECK, FLOOR ROOF							3"+1" 1⅛"-2"	

* At 20' above floor, open steel structure does not need fire protection.

___ 3. Fire-resistive materials may be applied to structural members to protect from fire. Use the above table, as well as the following:
 ___ *a.* Concrete: 1" ≈ 2 hr. 2" to 3" ≈ 4 hr.
 ___ *b.* Solid masonry: 2" ≈ 1 hr., add 1"/hr to 4" ≈ 4 hr.
 ___ *c.* Plaster: 1" ≈ 1 hr., add 1"/hr.
 ___ *d.* Vermiculite (spray-on): 1" ≈ 4 hr.
 ___ *e.* Gypsum wallboard: 2 layers ½" type "X" or 1 layer of ⅝" type "X" ≈ ¾ to 1 hr.

Costs: Spray-on vermiculite: $0.75 to 1.00/SF surface/inch thickness

___ 4. Flame Spread: The UBC requires finish materials to resist the spread of fire as follows:

    ___ *a.* Maximum flame-spread class

Occupancy Group	Enclosed Vertical Exitways	Other Exitways(1)	Rooms or Areas
A	I	II	II (2)
B	I	II	III
E	I	II	III
H	I	II	III (3)
I-1.1, I-1.2, I-2	I	I (4)	II (5)
I-3	I	I (4)	I (5)
M	I	II	III
R-1	I	II	III
R-3	III	III	III (6)
S-1, S-2	II	II	III
S-3, S-4, S-5	I	II	III
U	No restrictions		

Notes: (1) Finish classification is not applicable to interior walls and ceilings of exterior exit balconies.

(2) In Group A, Division 3 and 4 Occupancies, Class III may be used.

(3) Over 2 stories shall be Class II.

(4) In Group I, Divisions 2 and 3 Occupancies, Class II may be used.

(5) Class III may be used in administrative spaces.

(6) Flame-spread provisions are not applicable to kitchens and bathrooms of Group R, Division 3 Occupancies.

    ___ *b.* Flame-spread classification

Class	Flame-spread index
I	0 to 25
II	26 to 75
III	76 to 200

    ___ *c.* Use finishes to meet above requirements

        ___ (1) For woods, see p. 274.

        ___ (2) Aluminum: 5 to 10

        ___ (3) Masonry or Concrete: 0

        ___ (4) Gypsum wallboard: 10 to 25

        ___ (5) Carpet: 10 to 600

        ___ (6) Mineral-fiber sound-absorbing panels: 10 to 25

___ (7) Vinyl tile: 10 to 50
___ (8) Chemically treated wood fiberboard: 20 to 25
___ 5. Fire Loads: Interior building contents that will start or contribute to a fire. These typically range from 10 (residential) to 50 PSF (office), and can be reduced 80% to 90% by use of metal storage containers for paper.

___ E. OPERABLE PARTITIONS ④

___ 1. Types

CENTER TRACK   EDGE TRACK   STACKING POCKET   STACKING WITH SWITCHES

___ 2. Data
   ___ (1) Stack widths:
      ___ (*a*) Accordion: 5″ to 12″
      ___ (*b*) Panels: 15″ to 17″
   ___ (2) Stack depths: Usually ⅙ to ⅛ of opened width.
   ___ (3) Panels usually 48″ wide.
   ___ (4) Acoustic: STC 43 to 54 available.
   ___ (5) Flame spread: Class I available.

Costs:

   ___ **Folding, acoustical, vinyl, wood-framed: $55 to $75/SF (70% M and 30% L) Variation: −35% to +50%.**
   ___ **Accordion, vinyl-faced: $15 to $40/SF, Variation: ±20%**

___ F. BATHROOM ACCESSORIES

Costs given are for average quality. For better finishes (i.e., brass), add 75% to 100%:

___ **Mirrors**	**$30/SF (90% M and 10% L) variation of ±25%**
___ **Misc. small items (holders, hooks, etc.)**	**$15 to $30/ea. (double, if recessed)**
___ **Bars**	
Grab	**$30 to $35/ea.**
Towel	**$15 to $25/ea.**
___ **Medicine cabinets**	**$60–$300/ea.**
___ **Tissue dispensers**	**$30 to $60/ea.**
___ **Towel dispensers**	**$120/ea. (increase by 2½ times if waste receptacle included)**

__ 1. Types

    __ *a.* Horizontal (usually best on south side)

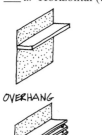

OVERHANG   TRELLIS   AWNING

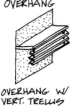   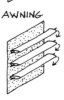

OVERHANG W/   SCREEN   HORZ. LOUVERS
VERT. TRELLIS

    __ *b.* Vertical (usually best on east and west sides)

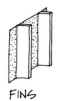

FINS   ANGLED FINS   MOVABLE FINS

    __ *c.* Egg crates (best for hot climates)

RECTILINEAR   ANGLED VERTICALS   ANGLED HORZ.

Costs:

__ **Canvas awnings**	**$7 to $50/SF (70% M and 30% L)**
	Variation −75%, +300%
	Other types of awnings (alum., painted, plastic, or security) are 1½ to 2½ times.
__ **Cloth patio covers**	**≈$3.50/SF (55% M and 45% L)**
__ **Metal carports**	**See p. 199.**

NOTES

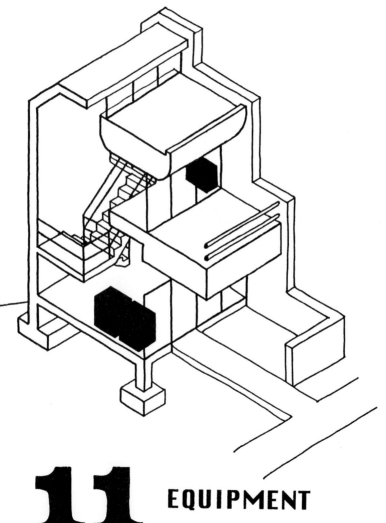

11 EQUIPMENT

NOTES

(See p. 142, Energy Conservation)

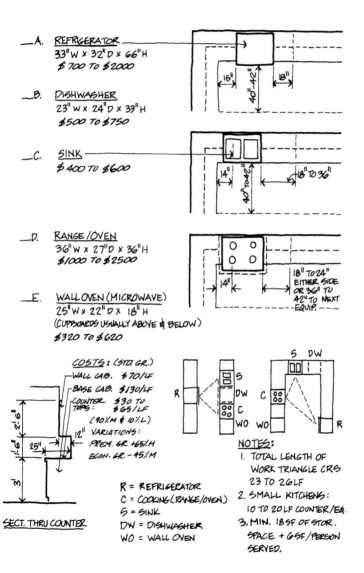

__A. REFRIGERATOR
33"W × 32"D × 66"H
$700 TO $2000

__B. DISHWASHER
23"W × 24"D × 39"H
$500 TO $750

__C. SINK
$400 TO $600

__D. RANGE/OVEN
36"W × 27"D × 36"H
$1000 TO $2500

__E. WALL OVEN (MICROWAVE)
25"W × 22"D × 18"H
(CUPBOARDS USUALLY ABOVE & BELOW)
$320 TO $620

COSTS: (STD. GR.)
WALL CAB. $70/LF
BASE CAB. $130/LF
COUNTER $30 TO
TOPS: $65/LF
(90%M & 10%L)
VARIATIONS:
PREM. GR. +65%M
ECON. GR. -45%M

SECT. THRU COUNTER

R = REFRIGERATOR
C = COOKING (RANGE/OVEN)
S = SINK
DW = DISHWASHER
WO = WALL OVEN

NOTES:
1. TOTAL LENGTH OF
   WORK TRIANGLE CRS
   23 TO 26 LF
2. SMALL KITCHENS:
   10 TO 20 LF COUNTER/EQ.
3. MIN. 18 SF OF STOR.
   SPACE + 6 SF/PERSON
   SERVED.

___ B. RESIDENTIAL LAUNDRIES ④

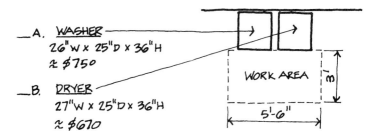

___ A. WASHER
26"W x 25"D x 36"H
≈ $750

___ B. DRYER
27"W x 25"D x 36"H
≈ $670

WORK AREA

3'

5'-6"

___ C. MISCELLANEOUS COSTS

(Also see item F, p. 507)

___ 1. **Bank Counter**	**$2000 to $4000/teller**
___ 2. **Barber**	
Total equipment	**$2500 to $5250/chair**
___ 3. **Cash Register**	**$550 to $2500/reg.**
___ 4. **Commercial Kitchen Equip.**	
By area:	
(Office)	**$60 to $95/SF kit.**
(Restaurant)	**$74 to $120/SF kit.**
(Hospital)	**$80 to $130/SF kit.**
By item:	
Work tables	**$265 to $335/LF**
Serving fixtures	**$275 to $355/LF**
Walk-ins	**$50 to $165/SF (add $1600/ ton for refrigeration machinery)**
___ 5. **Fire Extinguishers**	
Extinguishers	**$125 to $300/ea.**
Cabinets	**$450 to $600/ea.**
Hose and cabinets	**$450 to $600/ea.**
___ 6. **Library**	
Shelf	**$125/LF (−20%, +10%)**
Carrels	**$600 to $850/ea.**
Card catalog	**$65/tray**

___ 7. **Religious**
    Wood altar $1500 to $9000
    For pews, see p. 378

___ 8. **Safes**
    (Office) 4 hr.,
        1.5′ × 1.5′ × 1.5′ $3500
    (Jeweler's) 63″ × 25″ × 18″ $20,900

___ 9. **Theater**
    Total equipment $80 to $420/SF stage
    For seating, see p. 378

___ 10. **Trash Compactors** $650 to $8000/ea.

___ 11. **Vacuum Cleaning Equip.** $775 for first 1200 SF; then
                                   add $0.15/SF

NOTES

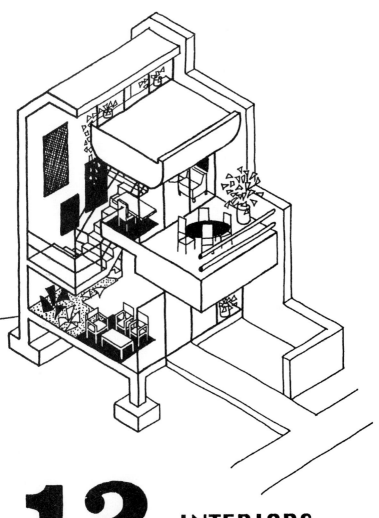

12 INTERIORS

NOTES

___ A. GENERAL COSTS

Costs for furniture and interior objects will vary more than any other item for buildings. These can vary as much as −75% to +500% (or more). Costs given in this part are a reasonable middle value and are "for trade" wholesale. Retail can go up 60% to 175%. Cost location factors given in App. B, line V will not apply as furniture costs are rather uniform across country.

___ B. MISCELLANEOUS OBJECTS

___ 1. Artwork (photos, reproductions, etc.): **$45 to $250/ea.**
___ 2. Ash urns and trash receptacles: **$90 to $290/ea.**
___ 3. Blinds: **$4.20 to $6.70/SF**
___ 4. Draperies: **$20 to $105/SY**
___ 5. Rugs and mats: **$20 to $100/SY**
___ 6. Interior plants: see p. 201. **For artificial silk plants, double or triple landscape costs.**
___ 7. Fabrics: Association of Contract Textiles (ACT) recommendations. Check for following:

    ___ *a.* Flammability
    Upholstery must pass CAL 117.
    Drapery must pass NFPA 701.
    Wall covering must pass ASTM E-84.

    ___ *b.* Abrasion resistance

a	A	Test
15,000 double rubs	30,000 double rubs 40,000	Wyzenbeek Martindale

    ___ *c.* Colorfastness to light
    Must pass Class 4 (40 to 60 hours exposure for UV).

    ___ *d.* Colorfastness to wet and dry crocking (Pigment colorfastness in fabric).

___ *e.* Miscellaneous other physical properties
    ___ (1) Brush pill test: measures tendency for ends of a fiber to mat into fuzz balls.
    ___ (2) Yard/seam slippage test: establishes fabric's likeliness to pull apart at seams. Must pass 25 lbs for upholstery and 15 lbs on drapery.
    ___ (3) Breaking/tensile strength test: evaluates fabric's breaking or tearing. Must pass:

Upholstery	50 lbs
Panel fabrics	35 lbs
Drapery over 6 oz	25 lbs
under 6 oz	15 lbs

___ C. FURNITURE

(Also see Item F, p. 507)
___ 1. Miscellaneous

___ *a.*	Theater	**$120 to $225/seat**
___ *b.*	Church Pews	**$70 to $110/seat**
___ *c.*	Dormitory	**$1900 to $3600/student**
___ *d.*	Hospital Beds	**$825 to $1340/bed**
___ *e.*	Hotel	**$1500 to $7850/room**
___ *f.*	Multiple Seating	
	Classroom	**$65 to $120/seat**
	Lecture Hall	**$130 to $370/seat**
	Auditorium	**$100 to $200/seat**

___ 2. <u>Living/Waiting</u>

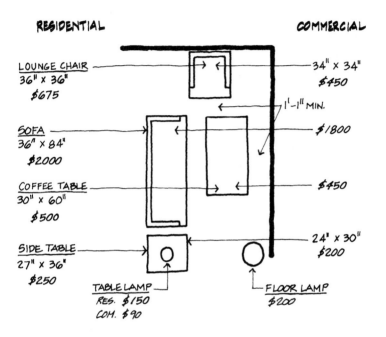

RESIDENTIAL   **COMMERCIAL**

<u>LOUNGE CHAIR</u>
36" x 36"
$675

34" x 34"
$450

1'-1" MIN.

<u>SOFA</u>
36" x 84"
$2000

$1800

<u>COFFEE TABLE</u>
30" x 60"
$500

$450

<u>SIDE TABLE</u>
27" x 36"
$250

24" x 30"
$200

<u>TABLE LAMP</u>
RES. $150
COM. $90

<u>FLOOR LAMP</u>
$200

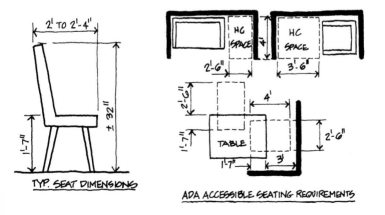

2' TO 2'-4"

± 32"

1'-7"

<u>TYP. SEAT DIMENSIONS</u>

HC SPACE   HC SPACE

2'-6"   3'-6"

2'-6"

4'

1'-7"   TABLE   2'-6"

1'-7"   3'

<u>ADA ACCESSIBLE SEATING REQUIREMENTS</u>

___ 3. <u>Bedroom/Guestroom</u>

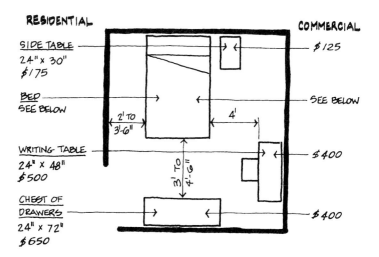

RESIDENTIAL   **COMMERCIAL**

<u>SIDE TABLE</u> $125
24" x 30"
$175

<u>BED</u>   SEE BELOW
SEE BELOW

2' TO 3'-6"   4'

<u>WRITING TABLE</u> $400
24" X 48"
$500   3' TO 4'-6"

<u>CHEST OF DRAWERS</u> $400
24" X 72"
$650

<u>BED SIZES</u>   *COST*: BEDS: $500 TO $1000/EA

	W	L
KING	72	84
QUEEN	60	82
DOUBLE	54	82
SINGLE	39	82
DAY BED	30	75
CRIB	30	53

___ 4. <u>Dining/Conference</u>

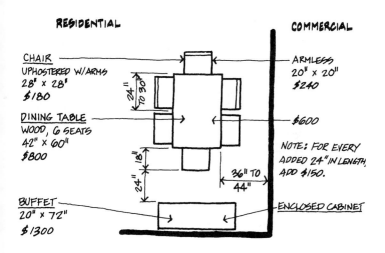

RESIDENTIAL

COMMERCIAL

<u>CHAIR</u>
UPHOSTERED W/ARMS
28" x 28"
$180

ARMLESS
20" x 20"
$240

<u>DINING TABLE</u>
WOOD, 6 SEATS
42" x 60"
$800

24" TO 30"

$600

NOTE: FOR EVERY
ADDED 24" IN LENGTH,
ADD $150.

18"
24"

36" TO
44"

<u>BUFFET</u>
20" x 72"
$1300

<u>ENCLOSED CABINET</u>

___ 5. <u>Restaurant Seating</u>

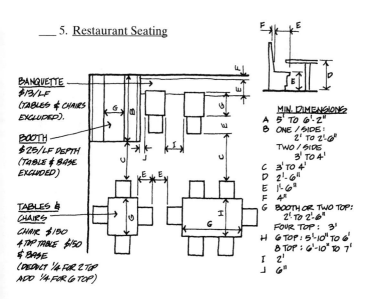

<u>BANQUETTE</u>
$13/LF
(TABLES & CHAIRS
EXCLUDED).

<u>BOOTH</u>
$25/LF DEPTH
(TABLE & BASE
EXCLUDED)

<u>TABLES &</u>
<u>CHAIRS</u>
CHAIR $150
4 TOP TABLE $150
& BASE
(DEDUCT ¼ FOR 2 TOP
ADD ¼ FOR 6 TOP)

F   E

D

E

<u>MIN. DIMENSIONS</u>
A 5' TO 6'-2"
B ONE / SIDE:
       2' TO 2'-6"
   TWO / SIDE
       3' TO 4'
C 3' TO 4'
D 2'-6"
E 1'-6"
F 4"
G BOOTH OR TWO TOP:
       2' TO 2'-6"
   FOUR TOP: 3'
H 6 TOP: 5'-10" TO 6'
   8 TOP: 6'-10" TO 7'
I 2'
J 6"

___ 6. <u>Office</u>

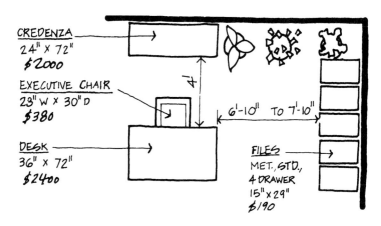

<u>CREDENZA</u>
24" × 72"
$2000

<u>EXECUTIVE CHAIR</u>
23" W × 30" D
$380

<u>DESK</u>
36" × 72"
$2400

6'-10" TO 7'-10"

<u>FILES</u>
MET., STD.,
4 DRAWER
15" × 29"
$190

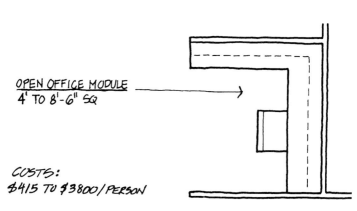

<u>OPEN OFFICE MODULE</u>
4' TO 8'-6" SQ

COSTS:
$415 TO $3800/PERSON

D. HUMAN DIMENSIONS

Note: All dimensions are in inches.

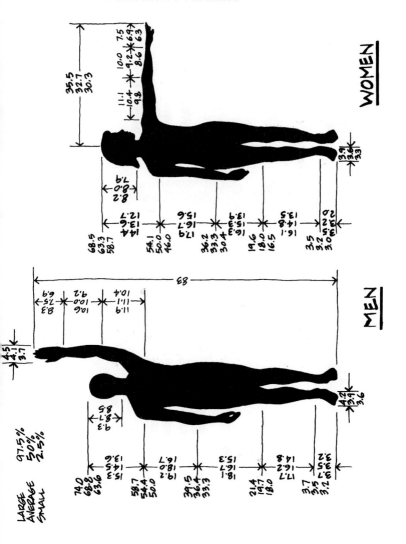

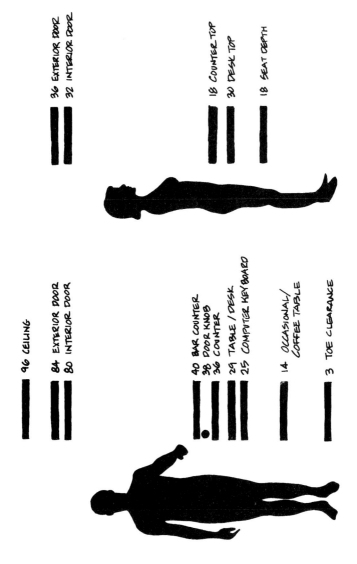

HEIGHTS

96 CEILING

84 EXTERIOR DOOR
80 INTERIOR DOOR

40 BAR COUNTER
38 DOOR KNOB
36 COUNTER
29 TABLE / DESK
25 COMPUTER KEYBOARD

14 OCCASIONAL/
COFFEE TABLE

3 TOE CLEARANCE

WIDTHS

36 EXTERIOR DOOR
32 INTERIOR DOOR

18 COUNTER TOP
30 DESK TOP

18 SEAT DEPTH

PARTITION HEIGHTS

70.5

52

42

WORKSTATION

30

17

18

30

8

27

385

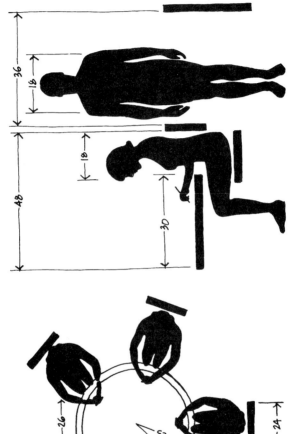

CORRIDOR / CLEARANCE

CONFERENCE

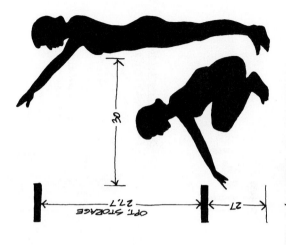

OVERHEAD / UNDER COUNTER REACH

30

OPT. STORAGE 27.7

27

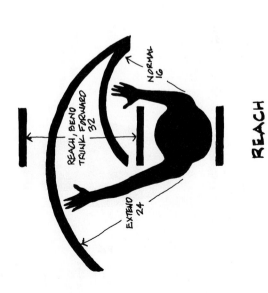

REACH

REACH, BEND TRUNK FORWARD 32

NORMAL 16

EXTEND 24

387

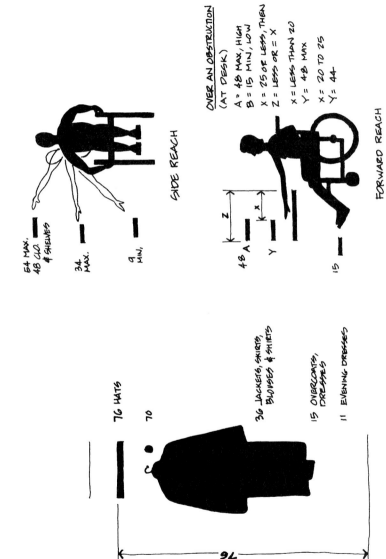

SIDE REACH

54 MAX.
48 CLO.
4 SHELVES

34. MAX.

9 MIN.

OVER AN OBSTRUCTION
(AT DESK)

A = 48 MAX, HIGH
B = 15 MIN, LOW
X = 25 OF LESS, THEN
Z = LESS OR = X

X = LESS THAN 20
Y = 48 MAX

X = 20 TO 25
Y = 44

FORWARD REACH

48 A

Z

X

Y

15

WHEELCHAIR (ADA)

76 HATS

70

36 JACKETS, SKIRTS,
BLOUSES & SHIRTS

15 OVERCOATS,
DRESSES

11 EVENING DRESSES

76

CLOSET

NOTES

NOTES

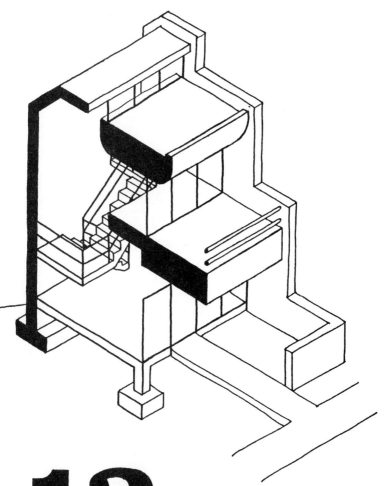

13 ASSEMBLIES

NOTES

__ A. ROOF STRUCTURE ASSEMBLIES

Use the tables on pp. 394–397 to help select a *roof structure assembly*. See p. 297 for roof coverings. Cross-sections on each table illustrate various assemblies, with *depth* of assembly in inches. Columns bearing the following numbers on each table show:

- ___ 2. *Standard member sizes* in inches
- ___ 3. *Dead loads* in pounds per square foot
- ___ 4. Suitable *live load* range in pounds per square foot
- ___ 5. Span range in feet
- ___ 6. Typical bay size
- ___ 7. Suitable for *inclined roofs:*
    Y = yes
    N = no
- ___ 8. Service plenum notes
    Between structural members
    Under structure
- ___ 9. *Acoustical:* Comparative resistance to sound transmission:
    Impact   E = Excellent   F = Fair
    Airborne G = Good   P = Poor
- ___ 10. *Construction type classification* by code (UBC)
- ___ 11. **Total costs in $/SF of roof area**

ROOF STRUCTURE ASSEMBLIES

	SIZES (inches)	DEAD LOAD (PSF)	LIVE LOAD (PSF)	SPANS (FT)	BAY SIZE	SUITABLE FOR SLOPE	SERVICE PLENUM	ACOUSTICAL IMPACT	ACOUSTICAL AIR	CONST. TYPE (UBC)	COST ($/SF)
A. WOOD RAFTER OR JOIST	2x4, 6, 8, 10 & 12	4 to 8	30 to 50	10 to 22		Y	BETW'N RAFTERS, ONE WAY	P	F	V	2.70 – 2.95
B. WOOD BEAM & PLANK	2, 3, or 4 PLANKS or 8 to 14	5 to 12	30 to 50	8 to 34		Y	UNDER STRUCTURE OR ONE WAY BETWN BEAMS	P	F	IV	2.75 – 4.00
C. WOOD TRUSSES (OR TRUSS JOIST)	12 to 14	5 to 15	20 to 50	30 to 50		Y	BETW'N & THRU TRUSSES	P	F	V	2.00 – 3.00
D. STEEL JOIST	8 to 30	8 to 20	20 to 50	10 to 40	35'SQ TO 40'SQ	Y	BETWIN & THRU BAR JOISTS	P	F	III	4.00 – 5.00
E. STEEL JOIST	8 to 72	6 to 24	20 to 50	35 to 60		Y	BETW'N & THRU BAR JOIST	E w/ INSUL ON DECK	G	III	1.50 – 3.00

ROOF STRUCTURE ASSEMBLIES

	SIZES (INCHES)	DEAD LOAD (PSF)	LIVE LOAD (PSF)	SPANS (FT.)	BAY SIZE (FT. SQ.)	SUITABLE FOR SLOPE	SERVICE PLENUM	ACOUSTICAL IMPACT	ACOUSTICAL AIR	CONST. TYPE (UBC)	COST ($/SF)
F. STEEL TRUSSES (METAL DECK, STD. PURLIN, STEEL TRUSS — 12" to 20")	VARIES	15 TO 25	20 TO 60	100 TO 200		Y (PITCH TRUSSES)	BETW'N & THRU TRUSSES	F	F	III	10.50 - 15.00 / 8.20 - 9.60
G. STEEL FRAME (P.C. CONC. PLANK, STEEL BEAM — 12" to 20")	4-16 PLANK / 12-48 M.D.	40 TO 75	30 TO 70	20 TO 60	30 TO 40	Y	UNDER STRUCTURE	F	F	II	8.20 - 9.60
H. PRECAST CONC. (P.C. CONC. PLANK, CONC. BEAM — 12" to 20")	4-16 PLANK / 12-48 M.D.	40 TO 75	30 TO 70	20 TO 60	30 TO 40	Y	UNDER STRUCTURE	F	F	I	11.70
I. ONE-WAY CONC. SLAB (CONC. SLAB, CONC. BEAM — 12" to 18")		50 TO 120	>100	10 TO 25	20	N	UNDER STRUCTURE	G	G	I	9.85
J. TWO-WAY CONC. SLAB (CONC. SLAB, CONC. BEAM — 12" to 18")		50 TO 120	>100	10 TO 30		N	UNDER STRUCTURE	G	G	:	9.25

ROOF STRUCTURE ASSEMBLIES

1	2 SIZES (INCHES)	3 DEAD LOAD (PSF)	4 LIVE LOAD (PSF)	5 SPANS (FT.)	6 BAY SIZE (FT. Sq.)	7 SUITABLE FOR SLOPE	8 SERVICE PLENUM	9 ACOUSTICAL IMPACT	9 ACOUSTICAL AIR	10 CONST. TYPE (UBC)	= COST ($/SF)
K. ONE-WAY RIBBED CONC. SLAB	6 TO 20 D, 20 & 30 W	40 TO 105	< 100	15 TO 50	3 TO 30	N	BETW'N. RIBS, ONE-WAY	G	G	—	6.80 - 10.26
L. CONC. WAFFLE SLAB (2 WAY RIB)	6 TO 20 D, 19 oR 30 30 W	75 TO 85	< 100	25 TO 60	35	N	UNDER STRUCTURE	G	G	—	9.35 - 11.90
M. PRE-CAST CONC. TEE	16 TO 36 D	65 TO 85	20 TO 80	8 TO 100		Y	BETW'N RIBS, ONE WAY	F	G	—	8.00 w/out topping
N. PRE-CAST DOUBLE TEE	6 TO 16 D, 4.5',6',8',10' W	35 TO 55	20 TO 60	20 TO 75		Y	BETW'N RIBS, ONE WAY	F	G	—	5.00 - 6.00 w/out topping
O. CONC. FLAT SLAB		50 TO 160	< 100	35	35	N	UNDER STRUCTURE	G	G	—	7.20 - 9.00

1. ROOF STRUCTURE ASSEMBLIES	2. SIZES (INCHES)	3. DEAD LOAD (PSF)	4. LIVE LOAD (PSF)	5. SPANS (FT.)	6. BAY SIZE (FT. SQ.)	7. SUITABLE FOR SLOPE	8. SERVICE PLENUM	9. ACOUSTICAL IMPACT	9. ACOUSTICAL AIR	10. CONST. TYPE (UBC)	11. COST ($/SF)
P. CONC. FLAT SLAB W/ DROP PANEL	4 TO 5 SLAB	50 TO 200	< 100	40	35	N	UNDER STRUCTURE	G	G	—	7.45 – 9.50

NOTES

__ B. FLOOR STRUCTURE ASSEMBLIES

Use the tables on pp. 400–403 to help select a *floor structure assembly*. Cross-sections on each table illustrate various assemblies, with *depth* of assembly in inches. Columns bearing the following numbers on each table show:

___ 2. *Standard member sizes* in inches
___ 3. *Dead loads* in pound per square foot
___ 4. Suitable *live load* range in pounds per square foot
___ 5. *Span* range in feet
___ 6. Typical bay size
___ 7. Service *plenum* notes
       Between structural members
       Under structure
___ 8. Acoustical: Comparative resistance to sound transmission:
       Impact   E = Excellent   F = Fair
       Airborne   G = Good   P = Poor
___ 9. *Fire*-resistive ratings, in hours, per code and Underwriters:
___ 10. *Construction type classification* by code (UBC)
___ 11. **Total costs in $/SF of floor area**

FLOOR STRUCTURE ASSEMBLIES

#	Attribute	A. WOOD JOIST	B. WOOD TRUSS OR PLYWOOD JOIST	C. WOOD BEAM & PLANK	D. GLU-LAM BEAM & PLANK	E. STEEL JOIST
1	(assembly)	PLYWD SUB-FL.; JOIST (7" to 13")	PLYWD SUB-FL.; TRUSS OR JOIST (13½" to 12")	WOOD PLANK; WOOD BEAM (8" to 22")	WOOD PLANK; GLU-LAM BEAM (8" to 22")	PLYWD SUB-FL.; STEEL BAR JOIST (6" to 31")
2	SIZE (INCHES)	2×6,8,10,12 @12	12,14,16,18 / PLYWD JOISTS	2,3,4 & PLANK	2,3,4 & PLANK	8 to 30 D JOIST
3	DEAD LOAD (PSF)	5 to 8	6 to 12	6 to 16	6 to 20	8 to 20
4	LIVE LOAD (PSF)	30 to 40	30 to 40	30 to 40	30 to 40	30 to 40
5	SPAN (FT.)	10 to 18	12 to 30	10 to 22	8 to 34	16 to 40
6	BAY SIZE (FT. SQ.)			15 to 20	20 to 25	25 to 30
7	SERVICE PLENUM	BETWEEN JOISTS, ONE-WAY	BETWEEN & THRU TRUSSES	UNDER STRUCTURE	UNDER STRUCTURE	BETWEEN & THRU JOIST
8	ACOUSTICAL — IMPACT	P	P	P	P	P
8	ACOUSTICAL — AIR	F	F	F	F	P
9	FIRE RATING (HR.)					
10	CONST. TYPE (UBC)	V	V	≥	≥	III
	COST ($/SF) =	4.15 - 7.45	7.00 - 7.85	5.45 - 7.65	2.65 - 3.85	2.00 - 4.00

FLOOR STRUCTURE ASSEMBLIES

1	2 SIZE (INCHES)	3 DEAD LOAD (PSF)	4 LIVE LOAD (PSF)	5 SPAN (FT.)	6 BAY SIZE (FT. SQ.)	7 SERVICE PLENUM	8 ACOUST-ICAL IMPACT	8 ACOUST-ICAL AIR	9 FIRE RATING (HRS)	10 CONST. TYPE (UBC)	11 COST ($/SF)
F. STEEL JOIST	JOIST 8 TO 15 D	30 to 110	60 to 100	16 to 40	25 TO 30	BETW'N & THRU JOIST	P	F		=	6.25
G. LIGHT WEIGHT STEEL FRAME		6 to 20	30 to 60	10 to 22	10 TO 15	UNDER STRUCTURE	P	P		≡	3.20 - 4.20
H. STEEL FRAME		35 to 60	30 to 100	16 to 35	30 TO 35	UNDER STRUCTURE	P	F	1 (SLAB)	=	9.00 - 12.10
I. STEEL FRAME	PLANK 4 TO 12 D, 16 TO 48 W	40 to 75	60 to 150	15 to 20	30 TO 40	UNDER STRUCTURE	F	F	1 to 2 (SLAB)	=	10.90 - 12.80
J. PRE CAST CONCRETE	PLANK 4 TO 12 D, 16 TO 48 W	40 to 75	60 to 150	35 to 60	30 x 40	UNDER STRUCTURE	F	F	2 to 4	—	13.75

FLOOR STRUCTURE ASSEMBLIES

	1	2 SIZE (INCHES)	3 DEAD LOAD (PSF)	4 LIVE LOAD (PSF)	5 SPAN (FT.)	6 BAY SIZE (FT. SQ.)	7 SERVICE PLENUM	8 ACOUSTICAL IMPACT	8 ACOUSTICAL AIR	9 FIRE RATING (HR.)	10 CONST. TYPE (UBC)	11 COST ($/SF)
K. ONE-WAY CONCRETE SLAB	CONC. SLAB / CONC. BEAM (10")		50 TO 120	40 TO 150	10 TO 20	20	UNDER STRUCTURE	6	6	2 TO 4	—	11.70
L. TWO-WAY CONCRETE SLAB	CONC. SLAB / CONC. BEAM (10")		50 TO 120	40 TO 250	10 TO 30		UNDER STRUCTURE	6	6	2 TO 4	—	10.90
M. ONE-WAY RIBBED CONCRETE	CONC. SLAB / CONC. RIB (JOIST) (8" 22")	6 TO 20 W 20 & 30	40 TO 90	40 TO 150	15 TO 50	20 TO 30	UNDER STRUCTURE	6	6	1 TO 2	—	12.00
N. CONCRETE WAFFLE SLAB	CONC. SLAB / CONC. RIB (8" 22")	6 TO 20 W 19 20 & 30	75 TO 105	60 TO 200	25 TO 40	35	UNDER STRUCTURE	6	6	1 TO 2	—	11.00 - 14.00
O. PRE-CAST CONCRETE DOUBLE TEE	CONC. TOPPING / P.C. CONC. DOUBLE TEE BM. (8" 18")	4 TO 16 M 4'-5', 6', 8'	50 TO 80	40 TO 150	20 TO 50		UNDER STRUCTURE	F	6	1 TO 2	—	5.75 - 7.75

FLOOR STRUCTURE ASSEMBLIES

	SIZE (INCHES)	DEAD LOAD (PSF)	LIVE LOAD (PSF)	SPAN (FT.)	BAY SIZE (FT.SQ.)	SERVICE PLENUM	ACOUSTICAL IMPACT	ACOUSTICAL AIR	FIRE RATING (HR.)	CONST. TYPE (UBC)	COST ($/SF)
P. PRE-CAST CONCRETE SINGLE TEE	TEE BEAM 16 to 36 D	50 to 90	40 to 150	26 to 65		UNDER STRUCTURE	F	G	1 to 2	—	9.75
Q. CONCRETE FLAT PLATE		60 to 125	60 to 200	18 to 35	35	UNDER STRUCTURE	G	G	2 to 4	—	8.00 - 10.00
R. CONCRETE SLAB W/ DROP PANEL	4 to 5 D SLAB	75 to 170	60 to 250	20 to 40	35	UNDER STRUCTURE	G	G	2 to 4	—	8.25 - 10.50

P. PRE-CAST CONCRETE SINGLE TEE — CONC. TOPPING, P.C. CONC. TEE BEAM, 18" to 36"

Q. CONCRETE FLAT PLATE — CONC. SLAB, COLUMN, BEYOND, 5" to 14"

R. CONCRETE SLAB W/ DROP PANEL — CONC. SLAB, DROP PANEL, COL. BEYOND

NOTES

__ C. WALLS (4)

___ 1. Use the tables on pp. 406–407 to help select a *wall assembly*. See Part 9 for finishes. Cross-sections on each table illustrate various assemblies; columns bearing the following numbers show:

___ 2. Overall *thickness* in nominal inches

___ 3. *Weight* in pounds per square foot

___ 4. Vertical *span* range for unsupported height in feet

___ 5. Heat transmission coefficient *U value* in BTU/hr/SF/°F (see p. 292)

___ 6. Resistance to airborne *sound* transmission (see p. 156)

___ 7. *Fire* resistance rating in hours (see pp. 82 and 363)

___ 8. UBC *construction type* (see p. 77)

___ 9. **Costs in $/SF of wall surface (one side). Wall finishes (paint, etc.) are not included.**

WALL ASSEMBLIES

	THICKNESS (IN.)	WEIGHT (PSF)	VERT SPAN (FT)	U VALUE	ACOUSTICAL	FIRE (HRS)	CONST TYPE	COST; ($/SF)
A C.M.U. — C.M.U.	8	55	UP TO 13	0.56	FAIR TO GOOD	2-4	I & II	$6.50
	12	85	UP TO 20	0.49	FAIR TO GOOD	4		$8.25
B CMU & INSUL. — CMU / INSULATION / GYPB'D.	8+	60	UP TO 13	0.21	EXCELLENT	2-4		$8.35
	12+	90	UP TO 20	0.20		4		$10.10
C CMU & BRICK — BRICK VENEER / C.M.U. / INSULATION / GYPB'D.	4+4	75	UP TO 13	0.19	EXCELLENT	3-4		$16.35
	4+8	100	UP TO 20	0.18		4		$17.85
D CAVITY — BRICK VENEER / AIR SPACE / INSULATION / C.M.U. / GYPB'D.	4+2+4	75	UP TO 9	0.12	EXCELLENT	4		$18.00
	4+2+8	100	UP TO 13	0.11				$16.60
E CMU & STUCCO — STUCCO / CMU / INSULATION / GYPB'D.	8+	67	UP TO 13	0.16	GOOD	2-4	→	$10.35
F WOOD STUD — PLYWOOD / WOOD STUDS / INSUL. W/ VAPOR BARRIER / GYPB'D.	4	12	UP TO 14	0.06	POOR TO FAIR	1	V	$3.10 to $3.40
	6	16	UP TO 20	0.04				
G BRICK, WOOD STUD — BRICK VENEER / PLYWOOD / WOOD STUDS / INSULATION / GYPB'D.	4+4	52	UP TO 14	0.07	GOOD TO EXCELLENT	1-2	V	$11.65 to $11.95
H METAL STUD — EXT. WALL FIN. / METAL STUDS / INSULATION W/ VAPOR BARRIER / GYPB'D.	4	14	UP TO 13	0.06	POOR TO FAIR	1-2	II-I	$3.75 to $4.10 EXT. FIN. EXCLU.
	5	18	UP TO 17	0.04				
I BRICK, METAL STUD — BRICK VENEER / PLYWOOD / METAL STUDS / INSUL. W/ VAPOR BARRIER / GYPB'D.	4+4	54	UP TO 15	0.07	GOOD TO EXCELLENT	2-1	II-I	$14.25 to $14.60

WALL ASSEMBLIES

1	2 THICKNESS (IN)	3 WEIGHT (PSF)	4 VERT SPAN (FT)	5 U VALUE	6 ACOUSTICAL	7 FIRE (HRS)	8 CONST TYPE (I-IV)	9 COST: ($/SF)
J INSULATED SANDWICH PANEL — METAL SKIN, AIRSPACE, INSULATED CORE, METAL SKIN	5	6		0.05	POOR TO GOOD		II-IV	$4.00
K CONCRETE — REINF. CONCRETE	8 / 12	92 / 138	UP TO 17 / UP TO 25	0.68 / 0.55	GOOD	4 / 4	I	$13.55 to $14.35
L CONCRETE & INSULATION — REINF. CONCRETE, INSULATION, GYPBD.	8+	97	UP TO 17	0.19	GOOD	4	III	$14.60
M BRICK, CONCRETE, INSULATION — BRICK VENEER, REINF. CONCRETE, INSULATION, GYPBD.	4+8	112	UP TO 17	0.13	EXCELLENT	4	III	$17.90 to $24.90
N PRECAST CONCRETE — REINF. CONCRETE, INSULATION, GYPBD.	2+ / 4+	23 / 46	UP TO 6 / UP TO 12	0.99 / 0.85	POOR TO FAIR	1-3	III	$7.05 to $14.85
O PRECAST CONCRETE SANDWICH — CONCRETE, INSULATION	5	45	UP TO 14	0.14	FAIR	1-3	I & II	$80 TO 90
P GLAZED CURTAIN WALL — ALUM. FRAME, GLAZING	5				POOR			SG $35 / DG $50 / MAX $110

NOTES

CEILING SELECTION TABLE

ASSEMBLY	COST COMPARISON	WEIGHT (LBS/SF)	SOUND ABSORB.	SOUND TRANSM.	LATERAL LOAD	IMPACT	UPLIFT	DEFLECTION	HUMIDITY	FINISH PRE-	FINISH TEXT.	FINISH IN PLACE PAINT	NOTES
SUSP. ACOUSTIC TILE W/ EXPOSED GRID	1 TO 2	2 TO 3	G	F TO P	F TO P	P TO F	P TO G	G	P TO F	●			
SUSP. ACOUSTIC TILE W/ CONCEALED GRID	4 TO 5	→	→	→	F	P	G	→	P	●			
SUSP. PLASTER	3 TO 5	4 TO 6	P	G	P	→	→	F TO P	P		●	●	
SUSP. GYPBOARD	2 TO 3	3 TO 4+	→	→	G	→	→	→	F TO P		●	●	
ACOUSTIC TILE ATTACHED	4 TO 5	2 TO 3	G	G	P	N/A	N/A	N/A	P TO F			●*	* "NON-BRIDGING" PAINT
SPRAY ON	1 TO 2	.2 TO .3	G	G	→	→	→	→	P		●		

● DENOTES COMMON USAGE
P = POOR
F = FAIR
G = GOOD

FLOOR TO CEILING SPACE

FLOOR
SEE STRUCT.
STRUCT.
HVAC DUCTS
LIGHTS
CEILING (±1" thick)
8-10" TYP.
6-8" TYP.
14 TO 20" TYP.
Also, See p. 454.

FLOORING SELECTION TABLE

TYPE	COST COMPARISON	WEIGHT (PSF)	COMFORT	MOISTURE DRY	OCC. WET	FREQ. WET	TRAFFIC FOOT LOW	MOD	HIGH	WHEEL RUB	STEEL	IMPACT	CLEANING MILD	HEAVY	LOCATION OUTSIDE	BELOW GR.	ON GRADE	ABOVE GR.	SUBSTRATE WOOD	CONC.	SLIP RESIST *	CONDUCTIVE	OTHER
STONE	.9 to 3	15 to 40	P	●	●	●	○	●	●	○		●	●	○	●	●	●	●		●	○		
BRICK	4-10.9	20 to 40	P	●	●	●	●	●	●	●		●	●	●	●	●	●	●	●	●	○		
CONCRETE	1.2-2.5	10 to 75	P	●	●	●	●	●	●	●	○	●	●	●	●	●	●	●	●	●	●	○	
C.T.	2-4	4-6	P	●	●	●	●	●	●	●			●	●	●	●	●	●	●	●	●	●	
Q.T.	4-5.5	4-6	P	●	●	●	●	●	●	○			●	●	●	●	●	●	●	●	●	●	
RESILIENT	.6-2	1-2	G	●	●		●	●	●	○	○	●	●	●		●	●	●	●	●	●	●	
WOOD	3-5	1-10	F	●	●		●	●	●	◐		○	●				●	●	●	●	●		
CARPET	1.5-5	.5-1	G	●			●	●	●	●		●	●				●	●	●	●	●	○	
EPOXY	3-5	3-7	F	●	●	●	●	●	●	●	●	●	●	●	●	●	●	●	●	●	●	●	

● DENOTES COMMON USAGE OR SUITABILITY

○ DENOTES POSSIBLE OR LIMITED USAGE OR SUITABILITY

* SLIP RESISTANCE

RECOMMENDATIONS FOR STATIC COEFFICIENT OF FRICTION:
NORMAL = 0.5 MIN., H.C. (ADA) = 0.6 MIN., RAMP = 0.8 MIN.

0.2 OR LESS IS VERY SLICK. 0.3 TO 0.4 IS SMOOTH. BROOM FINISH CONCRETE IS USUALLY 0.5 TO 0.7. GRIT STRIPES FOR STAIRS OR RAMPS ARE 0.8 OR ABOVE.

THE COEFFICIENT OF FRICTION IS THE RATIO OF HORIZONTAL FORCE TO VERTICAL FORCE. WAXES SHOULD MEET ASTM D-2047.

NOTES

NOTES

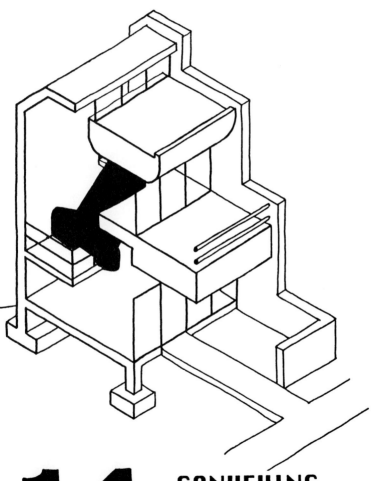

14 CONVEYING SYSTEMS

NOTES

__ A. ELEVATORS (10)

___ 1. <u>Hydraulic:</u> The least expensive and slower type. They are moved up and down by a piston. This type is generally used in low-rise buildings (2 to 4 stories) in which it is not necessary to move large numbers of people quickly.

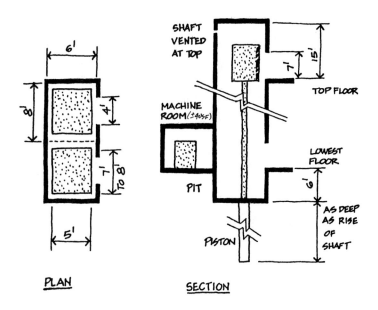

PLAN   SECTION

Costs:

Passenger elevators	$46,300 (50 fpm, 2000 lbs) to $64,000 (150 fpm, (3000 lbs) per shaft. 3 stops, 3 openings. Add: 50 fpm/stop = +$3500; 500 lb/stop = +$3500; stop = +$5300; custom interior = +$5000.
Hydraulic freight elevators	$56,750 (50 fpm, 3000 lbs) to $86,100 (150 fpm, 6000 lbs).

___ 2. <u>Traction Elevators:</u> Traction elevators hang on a counter-weighted cable and are driven by a traction machine that pulls the cable up and down. They operate smoothly at fast speeds and have no limits.

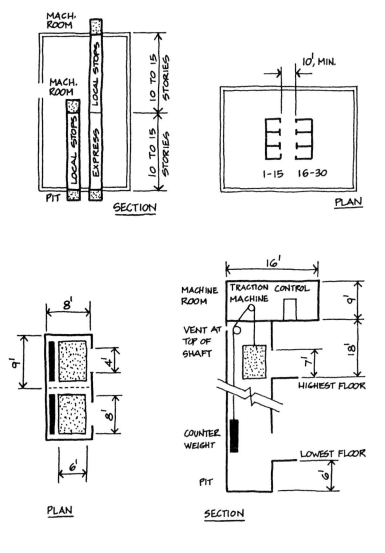

Costs:

Passenger elevators/shaft	**$64,280 (50 fpm, 2000 lbs) to $103,740 (300 fpm, 4000 lbs) for 6 stops, 6 openings. Add: stop = +$4000; 50 fpm/stop = +$2000; 500 lb/stop = +$2000; opening per stop = +$4500; custom interior = +$4800.**
Freight elevators (2 stops)/shaft	**$132,000 (50 fpm, 3500 lbs) to $139,400 (200 fpm, 5000 lbs).**

___ 3. Elevator Rules of Thumb
 ___ *a.* Commercial
  ___ (1) One passenger elevator for each 30,000 SF of net floor area.
  ___ (2) One service elevator for each 300,000 SF of net floor area.
  ___ (3) Lobby width of 10′ minimum.
  ___ (4) Banks of elevators should consist of 4 or fewer cars so that people can respond easily to the arrival of an elevator.
  ___ (5) In high buildings, the elevator system is broken down into zones serving groups of floors, typically 10 to 15 floors. Elevators that serve the upper zones express from the lobby to the beginning of the upper zone. The elevators that serve the lower zones terminate with a machine room above the highest floor served.
  ___ (6) Very tall buildings have sky lobbies served by express elevators. People arriving in the lobby take an express elevator to the appropriate sky lobby where they get off the express elevator and wait for the local elevator system.
  ___ (7) Lay out so that maximum walk to an elevator does not exceed 200′.
  ___ (8) Per ADA, accessible elevators *are* required at *shopping centers* and offices of *health care* providers. Elevators are *not* required in facilities that are less than 3 stories or less than 3000 SF per floor. But, if elevators are provided, at least one will be accessible (see p. 418).

  ___ *b.* Residential

      ___ (1) In hotels and large apartment buildings, plan on one elevator for every 70 to 100 units.

      ___ (2) In a 3- to 4-story building, it is possible to walk up if the elevator is broken, so one hydraulic elevator may be acceptable.

      ___ (3) In the 5- to 6-story range, two elevators are necessary. These will be either hydraulic (slow) or traction (better).

      ___ (4) In the 7- to 12-story range, two traction elevators are needed.

      ___ (5) Above 12 stories, two to three traction elevators are needed.

      ___ (6) Very tall buildings will require commercial-type applications.

      ___ (7) Plan adequate space and seating at lobby and hallways.

  ___ *c.* ADA-accessible elevators (see item 8, p. 417):

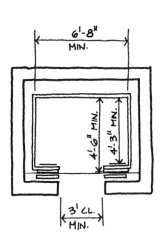
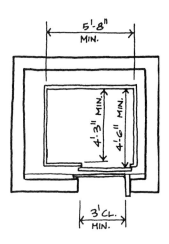

__ B. ESCALATORS

When the building design requires moving large numbers of people up and down a few floors, escalators are a good choice.

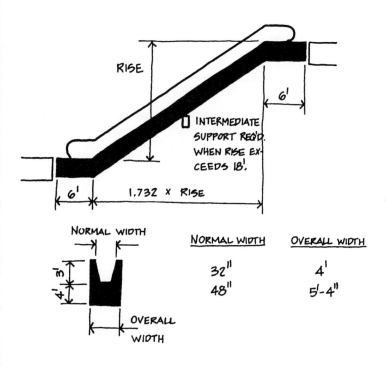

NORMAL WIDTH	OVERALL WIDTH
32"	4'
48"	5'-4"

Costs:
Escalator costs range from $88,800 for 12' rise, 32" width, to $139,500 for 25' rise, 48" width. For glass side enclosure add $11,500 to $13,500.

Rules of Thumb

1. All escalators rise at a 30-degree angle.
2. There needs to be a minimum of 10′ clear at top and bottom landings.
3. Provide beams at top and bottom for the escalator's internal truss structure to sit on.
4. The escalator will require lighting that does not produce any distorting shadows that could cause safety problems.
5. Escalators need to be laid out with a crowded flow of people in mind. Crossover points where people will run into each other must be avoided.
6. Current trends in the design of retail space use the escalators as a dramatic and dynamic focal feature of open atrium spaces.
7. Because escalators create open holes through building floor assemblies, special smoke and fire protection provisions are necessary.

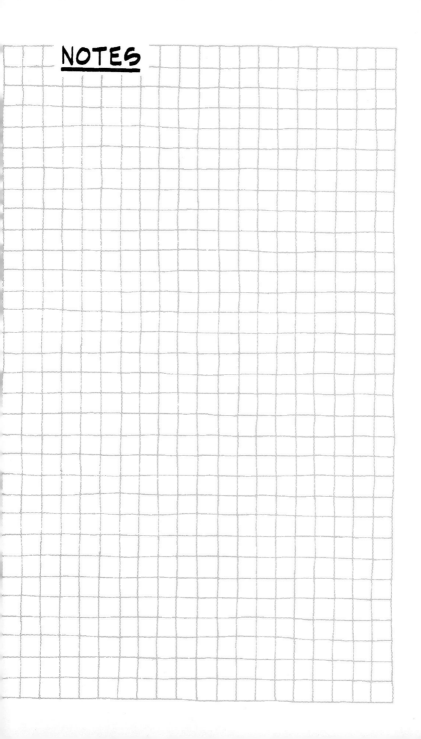

NOTES

<u>NOTES</u>

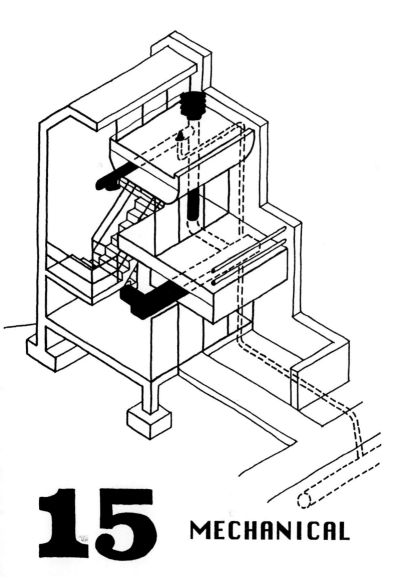

15 MECHANICAL

NOTES

__ A. THE PLUMBING SYSTEM

$\textcircled{1}$ $\textcircled{4}$ $\textcircled{7}$ $\textcircled{10}$ $\textcircled{20}$ $\textcircled{24}$ $\textcircled{25}$

See p. 193 for exterior utilities.
See p. 425 thru 428 for toilet rms.
See p. 430 for fixture count (1997 UBC and 1997 UPC).

The following systems need to be considered:

___ 1. Water supply (p. 429)
___ 2. Plumbing fixtures (p. 430)
___ 3. Sanitary sewer (p. 430)
___ 4. Rain water/storm sewer
    (p. 431)
___ 5. Fire protection (p. 433)
___ 6. Landscape irrigation (p. 437)
___ 7. Gas (p. 437)
___ 8. Other specialties (process, etc.)

RESIDENTIAL BATHROOMS

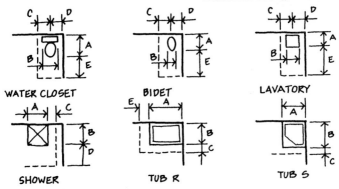

WATER CLOSET   BIDET   LAVATORY

SHOWER   TUB R   TUB S

FIXTURE SIZES AND CLEARANCES (INCHES)

FIXTURE	A MIN.	A LIB.	B MIN.	B LIB.	C MIN.	C LIB.	D MIN.	D LIB.	E MIN.	E LIB.
WATER C.	27	31	19	21	12	18	15	22	18	34 - 36
BIDET	25	27	14	14	12	18	15	22	18	34 - 36
LAVATORY	16	21	18	30	2	6	14	22	18	30
SHOWER	32	36	34	36	2	8	18	34		
TUB R	60 STD	72	30 STD	42	2	8	18 - 20	30 - 34	2	8
TUB S	38		39		2	4				

NOTE: FOR H.C. ACCESSIBILITY, SEE FOLLOWING PAGES.

TOILET ROOMS

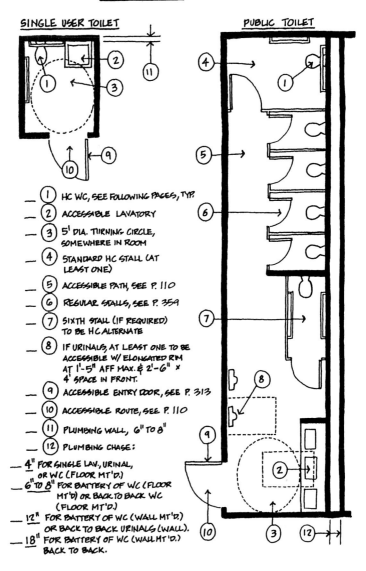

SINGLE USER TOILET

PUBLIC TOILET

__ ① HC WC, SEE FOLLOWING PAGES, TYP.

__ ② ACCESSIBLE LAVATORY

__ ③ 5' DIA. TURNING CIRCLE, SOMEWHERE IN ROOM

__ ④ STANDARD HC STALL (AT LEAST ONE)

__ ⑤ ACCESSIBLE PATH, SEE P. 110

__ ⑥ REGULAR STALLS, SEE P. 359

__ ⑦ SIXTH STALL (IF REQUIRED) TO BE HC ALTERNATE

__ ⑧ IF URINALS, AT LEAST ONE TO BE ACCESSIBLE W/ ELONGATED RIM AT 1'-5" AFF MAX. & 2'-6" × 4' SPACE IN FRONT.

__ ⑨ ACCESSIBLE ENTRY DOOR, SEE P. 313

__ ⑩ ACCESSIBLE ROUTE, SEE P. 110

__ ⑪ PLUMBING WALL, 6" TO 8"

__ ⑫ PLUMBING CHASE:

__ 4" FOR SINGLE LAV., URINAL, OR WC (FLOOR MT'D.)

__ 6" TO 8" FOR BATTERY OF WC (FLOOR MT'D) OR BACK TO BACK WC (FLOOR MT'D.)

__ 12" FOR BATTERY OF WC (WALL MT'D.) OR BACK TO BACK URINALS (WALL).

__ 18" FOR BATTERY OF WC (WALL MT'D.) BACK TO BACK.

ACCESSIBLE TOILET STALLS (ADA)

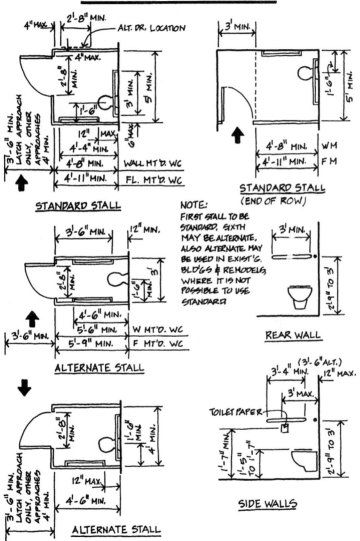

STANDARD STALL

STANDARD STALL
(END OF ROW)

NOTE:
FIRST STALL TO BE STANDARD. SIXTH MAY BE ALTERNATE, ALSO ALTERNATE MAY BE USED IN EXIST'G. BLD'GS & REMODELS, WHERE IT IS NOT POSSIBLE TO USE STANDARD.

ALTERNATE STALL

REAR WALL

ALTERNATE STALL

SIDE WALLS

ACCESSIBLE FIXTURES (ADA)

WATER CLOSETS

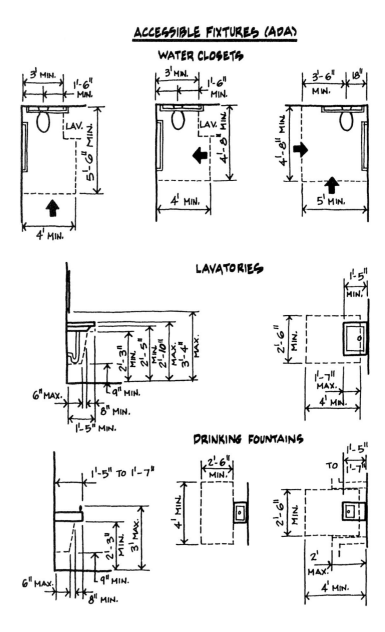

LAVATORIES

DRINKING FOUNTAINS

Costs: **As a rough rule of thumb, estimate $800 to $1200/fixture (50% M and 50% L) for all plumbing within the building. Assume 30% for fixtures and 70% for lines. Also, of the lines, assume 40% for waste and 60% for supply. For more specifics on fixtures, only:**

	Residential			
Fixture	**Low**	**Medium**	**High**	**Commercial**
WC	**$150**	**$500**	**$850**	**$100 to $300**
Lavatories	**$100**	**$150**	**$250**	**same**
Tub/shower	**$100**	**$400**	**$800**	
Urinals				**$250 to $600**
Kitchen sinks	**$150**	**$300**	**$450**	

___ 1. *Water Supply*

The water supply is under pressure, so there is flexibility in layout of the water main to the building. In warm climates the *water meter* can be outside, but in cold climates it must be in a heated space. For small buildings allow a space of *20″ W × 12″ D × 10″ H*. After entering the building the water divides into a hot- and cold-water distribution system at the hot water heater. For small buildings allow for a *gas heater* a space *3′ sq. dia. × 60″ H* and for *electric heaters, 24″ dia. × 53″ H*. Where bathrooms are spread far apart, consideration should be given to multiple hot water heaters or circulated hot water.

Costs: **Residential: $500 to $1500/ea.**
Commercial: $1500 to $3000/ea. (80% M and 20% L).

Electric is cheaper for small buildings but high for large buildings.

___ If the water is "hard" (heavy concentration of calcium ions), a *water softener* may be needed. Provide *18″ dia. × 42″ H* space.

Costs: ≈ **$2000 to $10,000**

___ If water is obtained from a private *well,* a pump is needed. If the well is *deep,* the pump is usually at the bottom of the well. For this case provide space for a pressure tank that is *20″ dia. × 64″H*. If the well is *shallow* (20′ to 25′ deep) the pump may be provided inside the building. Space for pump and tank should be *36″W × 20″D × 64″H*.

Costs: **$140 to $200 per LF of well shaft**

___ Water supply *pipes* are usually copper or plastic and range from ½″ to 2″ for small buildings, but 2½″ to 6″ for larger buildings or higher-water-use buildings. Hot and cold pipes are usually laid out parallel. Piping should be kept out of exterior walls in cold climates to prevent winter freeze-ups.

___ The city water pressure will push water up 2 or 3 stories. Buildings taller than this will need a *surge tank and water pressure pumps*. This equipment takes approximately *100 to 200 SF* of space.

Costs: $5000 to $20,000

___ 2. *Plumbing Fixtures*

The men's and women's *restrooms* need to be laid out to determine their size and located in the building. Economical solutions are shared plumbing walls (toilet rooms back to back) and for multistory buildings, stacked layouts.

___ See UBC Table A-29-A (p. 438) or UPC Table 4-1 (p. 442) for *toilet requirements* (WC, lavatories, urinals, and drinking fountains) based on occupancy type. The number of fixtures calculated is the minimum required, not the suggested quantity for good design. Check the site jurisdiction as to which of the two tables applies. A check of the local ordinance should be made to be sure there are not further restrictions. Typical toilet room layouts, including requirements for the handicapped, are shown on p. 426.

___ In *cold* climates, chases for plumbing lines should not be on exterior walls, or if so, should be built in from exterior wall insulation.

Costs: See p. 429.

___ 3. *Sanitary Sewer*

Horizontal runs of drainage piping are difficult to achieve inside the building. The best arrangement is to bring the plumbing straight down (often along a column) and make connections horizontally under the building.

___ The *sanitary drainage system* collects waste water from the plumbing fixtures, which flows by gravity down through the building and out into the city sewer. Because of the slope requirement, long horizontal runs of drainage pipe will run out of ceiling space to fit in. Ideally, sanitary drainage pipes (called plumbing stacks) should run vertically down through the building collecting short branch lines from stacked bathrooms. A *4″* stack can serve approx. *50* WCs and accompanying lavatories. A *6″* stack can serve approximately *150*

WCs and lavatories. Pipes are typically of cast iron or plastic (ABS). Each fixture is drained through a "P" trap with a water seal. This, and venting the system to the roof, keeps sewer gases from entering the building.

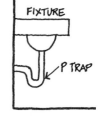

___ The *building drain* runs horizontally under the building collecting waste water from multiple vertical stacks. A *4″ to 6″* pipe requires a minimum slope of *1%*, and an *8″* pipe requires a minimum slope of $\frac{1}{2}$%. The lowest (or basement) *floor elevation* needs to be set higher than the rim elevation of the next upsteam manhole of the sewer main. If the building drain is below the sewer main, an automatic underground *ejector pump* is needed.

___ At sites where city sewer mains do not exist, a *septic system* will be needed. The size and configuration of private disposal systems vary widely depending on soil conditions, topography, local laws, and the regulated capacity of the system. The most common type includes a *septic tank* (usually 1000 to 1500 gallons) and a *disposal field* of open-joint pipe below the ground. Soil saturation at the wettest time of the year determines final design. As a starting point, allow an area of nearly level ground *40′ × 80′* with short side against building. No part of this area may be closer than *100′* to a well, pond, lake, stream, or river. Also see p. 187.

Costs: $3800 to $6000

___ *Solid waste* is often handled by a *compactor* for larger buildings. A compactor room of *60 SF* is sufficient for a small apartment building; *150 to 200 SF* for a larger building; and much larger for industrial. If a chute is used, plan on *15″ to 30″ diameter, with 24″* a typical dimension.

Costs: See p. 373.

___ 4. *Rainwater/Storm Sewer*

The rainwater that falls on the roof and the grounds of a building needs to be collected and channeled into the city storm drain system. If there is none, the site is drained to the street or to retention basins (if required). See page 176.

___ The *roof* slope must be arranged to channel water to drain points, where drainage pipes can carry the water down through the building and out into the storm drainage system (or sheet-drained on to the site).

___ The storm drainage water is kept separate from the sanitary drainage water so the sewage treatment system will not become overloaded in a rain. The following *guidelines* can be used in planning a storm drainage system:

___ *a.* "*Flat" roofs* need a minimum slope of *2%*.

___ *b.* Except for small roof areas there should be more than one drain point on a roof area.

___ *c.* *Roof drain leaders* are best *located* near exterior walls or interior columns, not at midspans of the structures.

___ *d.* *Backup drains or scuppers* should be provided in case main drains become clogged. These should be *4″* up slope or *2″* above drain. For small buildings, scuppers at exterior walls may be used.

___ *e.* At *sloped roofs,* water may shed off the edge, or to avoid this, roof *gutter and downspouts* may be used. Downspouts typically range from *3″ to 6″* in *1″* increments. Common provision for average rain conditions is *1 square inch* of cross section for each *150 SF* of roof area. Where parapets are long or tall, include ½ of their surface area to catch driving rain from one direction.

___ *f.* Horizontal *storm drain* pipes have a minimum slope of *1%*. The best strategy is to route them vertically down through the building, with a minimum of horizontal lines.

___ *g.* For estimating drain lines and downspouts:

Intensity, inch/hr. (see App. B, item J)	SF roof per sq. in, downspout or drain
2	600
3	400
4	300
5	240
6	200
7	175
8	150
9	130
10	120
11	110

Costs: $120 to $250/roof drain (for gutter and downspouts, assume ½ to ⅔ cost)

EXAMPLE:

PROBLEM:

FIGURE ROOF DRAINAGE FOR A ROOF THAT IS 50' x 100' IN MIAMI, FLORIDA. THE ROOF HAS A CENTER RIDGE AND IS TO BE SLOPED TO DOWNSPOUTS AT EXTERIOR WALLS.

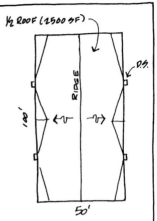

½ ROOF (2500 SF)

D.S.

RIDGE

100'

50'

SOLUTION:

1. AREA OF ROOF = 50' x 100' ÷ 2 SYSTEMS = 2500 SF
2. FOR MIAMI, FL (APP. B, ITEM J, P. 528) RAIN = 7.8"/HR.
3. ASSUME 3" x 3" DOWNSPOUTS = 9 SQ in / D.S.
4. NUMBER OF DOWNSPOUTS (SEE P. 432) @ 8"/HR = 150 SF/SQ IN/DS

$$\frac{2500 \text{ SF ROOF SYSTEM}}{150 \text{ SF/IN}} = 16.6 \text{ SQ IN.}$$

$$\frac{16.6 \text{ SQ IN}}{9 \text{ SQ IN/D.S}} = 2 \text{ DOWNSPOUTS PER SIDE}$$

___ 5. *Fire Protection*
(See p. 195 for fire hydrants)

   ___ *a.* A *sprinkler system* is the most effective way to provide fire safety.
      ___ (1) The UBC requires sprinklers at certain occupancies (see p. 81). Also see item I in App. A.
      ___ (2) Sprinkler *spacing* (maximum coverage per sprinkler):
         ___ Light hazard
            200 SF for smooth ceiling and beam-and-girder construction
            225 SF if hydraulically calculated for smooth ceiling, as above

130 SF for open wood joists

168 SF for all other types of construction

___ Ordinary hazard

130 SF for all types of construction, except:

100 SF for high-pile storage (12′ or more).

___ Extra hazard

90 SF for all types of construction

100 SF if hydraulically calculated.

___ (3) Notes

___ (*a*) Most buildings will be the *225 SF* spacing.

___ (*b*) Maximum spacing for light and ordinary hazard = 15′

High-pile and extra hazard = 12′

___ (*c*) Small rooms of light hazard, not exceeding *800 SF:* locate sprinklers max. of *9′* from walls.

___ (*d*) Maximum distance from walls to last sprinkler is *½ spacing* (except at small rooms). Minimum is *4″*.

___ (*e*) City ordinances should be checked to verify that local rules are not more stringent than UBC requirements.

___ (*f*) The sprinkler riser for small buildings usually takes a space about *2′6″ square*. Pumps and valves for larger buildings take up to about *100 to 500 SF.*

Costs: Wet pipe systems: $1.00 to $3.50/SF
For dry pipe systems, add $.050/SF.

___ *b.* Large buildings often also require a *stand-pipe,* which is a large-diameter water pipe extending vertically through the building with fire-hose connections at every floor.

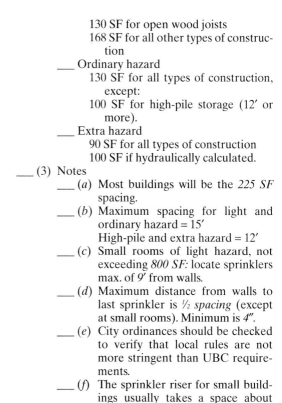

The system is either wet or dry. The UBC defines three classes (see p. 436):

___ (1) *Class I* is dry with 2½″ outlets. There is a connection point on every landing of every required stairway above or below grade, and on both sides of a horizontal exit door. This type of standpipe is for the fire department to connect their large hoses to.

___ (2) *Class II* is wet with 1½″ outlets and a hose. This type is located so that every part of the building is within 30′ of a nozzle attached to 100′ of hose. This type is for use by building occupants or the fire department.

___ (3) *Class III* is wet with 2½″ outlets and 1½″ hose connections. These are located according to the rules for both Class I and II.

SIAMESE FITTING

Often, two *Siamese* fittings are required in readily accessible locations on the outside of the building to allow the fire department to attach hoses from pumper trucks to the dry standpipe and to the sprinkler riser.

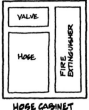

HOSE CABINET

Also, when required, *fire hose cabinets* will be located in such a way that every point on a floor lies within reach of a *30′* stream from the end of a *100′* hose. A typical recessed wall cabinet for a wet standpipe hose and fire extinguisher is *2′9″ W × 9″ D × 2′9″ H.* See UBC Table 9-A below for standpipe requirements.

TABLE 9-A—STANDPIPE REQUIREMENTS

OCCUPANCY	NONSPRINKLERED BUILDING[1]		SPRINKLERED BUILDING[2,3]	
× 304.8 for mm × 0.0929 for m²	Standpipe Class	Hose Requirement	Standpipe Class	Hose Requirement
1. Occupancies exceeding 150 feet in height and more than one story	III	Yes	I	No
2. Occupancies four stories or more but less than 150 feet in height, except Group R, Division 3[6]	[I and II[4]] (or III)	[5] Yes	I	No
3. Group A Occupancies with occupant load exceeding 1,000[7]	II	Yes	No requirement	No
4. Group A, Division 2.1 Occupancies over 5,000 square feet in area used for exhibition	II	Yes	II	Yes
5. Groups I; H; S; M; F, Division 1 Occupancies less than four stories in height but greater than 20,000 square feet per floor[6]	II[4]	Yes	No requirement	No
6. Stages more than 1,000 square feet in area	II	No	III	No

[1]Except as otherwise specified in Item 4 of this table, Class II standpipes need not be provided in basements having an automatic fire-extinguishing system throughout.

[2]The standpipe system may be combined with the automatic sprinkler system.

[3]Portions of otherwise sprinklered buildings that are not protected by automatic sprinklers shall have Class II standpipes installed as required for the unsprinklered portions.

[4]In open structures where Class II standpipes may be damaged by freezing, the building official may authorize the use of Class I standpipes that are located as required for Class II standpipes.

[5]Hose is required for Class II standpipes only.

[6]For the purposes of this table, occupied roofs of parking structures shall be considered an additional story. In parking structures, a tier is a story.

[7]Class II standpipes need not be provided in assembly areas used solely for worship.

___ 6. *Landscape Irrigation*: See p. 203.
___ 7. *Gas:* To allow for the gas meter and piping, provide a space
     1'6" W × 1'D × 2'H.
___ 8. *Solar Hot Water Systems*
        ___ *a.* In U.S., average person uses *20 gal.* of HW/day.
        ___ *b.* Mount collectors at tilt equal to about the site latitude.
        ___ *c.* Typical collectors are 4' × 8' and 4' × 10'.
        ___ *d.* Typical relationship between collector area and stor-
             age volume is *1:3* to *1:7* gal. per SF of collector.
        ___ *e.* Type of systems
             ___ (1) *Open loop, recirculation:* The most widely
                  used system in climates where freezing is of
                  little concern.
             ___ (2) *Open loop, drain down:* Includes valving
                  arrangement from collectors and piping
                  when water temperature approaches freez-
                  ing.
             ___ (3) *Closed loop, drain back:* Use of separate
                  fluid (such as water) circulated through col-
                  lectors where it is heated and transferred to
                  HW storage through heat exchanger.
             ___ (4) *Closed loop, antifreeze:* Most widely used
                  with heat exchanger.
        ___ *f.* Auxiliary heat: Typically an electric element in HW
             tank top.
        ___ *g.* For rough estimates:
             ___ (1) Northeast U.S.: 60 SF collector and 80 gal-
                  lon tank will provide 50% to 75% need of a
                  family of four.
             ___ (2) Southwest U.S.: 40 SF of collector will do
                  same.

Costs: $3300 to $6300 per system

TABLE A-29-A—MINIMUM PLUMBING FIXTURES[1,2,3]

Each building shall be provided with sanitary facilities, including provisions for accessibility in accordance with Chapter 11. Plumbing fixtures shall be provided for the type of building occupancy with the minimum numbers as shown in Table A-29-A. The number of fixtures are the minimum required as shown in Table A-29-A and are assumed to be based on 50 percent male and 50 percent female. The occupant load factors shall be as shown in Table A-29-A.

EXCEPTION: Where circumstances dictate that a different ratio is needed, the adjustment shall be approved by the building official.

TYPE OF BUILDING OR OCCUPANCY[4]	WATER CLOSETS[5] (fixtures per person) MALE	FEMALE	LAVATORIES[6] (fixtures per person) MALE	FEMALE	BATHTUB OR SHOWER (fixtures per person)
For the occupancies listed below, use 30 square feet (2.78 m²) per occupant for the minimum number of plumbing fixtures.					
Group A Conference rooms, dining rooms, drinking establishments, exhibit rooms, gymnasiums, lounges, stages and similar uses including restaurants classified as Group B Occupancies	1:1-25 2:26-75 3:76-125 4:126-200 5:201-300 6:301-400 Over 400, add one fixture for each additional 200 males or 150 females.	1:1-25 2:26-75 3:76-125 4:126-200 5:201-300 6:301-400	one for each water closet up to four; then one for each two additional water closets		
For the assembly occupancies listed below, use the number of fixed seating or, where no fixed seating is provided, use 15 square feet (1.39 m²) per occupant for the minimum number of plumbing fixtures.					
Assembly places— Auditoriums, convention halls, dance floors, lodge rooms, stadiums and casinos	1:1-50 2:51-100 3:101-150 4:151-300 Over 300 males, add one fixture for each additional 200, and over 400 females add one for each 125.	3:1-50 4:51-100 6:101-200 8:201-400	1:1-200 2:201-400 3:401-750 Over 750, add one fixture for each additional 500 persons.	1:1-200 2:201-400 3:401-750	

(Continued)

97 UBC FIXTURE COUNT

For the assembly occupancies listed below, use the number of fixed seating or, where no fixed seating is provided, use 30 square feet (2.29 m²) per occupant for the minimum number of plumbing fixtures.

Occupancy			
Worship places Principal assembly area	one per 150	one per 75	one per two water closets
Worship places Educational and activity unit	one per 125	one per 75	one per two water closets

For the occupancies listed below, use 200 square feet (18.58 m²) per occupant for the minimum number of plumbing fixtures.

| **Group B**
Offices or public buildings | 1:1-15
2:16-35
3:36-55
Over 55, add one for each 50 persons. | 1:1-15
2:16-35
3:36-55
Over 55, add one for each 50 persons. | one per two water closets |

For the occupancies listed below, use 50 square feet (4.65 m²) per occupant for the minimum number of plumbing fixtures.

Group E Schools—for staff use All schools	1:1-15 2:16-35 3:36-55 Over 55, add one fixture for each additional 40 persons.	1:1-15 2:16-35 3:36-55 Over 55, add one fixture for each additional 40 persons.	one per 40
Schools—for student use Day care	1:1-20 2:21-50 Over 50, add one fixture for each additional 50 persons.	1:1-25 2:26-50 Over 50, add one fixture for each additional 50 persons.	1:1-25 2:26-50 Over 50, add one fixture for each additional 50 persons.
Elementary	one per 30	one per 25	one per 35
Secondary	one per 40	one per 30	one per 40

For the occupancies listed below, use 50 square feet (4.65 m²) per occupant for the minimum number of plumbing fixtures.

| **Education Facilities other than Group E**
Others (colleges, universities, adult centers, etc.) | one per 40 | one per 30 | one per 40 |

(Continued)

TABLE A-29-A—MINIMUM PLUMBING FIXTURES[1,2,3]—(Continued)

TYPE OF BUILDING OR OCCUPANCY[4]	WATER CLOSETS[5] (fixtures per person) MALE	FEMALE	LAVATORIES[6] (fixtures per person) MALE	FEMALE	BATHTUB OR SHOWER (fixtures per person)
For the occupancies listed below, use 2,000 square feet (185.8 m²) per occupant for the minimum number of plumbing fixtures.					
Group F Workshop, foundries and similar establishments, and Group H Occupancies	1:1-10 2:11-25 3:26-50 4:51-75 5:76-100 Over 100, add one fixture for each additional 300 persons.	1:1-10 2:11-25 3:26-50 4:51-75 5:76-100	one for each two water closets		one shower for each 15 persons exposed to excessive heat or to skin contamination with irritating materials
For the occupancies listed below, use the designated application and 200 square feet (18.58 m²) per occupant of the general use area for the minimum number of plumbing fixtures.					
Group I Hospital waiting rooms Hospital general use areas	one per room (usable by either sex) 1:1-15 2:16-35 3:36-55 Over 55, add one fixture for each additional 40 persons.	1:1-15 3:16-35 4:36-55	one per room one per each two water closets		
Hospitals Patient room Ward room	one per room one per eight patients		one per room one per 10 patients		one per room one per 20 patients
Jails and reformatories Cell Exercise room	one per cell one per exercise room		one per cell one per exercise room		
Other institutions (on each occupied floor)	one per 25	one per 25	one per 10	one per 10	one per eight

(Continued)

For the occupancies listed below, use 200 square feet (18.58 m²) per occupant for the minimum number of plumbing fixtures.

Occupancy	Water closets	Lavatories	Bathtubs or Showers
Group M Retail or wholesale stores	1:1-50 2:51-100 3:101-400 Over 400, add one fixture for each additional 500 males and one for each 150 females.	one for each two water closets	

For Group R Occupancies, dwelling units and hotel guest rooms, use the chart. For congregate residences, use 200 square feet (18.58 m²) for Group R, Division 1 Occupancies and 300 square feet (27.87 m²) for Group R, Division 3 Occupancies for the minimum plumbing fixtures.

Occupancy	Water closets	Lavatories	Bathtubs or Showers
Group R Dwelling units	one per dwelling unit	one per dwelling unit	one per dwelling unit
Hotel guest rooms	one per guest room	one per guest room	one per guest room
Congregate residences	one per 10 Add one fixture for each additional 25 males and one for each additional 20 females. one per 8	one per 12 one per 12 Over 12, add one fixture for each additional 20 males and one for each additional 15 females	one per eight For females, add one bathtub per 30. Over 150, add one per 20.

For the occupancies listed below, use 5,000 square feet (464.5 m²) per occupant for the minimum number of plumbing fixtures.

Occupancy	Water closets	Lavatories	Bathtubs or Showers
Group S Warehouses	1:1-10 2:11-25 3:26-50 4:51-75 5:76-100 Over 100, add one for each 300 males and females.	one per 40 occupants of each sex	one shower for each 15 persons exposed to excessive heat or to skin contamination with poisonous, infectious or irritating materials

NOTE: Occupant loads over 30 shall have one drinking fountain for each 150 occupants.

[1]The figures shown are based on one fixture being the minimum required for the number of persons indicated or any fraction thereof.

[2]Drinking fountains shall not be installed in toilet rooms.

[3]When the design occupant load is less than 10 persons, a facility usable by either sex may be approved by the building official.

[4]Any category not mentioned specifically or about which there are any questions shall be classified by the building official and included in the category which it most nearly resembles, based on the expected use of the plumbing facilities.

[5]Where urinals are provided, one water closet less than the number specified may be provided for each urinal installed, except the number of water closets in such cases shall not be reduced to less than one half of the minimum specified.

[6]Twenty-four inches (610 mm) of wash sink or 18 inches (457 mm) of a circular basin, when provided with water outlets for such space, shall be considered equivalent to one lavatory.

Minimum Plumbing Facilities[1]

Each building shall be provided with sanitary facilities, including provisions for the physically handicapped as prescribed by the Department having jurisdiction. For requirements for the handicapped, ANSI A117.1-1992, Accessible and Usable Buildings and Facilities, may be used.

The total occupant load shall be determined by minimum exiting requirements. The minimum number of fixtures shall be calculated at fifty (50) percent male and fifty (50) percent female based on the total occupant load.

Type of Building or Occupancy[2]	Water Closets[14] (Fixtures per Person)		Urinals[5, 10] (Fixtures per Person)	Lavatories (Fixtures per Person)		Bathtubs or Showers (Fixtures per Person)	Drinking Fountains[3, 13] (Fixtures per Person)
	Male	Female	Male	Male	Female		
Assembly Places – Theatres, Auditoriums, Convention Halls, etc. – for permanent employee use	1: 1-15 2: 16-35 3: 36-55 Over 55, add 1 fixture for each additional 40 persons.	1: 1-15 3: 16-35 4: 36-55	0: 1-9 1: 10-50 Add one fixture for each additional 50 males.	1 per 40	1 per 40		
Assembly Places – Theatres, Auditoriums, Convention Halls, etc. – for public use	1: 1-100 2: 101-200 3: 201-400 Over 400, add one fixture for each additional 500 males and 1 for each additional 125 females.	3: 1-50 4: 51-100 8: 101-200 11: 201-400	1: 1-100 2: 101-200 3: 201-400 4: 401-600 Over 600 add 1 fixture for each additional 300 males.	1: 1-200 2: 201-400 3: 401-750 Over 750, add one fixture for each additional 500 persons.	1: 1-200 2: 201-400 3: 401-750		1: 1-150 2: 151-400 3: 401-750 Over 750, add one fixture for each additional 500 persons.
Dormitories[9] School or Labor	1 per 10 Add 1 fixture for each additional 25 males (over 10) and 1 for each additional 20 females (over 8).	1 per 8	1 per 25 Over 150, add 1 fixture for each additional 50 males.	1 per 12 Over 12 add one fixture for each additional 20 males and 1 for each 15 additional females.	1 per 12	1 per 8 For females, add 1 bathtub per 30. Over 150, add 1 per 20.	1 per 150[12]
Dormitories – for staff use	1: 1-15 2: 16-35 3: 36-55 Over 55, add 1 fixture for each additional 40 persons,	1: 1-15 3: 16-35 4: 36-55	1 per 50	1 per 40	1 per 40	1 per 8	

97 UPC FIXTURE COUNT

Type of Building or Occupancy	Water Closets	Urinals	Lavatories	Bathtubs or Showers	Drinking Fountains
Dwellings[4] Single Dwelling, Multiple Dwelling or Apartment House	1 per dwelling		1 per dwelling or apartment unit	1 per dwelling or apartment unit	
Hospital Waiting rooms	1 per room				1 per 150[12]
Hospitals – for employee use	**Male** 1: 1-15, 2: 16-35, 3: 36-55 / **Female** 1: 1-15, 3: 16-35, 4: 36-55 / Over 55, add 1 fixture for each additional 40 persons.	**Male** 0: 1-9, 1: 10-50 / Add one fixture for each additional 50 males.	**Male** 1 per 40, **Female** 1 per 40		
Hospitals Individual Room / Ward Room	1 per room / 1 per 8 patients		1 per room / 1 per 10 patients	1 per room / 1 per 20 patients	1 per 150[12]
Industrial[6] Warehouses, Workshops, Foundries and similar establishments – for employee use	**Male** 1: 1-10, 2: 11-25, 3: 26-50, 4: 51-75, 5: 76-100 / **Female** 1: 1-10, 2: 11-25, 3: 26-50, 4: 51-75, 5: 76-100 / Over 100, add 1 fixture for each additional 30 persons	**Male** 0: 1-9, 1: 10-50 / Add one fixture for each additional 50 males.	Up to 100, 1 per 10 persons / Over 100, 1 per 15 persons[7, 8]	1 shower for each 15 persons exposed to excessive heat or to skin contamination with poisonous, infectious, or irritating material	1 per 150[12]
Institutional – Other than Hospitals or Penal Institutions (on each occupied floor)	**Male** 1 per 25, **Female** 1 per 20	**Male** 0: 1-9, 1: 10-50 / Add one fixture for each additional 50 males.	**Male** 1 per 10, **Female** 1 per 10	1 per 8	1 per 150[12]

(Continued)

Minimum Plumbing Facilities[1] (Continued)

Type of Building or Occupancy[2]	Water Closets[14] (Fixtures per Person)		Urinals[5,10] (Fixtures per Person)	Lavatories (Fixtures per Person)		Bathtubs or Showers (Fixtures per Person)	Drinking Fountains[3,13] (Fixtures per Person)
Institutional – Other than Hospitals or Penal Institutions (on each occupied floor) – for employee use	Male 1: 1-15 2: 16-35 3: 36-55 Over 55, add 1 fixture for each additional 40 persons.	Female 1: 1-15 3: 16-35 4: 36-55	Male 0: 1-9 1: 10-50 Add one fixture for each additional 50 males.	Male 1 per 40	Female 1 per 40	1 per 8	1 per 150[12]
Office or Public Buildings	Male 1: 1-100 2: 101-200 3: 201-400 Over 400, add one fixture for each additional 500 males and 1 for each additional 150 females.	Female 3: 1-50 4: 51-100 8: 101-200 11: 201-400	Male 1: 1-100 2: 101-200 3: 201-400 4: 401-600 Over 600 add 1 fixture for each additional 300 males.	Male 1: 1-200 2: 201-400 3: 401-750 Over 750, add one fixture for each additional 500 persons	Female 1: 1-200 2: 201-400 3: 401-750		1 per 150[12]
Office or Public Buildings – for employee use	Male 1: 1-15 2: 16-35 3: 36-55 Over 55, add 1 fixture for each additional 40 persons.	Female 1: 1-15 3: 16-35 4: 36-55	Male 0: 1-9 1: 10-50 Add one fixture for each additional 50 males.	Male 1 per 40	Female 1 per 40		
Penal Institutions – for employee use	Male 1: 1-15 2: 16-35 3: 36-55 Over 55, add 1 fixture for each additional 40 persons.	Female 1: 1-15 3: 16-35 4: 36-55	Male 0: 1-9 1: 10-50 Add one fixture for each additional 50 males.	Male 1 per 40	Female 1 per 40		1 per 150[12]

(Continued)

Type of Building or Occupancy	Water Closets (Male / Female)	Urinals (Male)	Lavatories (Male / Female)	Drinking Fountains
Penal Institutions – for prison use				
Cell	1 per cell		1 per cell	1 per cell block floor
Exercise Room	1 per exercise room	Male 1 per exercise room	1 per exercise room	1 per exercise room
Restaurants, Pubs and Lounges[11]	Male 1: 1-50 2: 51-150 3: 151-300 Over 300, add 1 fixture for each additional 200 persons Female 1: 1-50 2: 51-150 3: 151-300 4: 151-300	Male 1: 1-150 Over 150, add 1 fixture for each additional 150 males	Male 1: 1-150 2: 151-200 3: 201-400 Over 400, add 1 fixture for each additional 400 persons Female 1: 1-150 2: 151-200 3: 201-400	
Schools – for staff use				
All schools	Male 1: 1-15 2: 16-35 3: 36-55 Over 55, add 1 fixture for each additional 40 persons Female 1: 1-15 2: 16-35 3: 36-55	Male 1 per 50	Male 1 per 40 Female 1 per 40	
Schools – for student use				
Nursery	Male 1: 1-20 2: 21-50 Over 50, add 1 fixture for each additional 50 persons Female 1: 1-20 2: 21-50		Male 1: 1-25 2: 26-50 Over 50, add 1 fixture for each additional 50 persons Female 1: 1-25 2: 26-50	1 per 150[12]
Elementary	Male 1 per 30 Female 1 per 25	Male 1 per 75	Male 1 per 35 Female 1 per 35	1 per 150[12]
Secondary	Male 1 per 40 Female 1 per 30	Male 1 per 35	Male 1 per 40 Female 1 per 40	1 per 150[12]
Others (Colleges, Universities, Adult Centers, etc.)	Male 1 per 40 Female 1 per 30	Male 1 per 35	Male 1 per 40 Female 1 per 40	1 per 150[12]
Worship Places Educational and Activities Unit	Male 1 per 150 Female 1 per 75	Male 1 per 150	1 per 2 water closets	1 per 150[12]
Worship Places Principal Assembly Place	Male 1 per 150 Female 1 per 75	Male 1 per 150	1 per 2 water closets	1 per 150[12]

(Continued)

445

1. The figures shown are based upon one (1) fixture being the minimum required for the number of persons indicated or any fraction thereof.

2. Building categories not shown on this table shall be considered separately by the Administrative Authority.

3. Drinking fountains shall not be installed in toilet rooms.

4. Laundry trays. One (1) laundry tray or one (1) automatic washer standpipe for each dwelling unit or one (1) laundry tray or one (1) automatic washer standpipe, or combination thereof, for each twelve (12) apartments. Kitchen sinks, one (1) for each dwelling or apartment unit.

5. For each urinal added in excess of the minimum required, one water closet may be deducted. The number of water closets shall not be reduced to less than two-thirds (2/3) of the minimum requirement.

6. As required by ANSI Z4.1-1968, Sanitation in Places of Employment.

7. Where there is exposure to skin contamination with poisonous, infectious, or irritating materials, provide one (1) lavatory for each five (5) persons.

8. Twenty-four (24) lineal inches (610 mm) of wash sink or eighteen (18) inches (457 mm) of a circular basin, when provided with water outlets for such space, shall be considered equivalent to one (1) lavatory.

9. Laundry trays, one (1) for each fifty (50) persons. Slop sinks, one (1) for each hundred (100) persons.

10. General. In applying this schedule of facilities, consideration must be given to the accessibility of the fixtures. Conformity purely on a numerical basis may not result in an installation suited to the need of the individual establishment. For example, schools should be provided with toilet facilities on each floor having classrooms.

    a. Surrounding materials, wall and floor space to a point two (2) feet (610 mm) in front of urinal lip and four (4) feet (1219 mm) above the floor, and at least two (2) feet (610 mm) to each side of the urinal shall be lined with non-absorbent materials.

    b. Trough urinals are prohibited.

11. A restaurant is defined as a business which sells food to be consumed on the premises.

    a. The number of occupants for a drive-in restaurant shall be considered as equal to the number of parking stalls.

    b. Employee toilet facilities are not to be included in the above restaurant requirements. Hand washing facilities must be available in the kitchen for employees.

12. Where food is consumed indoors, water stations may be substituted for drinking fountains. Offices, or public buildings for use by more than six (6) persons shall have one (1) drinking fountain for the first one hundred fifty (150) persons and one (1) additional fountain for each three hundred (300) persons thereafter.

13. There shall be a minimum of one (1) drinking fountain per occupied floor in schools, theatres, auditoriums, dormitories, offices or public building.

14. The total number of water closets for females shall be at least equal to the total number of water closets and urinals required for males.

EXAMPLE:

PROBLEM: FIGURE THE REQUIRED PLUMBING FIX-
TURES FOR A 10000 SF OFFICE SPACE.
FIGURE FOR BOTH THE UBC AND THE U.P.C.

SOLUTION:

A. <u>BY U.B.C.</u> (TABLE A·29-A OF UBC, SEE P. 439)

  1. GROUP B: 10000 SF ÷ 200 SF/OCC = 50 OCC

    ÷ 2 = 25/SEX

  2. FIXTURES

	M (25)	W (25)
WC	~~2~~ 1	2
LAV	2	2
UR	1	

    ALSO: 1 DF REQ'D.

B. <u>BY U.P.C.</u> (TABLE 4-1 OF U.P.C., SEE P. 444)

  1. FIGURE OCC. LOAD FOR EXITING (SEE TABLE 10-A
OF UBC. ON P. 105).

    10000 SF ÷ 100 SF/OCC = 100 OCC ÷ 2 = 50/SEX

  2. FIXTURES

	M (50)	W (50)
WC	~~3~~ 2	3
LAV	2	2
UR	~~1~~ 2	

NOTES

__ B. HEATING, VENTILATION, AND AIR CONDITIONING (HVAC) ① ⑩

See p. 451 for selection and **cost** table.

Costs: Equipment 20% to 30%; distribution system 80% to 70%; see p. 451 for cost of different systems. See App. A, item K for % of total construction costs.

During programming it is useful to do a functional partitioning of the building into major zones for:

___ 1. Similar schedule of use
___ 2. Similar temperature requirements
___ 3. Similar ventilation and air quality
___ 4. Similar internal heat generation
___ 5. Similar HVAC needs

During design, if possible, locate spaces with similar needs together. See App. A, item J for SF/ton estimates by building type. See p. 142 for energy conservation and equipment efficiency.

___ 1. *General*

HVAC systems can be divided into four major parts:

___ *a.* The *boiler and chiller* to create heat and cold for the system to use. (In small package systems this is an internal electric coil, gas furnace, or refrigeration compressor).

___ *b.* *Cooling tower* (or air-cooled condenser) located outside to exhaust heat.

___ *c.* *Air handlers* to transfer heat and cold to air (or at least fresh air) to be blown into the building zones. In large buildings this is in a fan room. (In small package systems this is an internal fan).

___ *d.* The *delivery system* of ducts, control boxes, and diffusers to deliver conditioned air to the spaces.

___ 2. *Systems for Small Buildings*

___ *a.* *Roof-mounted "package systems"* are typically used for residential and small to medium commercial buildings. They are AC units that house the first three parts in one piece of equipment that usually ends up on the roof. Used usually in warm or temperate climates. Typical sizes:

Size	Area served	Dimensions	System
2 to 5 tons	600 to 1500 SF	6'L × 4'W × 4'H	Single zone constant
5 to 10 tons	1500 to 4500 SF	10'L × 7'W × 5'H	vol. delivery system; can serve more than
15 to 75 tons	4500 to 22,500 SF	25'L × 9'W × 6'H	one zone with variable air vol. delivery system

Notes:
1. Units should have *3' to 4'* of clearance around.
2. A *ton is 12,000 Btu* of refrigeration.
3. Each *ton is equal to 400 CFM.*

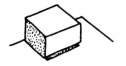

Roof Mounted
"Package" Unit

HVAC SYSTEMS AND COSTS

TYPE	HEATING	COOLING	BUILDING SMALL	BUILDING LARGE	FUEL ELECT.	FUEL GAS	FUEL OTHER	DELIVERY AIR	DELIVERY PIPES	MIN. OPERATING COST IN COLD CLIMATE	MIN. OPERATING COST IN MODERATE CLIMATE	MAX. CONTROL OF AIR VELOCITY & QUALITY	MAX. INDIVIDUAL CONTROL OF TEMP.	MINIMUM NOISE	MINIMUM VISUAL OBTRUSIVENESS	MIN. SPACE FOR EQUIP	MIN. MAINTENANCE	MIN. FL. TO FL. HT.	MAX. FLEXIBILITY OF RENTAL SPACE	$ PER SF (50% H & 50% L)	$ TON OF AC (±10%)
1 ROOF MT'D "PACKAGE" UNITS	•	•	•		•	•		•		•		•			•					5	1400
2 CENTRAL FORCED AIR (& "SPLIT" SYSTEMS)	•	•	•		•	•		•		•		•		•	•		•			6.25	1200
3 FORCED HOT WATER	•		•		•	•			•					•	•	•	•			6.25	1600
4 EVAPORATIVE COOLING		•	•		•			•			•		•			•				5	2000
5 THROUGH WALL UNITS	•	•	•		•			•					•	•		•				2	600
6 ELECTRIC BASE BOARD	•		•		•								•			•	•			1.50	600
7 ELECT. FAN UNIT HEATERS	•		•		•									•	•	•	•			1.25	
8 RADIANT	•	•	•		•				•	•	•	•		•	•	•				2.50	
9 WALL FURNACE	•		•		•	•				•	•				•	•	•			1.50	
10 PASSIVE SOLAR	•		•		•						•									2.50	
11 ACTIVE SOLAR	•		•		•				•	•	•										
12 STOVES	•		•				•														
13 SINGLE ZONE CONSTANT VOL.	•	•		•	•	•	•	•				•		•	•		•			6.25	2200
14 MULTI ZONE CONSTANT VOL.	•	•		•	•	•	•	•				•	•							8.75	2500
15 VARIABLE AIR VOLUME	•	•		•	•	•	•	•					•	•	•	•			•	10	2700
16 DOUBLE DUCT	•	•		•	•	•	•	•			•	•	•	•	•				•	12.50	3000
17 INDUCTION	•	•		•	•	•	•	•	•		•	•	•	•	•				•	10	2700
18 FAN COIL WITH AIR	•	•		•	•	•	•	•	•		•	•	•	•	•			•	•	10	2500
19 FAN COIL UNITS	•	•		•	•	•	•		•	•	•	•	•	•	•			•	•	8.75	2200
20 HOT WATER BASE BOARDS	•		•	•	•	•	•		•		•		•			•				5	

___ b. <u>Forced-air central heating</u> is typically used for residential and light commercial buildings. It heats air with gas, oil flame, or elect. resistance at a furnace. A fan blows air through a duct system. The furnace can be upflow (for basements), side flow, or down flow (for attic). The furnace must be vented. Furnace sizes range between *2′W × 2.5′D × 7′H* to *4′W to 7′D × 7′H*. Main ducts are typically *1′ × 2′* horizontal and *1′ × .33′* vertical.

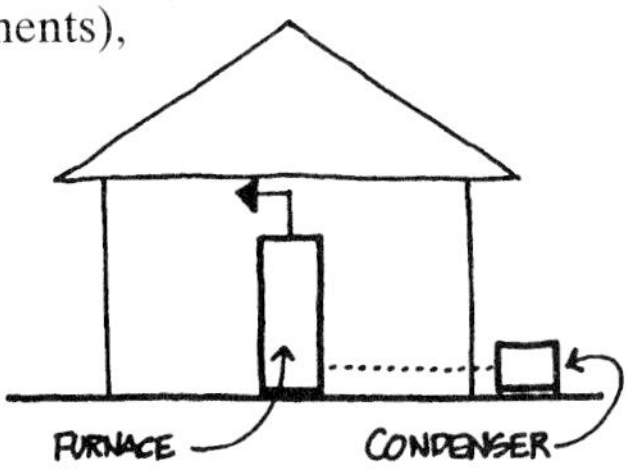

Furnace ─   Condenser ─

Can add cooling with a "*split system*" by adding evaporator coils in the duct and an exterior condenser. Typical condensers range from *2′W × 2′D × 2′H* to *3.5′W × 4′D × 3′H.*

___ c. <u>Forced hot water heating</u> is typically used for residential buildings and commercial offices. A burner or electric resistance heats water to fin tube convectors (or fan coil unit with blowers). The fueled boiler must be vented and provided with combustible air. Boiler sizes range from *2′W × 2′D × 7′H* to *3′W × 5′D × 7′H.* Fin tube convectors are typically *3″D × 8″H.* Fan coils are *2′W × 2.5′H.* There is *no* cooling.

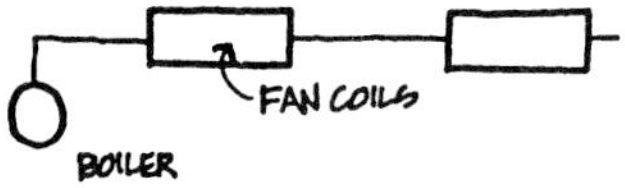

FAN COILS

BOILER

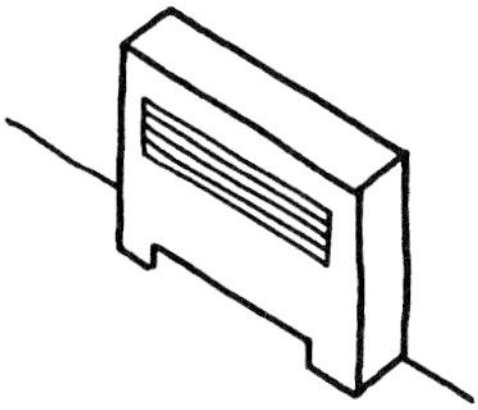

___ *d.* *Evaporative cooling* is typically used for residential buildings. It works only in hot, dry climates. A fan draws exterior air across wet pads and into the duct system. There is *no*

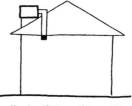

heating. Cooler size typically is *3'W × 3'D × 3'H.* Main duct is typically *1.5'W × 1.5'D.*

___ *e.* *Through-wall units and package terminal units* are typically used for motels/ hotels as well as small offices. They are self-contained at an exterior wall and are intended for small spaces. These are usually electric (or *heat*

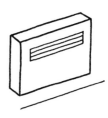

pump in mild climates), which are used for *both* heating and cooling. Interior air is recirculated and outside air is added. Typical sizes:

Package Terminal Units   3.5'W × 1.5'D × 1.3'H
Through-Wall Units   2'W × 2'D × 1.5'H

___ *f.* *Electric baseboard convectors* are typically used for residential buildings and commercial offices. They heat by electrical resistance

in *3"D × 8"H* baseboards around the perimeter of the room. There is *no cooling.*

___ *g.* *Electric fan-forced unit heaters* are much like item *f* above, but are larger because of internal fans recirculating the air. There is *no cooling.* Typical sizes range from *1.5' W × 8"D × 8"H* to *2'W × 1'D × 1.8'H.*

___ *h.* *Radiant heating:* Electrical resistance wires are embedded in floor or ceiling. There is *no cooling.* An alternative is to have recessed radiant panels, typically *2' × 2'* or *2' × 4'.* For alternative cooling and heating use water piping. These are typically residential applications.

___ *i.* <u>*Wall furnaces*</u> are small furnaces for small spaces (usually residential). They must be vented. There is *no cooling.* They may be either gas or electric. The typical size is *14″W × 12″D × 84″H.*

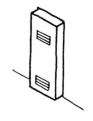

___ *j.* <u>Other</u> miscellaneous small systems (typically residential):

___ Passive solar heating (see p. 138)

___ Active solar heating

___ Heating stoves (must be properly vented!)

___ 3. <u>*Custom Systems for Large Buildings*</u>

These are where the first three parts (see p. 449) must have areas allocated for them in the floor plan. In tall buildings due to distance, mechanical floors are created so that air handlers can move air up and down *10 to 15* floors. Thus mechanical floors are spaced *20 to 30* floors apart.

A decentralized chiller and boiler can be at every other mechanical floor or they can be centralized at the top or base of the building with one or more air handlers at each floor. See p. 455 for equipment rooms.

___ *a.* <u>Delivery systems</u>

___ (1) <u>*Air delivery systems:*</u>

Because of their size, <u>*ducts*</u> are a great concern in the preliminary design of the floor-to-ceiling space. See p. 409. The main supply and return ducts are often run above main hallways because ceilings can be lower and because this provides a natural path of easy access to the majority of spaces served.

Air rates for buildings vary from *1 CFM/SF to 2 CFM/SF* based on usage and climate. Low-velocity ducts require *1 to 2 SF of area per 1000 SF* of building area served. High-velocity ducts require *0.5 to 1.0.* Air returns are required and are about the same size, or slightly larger, than the main duct supply. (The above-noted dimensions are interior. Typically, ducts are externally lined with 1″ or 2″ of insulation.)

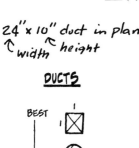

24″ x 10″ duct in plan
↑ width   ↑ height

<u>DUCTS</u>

BEST

1

2

4

WORST
(6″ MIN.)

LARGE SYSTEMS

DELIVERY SYSTEM (SEE FOLLOWING PAGES)

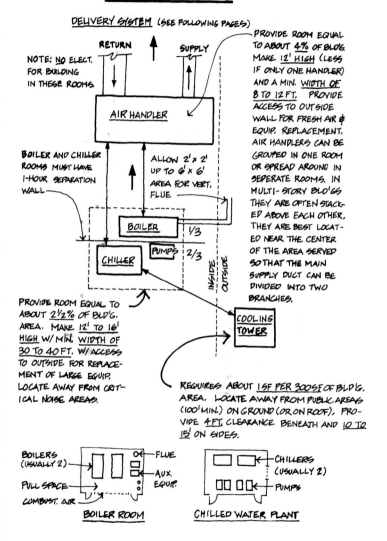

RETURN   SUPPLY

NOTE: NO ELECT. FOR BUILDING IN THESE ROOMS.

AIR HANDLER

PROVIDE ROOM EQUAL TO ABOUT 4% OF BLD'G. MAKE 12' HIGH (LESS IF ONLY ONE HANDLER) AND A MIN. WIDTH OF 8 TO 12 FT. PROVIDE ACCESS TO OUTSIDE WALL FOR FRESH AIR & EQUIP. REPLACEMENT. AIR HANDLERS CAN BE GROUPED IN ONE ROOM OR SPREAD AROUND IN SEPERATE ROOMS. IN MULTI-STORY BLD'GS THEY ARE OFTEN STACKED ABOVE EACH OTHER. THEY ARE BEST LOCATED NEAR THE CENTER OF THE AREA SERVED SO THAT THE MAIN SUPPLY DUCT CAN BE DIVIDED INTO TWO BRANCHES.

BOILER AND CHILLER ROOMS MUST HAVE 1-HOUR SEPARATION WALL

ALLOW 2' x 2' UP TO 6' x 6' AREA FOR VERT. FLUE

BOILER   1/3

PUMPS   2/3

INSIDE   OUTSIDE

CHILLER

PROVIDE ROOM EQUAL TO ABOUT 2½% OF BLD'G. AREA. MAKE 12' TO 16' HIGH W/ MIN. WIDTH OF 30 TO 40 FT. W/ACCESS TO OUTSIDE FOR REPLACEMENT OF LARGE EQUIP. LOCATE AWAY FROM CRITICAL NOISE AREAS.

COOLING TOWER

REQUIRES ABOUT 1 SF PER 300SF OF BLD'G. AREA. LOCATE AWAY FROM PUBLIC AREAS (100' MIN.) ON GROUND (OR ON ROOF), PROVIDE 4 FT. CLEARANCE BENEATH AND 10 TO 15' ON SIDES.

BOILERS (USUALLY 2)

FLUE

AUX. EQUIP.

PULL SPACE

COMBUST. AIR

BOILER ROOM

CHILLERS (USUALLY 2)

PUMPS

CHILLED WATER PLANT

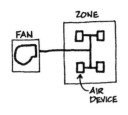

___ (*a*) *Single-zone constant-volume systems* serve only one zone and are used for large, open-space rooms without diverse exterior exposure. This is a low-velocity system.

___ (*b*) *Multizone constant-volume systems* can serve up to eight separate zones. They are used in modest-sized buildings where there is a diversity of exterior exposure and/or diversity of interior loads. This is a low-velocity system.

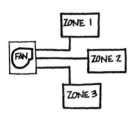

___ (*c*) *Subzone box systems* often modify single-zone systems for appended spaces. They use boxes that branch off the main supply duct to create separate zones. The size of the boxes can be related to the area served:

Box	Area served
4′L × 3′W × 1.5′H	500 to 1500 SF
5′L × 4′W × 1.5′H	1500 to 5000 SF

The main ducts can be high-velocity, but the ducts after the boxes at each zone (as well as the return air) are low-velocity.

___ (*d*) *Variable air-volume* single duct can serve as many subzones as required. It is the dominant choice in many commercial buildings because of its flexibility and energy savings. It is most effectively used for interior zones. At exterior zones hot water or electrical reheat coils are added to the boxes. Each zone's temperature is controlled by the volume of air flowing through its box. Typical above ceiling boxes are:

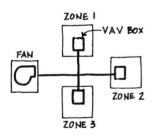

8″ to 11″H for up to 1500 SF
served (lengths up to 5′)
up to 18″H for up to 7000 SF

___ (*e*) <u>Double-duct systems</u> can serve as a good choice where *air quality control* is important. The air handler supplies hot air for one duct and cold air for the other. The mixing box controls the mix of these two air ducts. This system is not commonly used except in retrofits. It is a "caddie" but also a "gas guzzler."

___ (*f*) <u>Variable air-volume dual-duct systems.</u> This system is high-end first cost and most likely used in a retrofit. One duct conveys cool air, one other hot air. This system is most common where a dual-duct constant volume system is converted to VAV. The box is generally controlled to provide either heat or cool air as required in varying quantities.

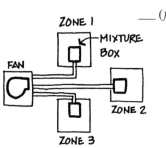

___ (2) <u>Air/water delivery systems</u>

These types of systems *reduce the ductwork* by tempering air near its point of use. Hot and cold water are piped to remote induction or fan coil units. Since the air ducts carry only fresh air, they can be sized at *0.2 to 0.4 SF per 1000 SF* of area served. The main hot and cold water lines will be *2 to 4 inches* diameter, including insulation, for medium size buildings.

___ (*a*) <u>Induction</u> is often used for the *perimeter of high-rise office buildings* and is *expensive*. Air from a central air handler is delivered through high-velocity ducts to each induction unit. Hot and cold lines run to each unit. Each unit is located along the outside wall, at the base of the windows. They are *6 to 12 inches deep* and *1 to 3 feet high.*

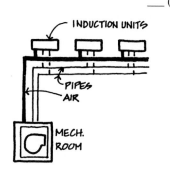

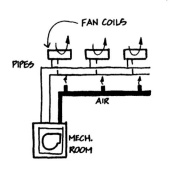

___ (b) *Fan coils with supplementary air* are used where there are *many small rooms needing separate control.* Hot and cold water lines are run through the coils. A fan draws room air through the coil for heating and cooling. A separate duct system supplies fresh air from a remote air handler.

The fan coils are *6 to 12 inches deep and 1 to 3 feet high.* They can also be a vertical shape ($2' \times 2' \times 6'$ *high*) to fit in a closet. They are often stacked vertically in a tall building to reduce piping. Fan coil units can be located in ceiling space.

___ (3) *Water delivery systems* use hot and cold water lines only. No air is delivered to the areas served.

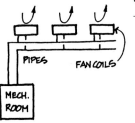

___ (a) *Fan coil units* can have hot and/or cold water lines with fresh air from operable windows or an outdoor air intake at the unit.

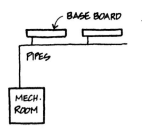

___ (b) *Hot water baseboards* supply only heat. Often used in conjunction with a cooling-only VAV system for perimeter zones. Baseboards are *6 inches high by 5 inches deep* and as long as necessary.

___ 4. Diffusers, Terminal Devices, and Grilles: Interface the HVAC system with the building interiors for visual impact and thermal comfort. Grilles are side wall devices. Opposite wall should be no greater than about *16′ to 18′* away (can throw up to 30′ in high rooms with special diffusers). Diffusers are down-facing and must be coordinated with the lighting as well as uniformly spaced (at a *distance apart of approximately the floor-to-ceiling height*). Returns should be spaced so as to not interfere with air supply. Assume return air grilles at one per 400 SF to 600 SF.

GRILLE

DIFFUSER

EXAMPLE:

PROBLEM:

HVAC
SYSTEM

DESIGN A PRELIMINARY LAYOUT FOR A
50' × 100', 1 STORY, OFFICE BUILDING
WITH A "FLAT" ROOF. THE BUILDING IS
TO BE DIVIDED INTO TWO OFFICE AREAS
(AND TWO AC ZONES) BY A 5' WIDE HALL
RUNNING DOWN THE CENTER. WORK OUT
A PRELIMINARY STRUCTURAL ROOF SYS-
TEM (THAT FULLY SPANS THE BUILDING) TO
BE SURE THE DUCTING WILL FIT THROUGH.
OFFICE CEILING HEIGHT TO BE 9' AND
HALL TO BE 8'. DO A PRELIMINARY COST
ESTIMATE OF THE HVAC SYSTEM.

SOLUTION: 450

1. SELECT SYSTEM: SELECT ROOF MOUNTED PACKAGE
   UNITS (SEE P. 449).
2. SIZE SYSTEM:
   A. FROM BUILDING TYPE (SEE APP. A, ITEM J, P. 516),
      250 TO 300 SF/TON
      (50' × 100' − 5' × 100') ÷ 2 = 2250 SF/ZONE
       BLDG   HALL   ZONES

$$\frac{2250 \text{ SF/ZONE}}{250 \text{ TO } 300 \text{ SF/TON}} = 9 \text{ TO } 7.5 \text{ TONS}$$

   B. FROM SYSTEM TYPE (P. 450):
      5 TO 10 TONS = 1500 TO 4500 SF
      BY PROPORTIONS (SEE P. 49) = 6.25 TONS

   C. ESTIMATE 8 TONS/ZONE (THIS WILL BE A
      ROOF MOUNTED UNIT OF ABOUT 10' × 7')

3. LOCATE SUPPLY DIFFUSERS (SD) AND RETURN
   AIR GRILLES (RAG)
   A. SUPPLY (P. 459): SD AT ABOUT CEILING HT
      OF 9'. SAY 10' ON MODULE.
              (SEE SKETCH)   −CONTINUED−

B. RETURN (P. 459)
ASSUME RAG FOR EVERY 400 TO 600 SF
400 - 600 SF ÷ 22.5' (WIDTH OF ZONE) = 18 TO 27'
ASSUME RAG AT EACH 22.5' × 25'

4. DUCT SIZES
A SUPPLY
(1) TRUNK (P.454) : $\frac{2250 \, SF/ZONE}{1000 \, SF}$ = 2.25

2.25 × 1 TO 2 SF OF DUCT = 2.25 TO 5 SF
SAY 3.5 SF = 2'⌀ OR 1'-10" SQ OR 12" × 3.5"
(2) LINE : ASSUME ½ TRUNK
SAY 1.75 SF = 1.5'⌀ OR 1.3' SQ OR 12" × 1'-9"
(3) BRANCH : ASSUME TRUNK OF 3.5 SF ÷ 9 EA
BRANCHES = .4 SF
SAY .5 SF = .8 ⌀ OR 0.3" SQ OR 12" × 10"

B. RETURN
(1) TRUNK : SAME AS SUPPLY OR SLIGHTLY LARGER
(SEE P. 454). THEREFORE :
SAY 3.5 SF = 2'⌀ OR 1'-10" SQ OR 12" × 3.5'
(2) BRANCH : ½ TRUNK
SAY 1.75 SF = 1.5'⌀ OR 1.22' SQ OR 1' × 1'-9" OR 10" × 2'

5. SIZE STRUCTURE
A. SELECT TRUSS JOIST ASSEMBLY (C ON P. 394).
B. SELECT OPEN WEB T.J.L. (P. 280).
C. SPACING = 2' O.C.
D. DEPTH = SPAN ÷ S.D.R. = 50' ÷ 17 TO 18 = 2.9' TO 2.8'
SAY 2'-10" DEEP

6. FIT TOGETHER
SELECT 12" × 1'-9" SUPPLY LINE UNDER 12" × 1'-9"
R.A. BRANCH. SEE SKETCH
7. ESTIMATE OF H.V.A.C. COST (P. 451)
$5/SF × 5000 SF = $25000
- CONTINUED -

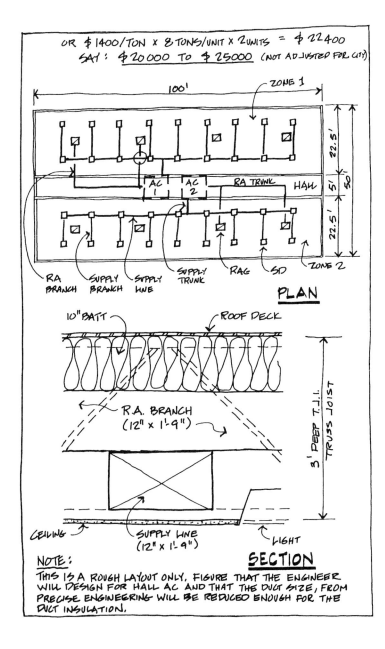

OR $1400/TON × 8 TONS/UNIT × 2 UNITS = $22400
SAY: $20000 TO $25000 (NOT ADJUSTED FOR CITY)

ZONE 1

100'

22.5'

5' 50'

AC 1   AC 2   RA TRUNK   HALL

22.5'

ZONE 2

RA BRANCH   SUPPLY BRANCH   SUPPLY LINE   SUPPLY TRUNK   RAG   SD

PLAN

10" BATT   ROOF DECK

R.A. BRANCH (12" × 1'-9")

3' DEEP T.J.I. TRUSS JOIST

CEILING   SUPPLY LINE (12" × 1'-9")   LIGHT

SECTION

NOTE:
THIS IS A ROUGH LAYOUT ONLY. FIGURE THAT THE ENGINEER WILL DESIGN FOR HALL AC AND THAT THE DUCT SIZE, FROM PRECISE ENGINEERING WILL BE REDUCED ENOUGH FOR THE DUCT INSULATION.

NOTES

NOTES

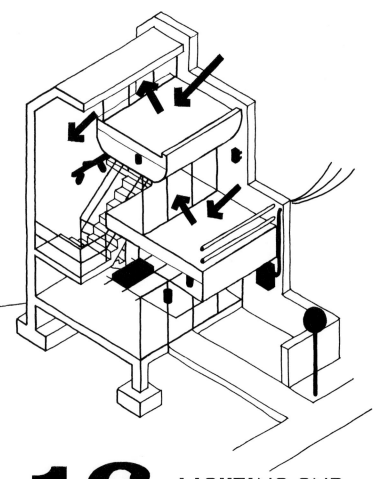

16 LIGHTING AND ELECTRICAL

NOTES

__ A. LIGHTING $\quad$ (10) (41)

__ 1. *General*
$\qquad$ *a.* Lighting terms and concepts using the analogy of a sprinkler pipe

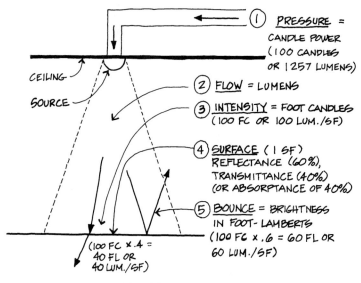

$\qquad$ (1) Visible light is measured in lumens.
$\qquad$ (2) One lumen of light flux spread over one square foot of area illuminates the area to one *footcandle.*
$\qquad$ (3) The ratio of lumens/watts is called *efficacy,* a measure of *energy efficiency.*
$\qquad$ (4) The incident angle of a light beam always equals the reflectance angle on a surface.
$\qquad$ *b.* Considerations in seeing
$\qquad$ (1) *Contrast* between the object or area being viewed and its surroundings will help vision. Too little will wash out the object. Too much will create glare. Recommended maximum ratios:

__ Task to adjacent area	3 to 1
__ Task to remote dark surface	3 to 1
__ Task to remote light surface	1 to 1
__ Window to adjacent wall	20 to 1
__ Task to general visual field	40 to 1
__ Focal point: up to	100 to 1

___ (2) *Brightness* (How much light?). For recommended lighting levels, see d, below, or p. 470.

___ (3) *Size* of that viewed. As the viewing task becomes smaller, the brightness needs to increase and vice versa.

___ (4) *Time:* As the view time is decreased, the brightness and contrast needs to increase and vice versa.

___ (5) *Glare:* Not only can too much contrast create glare, but light sources at the wrong angle to the eye can create glare. Typically, the non-glare angles are from 30° to 60° from the vertical.

"VEILING REFLECTIONS"

___ (6) *Color:* See p. 355.

___ (7) *Interest.*

___ c. Types of overall light sources

___ (1) *Task lighting* is the brightest level needed for the immediate task, such as a desk lamp. Select from table on p. 470.

___ (2) *General lighting* is the less bright level of surroundings for both general seeing and to reduce contrast between the task and surroundings. It is also for less intense tasks, such as general illumination of a lobby. This type of lighting can be both natural or artificial.

___ (3) As a *general rule,* general lighting should be about ⅓ that of task lighting down to *20 fc.* Noncritical lighting (halls, etc.) can be reduced to ⅓ of general lighting down to *10 fc.* For more detail, see p. 470.

___ d. Typical amounts of light

___ (1) Residential

___ *Casual* activities: 20 fc

___ *Moderate* activities (grooming, reading, and preparing food): up to 50 fc

___ *Extended* activities (hobby work, household accounts, prolonged reading): up to 150 fc

___ *Difficult* activites (sewing): up to 200 fc

___ (2) Commercial
    ___ *Circulation:*   up to 30 fc
    ___ *Merchandising:*   up to 100 fc
    ___ *Feature* displays: up to 500 fc
    ___ *Specific* activities
       (i.e., drafting):   200 fc to 2000 fc
___ (3) For more detailed recommendations, see p. 470.
___ *e.* For recommended room reflectances, see p. 355.
___ *f.* *Calculation* of a point source of light on an object can be estimated by:

$$\text{Foot candles} = \frac{\text{Source}}{\text{distance}^2} \times \text{Cosine of incident angle}$$

SOURCE CAN
BE IN CANDLES,
LUMENS, OR
FOOT-LAMBERTS

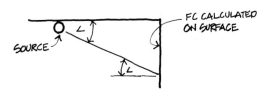

SOURCE

FC CALCULATED
ON SURFACE

Light hitting a surface at an angle will illuminate the surface less than light hitting perpendicular to the surface. The cosine of the incident angle is used to make the correction. Doubling the distance from source to surface cuts the illumination of the surface by ¼. Also, see page 492 for other calculations.

DESIGN LIGHTING LEVELS

	TYPE OF ACTIVITY	TYPE OF LIGHTING	FOOTCANDLES			TYPICAL SPACES
			X	Y	Z	
A	PUBLIC SPACES W/ DARK SURROUNDINGS	GENERAL AREA LIGHTING THROUGHOUT SPACES	2	3	5	THEATER, STORAGE
B	SIMPLE ORIENTATION FOR SHORT TEMPORARY VISITS		5	7.5	10	DINING, CORRIDORS, CLOSETS, STORAGE
C	WORKING SPACES WHERE VISUAL TASKS ARE ONLY OCCASIONALLY PERFORMED		10	15	20	WAITING, EXHIBITION, LOBBIES, LOCKERS, RESIDENTIAL DINING, STAIRS, TOILETS, ELEVATORS, LOADING DOCKS
D	PERFORMANCE OF VISUAL TASKS OF HIGH CONTRAST OR LARGE SIZE	ILLUMINATION ON TASK	20	30	50	GENERAL OFFICE, EXAM ROOMS, MANUFACTURING, READING ROOMS, DRESSING, DISPLAY
E	PERFORMANCE OF VISUAL TASKS OF MEDIUM CONTRAST OR SMALL SIZE		50	75	100	DRAFTING, LABS, KITCHENS, EXAM ROOM, SEWING, DESKS, FILES, WORK BENCH, READING, MANUFACTURING, CLASSROOMS
F	PERFORMANCE OF VISUAL TASKS OF LOW CONTRAST OR VERY SMALL AREA		100	150	200	ARTWORK AND DRAFTING, DEMONSTRATION, INSPECTION, SURGERY, LABS, FITTING, RECORDS, CRITICAL AT WORK BENCH, DIFFICULT SEWING, MANUFACTURE ASSEMBLY
G	PERFORMANCE OF VISUAL TASKS OF LOW CONTRAST AND VERY SMALL SIZE OVER A PROLONGED PERIOD.	ILLUMINATION ON TASK BY COMBINATION OF GENERAL AND LOCAL LIGHTING	200	300	500	CRITICAL SURGERY, VERY DIFFICULT MANUFACTURING ASSEMBLY, CLOSE INSPECTION
H	PERFORMANCE OF VERY PROLONGED & EXACTING VISUAL TASK		500	750	1000	
I	PERFORMANCE OF VERY SPECIAL TASKS OF EXTREMELY LOW CONTRAST AND SMALL SIZE		1000	1500	2000	

	AGE	% REFL.	SPEED &/OR ACCURACY
X	<40	>70	NOT IMPORT.
Y	40-55	30-70	IMPORT.
Z	>50	<30	CRITICAL

NOTES

NOTES

___ 2. _Daylighting (Natural Lighting)_ (5a) (10) (21a)

   ___ *a.* Before undertaking the design of electric lighting, *daylighting* should be considered. Daylighting is an important connection with the outside world. Even if daylight is not to be used as a primary lighting source, in most buildings there should be some penetration of daylight. The architectural program can be partitioned into spaces where daylighting can or should be used and spaces where daylight will not be a major factor. The best opportunities for daylight use are in areas where task lighting is not the primary consideration. As the task lighting needs to be more controlled, daylighting becomes more problematic as a lighting solution. Good daylighting opportunities happen where task-lighting needs are not too critical, as in corridors, lobbies, residences. Daylighting is probably not a good idea where task-light constraints are very restrictive, as in a lecture room or hospital operating room.

   ___ *b.* Daylighting components
      ___ (1) Direct sun
      ___ (2) Diffuse sky
      ___ (3) Indirect sun (sunlight reflected from ground or adjacent structures)

   ___ *c.* There are many ways to introduce natural light into buildings, ranging from fairly obvious and common methods to new and emerging technologies:
      ___ (1) *Perimeter lighting* involves the size and placement of windows and the use of light shelves.
      ___ (2) *Top lighting* includes the use of skylights and roof monitors, and even translucent membrane roofs.
      ___ (3) *Core lighting* involves the use of atriums and light wells.
      ___ (4) *Optical lighting* includes the use of fiber optics, prisms, mirrors, parabolic reflectors, and other means.

THREE WAYS TO DAYLIGHT

___ *d.* <u>General rules of thumb:</u>

___ (1) Daylighting, even more than artificial lighting, needs to be considered early in the design process.

___ (2) A useful conceptual approach to conceiving a daylighting scheme is to think in terms of bouncing the daylight off interior surfaces into the area to be lit.

___ (3) Direct sunlight is almost always too bright to work under.

___ (4) Direct sunlight on critical task areas should be avoided.

___ (5) Direct skylight and sunlight should be used sparingly in noncritical areas.

___ (6) For the best daylight, consider increasing the number of windows, rather than just increasing the size of one window.

___ (7) Daylight should be bounced off surrounding surfaces. In hot climates this should be outside (roofs, ground, walls, etc.) to reduce heat gain.

___ (8) Daylight should be brought in high and let down softly.

___ (9) Daylight can be filtered through drapes, screens, trees, and plants.

___ (10) Daylight from one side of a room can cause a glare problem. Daylight admitted from two or more sides will tend to balance the light in the room.

___ (11) Office building window daylighting usually affects the 15' perimeter of the plan.

___ (12) North-facing windows, skylights, or clearstories give the best daylight (but may allow excessive heat loss in cold climates with northerly winds).

___ (13) Northern orientations will receive only minor direct solar penetration in the early morning and late afternoon in the summer.

___ (14) North light should be used where soft, cool, uniform illumination is needed.

___ (15) South light should be allowed only where intense warm, variable illumination is appropriate.

___ (16) Southern orientations are relatively easy to shield from direct solar penetrations by using horizontal louvers or overhangs, provided the "cooling season" is not too long, as in extremely hot climates.

___ (17) Eastern and western orientations are almost impossible to protect from direct solar penetrations (heat and glare) while at the same time allowing occupants to see out the window.

___ (18) See p. 141 for solar control of south-, east-, and west-facing glass.

___ (19) Skylights can be a problem due to heat gain from too much sunlight.

___ (20) Skylights and clearstories can be used to deliver light deep into the interior of a building. Clearstories can be designed to best avoid direct sunlight.

THIS WALL REFLECTS
LIGHT FROM "GUNSLOT".

"GUNSLOT".

___ (21) "Gun slots" against wall can provide illumination at minimum heat gain.

___ (22) To be economically effective, office daylighting strategies may require *automatic controls* that adjust the level of electric lighting to complement the available natural light during the day. Controls may be photocells; 2- or 3-step lighting; continuous dimming; or motion detectors.

___ (23) New forms of daylighting are "light piping" (optic fiber technology) and translucent roof membranes.

___ *e.* Estimating illumination (daylight factors methods)

___ (1) Determine available daylight based on sky conditions (in fc on horizontal surface) and time of day:

	Noon	8 AM or 4 PM
	Clear Sky	
Summer	10,000 to 9000	5250
Spring/Fall	8500 to 7250	3750 to 3500
Winter	5750 to 4000	2500 to 1750
	Partly Cloudy Sky	
Summer	7000 to 6000	3250
Spring/Fall	5500 to 4500	2250 to 2000
Winter	3000 to 2500	1250 to 1000
	Overcast Sky	
Summer	4250 to 2750	2000 to 1500
Spring/Fall	2500 to 1750	1250 to 1000
Winter	1250 to 1000	500

Note: Higher numbers are for lower latitudes (32°N and less). Lower numbers are for higher latitudes (44°N and more).

(2) Calculate the "daylight factor" which ends up being a percentage applied against sky illumination available. This factor is based on a number of design variables, as follows:

___ (*a*) Top lighting

$$\text{Factor} = \frac{(F) \times (U) \times (Ag)}{Af}$$

where F = the window factor, given the amount of skylight incident on the roof. F is equal to 1 for an unobstructed site.

U = the coefficient of utilization-ratio of light reaching the reference plane.

	Average Interior Reflectance	
U Values	50%	20%
Monitors horizontal to 30°	0.4	0.3
Monitors at 60°	0.25	0.2
Vertical monitors	0.15–0.2	0.1–0.15

Ag = area of glazing
Af = area of floor

___ (*b*) Side lighting

$$\text{Factor} = \frac{10\,WH^2}{D(D^2 + H^2)} + \frac{4GR}{F(1 - R)}$$

where   F = floor area
H = height of top of window above reference plane.
W = width of window
D = distance of window to reference point.
R = reflectance of walls in % (see p. 355)
G = net area of glass

___ (3) Multiply sky illumination in (1) above by the daylight factor from either top lighting (*a*) or side lighting (*b*) to get illumination in fc on work plane.

Note: This method is mainly designed for overcast sky conditions, so the "cosine" method (see p. 469) may be best for direct sunlight.

REFLECT DAYLIGHT IN ORDER TO PENETRATE PERIMETER.

THE HEIGHT OF THE WINDOW AND ITS LOCATION INFLUENCE LIGHT DISTRIBUTION.

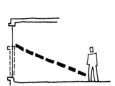

SILL HEIGHT HAS LITTLE EFFECT ON TASK LIGHTING, HOWEVER, IT PROVIDES FLOOR LIGHTING VARIANCES.

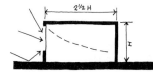

_____ *f.* Rules of thumb for *sizing glazing:* Daylight can be used to reduce the need for electrical lighting, but too much daylight can create glare, cause the air conditioning load of the building to rise, or lead to other overheating problems. The following list provides a useful guide to determining the approximate daylight aperture areas that will balance lighting and AC requirements:

   _____ (1) *Sidelighting*

Window openings	*10% (min.) to 25%* of floor area; *25% to 40%* of wall area
Room depth	*2 to 2½* times window height (usually *15′ to 20′*).

   _____ (2) *Top-lighting*

Skylights	*5% to 10% (max.)* of ceiling area.
	Space at *1 to 2* times ceiling-to-work-plane height.
Clearstories	*10%* of wall area.
	Space *1.5* times ceiling-to-work-plane height.
	At a point *15′* from rear wall:
	For overcast sky (1500 FC) climates, provide *15″* of glazing height per *10 FC* on ave. work plane.
	For clear climate (5000 FC), provide *2″*.

   Combinations

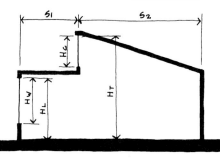

MAX. S_1 = 1 TO 1½ H_L
   OR = 2 H_L
      (FOR CONTINUOUS WINDOWS)
MIN. H_C = ½ H_W
MAX. S_2 = 2 H_T

SKY BRIGHTNESS VALUES COMBINED WITH THE COSINE EFFECT OF ORIENTATION CAN BE USED TO ESTIMATE SURFACE BRIGHTNESS LEVELS.

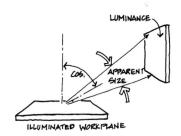

ILLUMINATED WORKPLANE

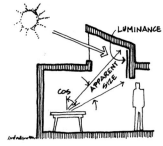

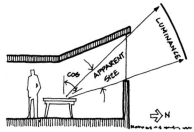

SLOPED, WHITE CEILING SOFFIT "SEES" SKY

DESK "SEES" CEILING BUT NOT SKY

Costs: Skylights = \$5.00 to \$160/SF (at average, 80% M and 20% L). Lower number is for large-area skylights and vice versa.

EXAMPLE:

PROBLEM:

ESTIMATE DAYLIGHTING
AT THE 3 LOCATIONS IN
THE ILLUSTRATED ROOM.
ESTIMATE THE 3 SKY
CONDITIONS. THE SITE
IS CHICAGO, IL. FIGURE
THE 3 SEASONS AND
2 TIMES A DAY.

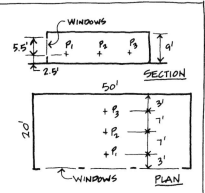

SOLUTION:

1. AVAILABLE ILLUMINATION FOR CHICAGO, AT LATITUDE
   41°-5 & 52% SUN (SEE APP. B, ITEMS A & K, P. 528)
   WOULD BE THE LOWER MIDDLE OF THE NUMBERS ON
   P. 476.   ASSUME:

	NOON	8 AM & 4 PM
CLEAR SKY		
SUMMER	9200 FC	5250 FC
SPRING / FALL	7500 FC	3600 FC
WINTER	4200 FC	1800 FC
PARTLY CLOUDY SKY		
SUMMER	6200 FC	3250 FC
SPRING / FALL	4700 FC	2100 FC
WINTER	2600 FC	1000 FC
OVERCAST SKY		
SUMMER	2800 FC	1600 FC
SPRING / FALL	1800 FC	1100 FC
WINTER	1100 FC	500 FC

SELECT BRIGHTEST = SUMMER, NOON = 9200 FC
SELECT DIMMEST = WINTER, 8AM OR 4 PM = 500 FC
ANALYZE THESE TWO EXTREMES

2. DAYLIGHT FACTOR FOR WINDOW "SIDE LIGHTING":

$$F = \frac{10 \ W H^2}{D(D^2 + H^2)} \ + \ \frac{4 \ \in R}{F(1-R)}$$

— CONTINUED —

WHERE: F = 20' × 50' = 1000 SF
  H = 5.5'
  W = 45'
  D = P.1 = 3', P.2 = 9', P.3 = 17'
  G = 5.5' × 45' = 247.5 SF
  R = ASSUME 50%

$$F = \frac{10\,(45)\,(5.5^2)}{(3, 9, \& 17)\,(D^2 + 30.25)} + \frac{4\,(247.5)\,(50)}{1000\,(1 - 50)}$$

F = P.1 = 115.6 = 1.156
     P.2 = 14.6 = .146
     P.3 =   3.5 = .035

3. ILLUMINATION = AVAILABLE DAYLIGHT OF 9200 FC &
   500 FC × FACTORS:

	SUMMER NOON	WINTER, AM & PM
P-1	10600 FC *	575 FC *
P-2	1340 FC	75 FC
P-3	322 FC	20 FC

* SINCE THESE NUMBERS ARE GREATER THAN THE
  AVAILABLE DAYLIGHT, TAKE 90% OF AVAILABLE DAY-
  LIGHT: 8280 FC   450 FC

• IF THE WINDOW IS FACING SOUTH, THE ILLUMINATION WILL
  BE TOO BRIGHT (AT LEAST AT P.1) AND BLINDS (OR
  SPECIAL GLASS) WILL HAVE TO BE USED IN SUMMER.

• IF THE WINDOW IS FACING NORTH, THE CLEAR SKY RE-
  SULTS ARE INVALID. USE PARTLY CLOUDY CONDITIONS.

• THE P-3 POSITION IN WINTER WILL PROBABLY NOT HAVE
  ENOUGHT 'NATURAL' ILLUMINATION, SO ELECTRIC LIGHTING
  WILL HAVE TO BE ADDED ALONG THE REAR WALL.

NOTES

___ 3. *Electric (Artificial) Lighting*

For energy conservation, see p. 142. For site-lighting costs, see p. 199.

___ *a.* Lamp types

___ (1) *Incandescent* lamps produce a warm light, are inexpensive and easy to use but have limited lumination per watt (*20 to 40*) and a short life. *Normal voltage* lamps produce a point source of light. Most common shapes are A, R, and PAR. *Low voltage* lamps produce a very small point of intense brightness that can be focused into a precise beam of light (for merchandise or art). These are usually PAR shapes or designed to fit into a parabolic reflector. Sizes are designated in ⅛ inch of the widest part of lamp. Tungsten-Halogen (quartz) and low voltage are a special type of incandescent.

A

(40 TO 150 W)

R

(30 TO 300 W)

PAR

(50 TO 250 W)

___ (2) *Gaseous discharge* lamps produce light by passing electricity through a gas. These lamps require a ballast to get the lamp started and then to control the current.

___ (*a*) *Fluorescent lamps* produce a wide, linear, diffuse light source that is well-suited to spreading light downward to the working surfaces of desks or displays in a commercial environment with normal ceiling heights (*8′ to 12′*). Lamps are typically 17, 25, or 32 watts. The deluxe lamps have good color-rendering characteristics and can be chosen to favor the *cool* (*blue*) or the *warm* (*red*) end of the spectrum. *Dimmers for fluorescents are expensive.* Fluorescent lamps produce more light per watt of energy (*70–85 lumens/watt*) than incandescent; thus operating costs are low. The purchase price and length of life of fluorescent lamps are greater than for incandescent and less than for HID. Four-feet lamp lengths utilize 40 watts and are most common. *Designations are F followed by wattage, shape, size, color, and a form factor.*

___ (*b*) <u>*High-intensity   discharge*</u> (*HID*) lamps can be focused into a fairly good beam of light. These lamps, matched with an appropriate fixture are well-suited to beaming light down to the working place from a high ceiling (*12′ to 20′*). *Dimming HID lamps is difficult. The lamps are expensive but produce a lot of light and last a long time.* If there is a power interruption, HID lamps will go out and cannot come on again for about *10 minutes* while they cool down. Therefore, *in an installation of HID lamps, a few incandescent or fluorescent lamps are needed to provide backup lighting.*

___ <u>*Mercury   vapor*</u> (the *bluish* street lamps). Deluxe version is warmer. *35 to 65* lumens/watt. This is not much used anymore.

___ <u>*Metal halide*</u> are often *ice blue cool* industrial-looking lamps. Deluxe color rendering bulbs are 50 to 400 watts, and almost as good as deluxe fluorescent for a warmer effect. Efficiency is *80 lumens/watt.*

___ <u>*High-pressure sodium*</u> produces a *warm golden yellow* light often used for highways. Bulbs are 35 to 400 watts. Deluxe color rendering is almost as cool as deluxe fluorescent for a cooler effect. Efficiency is *100 lumens/ watt.*

___ <u>*Low-pressure sodium*</u> produces a *yellow* color which makes all colors appear in shades of grey. Bulbs are typically 35 to 180 watts. Used for parking lots and roadways. Efficiency is *150 lumens/watt.*

___ (*c*) <u>*Cold cathode*</u> (neon) has a color dependent on the gas and the color of the tube. *Can be most any color.* Does not give off enough light for detailed visual tasks, but does give off enough light for *attracting attention,* indoors or out.

___ *b.*   <u>Lighting systems and fixture types</u>

Note: Costs include lamps, fixture, and installation labor, but not general wiring. As a rule of thumb, fixtures are 20% to 30%, and distribution (not included in following costs) is 30% to 70%.

___ (1) <u>*General room lighting*</u>
A large proportion of commercial space requires even illumination on the workplace. This can be done a number of ways.

___ (*a*) <u>*Direct lighting*</u> is the most common form of general room lighting.

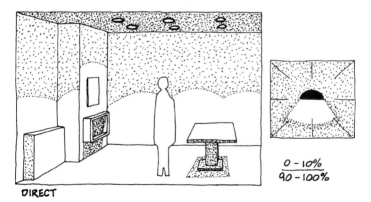

0 – 10%
90 – 100%

DIRECT

All recessed lighting is an example of a direct lighting system, but a pendant fixture could be direct if it emits virtually no light above the horizontal. Unless extensive wall washing, or high light levels (as with fluorescent for general office lighting) are used, the overall impression of a direct lighting system should be one of low general brightness with the possibility of higher intensity accents.

A guide to determine max. spacing is the *spacing-to-mounting-height ratio.* The mounting height is the height from the working place (*usually 2.5' above floor*) to the level of the height fixtures. Note that the ratio does not apply to the end of oblong fixtures due to the nature of their light distribution.

$$\text{Spacing} = \left(\frac{S}{MH} \right) \times (\text{Mounting Ht.})$$

EXAMPLE:

WHAT IS AN AVERAGE FLUORESCENT FIXTURE SPACING IF THE CEILING IS 9' AND THE S/MH RATIO IS TO BE 1.5?

SPACING = (1.5)(9' − 2.5') = 9.75'

SAY: 10'

Types of direct lighting are:

___ *Wide-beam diffuse lighting* is often fluorescent lights for normal ceiling heights (8' to 12'). The fixtures will produce a repetitive two-dimensional pattern that becomes the most prominent feature of the ceiling plane. Typical S/MH = *1.5.*

Typical recessed fluorescent fixture:

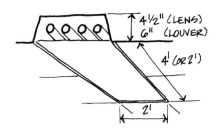

Costs: 2′ × 4′ = \$85 to \$135/ea. (85% M and 15% L), variation of −10%, +20%.

2′ × 2′ = 10% less

1′ × 4′ = +10% more

___ *Medium-beam downlighting* is produced with a fixture located in or on the ceiling that creates a beam of light directed downward. In the circulation and lobby areas of a building, *incandescent lamps* are often used. For large areas, *HID lamps* are often selected. In both cases the light is in the form of a *conical beam,* and *scallops* of light will be produced on wall surfaces.

S/MH is usually about *0.7 to 1.3*.

Typical fixture: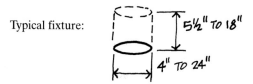

Cost: (per ea. fixture) (Variation of −10 to +35%).

	Res.	Comm.
Low voltage:	**\$145**	**\$300 (85% M and 15% L)**
Incandescent:	**\$65**	**\$300 (90% M and 10% L)**
Fluorescent:	**\$125**	**\$275 (85% M and 15% L)**
HID:	**\$145**	**\$450 (80% M and 20% L)**

___ *Narrow beam downlights* are often used in the same situation as above, but produce more of a spotlight effect at low mounting heights. This form of lighting is used to achieve even illumination where the ceiling height is relatively high. S/MH is usually *0.3 to 0.9*. Typical fixture same as above.

Cost: Same as medium-beam downlighting above.

___ (*b*) *Semidirect lighting*

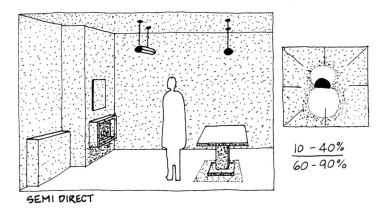

SEMI DIRECT

$$\frac{10-40\%}{60-90\%}$$

All systems other than direct ones necessarily imply that the lighting fixtures are in the space, whether pendant-mounted, surface-mounted, or portable. A semidirect system will provide good illumination on horizontal surfaces, with moderate general brightness.

Typical fixtures:

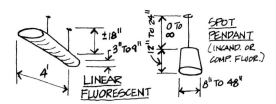

Costs: Fluor.: $325 to $750 (90% M and 10% L)
         Pendant: $150 to $450 (90% M and 10% L)

___ (c) *General diffuse lighting*

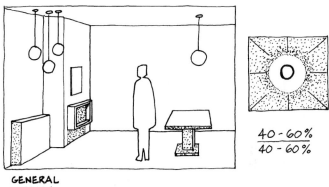

GENERAL
DIFFUSE

40 - 60%
40 - 60%

A general diffuse system most typically consists of suspended fixtures, with predominantly translucent surfaces on all sides. Can be incandescent, fluorescent, or HID.

Typical fixture: see sketch above

Costs: $75 to $550 (90% M and 10% L)

___ (d) *Direct-indirect lighting*

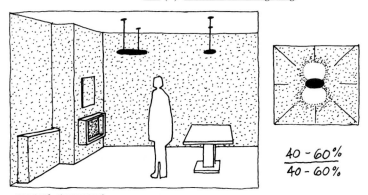

DIRECT - INDIRECT

40 - 60%
40 - 60%

A direct-indirect will tend to equally emphasize the upper and lower horizontal planes in a space (i.e., the ceiling and floor).

Typical fixture: same as semidirect

Costs: Same as Semidirect.

___ (e) *Semi-indirect lighting*

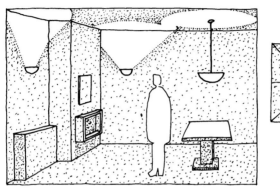

SEMI-INDIRECT

A semi-indirect system will place the emphasis on the ceiling, with some downward or outward-directed light.

Typical fixture:

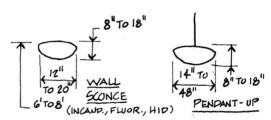

Costs: Wall sconce: $175 to $750 (90% M and 10% L)
Pendant: $350 to $2200 (85% M and 15% L)

_____ (*f*) _Indirect lighting_

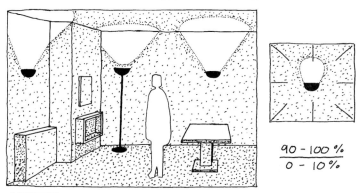

INDIRECT

$$\frac{90 - 100 \%}{0 - 10 \%}$$

A fully indirect system will bounce all the light off the ceiling, resulting in a low-contrast environment with little shadow.

Typical fixture: Same as Direct-Indirect.

Costs: Same as Direct-Indirect.

Note: ADA requires that, along accessible routes, *wall-mounted* fixtures protrude no more than *4″* when mounted lower than *6′8″* AFF.

_____ (*g*) _Accent or specialty lighting_

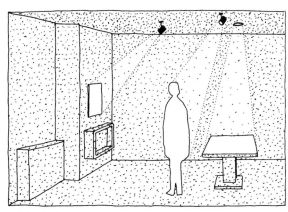

ACCENT

Used for special effects or spot lighting, such as lighting art objects or products on display.

Typical fixtures:

TRACK

RECESSED ACCENT

Costs: Track: $85 to $450 (90% M and 10%L)
Recessed accent: $145 to $1000 (80% M and 20% L)

___ *c.* Simplified calculations

___ (1) For estimating light from one source (such as a painting on a wall lit by a ceiling mounted spot) use the *Cosine Method* shown on on p. 469.

___ (2) For general room lighting use the *Zonal Cavity Method*.

ZONAL CAVITY CALCULATIONS METHOD FOR GENERAL LIGHTING

LIGHT FIXTURES

WORK PLANE

RM. CAVITY HT.

2.5'

$$\text{ROOM CAVITY RATIO (RCR)} = \frac{(5)(H)(\text{LENGTH} + \text{WIDTH})}{\text{LENGTH} \times \text{WIDTH}}$$

H = HEIGHT FROM THE WORK PLAN (2.5 FT. ABOVE FLOOR) TO BOTTOM OF LIGHT FIXTURES.

LENGTH & WIDTH = ROOM DIMENSIONS

$$\text{NUMBER OF FIXTURES} = \frac{(\text{FOOTCANDLES}) \times (\text{AREA OF ROOM})}{(\text{LUMENS PER FIXTURE}) \times (\text{CU}) \times (\text{MAINT. FACTOR})}$$

FOOTCANDLES = THE DESIRED ILLUMINATION ON THE WORK PLANE. SEE PART 1.

LUMENS PER FIXTURE = (LUMENS PER LAMP) × (NUMBER OF LAMPS IN THE FIXTURE).

CU = COEFFICIENT OF UTILIZATION
THE COEFFICIENT OF UTILIZATION EXPRESSES THE EFFICIENCY OF THE LIGHT FIXTURE ROOM COMBINATION. IT IS DEPENDENT ON FIXTURE EFFICIENCY, DISTRIBUTION OF LIGHT FROM THE FIXTURE, ROOM SHAPE, AND ROOM SURFACE REFLECTANCES. LIGHT FIXTURE MANUFACTURERS PRINT TABLES LISTING THE CU AS A FUNCTION OF ROOM CAVITY RATIO AND ROOM SURFACE REFLECTANCES FOR EACH INDIVIDUAL LIGHT FIXTURE. SEE NEXT PAGE.

MAINTENANCE FACTOR = VARIES FROM 0.85 TO 0.65. THE MAINT. FACTOR ADJUSTS THE CALCULATION FOR THE FACT THAT LAMPS PRODUCE LESS LIGHT AS THEY GET OLDER AND FIXTURES GET DIRTY AND REFLECT LESS LIGHT OUT OF THE FIXTURE.

TYPICAL COEFFICIENTS OF UTILIZATION

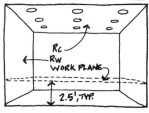

INCANDESCENT PATTERN DOWNLIGHT		
ROOM TYPE	HIGH REFL. FIN.	LOW REFL. FIN.
TYP. SMALLER RMS. (MOD. LOW CL'G.)	0.70 TO 0.80	0.60 TO 0.70
TYP. LARGER RMS.		
RELATIVELY HIGH CL'G.	0.85 TO 0.90	0.80 TO 0.85
RELATIVELY LOW CL'G.	0.90 TO 0.95	0.85 TO 0.90

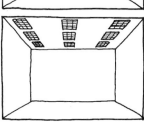

FLUORESCENT, 2×4, (PRISMATIC LENS)		
ROOM TYPE	HIGH REFL. FIN.	LOW REFL. FIN.
TYP. SMALLER RMS. (MOD. LOW CL'G.)	0.35 TO 0.45	0.30 TO 0.40
TYP. LARGER RMS.		
RELATIVELY HIGH CL'G.	0.50 TO 0.60	0.45 TO 0.50
RELATIVELY LOW CL'G.	0.60 TO 0.70	0.55 TO 0.60

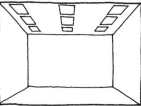

FLUORESCENT, 2×4, (PARABOLIC LOUVER)		
ROOM TYPE	HIGH REFL. FIN.	LOW REFL. FIN.
TYP. SMALLER RMS. (MOD. LOW CL'GS.)	0.30 TO 0.45	0.25 TO 0.35
TYP. LARGER RMS.		
RELATIVELY HIGH CL'G.	0.55 TO 0.65	0.45 TO 0.55
RELATIVELY LOW CL'G.	0.65 TO 0.75	0.55 TO 0.65

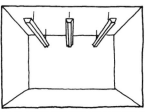

FLUORESCENT PATTERN OF INDIRECT LIGHTING		
ROOM TYPE	HIGH REFL. FIN.	LOW REFL. FIN.
TYP. SMALLER RMS. (MOD. LOW CL'GS.)	0.35 TO 0.50	0.15 TO 0.20
TYP. LARGER RMS.		
RELATIVELY HIGH CL'G.	0.40 TO 0.65	0.20 TO 0.30
RELATIVELY LOW CL'G.	0.50 TO 0.75	0.30 TO 0.40

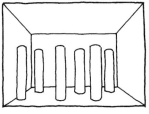

H.I.D. PATTERN OF INDIRECT LIGHTING		
ROOM TYPE	HIGH REFL. FIN.	LOW REFL. FIN.
TYP. SMALLER RMS. (MOD. LOW CL'GS)	0.28 TO 0.38	0.05 TO 0.15
TYP. LARGER RMS.		
RELATIVELY HIGH CL'G.	0.40 TO 0.55	0.10 TO 0.20
RELATIVELY LOW CL.	0.50 TO 0.65	0.10 TO 0.25

EXAMPLE :

PROBLEM:

DO A PRELM. DESIGN OF A
20' x 30' CLASS ROOM W/
DESK HEIGHT OF 2.5' AND
CEILING HEIGHT OF 9'. USE
2 x 4 LAYIN FLUOR. LIGHTS
WITH 4 - 32 WATT LAMPS,
ASSUME REFLECTANCE OF:
CEILINGS = 80%; WALLS =
50%; AND FLOORS = 40%

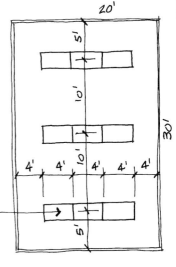

2x4 FLUOR. FIXTURE

SOLUTION:

1. NO. OF FIXTURES = $\dfrac{FC \times A}{LUM/FIX \times CU \times MF}$

WHERE: FC = DESIRED LIGHT LEVEL, SELECT 75 FC (P. 470)
A = AREA OF ROOM = 20' x 30' = 600 SF
LUM./FIX. = ASSUME 80 LUM/WATT (SEE P. 483)
× 32 WATTS × 4 LAMPS = $\dfrac{10\,240}{LUM./FIX.}$

CU = COEF. OF UTILIZATION. FROM TYPICAL CU's
ON P.   , AT FLUOR., 2x4, SELECT <u>0.6</u>
MF = MAINT. FACTOR (P.492), SELECT <u>0.8</u>

$= \dfrac{75 \times 600}{10240 \times 0.6 \times 0.8} = 9.15$ <u>SAY 9 FIX.</u>

2. SPACING (P.486) FOR DIRECT FLUOR = S/MH = 1.5
SPACING = (1.5)(9 - 2.5) = 9.75' <u>SAY 10'</u>

3. LAYOUT AS SHOWN ABOVE.

NOTES

NOTES

__ B. POWER AND TELEPHONE (1) (10) (20)

For Energy Conservation, see p. 142. For **Costs,** see App. A, item K.

___ 1. Electrical Power

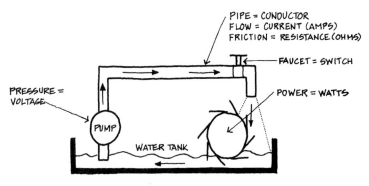

PIPE = CONDUCTOR
FLOW = CURRENT (AMPS)
FRICTION = RESISTANCE (OHMS)

FAUCET = SWITCH

PRESSURE = VOLTAGE

POWER = WATTS

PUMP

WATER TANK

___ *a.*   Water analogy (an electrical circuit)
   1 volt = Force needed to drive a current of 1 amp
      through a resistance of 1 ohm.
   1 watt = Rate at which electrical energy is consumed
      in a circuit with a force of 1 volt in a current
      of 1 amp.

___ *b.*   Basic formulas
   ___ Power formula: Watts = volts × amps
   Used to convert wattage ratings of devices to amps.
   Wires and circuits are rated by amps.
   ___ Ohm's law:

$$\text{Amps} = \frac{\text{volts}}{\text{ohms}}$$

   Devices may draw different amperage even though
   connected to the same voltage.

___ *c.*   *Building power systems* consist of:
   ___ *Transformer* to reduce voltage from utility
      power grid.
   ___ *Main switchboard* (sometimes called *service
      entrance section* or *switchgear*) with main dis-
      connect and distribution through circuit break-
      ers or fused switches.
   ___ *Subpanels and branch circuits* to distribute
      power throughout building.

497

More detailed description based on building size:

___ (1) _Residential and small commercial buildings_ typically use _120/240 volt, single-phase_ power.

    ___ (_a_) _Transformers_ are pole mounted (oil cooled, _18″ dia. × 3′ H_) or for underground system, dry type pad mounted on ground. Both outside building.

    ___ (_b_) _Main switchboard_ usually located at power entry to building and typically sized at _20″ W × 5″D × 30″H._

    ___ (_c_) _Branch circuits_ should not extend more than _100′_ from panel. Panel boards are approx. _20″ W × 5″D × 30″ to 60″H._ The max. no. of breakers per panel is _42._

    ___ (_d_) _Clearance_ in front of panels and switch boards is usually _3′ to 6′._

___ (2) _Medium-sized commercial buildings_ typically use _120/208 V, 3-phase_ power to operate large motors used for HVAC, etc., as well as to provide 120 V for lights and outlets.

    ___ (_a_) _Transformer_ is typically liquid-cooled, pad-mounted outside building and should have _4′_ clearance around and be within _30′_ of a drive. The size can be approximated by area served:

Area	No. res. units	Pad size
18,000 SF	50	_4′ × 4′_
60,000 SF	160	_4.5′ × 4.5′_
180,000 SF		_8′ × 8′_

    ___ (_b_) _Main switchboard_ for lower voltage is approx. _6′ W × 2′D × 7′H_ (for 2000 amps or less or up to 70,000 SF bld'g.). Provide _3′ to 6′_ space in front for access. Higher voltage require access from both sides. _3000 amps_ is usually the largest switchboard possible.

___ (c) _Branch panels:_ For _general_ lighting and outlets is same as for residential and small commercial except there are more panels and at least _one per floor._ The panel boards are generally related to the functional groupings of the building.

For _motor_ panels, see large buildings.

___ (3) _Large commercial buildings_ often use _277/480 V, 3-phase_ power. They typically purchase power at higher voltage and step down within the building system.

___ (a) _Transformer_ is typically owned by the building and located in a vault inside or outside (underground). Vault should be located adjacent to exterior wall, ventilated, fire-rated, and have two exits. Smaller dry transformers located throughout the building will step the 480 V down to 120 V. See below for size.

___ (b) _Main switchboard_ is approx. _10 to 15' W × 5' D × 7' H_ with _4' to 6'_ maintenance space on all sides. Typical sizes of transformer vaults and switchgear rooms:

Commercial building	Residential building	Transformer vault	Switchgear room
100,000 SF	200,000 SF	$20' \times 20' \times 11'$	$30' \times 20' \times 11'$
150,000 SF	300,000 SF	($30' \times 30' \times 11'$ combination)	
300,000 SF	600,000 SF	$20' \times 40' \times 11'$	$30' \times 40' \times 11'$
1,000,000 SF	2,000,000 SF	$20' \times 80' \times 11'$	$30' \times 80' \times 11'$

Over _3000 amp,_ go to multiple services. XFMR vaults need to be separated from rest of the building by at least _2-hr._ walls.

___ (c) _Branch panels_

___ Panels for lighting and outlets will be same as for medium-sized buildings except that they are often located in closets with telephone equip. The area needed is approx. *0.005* × the building area served.

___ Motor controller panel boards for HVAC equip., elev's., and other large equipment are often in (or next to) mechanical room, against a wall. A basic panel module is approx. *1'W × 1.5'D × 7'H.* One module can accommodate 2- to 4-motor control units stacked on top of one another. Smaller motors in isolated locations require individual motor control units approx. *1'W × 6"D × 1.5'H.*

___ (*d*) *Other:* In many buildings an emergency generator is required. Best location is outside near switchgear room. If inside, plan on a room 12'W × 18' to 22'L. If emergency power is other than for life safety, size requirements can go up greatly. In any case, the generator needs combustion air and possibly cooling.

___ *d.* Miscellaneous items on electrical

___ (1) Circuit symbols on electrical plans

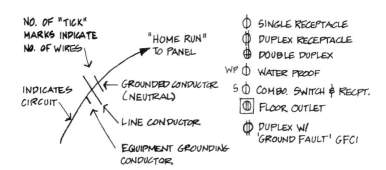

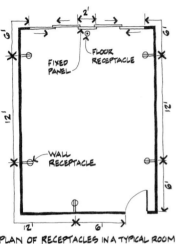

PLAN OF RECEPTACLES IN A TYPICAL ROOM

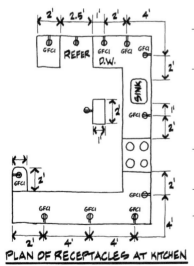

PLAN OF RECEPTACLES AT KITCHEN

___ (2) <u>Residential</u>

___ (a) Service drops (overhead lines) must be:

___ *10′* above ground or sidewalk

___ *15′* above driveways

___ *18′* above streets

___ (b) A min. of *1 wall switch* controlling lighting outlets required in all rooms (but convenience outlets may apply in main rooms).

___ (c) All rooms require a convenience outlet every 12′ along walls, 2′ or longer.

___ (d) Provide sufficient 15- and 20-amp circuits for min. of *3 watts of power/SF. One* circuit for every *500 to 600 SF.*

___ (e) A min. of *two* #12 wire (copper), *20-amp* small appliance circuits required pantry, dining, family, extended to kitchen.

___ (f) A min. of *one* #12 wire, 20-amp circuit required for *laundry* receptacle.

___ (g) A min. of *one* receptacle per *bathroom* with ground fault circuit interrupter protection (GFCI, required within *6′* of water outlet and at exteriors).

___ (h) A min. of *one* outlet (GFCI) required in *basement, garage, and patios.*

___ (i) Provide *smoke detector.* See p. 72.

___ (j) Mounting heights:

Switches, counter receptacles, bath outlets: *4′* AFF

Laundry: *3′6″* AFF

Wall convenience outlets: *12″* AFF

___ (3) For outlets and controls required to be *HC accessible,* per ADA, place between *18″ and 4′* AFF.

___ (4) Always check room switches against *door swings.*

___ (5) Check flush-mounted wall panels against *wall depth.*

___ (6) Building must always be *grounded* by connecting all metal piping to electrical system, and by connecting electrical system into the ground by either a buried rod or plate outside the building or by a wire in the footing (UFER).

___ (7) Consider *lightning protection* by a system of rods or masts on roof connected to a separate ground and into the building elect. ground system.

___ 2. Building Telephone and Signal Systems

   ___ *a.* Small buildings often have a telephone mounting board (TMB) of ¾″ plywood with size up to *4′ × 4′.*

   ___ *b.* Medium-size buildings often need a telephone closet of *4′ to 6′.*

   ___ *c.* Large buildings typically have a *400-SF* telephone terminal room. Secondary distribution points typical throughout building (one per area or floor) usually combined with electrical distribution closets (approx. *0.005 ×* area served).

   ___ *d.* ADA requires that where public phones are provided, at least *one* must be HC-accessible (1 per floor, 1 per bank of phones). See ADA for special requirements.

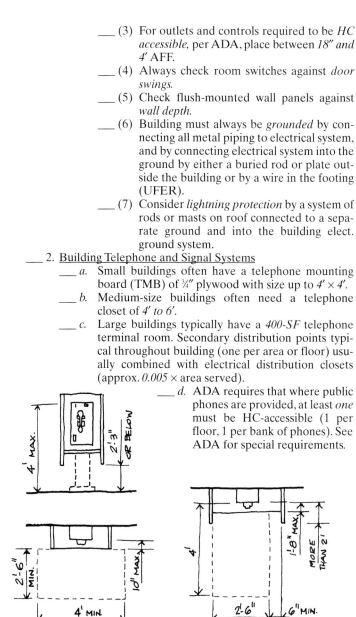

___ 3. <u>Solar Electric</u> (Photovoltaics)

    ___ *a.* Photovoltaics produce electrical energy from *sunlight* via solar electric *panels* facing sunlight (direct or reflected). Although it is most desirable to face these panels into direct sun, they can operate in any sky type of light. *Batteries* store the energy until needed.

    ___ *b.* Because photovoltaics are still *expensive,* they are still presently being used for *remote locations,* such as rural houses away from the power grid.

    ___ *c.* **These type of houses cost about *20% to 30%* above conventional houses. Of the extra cost, about *55% to 60%* is due to photovoltaics and the rest for added energy conservation features to reduce the electric load.**

    ___ *d.* Size collector area at about *10%* of floor area served (*7 to 12 watts/SF* of panel). For *retrofits* of less efficient homes, *double or triple* this. If the house is also tied into the *power grid,* then this can all be reduced.

    ___ *e.* Size battery and converter *storage area* at about *1 SF for every 12 SF* of collector area.

    ___ *f.* Collector area is made up of the PV panels, assembled into *modules* and in turn assembled into *arrays.* This should face south *with* a tilt angle within the range of ±*15 deg.* of the site latitude, and be roof- or ground-mounted. A typical PV panel ranges from *13″ × 4′ to 4′ × 6′,* but on average is about *6 SF.*

    ___ *g.* Other concerns are no year-around *shadows* on panels; keep collector undersides *cool;* steel-frame mounting for *wind* resistance and, if roof-mounted, prevention of *leaks.*

Costs: PV presently costs about *$12/watt* (95% M and 5% L). About half is the cost of the electronics and half the cost of structural support. The actual PV system for a house costs about *$10/SF* of the house area. About *10%* of this is for the storage batteries, which must be replaced about every *6* years.

NOTES

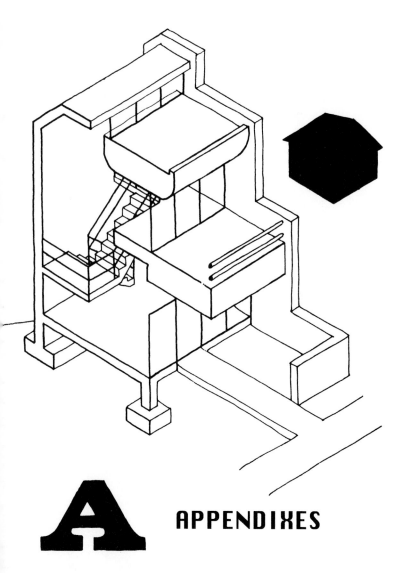

APPENDIXES

<u>NOTES</u>

___ APPENDIX A: BUILDING-TYPE DATA

Entries A through L in the tables on pp. 508–521 provide rough costs and other useful information, as described below, for the various listed types of buildings.

___ A. *Occupancy type* per UBC. See p. 77. (24)

___ B. *Efficiency ratio:* Average net-to-gross ratio as a percentage of total. Also see p. 29.

___ C. *Areas (SF):* Give typical building areas. (11) (17) (33) (40a)

___ D. *Costs ($/SF):* Typical SF costs based on areas in item C above. The projects do not include any site work or furniture, fixture, and equipment costs. See p. 165 for site work costs. (11) (17) (33) (40a)

___ E. *A/E (Architectural/Engineering)* fees (% of item D): Low figure equals minimal work, whereas high equals comprehensive, detailed services. A highest quality job may often go up another 5% from the high shown. In any case, these are rough numbers to begin an estimate of fees. See p. 3. (22)

___ F. *FF&E (Furniture, Fixture, and Equipment) costs ($/SF)* are over and above costs given in item D above, and are for items not generally provided by the general contractor. These numbers are for rough beginning planning. See pp. 372 and 378.

___ G. *Parking:* Although local zoning ordinances will give exact requirements, these numbers are national standards that can be used for beginning planning. See p. 165.

___ H. The average *partition density* (length of partition based on floor area) is on the left. The average *door density* (floor area per door) is on the right.

___ I. *Fire protection classification* designates what type of sprinklers to use, when required. See p. 433. (11)

___ J. *A/C (Air Conditioning) loads* are a range, given in SF/Ton. See p. 499. (7)

___ K. Average *mechanical* (HVAC and plumbing) costs to left and *electrical* costs to right. Both are given as % of total costs (D, above). (11)

___ L. *Typical power* requirements are given in watts/SF. Typically, lighting takes 20 to 25% of total power. See p. 497.

APARTMENT (100000 SF −)	Low	Ave.	High
A. Occupancy Type		R-1	
B. Efficiency Ratio		65	
C. Area (SF)	24000	42000	71500
D. Costs ($/SF)	47.50	63.50	73
E. A/E Fees (% of D)	5	6	8
F. FF&E Costs ($/SF)	10	15	20
G. Parking (CAR/P.L.)	0.3	1.0	1.5
H. Partition/Door	8-9 SF/LF		80-90 SF/DR
I. Fire Prot. Class		LIGHT	
J. A/C (SF/Ton)	400		500
K. Mech./Elect. Costs (% of D)	17% M		8% E
L. Power (Watts/SF)	20		25
M. Other			

APARTMENT (100000 SF +)	Low	Ave.	High
A. Occupancy Type		R-1	
B. Efficiency Ratio		65	
C. Area (SF)	114000	213000	456000
D. Costs ($/SF)	58.50	76.50	90.00
E. A/E Fees (% of D)	5	6	8
F. FF&E Costs ($/SF)	10	15	20
G. Parking (CAR/P.U.)	0.3	1.0	1.5
H. Partition/Door	8-9 SF/LF		80-90 SF/DR
I. Fire Prot. Class		LIGHT	
J. A/C (SF/Ton)	400		500
K. Mech./Elect. Costs (% of D)	15% M		8% E
L. Power (Watts/SF)	20		25
M. Other			

AUDITORIUMS	Low	Ave.	High
A. Occupancy Type	A-1		A-3
B. Efficiency Ratio		70	
C. Area (SF)	13500	26000	101500
D. Costs ($/SF)	98	134	155
E. A/E Fees (% of D)	6	7	9
F. FF&E Costs ($/SF)		35	
G. Parking			
H. Partition/Door			
I. Fire Prot. Class		LIGHT	
J. A/C (SF/Ton)	150		200
K. Mech./Elect. Costs (% of D)	12% M		13% E
L. Power (Watts/SF)	20		25
M. Other			

AUTO SALES	Low	Ave.	High
A. Occupancy Type			
B. Efficiency Ratio			
C. Area (SF)	11000	20500	27000
D. Costs ($/SF)	46	59.50	71
E. A/E Fees (% of D)			
F. FF&E Costs ($/SF)		5	
G. Parking			
H. Partition/Door			
I. Fire Prot. Class		ORDINARY	
J. A/C (SF/Ton)	250		300
K. Mech./Elect. Costs (% of D)	15% M		13.5% E
L. Power (Watts/SF)	15		25
M. Other			

BANKS

	Low	Ave.	High
A. Occupancy Type		B	
B. Efficiency Ratio		70	
C. Area (SF)	5500	8000	20500
D. Costs ($/SF)	102	130	169
E. A/E Fees (% of D)	6	10	12
F. FF&E Costs ($/SF)	10	15	20
G. Parking (PER 1000 SF)	2.5	3	3.5
H. Partition/Door	15-20 SF/LF		150-200 SF/OR
I. Fire Prot. Class		LIGHT	
J. A/C (SF/Ton)	250		
K. Mech./Elect. Costs (% of D)	11% M		10.5% E
L. Power (Watts/SF)	15		20
M. Other			

CAR WASH

	Low	Ave.	High
A. Occupancy Type			
B. Efficiency Ratio			
C. Area (SF)		2500	
D. Costs ($/SF)		65	
E. A/E Fees (% of D)			
F. FF&E Costs ($/SF)			
G. Parking			
H. Partition/Door			
I. Fire Prot. Class			
J. A/C (SF/Ton)			
K. Mech./Elect. Costs (% of D)			
L. Power (Watts/SF)			
M. Other			

BOWLING ALLEY

	Low	Ave.	High
A. Occupancy Type			
B. Efficiency Ratio			
C. Area (SF)		20000	
D. Costs ($/SF)		71.5	
E. A/E Fees (% of D)			
F. FF&E Costs ($/SF)			
G. Parking			
H. Partition/Door			
I. Fire Prot. Class			
J. A/C (SF/Ton)	200		300
K. Mech./Elect. Costs (% of D)			
L. Power (Watts/SF)	20		25
M. Other			

CHURCHES

	Low	Ave.	High
A. Occupancy Type	A-1		A-3
B. Efficiency Ratio		70	
C. Area (SF)	8000	14000	17300
D. Costs ($/SF)	76	105	117
E. A/E Fees (% of D)	4	7	9
F. FF&E Costs ($/SF)	5	10	20
G. Parking (PER 1000 SF)		0.4	
H. Partition/Door			
I. Fire Prot. Class		LIGHT	
J. A/C (SF/Ton)	100		200
K. Mech./Elect. Costs (% of D)	14% M		9% E
L. Power (Watts/SF)	20		25
M. Other			

CONVENIENCE MARKET	Low	Ave.	High
A. Occupancy Type			
B. Efficiency Ratio			
C. Area (SF)		5000	
D. Costs ($/SF)		72	
E. A/E Fees (% of D)			
F. FF&E Costs ($/SF)			
G. Parking			
H. Partition/Door			
I. Fire Prot. Class			
J. A/C (SF/Ton)			
K. Mech./Elect. Costs (% of D)	15		25
L. Power (Watts/SF)			
M. Other			

CLUB, COUNTRY	Low	Ave.	High
A. Occupancy Type	A-1		A-3
B. Efficiency Ratio			
C. Area (SF)	4500	9500	15000
D. Costs ($/SF)	64	95	100
E. A/E Fees (% of D)	4	7	9
F. FF&E Costs ($/SF)	15		75
G. Parking (PER 1000 SF)		0.4	
H. Partition/Door			
I. Fire Prot. Class		LIGHT	
J. A/C (SF/Ton)	100		200
K. Mech./Elect. Costs (% of D)	22.5% M		9.5% E
L. Power (Watts/SF)	20		25
M. Other			

CLUB, HEALTH	Low	Ave.	High
A. Occupancy Type			A-3
B. Efficiency Ratio			
C. Area (SF)	19000	27000	44500
D. Costs ($/SF)	65	92.50	107
E. A/E Fees (% of D)			
F. FF&E Costs ($/SF)			
G. Parking			
H. Partition/Door			
I. Fire Prot. Class		LIGHT	
J. A/C (SF/Ton)	100		250
K. Mech./Elect. Costs (% of D)	16% M		10.5% E
L. Power (Watts/SF)	20		30
M. Other			

CLUB, SOCIAL	Low	Ave.	High
A. Occupancy Type	A-1		A-3
B. Efficiency Ratio			
C. Area (SF)	6000	15000	20000
D. Costs ($/SF)	52	95	99
E. A/E Fees (% of D)			
F. FF&E Costs ($/SF)			
G. Parking			
H. Partition/Door			
I. Fire Prot. Class		LIGHT	
J. A/C (SF/Ton)	150		300
K. Mech./Elect. Costs (% of D)	18% M		9.5% E
L. Power (Watts/SF)	20		30
M. Other			

COLLEGE, CLASS RM. & ADM.

	Low	Ave.	High
A. Occupancy Type			
B. Efficiency Ratio		5	
C. Area (SF)	50,000	58,000	155,000
D. Costs ($/SF)	91	114	145
E. A/E Fees (% of D)	4	6.5	9
F. FF&E Costs ($/SF)	6		17
G. Parking (PER STUDENT)		0.45	
H. Partition/Door			
J. Fire Prot. Class		LIGHT	
J. A/C (SF/Ton)	150		200
K. Mech./Elect. Costs (% of D)		18.5% M	10% E
L. Power (Watts/SF)	15		25
M. Other			

COLLEGE, LABORATORY

	Low	Ave.	High
A. Occupancy Type			
B. Efficiency Ratio			
C. Area (SF)	13,000	40,500	80,000
D. Costs ($/SF)	150	170	200
E. A/E Fees (% of D)			
F. FF&E Costs ($/SF)	10		25
G. Parking			
H. Partition/Door			
J. Fire Prot. Class			
J. A/C (SF/Ton)	150		200
K. Mech./Elect. Costs (% of D)		27% M	10% E
L. Power (Watts/SF)	15		20
M. Other			

COLLEGE, STUDENT UNION

	Low	Ave.	High
A. Occupancy Type			
B. Efficiency Ratio		60	
C. Area (SF)	44,400	82,000	123,800
D. Costs ($/SF)	88	119	134
E. A/E Fees (% of D)	6		
F. FF&E Costs ($/SF)			18
G. Parking			
H. Partition/Door			
J. Fire Prot. Class		LIGHT	
J. A/C (SF/Ton)	200		300
K. Mech./Elect. Costs (% of D)		20.5% M	9% E
L. Power (Watts/SF)	20		25
M. Other			

COMMUNITY CENTER

	Low	Ave.	High
A. Occupancy Type			
B. Efficiency Ratio			
C. Area (SF)	11,900	18,800	32,600
D. Costs ($/SF)	77	99	134
E. A/E Fees (% of D)	6	8	12
F. FF&E Costs ($/SF)		15	
G. Parking (PER 1000 SF)	3	4	5
H. Partition/Door			
J. Fire Prot. Class		LIGHT	
J. A/C (SF/Ton)	150		200
K. Mech./Elect. Costs (% of D)		16.5% M	9.5% E
L. Power (Watts/SF)	20		25
M. Other			

COURT HOUSE

	Low	Ave.	High
A. Occupancy Type			
B. Efficiency Ratio		60	
C. Area (SF)	17800	32400	106000
D. Costs ($/SF)	93.50	114	125
E. A/E Fees (% of D)			
F. FF&E Costs ($/SF)		30	
G. Parking			
H. Partition/Door			
I. Fire Prot. Class		LIGHT	
J. A/C (SF/Ton)	150		200
K. Mech./Elect. Costs (% of D)	23% M		10% E
L. Power (Watts/SF)	20		25
M. Other			

DAY CARE CENTER

	Low	Ave.	High
A. Occupancy Type			
B. Efficiency Ratio			
C. Area (SF)		6000	
D. Costs ($/SF)		78	
E. A/E Fees (% of D)			
F. FF&E Costs ($/SF)		15	
G. Parking			
H. Partition/Door			
I. Fire Prot. Class			
J. A/C (SF/Ton)	200		300
K. Mech./Elect. Costs (% of D)			
L. Power (Watts/SF)	15		25
M. Other			

DEPARTMENT STORE

	Low	Ave.	High
A. Occupancy Type		M	
B. Efficiency Ratio		80	
C. Area (SF)	54000	111500	196500
D. Costs ($/SF)	43	65	76.50
E. A/E Fees (% of D)	4	6.5	8
F. FF&E Costs ($/SF)			
G. Parking (PER 1000 SF)	4	5	5.5
H. Partition/Door	60 SF/LF		175 SF/DR
I. Fire Prot. Class		ORDINARY	
J. A/C (SF/Ton)	200		300
K. Mech./Elect. Costs (% of D)	14.5% M		11% E
L. Power (Watts/SF)	10		15
M. Other SEE PART 14 ON ADA ELEV. REQ'MTS.			

DORMITORY

	Low	Ave.	High
A. Occupancy Type	R-1		
B. Efficiency Ratio		65	
C. Area (SF)	25000	505500	130000
D. Costs ($/SF)	70	101	114.50
E. A/E Fees (% of D)	4	6	8
F. FF&E Costs ($/SF)		20	
G. Parking			
H. Partition/Door	9 SF/LF		90 SF/DR
I. Fire Prot. Class		LIGHT	
J. A/C (SF/Ton)	400		500
K. Mech./Elect. Costs (% of D)	17% M		9% E
L. Power (Watts/SF)	10		15
M. Other			

FACTORES	Low	Ave.	High
A. Occupancy Type	F-1		F-2
B. Efficiency Ratio			
C. Area (SF)	31,000	54,500	109,500
D. Costs ($/SF)	39.50	60.50	73.50
E. A/E Fees (% of D)	4	8	12
F. FF&E Costs ($/SF)			
G. Parking (per 1000 sf)	0.75	1.5	2.5
H. Partition/Door	ORDINARY		EXTRA
I. Fire Prot. Class			
J. A/C (SF/Ton)	100		150
K. Mech./Elect. Costs (% of D)	16% M		12% E
L. Power (Watts/SF)	25		40
M. Other			

FIRE STATIONS	Low	Ave.	High
A. Occupancy Type			
B. Efficiency Ratio			
C. Area (SF)	5,500	6,500	8,800
D. Costs ($/SF)	95	110	124
E. A/E Fees (% of D)		15	
F. FF&E Costs ($/SF)			
G. Parking			
H. Partition/Door			
I. Fire Prot. Class			
J. A/C (SF/Ton)	200		300
K. Mech./Elect. Costs (% of D)	14.5% M		10% E
L. Power (Watts/SF)	10		15
M. Other			

FUNERAL HOME	Low	Ave.	High
A. Occupancy Type			
B. Efficiency Ratio			
C. Area (SF)	3,000	12,000	20,500
D. Costs ($/SF)	57	80	126
E. A/E Fees (% of D)			
F. FF&E Costs ($/SF)			
G. Parking			
H. Partition/Door	14-15 SF/LF		140-150 SF/DR
I. Fire Prot. Class		LIGHT	
J. A/C (SF/Ton)	200		300
K. Mech./Elect. Costs (% of D)	18% M		4.6% E
L. Power (Watts/SF)	2.0		2.5
M. Other			

GARAGE, PARKING	Low	Ave.	High
A. Occupancy Type			
B. Efficiency Ratio			
C. Area (SF)	121,000	176,000	320,000
D. Costs ($/SF)	21	33	42
E. A/E Fees (% of D)			
F. FF&E Costs ($/SF)			
G. Parking			
H. Partition/Door	30-60 SF/LF		300-600 SF/DR
I. Fire Prot. Class		ORDINARY	
J. A/C (SF/Ton)			
K. Mech./Elect. Costs (% of D)	12% M		5% E
L. Power (Watts/SF)	3		5
M. Other			

GARAGE, SERVICE

	Low	Ave.	High
A. Occupancy Type			
B. Efficiency Ratio		85	
C. Area (SF)	3500	9000	22000
D. Costs ($/SF)	26	52	57
E. A/E Fees (% of D)	3	5.5	8
F. FF&E Costs ($/SF)			
G. Parking	30 SF/LF		
H. Partition/Door		ORDINARY	300 SF/DR
I. Fire Prot. Class			
J. A/C (SF/Ton)			
K. Mech./Elect. Costs (% of D)	14.5% M		9% E
L. Power (Watts/SF)	10		15
M. Other			

GYMNASIUMS

	Low	Ave.	High
A. Occupancy Type			
B. Efficiency Ratio		70	
C. Area (SF)	56000	71000	136500
D. Costs ($/SF)	80	102.50	115
E. A/E Fees (% of D)	6	6.5	9
F. FF&E Costs ($/SF)			
G. Parking (per 1000 SF)		5	
H. Partition/Door			
I. Fire Prot. Class			
J. A/C (SF/Ton)	200		250
K. Mech./Elect. Costs (% of D)	15		
L. Power (Watts/SF)			25
M. Other			

HOSPITAL

	Low	Ave.	High
A. Occupancy Type		I-1	
B. Efficiency Ratio		55	
C. Area (SF)	65000	128500	203000
D. Costs ($/SF)	134	178	233.50
E. A/E Fees (% of D)	4	6.5	9
F. FF&E Costs ($/SF)	35		55
G. Parking (per bed)	0.75	1.8	3
H. Partition/Door			
I. Fire Prot. Class		LIGHT	
J. A/C (SF/Ton)	150		250
K. Mech./Elect. Costs (% of D)	24.5% M		13% E
L. Power (Watts/SF)	25		35
M. Other			

HOTEL

	Low	Ave.	High
A. Occupancy Type			
B. Efficiency Ratio			
C. Area (SF)	87000	166000	222500
D. Costs ($/SF)	92.50	114.50	127.50
E. A/E Fees (% of D)			
F. FF&E Costs ($/SF)			
G. Parking		20	
H. Partition/Door			
I. Fire Prot. Class			
J. A/C (SF/Ton)	300		400
K. Mech./Elect. Costs (% of D)	17.5% M		10.5% E
L. Power (Watts/SF)	20		30
M. Other			

LABS / PERSONS	Low	Ave.	High
A. Occupancy Type		1-3	
B. Efficiency Ratio		75	
C. Area (SF)	60500	64000	144500
D. Costs ($/SF)	119	158	177
E. A/E Fees (% of D)			
F. FF&E Costs ($/SF)			
G. Parking			
H. Partition/Door			
I. Fire Prot. Class		LIGHT	
J. A/C (SF/Ton)	250		300
K. Mech./Elect. Costs (% of D)	16%M	11%E	
L. Power (Watts/SF)	15		25
M. Other			

MEDICAL/DENTAL, CLINICS/OFF.	Low	Ave.	High
A. Occupancy Type			
B. Efficiency Ratio			
C. Area (SF)	9000	15000	33000
D. Costs ($/SF)	75	106	115
E. A/E Fees (% of D)	6	8	9
F. FF&E Costs ($/SF)	10	15	25
G. Parking (PER 1000 SF)	1.5	3	5
H. Partition/Door			
I. Fire Prot. Class		LIGHT	
J. A/C (SF/Ton)	250		300
K. Mech./Elect. Costs (% of D)	15.5% M	16.5% M	10.5% E
L. Power (Watts/SF)	15		20
M. Other	SEE PART 14 ON ADA ELEV. REQMTS		

LIBRARIES	Low	Ave.	High
A. Occupancy Type			
B. Efficiency Ratio			
C. Area (SF)	16500	24500	71000
D. Costs ($/SF)	57	106.50	125.50
E. A/E Fees (% of D)			
F. FF&E Costs ($/SF)			
G. Parking	20	60	100
H. Partition/Door	LIGHT		ORDINARY *
I. Fire Prot. Class		LIGHT	
J. A/C (SF/Ton)	250		300
K. Mech./Elect. Costs (% of D)	16% M	11% E	
L. Power (Watts/SF)	15		25
M. Other * AT STACKS			

MOTELS	Low	Ave.	High
A. Occupancy Type		R-1	
B. Efficiency Ratio		60	
C. Area (SF)	55500	68500	128000
D. Costs ($/SF)	53	71.50	79
E. A/E Fees (% of D)	8	4	6
F. FF&E Costs ($/SF)		20	
G. Parking (PER D.U.)	0.4	0.8	1.6
H. Partition/Door	7-8/SF/LF		70-80 SF/DR
I. Fire Prot. Class		LIGHT	
J. A/C (SF/Ton)	400		500
K. Mech./Elect. Costs (% of D)	17% M	9% E	
L. Power (Watts/SF)	15		20
M. Other			

MUSEUMS	Low	Ave.	High
A. Occupancy Type			
B. Efficiency Ratio			
C. Area (SF)	27600	31250	63000
D. Costs ($/SF)	126	138	146
E. A/E Fees (% of D)			
F. FF&E Costs ($/SF)			
G. Parking			
H. Partition/Door		LIGHT	
I. Fire Prot. Class			
J. A/C (SF/Ton)	250		300
K. Mech./Elect. Costs (% of D)	14% M		12% E
L. Power (Watts/SF)	20		25
M. Other			

NURSING HOMES	Low	Ave.	High
A. Occupancy Type	I-1		I-2
B. Efficiency Ratio			
C. Area (SF)	24500	38000	82500
D. Costs ($/SF)	89.50	106	136.50
E. A/E Fees (% of D)	5	8	11.5
F. FF&E Costs ($/SF)			
G. Parking (PER D.U.)	0.25	0.3	0.45
H. Partition/Door	85F/LF		90 SF/DR
I. Fire Prot. Class		LIGHT	
J. A/C (SF/Ton)	200		250
K. Mech./Elect. Costs (% of D)	25.5% M		10.5% E
L. Power (Watts/SF)	15		25
M. Other			

OFFICE (LESS THAN 50,000 SF)	Low	Ave.	High
A. Occupancy Type			
B. Efficiency Ratio		75	
C. Area (SF)	8500	17000	25000
D. Costs ($/SF)	63	82	108.50
E. A/E Fees (% of D)*	3	6.5	10
F. FF&E Costs ($/SF)	10	20	30
G. Parking (PER 1000 SF)	1.66	2.6	3.5
H. Partition/Door	20 SF/LF		200-500 SF/DR
I. Fire Prot. Class		LIGHT	
J. A/C (SF/Ton)	250		300
K. Mech./Elect. Costs (% of D)	15% M		10% E
L. Power (Watts/SF)	15		20
M. Other *INCLUDES T.I., SEE P. 41			

OFFICE (50,000 SF +)	Low	Ave.	High
A. Occupancy Type			
B. Efficiency Ratio		75	
C. Area (SF)	77500	87500	428000
D. Costs ($/SF)*	68.50	100	122
E. A/E Fees (% of D)	3	6.5	10
F. FF&E Costs ($/SF)	15	35	50
G. Parking (PER 1000SF)	1.66	2.6	3.5
H. Partition/Door	20 SF/LF		200-500 SF/DR
I. Fire Prot. Class		LIGHT	
J. A/C (SF/Ton)	250		300
K. Mech./Elect. Costs (% of D)	15% M		8% E
L. Power (Watts/SF)	15		20
M. Other *INCLUDES T.I., SEE P. 41			

POLICE STATION	Low	Ave.	High
A. Occupancy Type		B-2	
B. Efficiency Ratio			
C. Area (SF)	4000	10500	19000
D. Costs ($/SF)	87	114	144
E. A/E Fees (% of D)			
F. FF&E Costs ($/SF)			
G. Parking			
H. Partition/Door			
I. Fire Prot. Class		LIGHT	
J. A/C (SF/Ton)	250		300
K. Mech./Elect. Costs (% of D)	17.5% M		12% E
L. Power (Watts/SF)	15		20
M. Other			

RELIGIOUS EDUCATION	Low	Ave.	High
A. Occupancy Type			
B. Efficiency Ratio			
C. Area (SF)	6700	9800	13500
D. Costs ($/SF)	74.50	94.50	109
E. A/E Fees (% of D)			
F. FF&E Costs ($/SF)			
G. Parking			
H. Partition/Door			
I. Fire Prot. Class		LIGHT	
J. A/C (SF/Ton)	150		200
K. Mech./Elect. Costs (% of D)	14% M		10.6% E
L. Power (Watts/SF)	15		20
M. Other			

POST OFFICE	Low	Ave.	High
A. Occupancy Type			
B. Efficiency Ratio			
C. Area (SF)	7000	12500	30000
D. Costs ($/SF)	68	93	106
E. A/E Fees (% of D)			
F. FF&E Costs ($/SF)			
G. Parking			
H. Partition/Door			
I. Fire Prot. Class		LIGHT	
J. A/C (SF/Ton)	200		215
K. Mech./Elect. Costs (% of D)	14% M		9.5% E
L. Power (Watts/SF)	15		25
M. Other			

RESEARCH LABORATORY	Low	Ave.	High
A. Occupancy Type		H-6	
B. Efficiency Ratio		60	
C. Area (SF)	54000	64500	86000
D. Costs ($/SF)	96	127	159
E. A/E Fees (% of D)			
F. FF&E Costs ($/SF)			
G. Parking			
H. Partition/Door			
I. Fire Prot. Class		LIGHT	
J. A/C (SF/Ton)	100		250
K. Mech./Elect. Costs (% of D)	25% M		11% E
L. Power (Watts/SF)	15		25
M. Other			

RESIDENTIAL, SINGLE FAM.	Low	Ave.	High
A. Occupancy Type		R-3	
B. Efficiency Ratio			
C. Area (SF)	1800	2900	3900
D. Costs ($/SF) *	66	83	111.50
E. A/E Fees (% of D)			
F. FF&E Costs ($/SF)	5	15	50
G. Parking			
H. Partition/Door			
I. Fire Prot. Class			
J. A/C (SF/Ton)	300	400	450
K. Mech./Elect. Costs (% of D)	12% M		5% E
L. Power (Watts/SF)	5		10
M. Other See P. 40 FOR HIGHER COSTS			

RESTAURANTS	Low	Ave.	High
A. Occupancy Type	A-1 OR 2		B-2
B. Efficiency Ratio		70	
C. Area (SF)	4000	5500	9000
D. Costs ($/SF)	85	109.50	127
E. A/E Fees (% of D)	3.5	6	8
F. FF&E Costs ($/SF)	30	50	100
G. Parking (PER 1000 SF)	10	15	21.5
H. Partition/Door	20-25 SF/LF	150-250 SF/DR	
I. Fire Prot. Class	LIGHT	ORDINARY *	
J. A/C (SF/Ton)	150		200
K. Mech./Elect. Costs (% of D)	21% M		11% E
L. Power (Watts/SF)	15		30
M. Other * KITCHEN AREAS			

RETAIL STORES	Low	Ave.	High
A. Occupancy Type			
B. Efficiency Ratio		60	
C. Area (SF)	20500	46500	65500
D. Costs ($/SF)	52	71	92
E. A/E Fees (% of D)	4	6	9
F. FF&E Costs ($/SF)			
G. Parking (PER 1000 SF)	3.5	4.5	5.5
H. Partition/Door	10-60 SF/LF	300-600 SF/DR	
I. Fire Prot. Class		ORDINARY	
J. A/C (SF/Ton)	250		300
K. Mech./Elect. Costs (% of D)	12.5% M		11.5% E
L. Power (Watts/SF)	10		15
M. Other			

SCHOOL, ELEMENTARY	Low	Ave.	High
A. Occupancy Type			
B. Efficiency Ratio			
C. Area (SF)	28000	43500	62000
D. Costs ($/SF)	71	93	96
E. A/E Fees (% of D)	6	7.5	9
F. FF&E Costs ($/SF)	5		10
G. Parking			
H. Partition/Door			
I. Fire Prot. Class		LIGHT	
J. A/C (SF/Ton)	150		250
K. Mech./Elect. Costs (% of D)	18% M		10% E
L. Power (Watts/SF)	15		25
M. Other			

SCHOOLS, JR. HIGH

	Low	Ave.	High
A. Occupancy Type			
B. Efficiency Ratio			
C. Area (SF)	48500	85500	106500
D. Costs ($/SF)	76	98.50	101.50
E. A/E Fees (% of D)	6	7.5	9
F. FF&E Costs ($/SF)	5		10
G. Parking			
H. Partition/Door			
I. Fire Prot. Class		LIGHT	
J. A/C (SF/Ton)	150		250
K. Mech./Elect. Costs (% of D)	19% M		10% E
L. Power (Watts/SF)	15		25
M. Other			

SCHOOLS, SR. HIGH

	Low	Ave.	High
A. Occupancy Type			
B. Efficiency Ratio			
C. Area (SF)	50000	139000	249500
D. Costs ($/SF)	81.50	101	117
E. A/E Fees (% of D)	6	7.5	9
F. FF&E Costs ($/SF)	5		10
G. Parking (PER STUDENT)		0.5	
H. Partition/Door			
I. Fire Prot. Class		LIGHT	
J. A/C (SF/Ton)	150		250
K. Mech./Elect. Costs (% of D)	18% M		10.5% E
L. Power (Watts/SF)	15		25
M. Other			

SCHOOLS, VOCATIONAL

	Low	Ave.	High
A. Occupancy Type			
B. Efficiency Ratio			
C. Area (SF)		43500	
D. Costs ($/SF)		98.50	
E. A/E Fees (% of D)			
F. FF&E Costs ($/SF)	5		10
G. Parking			
H. Partition/Door			
I. Fire Prot. Class			
J. A/C (SF/Ton)	100		250
K. Mech./Elect. Costs (% of D)	19% M		11.5% E
L. Power (Watts/SF)			
M. Other			

SERVICE STATION

	Low	Ave.	High
A. Occupancy Type			
B. Efficiency Ratio			
C. Area (SF)	1000	1500	1700
D. Costs ($/SF)	76	81	99
E. A/E Fees (% of D)			
F. FF&E Costs ($/SF)			
G. Parking			
H. Partition/Door	15 SF/LE		150 SF/DR
I. Fire Prot. Class			
J. A/C (SF/Ton)			
K. Mech./Elect. Costs (% of D)			
L. Power (Watts/SF)	10		20
M. Other			

SPORTS ARENA

	Low	Ave.	High
A. Occupancy Type		A-4	
B. Efficiency Ratio			
C. Area (SF)	235,000	173500	320500
D. Costs ($/SF)	90	104.50	139
E. A/E Fees (% of D)			
F. FF&E Costs ($/SF)			
G. Parking			
H. Partition/Door			
I. Fire Prot. Class		LIGHT	
J. A/C (SF/Ton)	100		200
K. Mech./Elect. Costs (% of D)	14.5% M		9% E
L. Power (Watts/SF)	25		35
M. Other			

SUPERMARKETS

	Low	Ave.	High
A. Occupancy Type			
B. Efficiency Ratio			
C. Area (SF)	8500	22500	40000
D. Costs ($/SF)	47	59.50	69
E. A/E Fees (% of D)	3	7	7.5
F. FF&E Costs ($/SF)			
G. Parking (PER 1000 SF)		300-400 SF/PK	
H. Partition/Door	30 - 40 SF/LF		
I. Fire Prot. Class		ORDINARY	
J. A/C (SF/Ton)	100		250
K. Mech./Elect. Costs (% of D)	14.5% M		12.5% E
L. Power (Watts/SF)	20		25
M. Other			

THEATER

	Low	Ave.	High
A. Occupancy Type	A-1		A-3
B. Efficiency Ratio			
C. Area (SF)	10000	14500	20500
D. Costs ($/SF)	62	85.50	100
E. A/E Fees (% of D)			
F. FF&E Costs ($/SF)			
G. Parking (PER SEAT)	0.1	0.25	0.5
H. Partition/Door			
I. Fire Prot. Class		LIGHT *	
J. A/C (SF/Ton)	150		200
K. Mech./Elect. Costs (% of D)	13% M		8% E
L. Power (Watts/SF)	20		25
M. Other * EXCLUDING STAGE AREAS			

TOWN HALL

	Low	Ave.	High
A. Occupancy Type			
B. Efficiency Ratio			
C. Area (SF)	30500	47500	90000
D. Costs ($/SF)	87	108	139
E. A/E Fees (% of D)			
F. FF&E Costs ($/SF)			
G. Parking (PER 1000 SF)	1.0	3.5	8
H. Partition/Door			
I. Fire Prot. Class		LIGHT	
J. A/C (SF/Ton)	200		300
K. Mech./Elect. Costs (% of D)	13% M		10% E
L. Power (Watts/SF)	15		25
M. Other			

TRANSPORTATION	Low	Ave.	High
A. Occupancy Type			
B. Efficiency Ratio			
C. Area (SF)		175,000	
D. Costs ($/SF)	121	127.50	191
E. A/E Fees (% of D)			
F. FF&E Costs ($/SF)			
G. Parking			
H. Partition/Door			
I. Fire Prot. Class		LIGHT	
J. A/C (SF/Ton)	150		250
K. Mech./Elect. Costs (% of D)	15%M		13%E
L. Power (Watts/SF)	15		25
M. Other			

VETERINARY CLINIC	Low	Ave.	High
A. Occupancy Type			
B. Efficiency Ratio			
C. Area (SF)		20,000	
D. Costs ($/SF)		137	
E. A/E Fees (% of D)			
F. FF&E Costs ($/SF)			
G. Parking			
H. Partition/Door			
I. Fire Prot. Class			
J. A/C (SF/Ton)	100		300
K. Mech./Elect. Costs (% of D)	17%M		5.5%E
L. Power (Watts/SF)	20		30
M. Other			

WAREHOUSE	Low	Ave.	High
A. Occupancy Type			
B. Efficiency Ratio		95	
C. Area (SF)	36,000	67,000	157,500
D. Costs ($/SF)	29.50	41.00	52.50
E. A/E Fees (% of D)	4	5.5	8
F. FF&E Costs ($/SF)			
G. Parking (PER 1000 SF)	1.5	2	2.5
H. Partition/Door			
I. Fire Prot. Class	LIGHT		ORDINARY
J. A/C (SF/Ton)			
K. Mech./Elect. Costs (% of D)	9%M		8%E
L. Power (Watts/SF)	10		15
M. Other			

	Low	Ave.	High
A. Occupancy Type			
B. Efficiency Ratio			
C. Area (SF)			
D. Costs ($/SF)			
E. A/E Fees (% of D)			
F. FF&E Costs ($/SF)			
G. Parking			
H. Partition/Door			
I. Fire Prot. Class			
J. A/C (SF/Ton)			
K. Mech./Elect. Costs (% of D)			
L. Power (Watts/SF)			
M. Other			

___ APPENDIX B: LOCATION DATA

Entries A through V in the tables on pp. 526–539 provide useful architecturally related data, as described below, for various U.S. cities and nearby areas.

___ A. *Latitude* is given in degrees and minutes. ⑦

___ B. *Elevation* is in feet above sea level. See p. 136. ⑦

___ C. *Frost line* is inches below top of ground to frost line. See p. 190. ④

___ D. *Ground temperature* is the constant year-round temperature (in degrees F) at about 20 to 30 feet below the surface. See p. 138. ④

___ E. *Seismic* is UBC earthquake zones. See p. 122. ㉔

___ F. *Termite* lists zones of degree of infestation (with 1 being worst). See p. 191. ④

___ G. *Soils* are the predominant soils for the location. See p. 182. No data available at this publication.

___ H. *Plant zone* is for plant hardiness. See p. 202. ④

___ I. *Rain, average* in inches per year. ㉟ₐ

___ J. *Rain, intensity* is hourly intensity in inches/hour for 5-minute periods to be expected once in 10 years. Some storms have twice as much in some zones. See pp. 176 and 432. ④

___ K. *Percent sun* is yearly average of clear days. See p. 136. ㉟ₐ

___ L. *Heating degree days* (*HDD*), base 65°F. See p. 135. ㉟ₐ

___ M. *Cooling degree days* (*HDD*), base 65°F. See p. 136. ㉟ₐ

___ N. *Percent humidity* (*% RH*) *AM* is yearly average in mornings. See p. 136. ㉟ₐ

___ O. *Percent humidity* (*% RH*) *PM* is yearly average in afternoon/evenings. See p. 136. ㉟ₐ

___ P. *Winter temperature* is design winter dry-bulb temperature (99%) as recommended by ASHRAE. See p. 135.   (7)

___ Q. *Summer temperature* is design summer dry-bulb temperature (1%) as recommended by ASHRAE. See p. 135.   (7)

___ R. *Wind, average* is yearly average. See p. 136.   (35a)

___ S. *Wind, intensity* is design wind speed per UBC. See p. 121.   (24)

___ T. *Snow* is the ground snow load in LB/SF per UBC. See p. 115 where not given, establish from local authority.   (24)

___ U. *Insulation* is the recommended zone for minimum R value. See p. 292.   (7)

___ V. *Costs* are the city cost indexes to adjust cost given in this book. See p. 35.   (11)*

___ *Other:* (1) Possible radon-producing area. See p. 190.   (45)

---

*Data courtesy of BNI Building News. See latest BNI for current data.

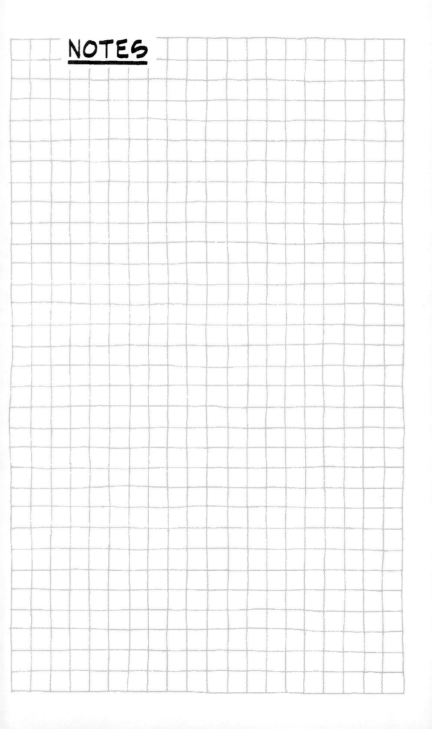

NOTES

LOCATION

Line No.	LOCATION	A LAT.	B ELEV.	C FROST LINE	D GD. TEMP.	E SEISMIC	F TERMITE	G SOILS	H PLANT ZONE	I RAIN AVE.	J RAIN INT.	K % SUN
1	AK ANCHORAGE	61-1	90			4	0		9	15		34
2												
3	AL BIRMINGHAM	33-3	610	3	64	1	1		8	52	7.2	58
4	HUNTSVILLE	34-4	619	3	62	1	1		7	55	6.3	55
5	MOBILE	30-4	211	0	70	0	1		9	65	7.8	60
6	MONTGOMERY	32-2	195	2	67	0	1		8	49	7.5	59
7												
8	AR FT. SMITH	35-2	449	7	64	1	2		7	40	7.4	60
9	LITTLE ROCK	34-4	257	4.5	64	1	2		7	49	7.2	60
10												
11	AZ PHOENIX	33-3	1117	0	72	1	2		8	7	4	81
12	TUCSON	32-1	2584	0	72	1	2		8	11	4	78
13												
14	CA BAKERSFIELD	35-2	495	0	64	4	2		9	6	3.6	75
15	FRESNO	36-5	326	0	64	3	2		9	11	3.6	73
16	LOS ANGELES	34-0	99	0	68	4	2		10	12	3.6	72
17	RIVERSIDE	33-5	1511	0	72	4	2		9		3.6	
18	SACRAMENTO	38-3	17	0	64	3	2		9	17	3.6	73
19	SANTA BARB.	33-4	33	0	64	4	2		10	16	3.6	
20	SAN DIEGO	32-4	19	0	72	4	2		10	9	3.6	72
21	SAN FRANCISCO	37-4	8	0	64	4	2		9	20	3.6	72
22	STOCKTON	37-5	28	0	64	3	2		9	14	3.6	
23												
24	CO COLO. SPRINGS	38-5	6173	10	54	1	3		5	15	4.8	68
25	DENVER	39-5	5283	10	54	1	3		5	15	4.8	67
26												
27	CT BRIDGEPORT	41-1	7	18	52	2A	2		6	42	6.3	56
28	HARTFORD	41-5	15	18	52	2A	2		6	44	6.3	52
29	NEW HAVEN	41-2	6	18	52	2A	2		6		6.3	
30												
31	DE WILMINGTON	39-4	78	6	56	1	2		7	41	6.6	
32												

DATA

L HDD	M CDD	N % RH AM	O % RH PM	P WINT TEMP	Q SUM TEMP	R WIND AVE.	S WIND INT.	T SNOW	U INSUL.	V COST*	OTHER	Line No.
10816	0	73	63	−23	71	7	90		6	130		1
												2
2943	1891	84	57	17	96	7	70	5	3	79		3
3279	1708	85	58	11	95	8	70	10	3	77	(1)	4
1695	2643	86	57	25	95	9	100	0	2	81		5
2277	2274	87	56	22	96	7	80	5	3	75		6
												7
3477	1969	85	56	12	101	8	70		3	74	(1)	8
3152	2045	84	57	15	99	8	70	5	3	78		9
												10
1442	3746	51	23	31	109	6	75	0	3	89	(1)	11
1734	2840	53	25	28	104	8	75	0	3	89		12
												13
2128	2347	65	38	30	104	6	70	0	3	97	(1)	14
2647	1769	78	40	28	102	6	70	0	3	98		15
1595	728	79	64	41	83	8	70	0	1	107	(1)	16
				29	100		70	0	2	97	(1)	17
2772	1198	83	45	30	101	8	70	0	4	100	(1)	18
2487	269	80	59			6	70	0	1	107		19
1284	842	76	62	42	83	7	70	0	1	102		20
3161	115	84	61	35	82	11	70	0	1	112		21
2674	1448	78	44	28	100	8	70	0	4	108	(1)	22
												23
6346	501	63	40	−3	91	10	75		5	92	(1)	24
6014	680	68	40	−5	93	9	75		5	95	(1)	25
												26
5501	746	76	60	6	84	12	85	25	4	103	(1)	27
6174	666			3	91	9	85	25	4	101	(1)	28
				3	88					102	(1)	29
												30
4986	1015	78	55	10	92	9	75	15	4	91		31
												32

*Data courtesy of BNI Building News. See latest BNI for current data.

LOCATION

Line No.	LOCATION	A LAT.	B ELEV.	C FROST LINE	D GD. TEMP.	E SEISMIC	F TERMITE	G SOILS	H PLANT ZONE	I RAIN AVE.	J RAIN INT.	K % SUN
1	DC WASHINGTON	38-5	14	8	58	1	2		7	40	6.6	54
2												
3	FL JACKSONVILLE	30-3	24	0	73	0	1		9	53	7.8+	61
4	MIAMI	25-5	7	0	76	0	1		10	58	7.8+	69
5	ORLANDO	28-3	106	0	74	0	1		9	48	7.8+	65
6	TAMPA	28-0	19	0	76	0	1		10	47	7.8+	67
7												
8	GA ATLANTA	33-4	1005	4	64	2A	1		7	49	7	59
9	COLUMBUS	33-2	242	3	66	1	1		8	51	7.5	59
10	SAVANNAH	32-1	52	0	68	2A	1		9	50	7.5	59
11												
12	HI HONOLULU	21-2	7							23		74
13												
14	IA DES MOINES	41-3	948	30	53	0	2		5	31	7	55
15	DAVENPORT	41-3		30	55	0	2		5		6.6	
16	SIOUX CITY	42-2	1095	35	52	1	3		4	25	7	57
17												
18	ID BOISE	43-3	2842	6	55	2B	3		5	12	3	58
19	POCATELLO	43-0	4444	20	53	2B	3		5	11	3.8	56
20												
21	IL CHICAGO	41-5	610	35	54	0	2		4	33	6.3	52
22	PEORIA	40-4	652	25	54	1	2		5		6.3	
23	ROCKFORD	42-1	724	35	54	0	2		5	37	6.3	53
24	SPRINGFIELD	39-5	587	18	56	1	2		5	34	6.3	54
25												
26	IN EVANSVILLE	38-0	381	7	58	1	2		6	42	6.5	55
27	FT. WAYNE	41-0	791	23	55	1	2		5	34	6.2	50
28	INDIANAPOLIS	39-4	793	20	56	1	2		6	39	6.3	51
29	SOUTH BEND	41-4	773	30	54	1	2		5	38	6.3	47
30	TERRE HAUTE	39-3	601	15	56	2A	2		6		6.3	
31												
32												

DATA

L HDD	M CDD	N % RH AM	O % RH PM	P WINT TEMP	Q SUM TEMP	R WIND AVE.	S WIND INT.	T SNOW	U INSUL.	V COST*	OTHER	Line No.
5004	970	83	55	14	93	7	75	20	4	95		1
												2
1402	2520	88	56	29	96	8	95	0	2	80		3
199	4095	84	61	44	91	9	110	0	2	86		4
656	3401	89	55	35	94	9	95	0	2	80		5
739	3324	88	58	36	92	8	100	0	2	82		6
												7
3021	1670	82	56	17	94	9	75	5	3	83	(1)	8
2356	2152	87	54	21	95	7	70	5	3	75	(1)	9
1921	2290	86	53	24	96	8	100	0	2	79		10
												11
0	4389	72	56	62	87	11				125		12
												13
6554	1019	80	60	−10	94	11	80	25	5	89		14
							75	25	5	87		15
6947	940	82	60	−11	95	11	85	35	5	85		16
												17
5802	742	69	43	3	96	9	70		4	92		18
7123	445	72	44	−8	94	10	70		4	88	(1)	19
												20
6455	740	80	60	−5	94	10	75	25	5	103		21
6226	948			−8	91	10	75	20	5	92		22
6952	714	83	61	−9	91	10	75	25	5	92		23
5654	1165	83	61	−3	94	11	75	20	4	89		24
												25
4729	1378	82	59	4	95	11	70	15	4	88	(1)	26
6320	786	82	62	−4	92	10	75		5	88	(1)	27
5650	988	84	62	−2	92	10	75	20	4	95		28
6377	710	82	62	−3	91	10	75	20	4			29
				−2	95		70	20	4	86	(1)	30
												31
												32

*Data courtesy of BNI Building News. See latest BNI for current data.

LOCATION

Line No.	LOCATION	A LAT.	B ELEV.	C FROST LINE	D GD. TEMP.	E SEISMIC	F TERMITE	G SOILS	H PLANT ZONE	I RAIN AVE.	J RAIN INT.	K % SUN
1	KS TOPEKA	39-0	877	15	58	2A	2		6	33	7.3	58
2	WICHITA	37-4	1321	12	60	1	2		6	29	7.3	62
3												
4	KY LEXINGTON	38-0	979	7	59	1	2		6	46	6.4	52
5	LOUISVILLE	38-1	474	6	58	1	2		6	44	6.4	53
6												
7	LA BATON ROUGE	30-3	64	0	70	0	1		9	56	7.8	60
8	LAKE CHARLES	30-1	14	0	72	0	1		9	53	7.8+	58
9	NEW ORLEANS	30-0	3	0	72	0	1		9	60	7.8+	60
10	SHREVEPORT	32-3	252	18	68	1	1		8	44	7.6	59
11												
12	MA BOSTON	42.2	15	30+	52	2A	2		6	44	5.7	55
13	LOWELL	42.3	90	35	48	2A	1		5		5.7	
14	NEW BEDFORD	41-4	70	18	54	2A	2		6		6.2	
15	SPRINGFIELD	42-1	247	25	52	2A	1		5		6.0	
16	WORCESTER	42.2	986	30	52	2A	2		5	48	5.7	54
17												
18	MD BALTIMORE	38-8	14	8	58	1	2		7	42	6.6	59
19												
20	ME LEWISTON	44-0	182	50	50	2A	3		5		5.2	
21	PORTLAND	43-4	61	48	50	2A	3		6	44	5.4	55
22												
23	MI DETROIT	42-2	633	30	50	1	3		5	31	5.8	50
24	FLINT	40-0	760	30	49	1	3		5	29	6.0	47
25	GRAND RAPIDS	42-5	681	20	50	0	3		5	34	6.0	44
26	KALAMAZOO	42-1	930	20	52	1	3		5		6.2	
27	LANSING	42-5	852	25	50	1	3		5	30	6.0	48
28												
29	MN DULUTH	46-5	1426	50	48	0	3		3	30	6.2	49
30	MINNEAPOLIS	44-5	822	50	46	0	3		4	26	6.4	54
31	ROCHESTER	44.0	1297	38	49	0	3		4	28	6.4	50
32												

DATA

L HDD	M CDD	N % RH AM	O % RH PM	P WINT TEMP	Q SUM TEMP	R WIND AVE.	S WIND INT.	T SNOW	U INSUL.	V COST*	OTHER	Line No.
5319	1380	83	59	0	99	10	80	20	4	83		1
4787	1684	80	55	3	101	12	80	15	4	81		2
												3
4814	1170	82	60	3	93	9	70	15	4	85	(1)	4
4525	1342	81	58	5	95	8	70	15	4	89	(1)	5
												6
1673	2605	88	59	25	95	8	90	0	2	84		7
1579	2682	91	63	27	95	9	100	0	2	82		8
1490	2686	88	63	29	93	8	100	0	2	86		9
2269	2444	88	58	20	99	8	70	0	3	78		10
												11
5593	699	72	58	6	91	13	85	30	5	101	(1)	12
				-4	91		80	35	5	94	(1)	13
				5	85		85	20	5	91	(1)	14
				-5	90		80	30	5	94	(1)	15
6950	359	74	57	0	89	10	80	30	5	96	(1)	16
												17
4706	1138	77	54	14	93	9	75	20	4	90		18
												19
				-7	88		80	70	6	87	(1)	20
7501	254	79	59	-6	87	9	85	60	5	89	(1)	21
												22
6563	615	81	60	3	91	10	75	25	5	95	(1)	23
7068	456	81	62	-4	90	10	75	30	5	91	(1)	24
6927	570	83	63	1	91	10	75	30	5	88	(1)	25
				1	92		75	30	5	86	(1)	26
8298	530	85	64	-3	90	10	75	30	5	88	(1)	27
												28
9901	150	81	63	-21	85	11	75		6	93	(1)	29
8007	662	79	60	-16	92	11	75		6	98		30
8277	479	83	65	-17	90	13	80		6	93		31
												32

*Data courtesy of BNI Building News. See latest BNI for current data.

LOCATION

Line No.	LOCATION	A LAT.	B ELEV.	C FROST LINE	D GD. TEMP.	E SEISMIC	F TERMITE	G SOILS	H PLANT ZONE	I RAIN AVE.	J RAIN INT.	K % SUN
1	MO KANSAS CITY	39-1	742	15	58	2A	2		6	35	7.4	60
2	ST. JOSEPH	39-5	809	20	55	2A	2		5		7.4	
3	ST. LOUIS	38-5	535	12	58	2A	2		6	34	6.6	55
4	SPRINGFIELD	37-1		8	59	1	2		6	39	7.4	58
5												
6	MS BILOXI	30-2	25	0	70	0	1		9		7.8	
7	JACKSON	32-2	330	1	67	1	1		8	53	7.5	59
8												
9	MT BILLINGS	45-5	3567	25	50	1	3		5	15	4.2	55
10	GREAT FALLS	47-3	3664	60	50	2B	3		5	15	3.6	51
11												
12	NC CHARLOTTE	35-0	735	5	62	2A	2		7	43	7.4	59
13	RALEIGH	35-5	433	3	62	2A	2		7	42	7.4	59
14	WINSTON-SALEM	36-1	967	4	62	2A	2		7	42	7.4	59
15												
16	ND FARGO	46-5	900	55	46	0	3		3	20	6.4	54
17												
18	NE LINCOLN	40-5	1150	28	54	1	2		5	27	7.2	59
19	OMAHA	41-2	978	30	53	1	2		5	30	7.2	60
20												
21	NH MANCHESTER	43-0	253	45	46	2A	3		5		5.6	
22												
23	NJ NEWARK	40-5	132	15	54	2A	2		6	44	6.3	64
24	TRENTON	40-1	144	12	55	2A	2		6		6.3	
25												
26	NM ALBUQUERQUE	35-0	5310	6	60	2B	2		5	8	4.6	76
27												
28	NV LAS VEGAS	36-1	2162	0	70	2B	2		8	5	3.8	80
29	RENO	39-3	4404	20	58	3	2		5	7	3.2	80
30												
31												
32												

DATA

L HDD	M CDD	N % RH AM	O % RH PM	P WINT TEMP	Q SUM TEMP	R WIND AVE.	S WIND INT.	T SNOW	U INSUL.	V COST*	OTHER	Line No.
5283	1333	81	59	2	99	11	75	20	4	86		1
				-3	96		75	25	4	84		2
4938	1468	83	59	2	97	10	70	20	4	90		3
4660	1374	82	58	3	96	11	70	15	4	84		4
												5
				28	31				2			6
2389	2320	91	58	21	97	7	80	5	3	81		7
												8
7212	553	66	44	-15	94	11	80		5	87		9
7766	391	67	45	-21	91	13			6	87		10
												11
3342	1546	82	54	18	95	7	70	10	3	79	(1)	12
3531	1394	85	54	16	94	8	75	15	3	77	(1)	13
3874	1303	83	55	16	94	8	75	15	3		(1)	14
												15
9343	476	81	62	-22	92	12	85	35	6	90		16
												17
6375	1124	82	58	-5	99	10	80	25	5	85		18
6194	1166	81	59	-8	94	11	80	25	5	87		19
												20
				-8	91		75		5	88		21
												22
4972	1091	73	53	11	92	9	80	20	4	102	(1)	23
				11	91		75	30	4	97	(1)	24
												25
4414	1254	60	29	12	96	9	70	10	4	86	(1)	26
												27
2532	3029	40	21	25	108	9	80	5	3	97		28
6030	357	70	31	5	95	7			3	100		29
												30
												31
												32

*Data courtesy of BNI Building News. See latest BNI for current data.

LOCATION

Line No.	LOCATION	A LAT.	B ELEV.	C FROST LINE	D GD. TEMP.	E SEISMIC	F TERMITE	G SOILS	H PLANT ZONE	I RAIN AVE.	J RAIN INT.	K % SUN
1	NY ALBANY	42-5	277	30+	46	2A	3		5	36	5.7	49
2	BINGHAMTON	42-1	1590	30+	51	1	2		5	37	5.8	42
3	BUFFALO	43-0	705	30+	51	1	3		6	38	5.7	43
4	NEW YORK	40-5	132	15	54	2A	2		6	44	6.3	64
5	ROCHESTER	43-1	543	30+	50	1	3		6	31	5.4	46
6	SYRACUSE	43-1	424	30+	50	1	3		6	39	5.4	44
7												
8	OH AKRON	40-1	1210	15	54	1	2		5	36	6.0	46
9	CINCINNATI	39-1	761	10	58	1	2		6		6.3	
10	CLEVELAND	41-2	777	23	54	1	2		5	35	6.0	45
11	COLUMBUS	40-0	812	10	56	1	2		5	37	6.2	48
12	DAYTON	39-5	997	10	54	1	2		5	35	6.2	49
13	TOLEDO	41-4	676	20	54	1	2		5	32	6.0	50
14	YOUNGSTOWN	41-2	1178	15	53	1	2		5	37	6.0	44
15												
16	OK LAWTON	34-3	1108	8	62	1	2		5/6		7.2	
17	OKLA. CITY	35-2	1280	8	64	2A	2		5/6	31	7.4	64
18	TULSA	36-1	650	8	62	1	2		5/6	39	7.5	63
19												
20	OR EUGENE	44-1	364	13	56	2B	3		7	46	3.4	43
21	PORTLAND	45-4	21	13	54	2B	3		8	37	3.4	39
22												
23	PA ALLENTOWN	40-4	376	15	53	2A	2		6	44	6.3	56
24	ERIE	42-1	732	25	51	1	2		6	39	5.7	44
25	HARRISBURG	40-1	335	18	52	1	2		6	39	6.3	54
26	PHILADELPHIA	39-5	7	12	54	2A	2		7	41	6.4	56
27	PITTSBURGH	40-3	1137	15	54	1	2		6	36	6.2	44
28	SCRANTON	41-2	940	25	51	2A	2		5		6.0	
29												
30	RI PROVIDENCE	41-4	55	18	54	2A	2		6	45	6.2	55
31												
32												

DATA

L HDD	M CDD	N %RH AM	O %RH PM	P WINT TEMP	Q SUM TEMP	R WIND AVE	S WIND INT	T SNOW	U INSUL	V COST*	OTHER	Line No.
6927	494	80	57	-6	91	9	70	30	5	87		1
7344	330	82	63	-2	86	10			5	83		2
6798	476	80	63	2	88	12			5	90	(1)	3
4868	1089	72	56	11	92	9	80	20	4	115	(1)	4
6713	531	81	61	1	91	10	70	40	5	90		5
6768	506	81	61	-3	90	9	70	35	5	87		6
												7
6241	625	80	61	1	89	10	75	15	5		(1)	8
5069	1080			1	92			15	4	83		9
6178	625	79	62	1	91	11			5	91	(1)	10
5686	862	80	59	0	92	8	70	20	4	89		11
5689	947	80	60	-1	91	10	70	20	4			12
6570	622	84	60	-3	90	9		15	5	89	(1)	13
6560	485	82	62	-1	88	10	75	25	5	85	(1)	14
												15
				12	101		80	5	3	77		16
3735	1914	80	54	9	100	12	75	10	3	83		17
3731	2043	81	56	8	101	10	70	10	3	81	(1)	18
												19
4799	261	91	60	17	92	8	80		4	90		20
4691	332	86	60	17	89	8	85		1	95		21
												22
5815	751	80	56	4	92	9	70	30	5	91	(1)	23
6768	402	78	66	4	88	11			5		(1)	24
5335	1006	76	54	7	94	7	70	25	4	85	(1)	25
4947	1075	76	55	10	93	10	75	25	4	98	(1)	26
5950	645	79	57	1	89	9	70	30	4	89		27
				1	90		70		5	87		28
												29
5908	574	75	55	5	89	11	90	20	4	98	(1)	30
												31
												32

*Data courtesy of BNI Building News. See latest BNI for current data.

LOCATION

Line No.	LOCATION	A LAT.	B ELEV.	C FROST LINE	D GD. TEMP.	E SEISMIC	F TERMITE	G SOILS	H PLANT ZONE	I RAIN AVE.	J RAIN INT.	K % SUN
1	SC CHARLESTON	32-5	9	0	67	2A	1		9	52	7.6	58
2	COLUMBIA	34-0	217	3	65	2A	1		8	49	7.4	60
3												
4	SD RAPID CITY	44-0	3165	28	50	1	3		4	16	5.4	62
5	SIOUX FALLS	43-4	1420	38	50	0	3		4	24	6.8	57
6												
7	TN CHATTANOOGA	35-0	670	5	63	2A	2		7	53	6.8	58
8	KNOXVILLE	35-5	980	8	60	2A	2		7	47	6.6	56
9	MEMPHIS	35-0	263	3	63	3	2		7	52	6.8	59
10	NASHVILLE	36-1	577	5	60	1	2		7	48	6.5	57
11												
12	TX ABILENE	32-3	1759	4	68	0	2		7	23	7.2	67
13	AMARILLO	35-1	3607	6	61	1	2		6	19	6.0	72
14	AUSTIN	30-2	597	3	73	0	1		8	32	7.4	63
15	BEAUMONT	30-0	18	0	70	0	1		9		8	
16	CORPUS CHRISTI	27-5	43	0	76	0	1		9	30	8	61
17	DALLAS	32-5	481	4	69	0	1		8	29	7.5	70
18	EL PASO	31-5	3918	2	68	1	2		6	8	4.8	80
19	HOUSTON	29-4	50	0	76	0	1		9	45	8	56
20	LUBBOCK	33-4	3243	5	64	0	2		7	18	6	72
21	SAN ANTONIO	29-3	792	1	76	0	1		9	29	7.8	62
22	WACO	31-4	500	4	71	0	1		8	31	7.6	63
23	WICHITA FALLS	34-0	994	8	66	1	2		7	27	7.2	67
24												
25	UT OGDEN	41-1	4455	18	55	3	3		5		4.5	
26	SALT LAKE	40-5	4220	16	55	3	3		5	15	4.5	62
27												
28	VA NORFOLK	36-5	26	2	60	1	1		8	45	7.2	58
29	ROANOKE	37-2	1174	15	57	1	2		7	39	6.6	59
30	RICHMOND	37-3	162	4	57	1	2		7/8	44	7.0	56
31												
32												

DATA

L HDD	M CDD	N % RH AM	O % RH PM	P WINT TEMP	Q SUM TEMP	R WIND AVE.	S WIND INT.	T SNOW	U INSUL.	V *COST	OTHER	Line No.
2147	2093	86	56	25	94	9	110	0	2	79		1
2629	2033	87	51	20	97	7	75	10	3	81	(1)	2
												3
7301	667	71	50	-11	95	11	80	15	5	81	(1)	4
7885	749	81	60	-15	94	11	80	40	5	83		5
												6
3583	1578	86	56	13	96	6	70	5	3	77	(1)	7
3658	1449	86	59	13	94	7	70	10	3	79	(1)	8
3207	2067	81	57	13	98	9	70	10	3	81		9
3756	1661	84	57	9	97	8	70	10	3	83	(1)	10
												11
2621	2467	74	50	15	101	12	80	5	3			12
4231	1428	73	45	6	98	14	80	15	4			13
1760	2914	84	57	24	100	9	70	5	2	80		14
				27	95		95	0	2			15
970	3574	90	62	31	95	12	100	5	2			16
2407	2809	82	56	18	102	11	70		3	82	(1)	17
2664	2096	57	28	20	100	9	70	5	3			18
1549	2761	90	60	27	96	8	100	0	2	86		19
3516	1676	75	47	10	98	12	80	10	3	78		20
1606	2983	84	55	25	99	9	80	0	2	80		21
2126	2891	84	57	21	101	11	70	5	3			22
3011	2506	82	51	14	103	12	80	5	3			23
												24
				1	93		70		5	85	(1)	25
5802	981	67	43	3	97	9	70		5	87	(1)	26
												27
3446	1458	78	57	20	93	11	90	10	3	83		28
4315	1085	78	53	12	93	8	70	25	4	81		29
3960	1336	78	57	14	95	8	75	15	3	85	(1)	30
												31
												32

*Data courtesy of BNI Building News. See latest BNI for current data.

LOCATION

Line No.	LOCATION	A LAT.	B ELEV.	C FROST LINE	D GD. TEMP.	E SEISMIC	F TERMITE	G SOILS	H PLANT ZONE	I RAIN AVE.	J RAIN INT.	K % SUN
1	VT BURLINGTON	44·3	331	50	46	2A	3		4/5	34	5.0	44
2	RUTLAND	43·3	620	50	46	2A	3		4/5		5.4	
3												
4	WA SPOKANE	47·4	2357	25	50	2B	3		6	17	3.0	47
5	SEATTLE	47·3	386	5	52	3	3		8	39	3.2	38
6												
7	WI GREEN BAY	44·3	683	50	49	0	3		4/5	28	6.0	52
8	MADISON	43·1	858	50	50	0	3		4/5	31	6.3	51
9	MILWAUKEE	43·0	672	50	50	0	3		5	31	6.2	52
10												
11	WV CHARLESTON	38·2	939	15	60	1	2		6	42	6.3	48
12	HUNTINGTON	38·2	565	15	60	1	2		6	41	6.3	44
13												
14	WY CHEYENNE	41·1	6126	24	52	1	3		4/5	13	4.8	64
15												
16												
17												
18												
19												
20												
21												
22												
23												
24												
25												
26												
27												
28												
29												
30												
31												
32												

DATA

L HDD	M CDD	N % RH AM	O % RH PM	P WINT TEMP	Q SUM TEMP	R WIND AVE.	S WIND INT.	T SNOW	U INSUL.	V COST*	OTHER	Line No.
7953	379	77	59	-12	88	9	75		6	94	(1)	1
				-13	87		75		5	87	(1)	2
												3
6882	411	78	52	-6	93	9	75		5	99	(1)	4
5121	184	83	62	21	84	9	80		1	106	(1)	5
												6
8143	381	82	63	-13	88	10	90	40	6	92		7
7642	467	84	61	-11	91	10	80	40	5	90		8
7326	470	80	64	-8	90	12		40	5	97		9
												10
4697	1007	83	56	7	92	6	70		4	87	(1)	11
4676	1121	83	58	5	94	7	70		4	89	(1)	12
												13
7310	309	65	44	-9	89	13	80		5	91		14
												15
												16
												17
												18
												19
												20
												21
												22
												23
												24
												25
												26
												27
												28
												29
												30
												31
												32

*Data courtesy of BNI Building News. See latest BNI for current data.

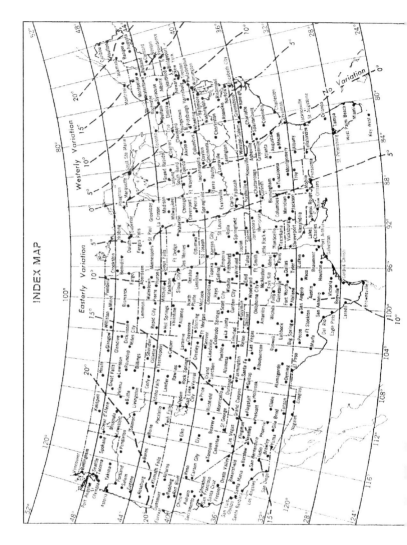

MAGNETIC VARIATION

The magnetic compass points to magnetic north rather than true north. In most localities magnetic north does not coincide with true north but is toward the east ("easterly variation") or toward the west ("westerly variation") from it

The heavy broken lines on this map connect points of equal magnetic variation, and present a generalized picture of magnetic variation in the United States. Due to "local attraction" it may be quite different in your locality. For more exact information consult your local surveyor.

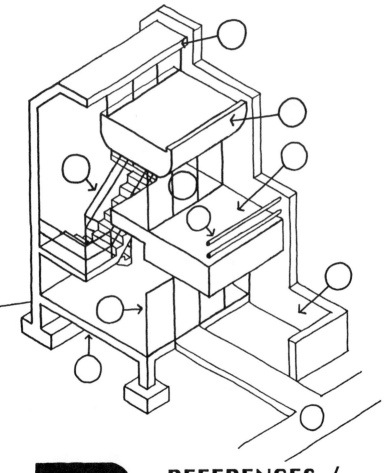

R REFERENCES / INDEX

NOTES

___ REFERENCES

This book was put together from a myriad of sources including the help of consultants listed on p. 547. References shown at the front of a section indicate general background information. A reference shown at a specific item indicates a copy from the reference. The major book references are listed as follows, and many are recommended for architects' libraries:

— (1) Allen, Edward, and Iano, Joseph, 1989. *The Architect's Studio Companion, Technical Guidelines for Preliminary Design.* New York: John Wiley & Sons.

— (2) Ambrose, James, 1981. *Simplified Design of Building Foundations.* New York: John Wiley & Sons.

— (2a) Ambrose, James, 1995, *Simplified Design for Building Sound Control.* New York: John Wiley & Sons.

— (3) American Institute of Architects, 6th ed., 1970. *Architectural Graphic Standards.* New York: John Wiley & Sons.

— (4) American Institute of Architects, 9th ed., 1994. *Architectural Graphic Standards.* New York: John Wiley & Sons.

— (5) American Institute of Architects, 1988. *The Architect's Handbook of Professional Practice,* David Haviland, editor.

— (5a) American Institute of Architects, 1982. *Architect's Handbook of Energy Practice—Daylighting.*

— (6) American Institute of Architects, 1981. *Energy in Architecture.*

— (7) Ballast, David Kent, 1988. *Architect's Handbook of Formulas, Tables, and Mathematical Calculations.* New Jersey: Prentice-Hall.

— (8) Ballast, David Kent. 1990. *Architect's Handbook of Construction Detailing.* New Jersey: Prentice-Hall.

— (9) Better Homes and Gardens, 1975. *Decorating Book.*

— (10) Bovill, Carl, 1991. *Architectural Design, Integration of Structural and Environmental Systems.* New York: Van Nostrand Reinhold Co.

— (11) Building News, 1997. *Facilities Manager's 1997 Cost Book.* William D. Mahoney, editor-in-chief.

— (12) Ching, Francis, 1975. *Building Construction Illustrated.* New York: Van Nostrand Reinhold Co.

— (13) Ching, Francis, 1990. *Drawing—A Creative Process.* New York: Van Nostrand Reinhold Co.

544   References

—   (14)   Clayton, George T., 1973. *The Site Plan in Architectural Working Drawings.* Chicago: Stipes Publishing Co.

—   (15)   Construction Specifications Institute, 1988. *Master-Format, Master List of Section Titles and Numbers.*

—   (16)   Craftsman Book Co., 1997. *1997 National Construction Estimator.* Edited by Martin D. Kiley and William M. Moselle.

—   (17)   Craftsman Book Co. 1997. *1997 Building Cost Manual.* Edited by Martin D. Kiley and Michael L. Kiley.

—   (17a)   Dept. of the Air Force, AFM 88-54. *Air Force Civil Engineer Handbook.*

—   (18)   Dept. of the Army, 1969. *FM-34 Engineer Field Data.*

—   (19)   Elliott, H. M., 1979. *How Structures Work, A Structural Engineering Primer,* unpublished.

—   (20)   Federal Register, 1991. *Americans with Disabilities Act* (ADA).

—   (21)   Foote, Rosslynn F., 1978. *Running an Office for Fun and Profit, Business Techniques for Small Design Firms.* Pennsylvania: Dowden, Hutchinson & Ross.

—   (21a)   Flynn, Kremers, Segil and Steffy, 3rd Edition. *Architectural Interior Systems.*

—   (22)   Guidelines Publications, 1990. *Design Services Appraiser.*

—   (23)   Guidelines Publications, 1975. *Architectural Rules of Thumb.*

—   (24)   International Conference of Building Officials. 1997. *Uniform Building Code.* Tables 3-A, 3-B, 5-A, 5-B, 6-A, 9-A, 10-A, 15-A, 16-A, 16-B, 16-C, 23-11-B-1, A-29-A, and graphic 24-1, reproduced from the 1997 edition of the *Uniform Building Code*™, copyright © 1997, with permission of the publisher, the International Conference of Building Officials.

—   (25)   International Association of Plumbing and Mechanical Officials, 1997. *Uniform Plumbing Code.* Table 4-1 is reprinted from the *Uniform Plumbing Code* with permission of the International Association of Plumbing and Mechanical Officials copyright © 1997.

—   (26)   International Conference of Building Officials, 1997. *Dwelling Construction Under the Uniform Building Code.*

— (27) Libbey-Owens-Ford Co., 1974. *Sun Angle Calculator.*

— (28) Lockard, William K., 1968. *Drawing as a Means to Architecture.* New York: Van Nostrand Reinhold.

— (29) Lockard, William K., 1982. *Design Drawing.* New York: Van Nostrand Reinhold.

— (30) Lynch, Kevin, 1962. *Site Planning.* Massachusetts: The MIT Press.

— (31) McGraw-Hill Book Co., 1993. *Sweet's Catalog File.*

— (32) McGraw-Hill Book Co., 1966. *Time Saver Standards.* John H. Callender, editor-in-chief.

— (33) Means, R. S. Co. Inc., 1997. *Means Building Construction Cost Data.*

— (34) Means, R. S. Co. Inc., 1997. *Means Assemblies Cost Data.*

— (35) Munsell, A. H., 1946. *A Color Notation.* Munsell Color Co., Inc.

— (35a) National Oceanic and Atmospheric Administration, 1992. *Comparative Climatic Data for the U.S.*

— (36) National Roofing Contractors Association, 1983. *Handbook of Accepted Roofing Knowledge.*

— (37) National Roofing Contractors Association, 1981. *The NRCA Roofing and Waterproofing Manual.*

— (38) Parker, Harry, and MacGuire, John, 1967. *Simplified Engineering for Architects and Engineers.* New York: John Wiley & Sons.

— (39) Parker, Harry, and MacGuire, John, 1954. *Simplified Site Engineering for Architects and Engineers.* New York: John Wiley & Sons.

— (40) Peña, William, with Parshall and Kelley, 1977. *Problem Seeking.* Washington, D.C.: A.I.A. Press.

— (40a) Saylor Publications, Inc., 1997. *1997 Current Construction Costs.*

— (41) Schiler, Marc, 1992. *Simplified Design of Building Lighting.* New York: John Wiley & Sons.

— (42) Stasiowski, Frank A., 1991. *Staying Small Successfully.* New York: John Wiley & Sons.

— (43) U.S. Navy, 1972. *Basic Construction Techniques for Houses and Small Buildings.* New York: Dover Publications.

— (44) Watson, Donald, and Labs, Kenneth, 1983. *Climatic Design.* New York: McGraw-Hill Book Co.

— (45) Wing, Charlie, 1990. *The Visual Handbook of Building and Remodeling.* Pennsylvania: Rodale Press.

— (46) Wood, R. S. and Co., 1985. *The Pocket Size Carpenter's Helper.*

Acknowledgments

Thanks to the following people for their professional expertise in helping with this book:

Special thanks to: Ray Beltran, Ed Denham, and Bill Mahoney.

Also, thanks to: Roger Alven, Steve Andros, Marcia and Ken Caldwell, Doug Collier, Bob Conley, Rick Goolsby, Peggy Gustave, Zamir Hasan, Glenn Heyes, Doug Hood, Tom Lepley, Norm Littler, Bill Lundsford, Randy Pace, Bert Rowe, Renee Tinsley, Craig Walling, Sandra Warner, and L. D. Womack.

NOTES

Index

NOTES

ABOUT THE AUTHOR

John Patten ("Pat") Guthrie, AIA, is a Principal of John Pat Guthrie Architects, Inc., of Scottsdale, Arizona. He has been a licensed architect in 13 states and now heads a broadbased practice that includes commercial, residential, industrial, medical, and religious facilities and that also specializes in restaurants and in passive solar energy design. Mr. Guthrie is author of *Cross-Check: Integrating Building Systems and Working Drawings,* published by McGraw-Hill, and *Desert Architecture.* He and his wife Janet are the parents of two grown children, Eric and Erin. Pat's hobbies include art, sailing, history, and world travel.

NOTES

NOTES

NOTES